MORAL BRAINS

Moral Brains

THE NEUROSCIENCE OF MORALITY

Edited by S. Matthew Liao

OXFORD
UNIVERSITY PRESS

OXFORD
UNIVERSITY PRESS

Oxford University Press is a department of the University of Oxford. It furthers
the University's objective of excellence in research, scholarship, and education
by publishing worldwide. Oxford is a registered trade mark of Oxford University
Press in the UK and certain other countries.

Published in the United States of America by Oxford University Press
198 Madison Avenue, New York, NY 10016, United States of America.

Library of Congress Cataloging-in-Publication Data
Names: Liao, S. Matthew, editor. Title: Moral brains : the neuroscience of morality /
edited by S. Matthew Liao. Description: New York, NY : Oxford University Press, [2016] |
Includes index. Identifiers: LCCN 2015044868| ISBN 9780199357666 (hardcover : alk. paper) |
ISBN 9780199357673 (pbk. : alk. paper)
Subjects: LCSH: Cognitive neuroscience. | Neuroscience—Social aspects.
Classification: LCC QP360.5 .M6684 2016 | DDC 612.8/233—dc23
LC record available at http://lccn.loc.gov/2015044868

For Wibke, Caitlin, and Connor

Contents

Acknowledgments

THIS VOLUME GREW out of a three-day conference that the New York University Center for Bioethics, in conjunction with the Duke University Kenan Institute for Ethics, the Yale University Interdisciplinary Center for Bioethics, and the Institute for Ethics and Emerging Technologies, organized in 2012, entitled "The Moral Brain." I am indebted to Bill Ruddick, Walter Sinnott-Armstrong, and Wendell Wallach for all their help with the conference, and to the NYU Center for Bioethics, Yale University's Interdisciplinary Center for Bioethics, the Institute for Ethics and Emerging Technologies, and the NYU Humanities Grant Initiative for financial support. Amanda Anjum and Zahra Ali, the administrative personnel for the NYU Center for Bioethics, merit special gratitude for their assistance in organizing and planning all facets of the conference. I am particularly grateful to Tom Carew, the Dean of the Faculty of Arts and Science at NYU, for providing the opening remarks for the conference, and to all the participants, James Blair, Paul Bloom, Molly Crockett, Joshua Greene, Jonathan Haidt, Guy Kahane, Walter Sinnott-Armstrong, James Woodward, Liane Young, Tamar Szabo Gendler, William Casebeer, James Giordano, James Hughes, Fabrice Jotterand, Joshua Knobe, Andrea Kuszewski, Maxwell Mehlman, Erik Parens, Wendell Wallach, Andre Fenton, Laura Franklin-Hall, Don Garrett, Joseph LeDoux, Victoria McGeer, Bill Ruddick, and Michael Strevens, for helping to make this conference a tremendous success.

Special thanks are owed to Walter Sinnott-Armstrong for suggesting the idea of producing a volume on the neuroscience of morality using some of the papers from the conference and for his intellectual support and guidance throughout the production of this volume. I would like to thank all the contributors for their excellent work and their patience. Peter Ohlin, my editor at Oxford University Press, has my special gratitude for his encouragement and care in seeing this book through to publication.

I have been greatly helped by a number of people who read and provided astute comments on various chapters in this book, including Rosa Cao, Peter DeScioli, Cressida Gaukroger, Jonathan Haidt, Bryce Huebner, Dan Khokhar, Collin O'Neil, Carolyn Plunkett, Regina Rini, Walter Sinnott-Armstrong, Joshua Stein, Carissa Véliz, and Liane Young. Chapter 4, Joshua Greene's "Beyond Point-and-Shoot Morality: Why Cognitive (Neuro)Science Matters for Ethics," is reprinted from *Ethics* 124 (2014): 695–726. I would like to thank the University of Chicago Press for permission to reprint this material. I also benefited greatly from A. J. Durwin's and Joshua Stein's research assistance and from Joshua's work on the index for the book.

Lastly, I thank my family—Wibke, Caitlin, and Connor—for their love, patience, and support while I completed this book.

Contributors

R. J. R. Blair, National Institutes of Health
Molly J. Crockett, University of Oxford
Stephen Darwall, Yale University
Julia Driver, Washington University in Saint Louis
Philip Gerrans, University of Adelaide
Joshua D. Greene, Harvard University
Soonjo Hwang, National Institutes of Health
Guy Kahane, University of Oxford
Jeanette Kennett, Macquarie University
S. Matthew Liao, New York University
Harma Meffert, National Institute of Mental Health
Jorge Moll, D'Or Institute for Research and Education
Ricardo de Oliveira-Souza, D'Or Institute for Research and Education
Jesse Prinz, Graduate Center, City University of New York
Jana Schaich Borg, Duke University
Walter Sinnott-Armstrong, Duke University
Stuart F. White, National Institutes of Health
James Woodward, University of Pittsburgh
Roland Zahn, Institute of Psychiatry at King's College

MORAL BRAINS

Morality and Neuroscience

PAST AND FUTURE

S. Matthew Liao

I.1. Introduction

A distinguishing characteristic of human beings is that most of us are moral agents. As moral agents, we have the capacity to make moral judgments and to act in light of these moral judgments. Accordingly, a central area of intellectual inquiry across different disciplines involves understanding the nature, practice, and reliability of moral judgments. For instance, an issue of perennial interest concerns what moral judgments are and how moral judgments differ from nonmoral judgments. Moral judgments such as "Torture is wrong" seem different from nonmoral judgments such as "Water is wet." But how do moral judgments differ from nonmoral, but normative judgments such as "The time on the clock is wrong" or "Talking with one's mouth full is wrong"? Can, for example, R. M. Hare's proposal that moral judgments are prescriptive, universalizable, and overriding distinguish moral judgments from nonmoral judgments? (Hare 1981).

Another issue of considerable interest is whether moral judgments are generated on the basis of deliberative reasoning or arise from emotions. A related debate is whether moral judgments are intrinsically motivating. Indeed, David Hume famously asserted that reason is a "slave to the passions" and that moral judgments are the product of emotions (Hume 1978). Immanuel Kant, on the other hand, argued that genuine moral requirements are derived from a principle of rationality, in particular, the Categorical Imperative (Kant 1964).

A further issue is concerned with the reliability of moral judgments generally and whether some moral judgments are more reliable or truth-tracking than others.[1] For instance, are moral judgments generated by emotions more reliable or truth-tracking than moral judgments generated by reasoning, or vice versa?

In the last fifteen years, there has been significant interest in studying the brain structures involved in moral judgments using novel techniques from neuroscience such as functional magnetic resonance imaging (fMRI). Many people, including a number of philosophers, believe that results from neuroscience have the potential to settle seemingly intractable debates concerning the nature, practice, and reliability of moral judgments. This has led to a flurry of scientific and philosophical activities, resulting in the rapid growth of the new field of moral neuroscience. There is now a vast array of ongoing scientific research devoted toward understanding the neural correlates of moral judgments, accompanied by a large philosophical literature aimed at interpreting and examining the methodology and the results of this research. My aim in this introduction is to identify some of the central topics in this field, take stock of some of the key discussions, and recommend some ways of taking these discussions further. The chapters in this volume will continue where I have left off by offering a wide variety of new perspectives, both philosophical and scientific, and representing the most up-to-date research in this area.

To start, in section 2, I shall present some of the key scientific findings and detail some of the latest scientific results. I shall focus in particular on studies that are widely cited in this collection, that have received significant discussions in the philosophical literature, and that purport to shed light on some of the philosophical questions discussed. Next, I shall examine two debates concerning the nature and practice of moral judgments and the way in which neuroscience has been employed to advance these debates. In sections 3–5, I shall discuss how neuroscience has contributed to the debate concerning whether moral judgments are the product of reasoning or emotions. In particular, section 3 will examine the issue of whether moral judgments are intrinsically motivating; section 4 will consider whether moral judgments tend to be the product of emotions or reasoning; and section 5 will discuss whether there is an innate moral faculty that can produce moral judgments without inputs from emotions or reasoning. In section 6, I shall discuss Joshua Greene's argument that neuroscientific evidence supports the idea that consequentialist judgments are more reliable or truth-tracking than nonconsequentialist judgments. Following these discussions, I shall provide a brief overview of the essays in the volume in section 7.

I.2. Cognitive Neuroscience and the Moral Brain

In a series of groundbreaking studies in the 1990s, Antonio Damasio and his colleagues sought to demonstrate the importance of emotions in decision-making by studying patients with damage to the ventromedial prefrontal cortex (VMPFC). VMPFC patients resemble Phineas Gage, an American railroad construction foreman who accidentally had a large iron rod driven through his medial prefrontal cortex and survived. Like Gage, VMPFC patients make very poor decisions in real life, yet appear to retain their intellectual and reasoning abilities; for example, they can perform normally on standard cognitive measures such as IQ tests and on Kohlberg's moral reasoning tests. Damasio et al. hypothesized that VMPFC patients made poor decisions because they were unable to generate the kind of emotions needed to make good decisions in real-life situations. To show this, Damasio et al. gave VMPFC patients the Iowa Gambling Task, a game designed to simulate real-world decision-making (Damasio 1994). In this task, subjects were presented with four decks of cards. Two decks were "high risk and high return," containing high-reward and high-penalty cards. Two decks were "low risk and low return," containing low-reward and low-penalty cards. The "high risk and high return" decks were considered "bad decks" in that they tended to lead to losses over the long run, while the "low risk and low return" decks were considered "good decks," because they tended to result in gains in the long run. The subjects were given a certain amount of money to start, and the objective of the game was to win as much money as possible. Damasio et al. found that while normal subjects were good at selecting the good decks after a certain number of losses, VMPFC patients often persevered with the bad decks, even though they knew that they were losing money. Moreover, measuring the skin conductance responses (SCRs)—a reliable measure of emotional arousal—before the subjects selected each card, Damasio et al. found that normal subjects generated anticipatory SCRs to the bad decks after only a few losses (Bechara et al. 1996). In contrast, VMPFC patients failed to generate anticipatory SCRs before selecting cards from the bad decks. Since the VMPFC is known to play an important role in regulating and inhibiting our response to emotions, and since damage to the VMPFC results in the deficit of emotions, Damasio et al. argued that this provides evidence that VMPFC patients have difficulty making good decisions in real-life situations as a result of their emotional deficits.

A number of other studies in the 1990s concerning psychopaths and other individuals with antisocial personality disorder further underscore the importance of emotions in *moral* decision-making. According to developmental psychologists, acquiring the ability to grasp the distinction between moral rules (e.g., rules against hitting someone) from conventional rules (e.g., rules against talking in class) is a key stage in the moral development of children. For instance, Elliot Turiel and others have found that children as young as three to four years of age appear to be able to make the moral/conventional distinction (see, e.g., Turiel 1983). In a classic study, James Blair took subjects who scored highly on Robert Hare's psychopathy test and assessed their ability to distinguish between moral and conventional transgressions (1995). Blair found that psychopaths tended to treat conventional and moral transgressions equivalently. Since psychopathy is a disorder that is characterized not just by antisocial behavior but also by emotional impairment such as the lack of guilt (Hare 1991), Blair argued that the emotional impairment of psychopaths can explain why they tended to treat conventional and moral transgressions equivalently.[2]

Damasio, Blair, and their colleagues investigated individuals who have abnormal brains using clinical observations and tasks. In a pioneering study in 2001, Jorge Moll and his colleagues studied healthy individuals using brain imaging (Moll et al. 2001). Moll et al.

asked subjects silently to judge as right or wrong certain moral and factual sentences while undergoing fMRI. An example of a moral sentence is "We break the law when necessary" and an example of a factual sentence is "Stones are made of water." Moll et al. found that judging moral sentences activated certain distinct regions of the brain, including the frontopolar cortex, medial frontal gyrus, right anterior temporal cortex, lenticular nucleus, and cerebellum, when compared with judging factual sentences. In another study in 2002, Moll and his colleagues presented subjects with a series of emotionally charged pictures with and without moral content (Moll et al. 2002). Emotionally charged pictures with moral content included pictures of physical assaults and poor children abandoned in the streets. Emotionally charged pictures without moral content included pictures of body lesions and dangerous animals. Moll et al. hypothesized that since damage to the orbitofrontal cortex can result in a lack of empathy and antisocial behaviors, this brain region would be more activated by emotionally charged pictures with moral content than by emotionally charged pictures without moral content. Indeed, Moll et al. found that viewing pictures with moral content increased the activation of the right medial orbitofrontal cortex and the medial frontal gyrus and the cortex surrounding the right posterior superior temporal sulcus (STS), when compared with viewing nonmoral, unpleasant stimuli. Moll et al. argued that these studies showed that "a remarkably consistent network of brain regions is involved in moral cognition" (2005, 799).

Moll et al.'s research emphasized the role of emotions in moral judgments. Also in 2001, and drawing on a dual-processing theory of moral judgment, according to which both intuitive, emotional responses and controlled, cognitive responses play crucial and sometimes competing roles in producing moral judgments, Joshua Greene and his colleagues asked subjects to make judgments about moral and nonmoral dilemmas while undergoing fMRI (Greene et al. 2001). Nonmoral dilemmas included questions about whether to travel by bus or by train given certain time constraints. Moral dilemmas were divided into "impersonal" and "personal" moral dilemmas. To illustrate this distinction, Greene et al. appealed to the classic trolley dilemmas (Foot 1967; Thomson 1985). Consider the following two trolley cases:

Switch: a runaway trolley is headed toward five people who will be killed. You can hit a switch that will turn the trolley onto another set of tracks where another person sits and where the trolley will kill this person instead of the five.

Footbridge: as before a runaway trolley is threatening to kill five people. You are standing next to a large man on a footbridge and you can push the large man off the bridge. The large man will die but his body will stop the trolley from reaching the five people, thereby saving the five.

According to Greene et al., Footbridge is considered a personal moral dilemma because the act of pushing the large man involves a kind of "up close and personal" harm. Moral dilemmas that are not personal moral dilemmas such as Switch are, according to Greene et al., classified as impersonal moral dilemmas. As Greene et al. noted, most people believe that it is appropriate to hit the switch in Switch, but that it is inappropriate to push the large man in Footbridge, even though in both cases the choice is between killing one person or letting five people die. At the same time, some people do hold the judgment that it is appropriate to push the large man in Footbridge, and some do say that it is wrong to hit the switch in Switch.

Greene et al. hypothesized that what makes people approve of killing the one for the purpose of saving the five in Switch, but not in Footbridge, is the different emotional engagement the two dilemmas elicit. In particular, they predicted that brain areas associated with emotions would be more active when people think about personal moral dilemmas such as Footbridge, when compared with impersonal moral dilemmas such as Switch. In addition, they hypothesized that people who reach an intuitively unappealing judgment regarding personal moral dilemmas, for example, judging that it is appropriate to push the large man in Footbridge, would take longer to reach their judgment because they would be using cognitive processes to override an automatic, emotional response in order to reach their final judgment.

Indeed, Greene et al. found that brain areas associated with emotional and social cognition such as medial frontal gyrus, posterior cingulate gyrus, and angular gyrus bilaterally exhibited greater activity in cases of personal moral dilemmas. By contrast, impersonal moral dilemmas and nonmoral dilemmas produced increased activity in more cognitive areas associated with working memory such as dorsolateral prefrontal and parietal areas. Moreover, Greene et al. found (or rather, thought that they had found then)[3] that in personal moral dilemmas, subjects who made the intuitively unappealing judgment, that is, judging that it is appropriate to push the large man off the footbridge in Footbridge, had longer reaction times than those who made the more emotionally congruent judgments. Since personal moral dilemmas typically elicit negative social emotional responses, and since subjects who made the intuitively unappealing judgment appeared to have overcome their negative emotional responses using more cognitive processes, Greene et al. interpreted this result as showing that reasoning can play an important role in cases in which reasoned considerations and automatic emotions conflict.

In a follow-up study in 2004, Greene and his colleagues presented subjects with "easy" and "difficult" personal moral dilemmas (Greene et al. 2004). Easy personal moral dilemmas are ones in which subjects answered quickly, that is, they had fast reaction times, and in which the subjects appeared to have uniform judgments on the matter. An example is infanticide in which a teenage mother must decide whether or not to kill her unwanted newborn infant. Difficult personal moral dilemmas are ones in which subjects did not answer quickly, that is, they had slow reaction times, and in which subjects did not appear to have uniform judgments regarding the matter. In addition, difficult personal moral dilemmas also have the following structure: in order to maximize good consequences, for example, to save the most lives, one must commit a personal moral violation. An example of a difficult personal moral dilemma is the crying baby dilemma, in which in order to save yourself and several others from being discovered by a group of enemy soldiers, you must smother your child to death.

Greene et al. classified the judgment that it is appropriate to perform a personal moral violation in order to achieve a greater good as making a "utilitarian" judgment. For instance, judging that it is appropriate to smother the baby in the crying baby dilemma in order to save yourself and others would count as making a utilitarian judgment. Greene et al. classified the judgment that it is not appropriate to perform a personal moral violation in order to achieve a greater good as making a "nonutilitarian" or "deontological" judgment. For example, judging that it is inappropriate to smother the baby in the crying baby dilemma would count as making a deontological judgment.

Greene et al. hypothesized that judging that the utilitarian action in difficult personal moral dilemmas is appropriate should be associated with greater activity in the cognitive regions of the brain, compared with judging that the utilitarian action in difficult personal moral dilemmas is inappropriate. Indeed, Greene et al. found that subjects who approved of the utilitarian choices had increased activity in brain regions associated with cognitive control such as the anterior dorsolateral prefrontal cortex (DLPFC) and the right inferior parietal lobe.

If Greene's hypothesis is correct, we should expect that modulation of the emotional response to moral dilemmas influences whether subjects make utilitarian judgments. In particular, increasing emotional intensity should decrease utilitarian judgments, as cognitive control decreases; and decreasing emotional intensity should correlate with utilitarian judgments. In fact, Greene's findings appear to find additional support in other studies. For instance, a number of research groups have found that patients with emotion-related, neurological deficits are more likely than a control population to make utilitarian decisions in trolley dilemmas. For instance, two research groups, Michael Koenigs, Liane Young, and colleagues, and Elisa Ciaramelli and colleagues, found that people with injuries in the VMPFC were more likely to endorse the utilitarian choice in personal moral dilemmas such as Footbridge (Koenigs et al. 2007; Ciaramelli et al. 2007). Likewise, Mario Mendez and colleagues found that patients with frontotemporal dementia, who are characterized by a lack of empathy for others, also tended to favor the utilitarian action in Footbridge (Mendez et al. 2005).

Other research groups found that increasing emotional responses in brain regions associated with emotions such as the amygdala and the VMPFC can increase nonutilitarian, deontological judgments. For instance, Molly Crockett and colleagues gave subjects citalopram, a selective serotonin-reuptake inhibitor (SSRI), which enhances serotonin function by blocking its reuptake after serotonin has been released into the synapse, thus prolonging serotonin's action (Crockett et al. 2010). Citalopram is used to treat a wide range of affective illnesses, including anxiety disorders. Crockett et al. found that subjects were more deontological, that is, less likely to endorse harming one to save many others. In contrast, Adam Perkins and colleagues found that giving subjects the antianxiety drug lorazepam increased the subjects' willingness to endorse responses that directly harm others in moral-personal dilemmas, compared with dilemmas in which harm is remotely inflicted (Perkins et al. 2013). These studies appear to support Greene's findings, because if people tended to disapprove of the utilitarian choice in moral dilemmas such as Footbridge as a result of negative social emotional responses, then it seems that increasing emotional intensity should decrease utilitarian judgments as cognitive control decreases; and decreasing emotional intensity should correlate with utilitarian judgments.

Before moving on, let me mention one other emergent area of research in this field. A key factor in judging whether an act of harm is right or wrong is whether the act is intentional or accidental. Some researchers have begun investigating how mental states such as intentions and beliefs are represented in the brain in the context of moral judgment. For instance, Liane Young, Rebecca Saxe, and colleagues compared the effect of outcome and the intention of the agent on moral judgment, using an example involving an agent, Grace, who puts a white substance in her friend's coffee. Young et al. presented subjects with four vignettes that varied according to whether Grace believes that the substance is sugar or toxic; and whether it is actually sugar or toxic and therefore whether the friend dies or not (Young et al. 2007):

a. Grace believes that the substance is toxic and it is toxic; friend dies (intentional harm).
b. Grace believes the substance is toxic but it is sugar; friend does not die (attempted harm).
c. Grace believes the substance is sugar but it is toxic; friend dies (accidental harm).
d. Grace believes the substance is sugar and it is sugar; friend does not die (neutral).

Subjects were then asked to judge the moral permissibility of Grace's action. Young et al. found that the right temporo-parietal junction (RTPJ), which is associated with attributions of beliefs to others, was significantly activated in all four conditions. In addition, Young et al. found that the RTPJ was particularly sensitive to attempted harms, that is, cases in which the protagonist believed that she would harm someone but in fact did not. In another study, Young and colleagues (2010) used transcranial magnetic stimulation (TMS) to disrupt neural activity in the RTPJ before moral judgment and during moral judgment. Young et al. found that applying TMS to the RTPJ caused subjects to judge attempted harms as less morally forbidden and more morally permissible, which seems to suggest that interfering with activity in the RTPJ can disrupt the capacity to use mental states in moral judgment, especially in the case of attempted harms.

As we shall see, these are some of the key scientific studies that are widely cited in this collection, that have received significant discussions in the philosophical literature, and that purport to shed light on some the philosophical questions discussed. There are other neuroscientific studies that are worthy of being discussed, but this brief overview should give one a sense of the richness of the work that has been done thus far.

I.3. Motivational Internalism and Neuroscience

As noted earlier, a classic issue concerning the role of emotions and reasoning in making moral judgments is whether motivation is intrinsic to, or a necessary component of, moral judgment. In this section, I shall consider how neuroscience has been employed to help advance this debate. To start, let me offer an overview of the debate.

According to internalism, moral judgment contains or entails moral motivation. For instance, if I judge that I ought to give money to Oxfam, according to internalism, I am necessarily motivated (e.g., as a matter of conceptual necessity, i.e., something that holds across all possible worlds) to some degree to do so. On internalism, if I am not motivated at all to give money to Oxfam, then I cannot possibly judge that I ought to give money to Oxfam. At best, I am only making this judgment in "inverted commas," that is, I am not really making a genuine moral judgment. In contrast, according to externalism, motivation is not a necessary component of moral judgment. On externalism, if I judge that I ought to give money to Oxfam, this judgment can be a genuine moral judgment whether or not I am motivated to give money to Oxfam. In other words, according to externalism, motivation is only contingently related to moral judgments.

Numerous philosophical arguments have been put forward in support of internalism, and others in support of externalism. For instance, an argument in favor of internalism is the following: Morality is practical; that is, when we judge that we ought to do something, we cannot be indifferent to bringing about this action. However, cognitive states without motivation cannot get us to bring about an action. Therefore, moral judgments cannot be exclusively cognitive. An argument in favor of externalism is that it seems possible to imagine beings who can make judgments about right or wrong but who are utterly unmoved by such judgments. An oft-used example is an amoralist, that is, someone who is perfectly competent with the concept of a moral judgment but who is not motivated to act morally. Other examples include psychopaths, who appear able to express moral judgments but who also appear not be moved by such judgments; and characters in fiction such as Spock from *Star Trek*, who is perfectly competent with the concept of moral judgment, who can make moral judgments, but who does not have any emotions, assuming (not uncontroversially) that emotions are necessary for motivation.

Recently, a number of people have argued that neuroscientific results can be used to advance the debate between internalism and externalism. For instance, Jesse Prinz (2006) argues that neuroscientific findings can, in conjunction with other evidence, be employed to support a form of internalism. In particular, Prinz believes that it can be shown that moral judgments necessarily have an emotional component, which, according to Prinz, explains why moral judgments characteristically give rise to motivational states. To demonstrate this, Prinz first argues that emotions co-occur with moral judgments. Citing Moll et al.'s studies, Prinz points out that areas of the brain that are associated with emotional responses were active when evaluating moral sentences such as "You should break the law when necessary," compared with evaluating factual sentences such as "Stones are made of water." Likewise, citing Greene et al.'s studies, Prinz notes that emotional areas of the brain were activated when subjects contemplated moral dilemmas. Next, Prinz defends that idea that emotions can influence moral judgments in a way such that "emotions are sufficient for moral appraisal" (2006, 31). Here Prinz draws on a number of behavioral studies conducted by Jonathan Haidt and his colleagues. For instance, in one study, Haidt et al. found that subjects who were seated at a dirty desk judged certain vignettes as more wrong than subjects who were seated at a clean desk (Schnall et al. 2008). In another study, Wheatley and Haidt (2005) hypnotized a group of subjects to feel a flash of disgust whenever they read the word "take," while another group was hypnotized to feel disgust at the word "often." Subjects then read six stories, each of which included either the word "take" or the word "often," and the subjects were asked to make moral judgments about these stories. Wheatley and Haidt found that compared to the control group, the flash of disgust that subjects felt when the key word was in the story made their moral judgments more severe. According to Prinz, "Such findings suggest that we can form the belief that something is morally wrong by simply having a negative emotion directed towards it" (2006, 31).

Lastly, Prinz argues that emotions are necessary for moral judgments. Prinz offers three arguments. First, he observes that emotions are needed for moral development. As Prinz points out, parents use various techniques to condition a child to experience negative emotions when the child misbehaves. Also, citing Blair's research on psychopaths, Prinz endorses the interpretation that because psychopaths are profoundly deficient in negative emotions, they are not amenable to fear conditioning, and as a result they are unable to develop the capacities to make genuine moral judgments. Second, Prinz argues that emotions are necessary for moral judgments "in a synchronic sense" (2006, 31). As Prinz explains, the necessity thesis he has in mind is "dispositional" (32). In support of the synchronic necessity thesis, Prinz says the following: "Can one sincerely attest that killing is morally wrong without being disposed to have negative emotions towards killing? My intuition here is that such a person would be confused or insincere" (32). Third, Prinz offers an argument from anthropological record. As he says, "If moral judgments were based on something other than emotions—something like reason or observation—we would expect more moral convergence cross-culturally. Reason and observation lead to convergence over time" (33). In other words, according to Prinz, the fact that moral values appear to be divergent across cultures lends support to the idea that "moral values do not have a purely cognitive source . . . [and that] they hinge on culturally inculcated passions" (33).

Has Prinz successfully shown that the empirical findings support internalism? Karen Jones (2006) raises at least two helpful points regarding Prinz's arguments. First, since the internalist claims that the motivation connection holds as a matter of conceptual necessity, Jones asks whether empirical evidence can really be used to support a necessity claim. As she explains,

> Empirical work is more obviously relevant to the externalist than the internalist in as much as showing that something is actual is one way of showing it possible;

whereas showing that something is actual does nothing to show that it is necessary. . . . Empirical debate can be relevant negatively; that is, closer examination of empirical facts can rebut an externalist's putative real-world counter-example, but it is not going to be able to lend independent support to the internalist position itself. (2006, 47)

Second, Jones questions Prinz's argument that emotions can influence moral judgments in a way such that they are sufficient for moral judgments. Recall that Prinz appealed to Haidt's various experiments to show that emotions can influence moral judgments. Granting these experimental results, Jones argues that it is an open question whether subjects in these experiments are making genuine moral judgments. As Jones points out, it is generally agreed that emotions can have distorting influences on moral judgments. Given this, according to Jones, if the subjects are told about how the hypnosis has influenced their moral judgments, and if nevertheless the subjects refuse to withdraw their judgment, then arguably, these subjects lack our moral concepts and are not making genuine moral judgments (2006, 48).

Let me mention three other issues regarding Prinz's arguments. First, consider Prinz's observation that emotions are necessary for moral development. Suppose that this is true. Does this thereby show that emotions are necessary when adults make moral judgments? To see why it might not be necessary, consider the following analogy. To learn how to ride a bicycle, most children need to have training wheels. It does not follow that to ride a bicycle, one, as an adult, therefore needs to have training wheels. In other words, what is necessary for moral development may not be necessary for making genuine moral judgments. Second, as we have seen, to support the claim that emotions are necessary "in a synchronic sense," Prinz asks, "Can one sincerely attest that killing is morally wrong without being disposed to have negative emotions towards killing? My intuition here is that such a person would be confused or insincere." Notice that Prinz is appealing to his intuition here to make this crucial point for his thesis. Although, at least in my view, there is nothing wrong with appealing to intuitions to support a particular theory, in this context, doing so is not using neuroscience to support internalism, and, also, presumably an externalist would simply disagree with this intuition. Third, recall that Prinz thinks that if moral judgments were based on reasoning, there would be more convergence in moral values cross-culturally. For one thing, it seems that a plausible case can be made that there is in fact such a convergence. For instance, the fact that more than 190 countries have ratified the Convention on the Rights of the Child seems to support the idea that there is some kind of moral convergence cross-culturally. Moreover, Prinz seems to assume that if two cultures disagree about a matter, and cannot resolve their differences, this fact implies that the disagreement is the result of their having different emotional responses regarding this matter. But why assume this? Suppose that two scientists disagree about whether black holes really exist and are unable to resolve their differences. Would it follow that their disagreement is the result of their having different emotional responses regarding whether black holes really exist? If not, it seems that Prinz needs to do more to show that cultural disagreements are in fact the result of what he calls "culturally inculcated passions."

While Prinz has used empirical evidence, including neuroscientific ones, to defend internalism, Adina Roskies argues that neuroscientific results demonstrate the falsity of internalism. Drawing on Damasio's work on patients with VMPFC damage, Roskies (2003) argues that VMPFC patients are "walking counterexamples" to internalism. As mentioned earlier and as Roskies elaborates, VMPFC patients retain declarative knowledge related to moral issues and appear to be able to reason morally at a normal level, but they make poor decisions in real life. Indeed, a number of VMPFC patients were divorced, bankrupt, unable to maintain employment, and bad at future planning. In addition, measuring the SCRs of normal subjects versus VMPFC patients when both were presented with emotionally charged or value-laden stimuli such as pictures of bodies mutilated by war, it has been found that normal subjects tended to produce SCRs, while VMPFC patients did not generally produce SCRs (Damasio et al. 1990). At the same time, VMPFC patients did produce normal SCRs in other tests that did not involve such emotionally charged stimuli, which suggests that their autonomic nervous system was not damaged.

According to Roskies, we can assume that a measurable SCR is evidence of the presence of motivation, and that the lack of an SCR is indicative of absence of motivation, because "the presence of the SCR is reliably correlated with cases in which action is consistent with judgment, and its absence is correlated with occasions in which the [VMPFC] patient fails to act in accord with his or her judgments. Thus, the SCR is a reliable indicator of motivation for action" (2002, 7). If so, given that VMPFC patients could engage in moral reasoning and have moral knowledge and beliefs but did not reliably display motivation in moral situations (supposing that the SCR tests showed this), Roskies argues that VMPFC patients are counterexamples to the claim that there is a necessary connection between moral judgments and motivation.

Jeanette Kennett and Cordelia Fine (2008) have offered several responses to Roskies. I shall mention four of them here. First, Kennett and Fine believe that no one would hold Roskies's version of internalism, according to which motivation is a necessary component of moral judgment. As they say, "Who, exactly, is the foe? Strict-motive internalists [as defined by Roskies] . . . are pretty hard to find" (179). Second, Kennett and Fine argue that while the kind of moral judgments at issue in deciding whether internalism or externalism is true should be first-person moral judgments, that is, they shouldn't be judgments about what someone else ought to do, internalism further requires that these first-person moral judgments be in situ judgments. As they explain,

I can surely believe that I ought to keep my promise but fail to form the in situ judgment that I ought to keep my promise. Maybe my belief or my promise isn't foregrounded in my deliberations about what to do. Maybe I fail to notice that what I'm planning to do—go to the football game this afternoon, say—would be inconsistent with keeping the promise I made two weeks ago to meet you in the mall at 3:00 on Saturday the 22nd. If I forget my promise to you, or I don't notice that the time to keep it is now, then, although I believe I ought to keep my promises, including this one, I fail to form a judgment about what I ought to do right now, and so I fail to meet you. Of course I ought to form the judgment, but my failure to do so is not a failure of motivation. As we have described it, it can be a failure of attention or memory or inference. We take it that this kind of mismatch between moral belief and motivation to act wouldn't be enough to refute motive internalism. The relevant judgments are first person, in situ. (Kennett and Fine 2008, 182)

Third, Kennett and Fine question whether Roskies is correct to regard the VMPFC patients' behaviors as exemplifying moral violations. As Kennett and Fine argue, bankruptcy, divorce, inability to maintain employment, and defective future planning do not seem to be "moral" violations. Kennett and Fine hypothesize that what VMPFC patients lacked was not moral motivations; instead their defect was a defect in decision-making (2008, 185). Fourth, Kennett and Fine disagree that the situations in which VMPFC patients failed to show SCRs were ethically charged. As they point out, the study in which VMPFC patients were asked to view social pictures such as pictures of social disaster, mutilation, and nudity was administered under two conditions, passive viewing, where the subjects were asked just to view the slides; and active viewing, where subjects were asked to comment on the slide and to say whether or not they liked it. According to Kennett and Fine, the relevant condition at issue should be active viewing, but under active viewing, VMPFC patients in fact showed normal SCRs (Damasio et al. 1990).

With respect to the first point that Roskies is attacking a straw version of internalism, Roskies has replied that the claim of necessity is "part of the standard view of internalism" (2008, 192). In support of Roskies on this point, it seems that Prinz is an internalist who would accept Roskies's characterization of internalism. With respect to Kennett and Fine's second point that internalism applies only to in situ moral judgments, Roskies has argued plausibly that internalism should apply also to hypothetical moral judgments. For example, if I judge that killing is wrong, it seems that an internalist should say that I would have the disposition to be motivated not to kill, whether I am actually in the position to kill someone or not. Regarding Kennett and Fine's third point, Roskies's response is that bankruptcy, divorce, the inability to maintain employment, and poor future planning are moral as well as social deficits. However, there are reasons to question Roskies on this score. Recall the distinction between moral and conventional transgressions. If this distinction is valid, arguably, a case can be made that social deficits such as bankruptcy, divorce, inability to maintain employment, and so on are just forms of conventional transgression. In any case, given this distinction, it seems that Roskies has to do more to show that social deficits are in fact also moral deficits. Lastly, with respect to Kennett and Fine's point that under active viewing, VMPFC patients did show normal SCRs, Roskies has in effect conceded this point (2008, 199). However, one might question whether making comments about whether one likes a particular image on a slide or not is the same thing as making a moral judgment about the content of the image. If not, this would call into question using these particular studies to determine whether VMPFC patients are motivated by their moral judgments. For future research, it seems that it would be good to ask VMPFC patients explicitly to make moral judgments about the moral content of certain images. Of course, such research would still assume that SCRs are a reliable indicator for motivation, which is an assumption that is worth examining further as well. Here it seems that we can draw two tentative conclusions. First, it remains an open question whether neuroscience can be used to advance the debate between internalism and externalism. Second, à la Jones, there are reasons to believe that neuroscientific evidence may be more relevant for the externalist than the internalist.

I.4. Emotions, Reasoning, and Moral Judgments

Whether emotions are a necessary component of moral judgments or not, do moral judgments tend to be generated by emotions or reasoning, or both? Relatedly, are moral judgments generated by emotions more reliable or truth-tracking than moral judgments generated by reasoning, or vice versa? Following the works of Kohlberg, a dominant perspective in psychology has been that moral judgments are derived from reasoning and that judgments derived from reasoning are more reliable or truth-tracking than judgments derived from emotions (Kohlberg 1969). Recently, however, some people have argued that moral judgments arise predominantly as a result of the emotional/intuitive process, and that the purpose of reasoning appears not to generate moral judgments but instead to provide a post hoc and biased basis for justification. As we shall see, among other things, neuroscientific results have been employed to support such a claim. In particular, Jonathan Haidt and his collaborators have defended a "social intuitionist model" of moral judgment, according to which moral judgments are initially the product of fast, nonconscious, automatic, affective, intuitive processing (Haidt 2001, 2007; Haidt and Bjorklund 2008a, 2008b). Conscious reasoning then takes place after a judgment has been made and is typically occupied with the task of justifying, in a biased, non-truth-seeking way, whatever judgments affect-laden intuitions have produced.

Haidt supports the social intuitionist model in at least four ways. First, Haidt appeals to the phenomenon of "moral dumbfounding" (Haidt and Hersh 2001). Moral dumbfounding occurs when people have moral convictions that they quickly provide but struggle to find a supporting reason for these convictions. As an example, Haidt presents subjects with the following case:

> Julie and Mark are brother and sister. They are travelling together in France on
> summer vacation from college. One night they are staying alone in a cabin near the

beach. They decide that it would be interesting and fun if they tried making love. At the very least it would be a new experience for each of them. Julie was already taking birth control pills, but Mark uses a condom too, just to be safe. They both enjoy making love, but they decide not to do it again. They keep that night as a special secret, which makes them feel even closer to each other. What do you think about that? Was it OK for them to make love? (Haidt 2001, 814)

Haidt found that most people quickly regarded the action of Julie and Mark as immoral. When asked to justify their judgment, people typically referred to the possibility of inbreeding and the possible psychological harm to the siblings. However, when it was pointed out to them that in this case, it is stipulated that birth control had been used and that there was no psychological harm to the siblings, Haidt found that many subjects would nevertheless continue to insist that the activity of the siblings was morally wrong. Moreover, Haidt discovered that some people would make up reasons, sometimes bad ones, to justify their condemnation, while others would concede that they cannot provide any further justification for their judgments (Haidt 2006, 64). According to Haidt, since these individuals were offering bad reasons or were not able to provide any further justification in support of their judgments, and yet they nevertheless continue to hold on to their judgments, it does not seem plausible to think that their judgments were generated by reasoning. Instead, so argues Haidt, it seems more likely that these individuals were using reasoning to justify, in a post hoc and biased way, a judgment that is generated by their affect-laden intuitions (Haidt 2001, 822).

Second, Haidt cites research that shows that altering an individual's emotions can alter moral judgments. As noted earlier, Wheatley and Haidt (2005) hypnotized one group of subjects to feel a flash of disgust whenever they read certain words, and they found that the subjects' judgments can be made more severe by the presence of a flash of disgust. According to Haidt, these findings support the idea that emotions can influence and generate moral judgments in a way suggested by the social intuitionist model (2001, 825).

Third, for our purpose, Haidt draws on the neuroimaging studies by Moll, Greene, and their colleagues to defend the social intuitionist model further. As noted earlier, Moll, Greene, and their colleagues found that when subjects were presented with claims that have moral content or when subjects made personal moral judgments, there was significant activity in, for example, the medial frontal gyrus, the posterior cingulate, and the STS. As Greene and Haidt (2002) note, among other things, the medial frontal gyrus is involved in the integration of emotion into decision-making and planning; the posterior cingulate is recruited in memory and processes involving imagery, especially affective imagery; and the STS is recruited in perception of representation of socially significant information. According to Greene and Haidt, these studies further support the idea that "emotion is a significant driving force in moral judgment" (2002, 522).

Fourth, to support the claim that reasoning is not just post hoc but also biased, Haidt appeals to the literature on motivated reasoning. In particular, Haidt points to two factors that, according to him, make reasoning biased. The first is relatedness motives, according to which we tend to be motivated to agree with our friends, and, as a result, we tend actually to agree with our friends (Haidt 2001, 821). Haidt cites studies by Chaiken and her colleagues that found that people who expected to discuss an issue with a partner whose attitudes were known tended to express attitudes that were evaluatively consistent with the partner's opinion (Chen et al. 1996; Chaiken et al. 1996). As Chen et al. explain, sometimes we are motivated to agree with our friends just because we do not want to come across as being disagreeable. For example, when the views of our friends are unknown, we might employ a "moderate opinions minimize disagreement" heuristic in order to have a smooth interaction with such a friend (Chen et al. 1996, 263). Or when the views of our friends are known, we might employ a "go along to get along" heuristic to serve the same goal (Chen et al. 1996, 263). As Haidt says, the existence of such a motive means that the "mere fact that your friend expresses a moral judgment against X is often sufficient to cause in you a critical attitude toward X" (Haidt 2001, 821), which, according to Haidt, is a kind of bias. The second kind of factor that makes reasoning biased is what Haidt calls coherence motives (2001, 821). According to these motives, we tend to try to keep our attitudes and beliefs congruent with the beliefs and attitudes that are central to our identity, and we tend to dismiss evidence that threatens attitudes and beliefs that are constitutive of our identity. Haidt cites studies that found that we tend to accept evidence supporting our prior beliefs with *less scrutiny* and we tend to subject opposing evidence to *greater scrutiny*. For example, in the classic study by Charles Lord, Lee Ross, and Mark Lepper (1979) in which two groups of people were selected, one strongly in favor of capital punishment and the other strongly opposed to capital punishment, the researchers gave people from both groups some "mixed evidence," namely, a piece of new research that suggested that capital punishment was an effective deterrent and a piece of new research that suggested that capital punishment was not an effective deterrent. The researchers found that people tended to regard the research that was consistent with their original views to be better conducted and more convincing than the research that conflicted with their original views. Moreover, the researchers found that people tended to hold on to their initial views even more strongly after having been presented with the mixed evidence. According to Lord, Ross, and Lepper, this belief polarization does not seem to be a rational response, because learning about research that conflicted with our views should cause us to have reduced, rather than increased, confidence in our views. Haidt argues that these studies of motivated reasoning show that "the roots of human intelligence, rationality, and ethical sophistication should not be sought in our ability to search for and evaluate evidence *in an open and unbiased way*" (2001, 821; my emphasis).

Haidt's social intuitionist model has been criticized in a number of ways. I shall highlight three kinds of critiques here. First, some question whether Haidt has shown that our moral judgments tend to be generated by affect-laden intuitions and that reasoning tends to take place post hoc. For instance, it seems that intuitive judgments could just reflect the automatization of judgments based on prior moral reasoning (Saltzstein and Kasachkoff 2004). Consider an analogy. Learning to how to play the piano is initially cognitively demanding and requires reasoning, but once the skills are learned, playing the piano becomes automatic. Also, there is evidence that reasoning can disrupt the automatic process of judgment formation described by the social intuitionist model, either by a slow, intentional, deliberative and effortful "after the fact" correction, or by an "upfront" preconscious control (Fine 2006). For instance, there is ample evidence that many of us have implicit biases in favor of members of our in-groups and against members of some out-groups. At the same time, there is also evidence that one can override one's implicit biases and produce a judgment in accordance with one's explicit preference for moral impartiality. If so, this seems to suggest that reasoning does not have to take place post hoc and that reasoning can in fact occur alongside affect-laden intuitive processes.

In response to this critique, Haidt accepts these empirical possibilities, but he asserts that their occurrences are rare (Haidt and Bjorklund 2008). However, it might be asked, what evidence does Haidt have that the occurrences of reasoning prior to intuitive judgments are rare? In addition, it seems that one could just as well claim that the phenomenon of moral dumbfounding, which Haidt has used to show that affective intuitions can come before reasoning, is rare. For example, it could be argued that Haidt's case of Julie and Mark, discussed above, is a special case of incest constructed by Haidt and that in more mundane cases of incest, the possibility of inbreeding and the possible psychological harm to the siblings would seem to support and justify the judgment that incest is wrong. When pressed about how common private reflection, that is, reasoning prior to intuitive judgments, takes place, Haidt concedes that "there is not at present evidence that would allow an answer to this question" (2003, 198). That said, to be fair, Haidt's critics also have not shown that occurrences of reasoning prior to intuitive judgments are not rare. This means that what appear to be judgments based on reasoning could in fact just be judgments that are the result of some prior intuition. Hence, the debate on this point appears to be at a standstill, at least for now.

Second, as we have seen, one of Haidt's claims is that reasoning is biased. There is no doubt that reasoning can sometimes be biased. Indeed, there is good evidence that we are not very reliable at detecting correlations; we tend to be overconfident about the power of our reasoning; and so on (Nisbett and Ross 1980; Trope and Liberman 1996). Also, our cognitive limitations, including limits on our memory and attention, can further contribute to the relative unreliability of our reasoning. If so, the relevant issue is whether reasoning is usually, or tends to be, biased.

With respect to this issue, some people like to point out that there are debiasing strategies that one can employ to reduce possible biases in the reasoning process. For example, one may be able to employ the following strategies proposed by Wilson and Brekke (1994): First, we must be aware of the biases. Second, we must be motivated to correct these biases. Third, even if we are motivated to correct the biases, we must also be aware of the direction and the magnitude of the bias. Finally, we must be aware of whether we have sufficient control over our responses to be able to correct these biases. Bishop and Trout (2005) have proposed that one should consider explanations for propositions that one does not believe; make statistical judgments in terms of frequencies rather than probabilities; and so on. Likewise, Neil Levy (2006) has argued that reasoning can be put in the open and be subjected to a "community-wide" scrutiny "led by moral experts" and that in doing so, one can counter possible biases in reasoning. However, there are studies that show that people become more biased in groups (Kerr et al. 1996). Also, there are studies that show that peer review (by experts in a particular area) may be subject to the kinds of motivated reasoning that are seen in individuals (Mahoney 1977). As an example, some people speculate that theoretical physics in the last twenty years has been dominated by advocates of string theories at the expense of other theories (Smolin 2006). If biases can take place at the community-wide level, then community-wide scrutiny may only have limited power in canceling out biases in reasoning.

Another possible response to Haidt is to question his claim that reasoning tends to be biased (Liao 2011). Recall that Haidt cites relatedness motives, according to which we tend to be motivated to agree with our friends and, as a result, tend actually to agree with our friends, to support his claim that reasoning tends to be biased. Haidt is assuming that relatedness motives are always biases. However, one can question whether this is true. Here is a reason why relatedness motives may not always be biases. A friend is typically someone whose judgments you have reasons to trust in general. That is, you have reasons to trust that when your friend disagrees with you, she will be honest with you, try to familiarize herself with the relevant available evidence that bears on the issue, exercise epistemic virtues such as intelligence and thoughtfulness, and so on. Suppose that you find yourself in a disagreement with your friend about a particular matter. Suppose further that you and she are both fallible and neither has any special epistemic advantage regarding the issue at stake. Can it be epistemically rational for you to reason that because she is your friend and because she disagrees with you, you should suspend your judgment or at least lose some confidence in your judgment? Arguably, given that you trust her judgments in general, it can be epistemically rational for you to believe that there is a chance you might be mistaken and that she might be correct on this particular occasion. Given this, it can be epistemically rational for you to lose some confidence in your judgment. In other words, the relatedness motives merely show that we have a tendency to be motivated to agree with our friends. But one should distinguish between

(a) our tendency to be motivated to agree with our friends because we want to be harmonious with our friends, and

(b) our tendency to be motivated to agree with our friends because we tend to trust our friends' judgments in general.

Both (a) and (b) can explain why we have the tendency to be motivated to agree with our friends. But while (a) may be epistemically irrational, (b) need not be, since it can be epistemically justified to trust a friend's judgment (e.g., based on how the friend has judged in the past about other matters). Given that (a) is Haidt's explanation for why we have the tendency to be motivated to agree with our friends, but (b) is a plausible alternative and is not epistemically irrational, the fact that we tend to be motivated to agree with our friends need not always be a bias. Similar things can be said about the coherence motives, though, owing to limited space, I shall not do so here. If relatedness motives and coherence motives are not always biases, then Haidt has not established that our reasoning tends to be biased. If so, this undercuts his claim that the purpose of reasoning is to provide a biased basis for justification.

Third, some people worry that if the social intuitionist model were an accurate description of how we arrive at our moral judgments, then the evidential weight of many of our moral judgments would be undercut. For instance, Alan Gibbard states that "if intuitions are the sorts of states that figure in Haidt's picture, [that is, if they are ones that reach moral conclusions all by themselves,] why place any stock in them?" (2008, 14). Likewise, Jeanette Kennett and Cordelia Fine (2009) argue that the social intuitionist model challenges our normative conception of ourselves as agents capable of grasping and responding to reasons, and that there can be no "real" moral judgments in the absence of a capacity for reflective shaping and endorsement of moral judgments. Let us consider Kennett and Fine's arguments in greater detail.

To make their case, Kennett and Fine first draw on Karen Jones's (2003) distinction between reason trackers and reason responders. Reason trackers are capable of registering reasons and behaving in accordance with them, but reason trackers need not possess the concept of a reason nor have a self-conception. Reason responders are agents capable of responding to reasons as reasons. As Kennett and Fine explain, nonhuman animals such as birds, reptiles, dogs, and young human beings such as small children may be reason trackers, but they do not have the cognitive capacity to respond to reasons as reasons, and are therefore not reason responders. Persons, on the other hand, are both reason trackers and reason responders.

Next, Kennett and Fine argue that the distinction between reason tracking and reason responding maps onto a dual-processing model of moral judgments such as Haidt's social intuitionist model. In particular, "Reason tracking is fast and automatic with only the results available to consciousness. Reason responding is a slower, controlled, deliberative process" (2009, 81). According to this line of thought, those who tend to use the affect-laden intuitive process to make moral judgments are reason trackers, while those who tend to use the reasoning process to make moral judgments are reason responders.

Kennett and Fine then argue that normative agency requires reason-responding capacities and not just reason-tracking capacities. In other words, beings with only reason-tracking capacities are not normative agents. For instance, they point out that birds, reptiles, dogs, and small children may be able to respond effectively and efficiently to cues in their environments. They are therefore reason trackers. However, they are not reason responders. As such, they are not normative agents.

Finally, Kennett and Fine argue that if the social intuitionist model were an accurate description of how we make moral judgments, then we would be reason trackers rather than reason responders. Given that normative agency requires that we be reason responders rather than reason trackers, it follows that if the social intuitionist model were true, then we would not be normative agents.

What are we to make of Kennett and Fine's argument? I shall offer two observations. First, it seems that they are relying on a fairly thin notion of the intuitive process, according to which if a cognitive process is fast, automatic, and unconscious, then it qualifies as an intuitive process. As we have seen, on their understanding of the intuitive process, even birds, reptiles, and dogs are capable of having such a cognitive process. To be fair to Kennett and Fine, Haidt and a number of people who accept a dual-processing model of moral judgments have tended to understand an intuitive process in something like this manner (or at least they have not argued that an intuitive process could not be understood in this manner). Given this, Kennett and Fine's arguments may in fact have some force against their views.

Arguably though, the kind of intuitive process that is of interest to philosophers is not so thin. There are many accounts of intuitions, including conceptual accounts, rationalist accounts, virtue-based accounts, and naturalistic accounts of intuitions.[4] However intuitions are understood, a case can be made that the kind of intuitive process that is of interest to philosophers need not be fast, automatic, and unconscious. For instance, consider the following thought experiment:

> **Brain Transplant:** Suppose that there are two human beings, Abbey and Brenda. Both have their cerebrums removed. The cerebrum that had been in Brenda is then destroyed, while the cerebrum that had been in Abbey is transplanted into the skull that had encased Brenda's cerebrum. Let us call the being that receives the cerebrum transplant "Brenbey" while the name "Cerebrumless" will refer to the now mindless body that had earlier contained Abbey's cerebrum. And let us suppose that Brenbey has Abbey's psychology and is now able to (quasi-)know and (quasi-)remember things that Abbey had known and remembered.

Suppose that one is asked about one's judgment regarding whether Abbey is Cerebrumless or Brenbey (or neither). It might take some time for one to understand this case, after which it might take still more time for one to form a judgment regarding whether Abbey is Cerebrumless or Brenbey (or neither). This would not mean that one's judgment was therefore not an intuitive judgment. Suppose that the judgment one makes is an intuitive judgment. This would mean that one need not form an intuitive judgment quickly and automatically.

In addition, it also does not seem necessary that an intuitive judgment must be formed unconsciously. Consider again Brain Transplant. It seems that one can consciously be thinking about whether Abbey is Cerebrumless or Brenbey (or neither) and that one can be aware that one is intuiting. As far as I can tell, this phenomenon seems ubiquitous; that is, in many cases, we know, through introspection, that we are intuiting. Also, there are a number of ways one can figure out whether one is intuiting or not. For example, we can eliminate incidences in which we are reasoning or employing cognitive processes other than intuiting (e.g., recall). If so, this suggests that one can form an intuitive judgment at least in part consciously.

A second thing to say about Kennett and Fine's argument is the following. Consider a paradigm example of an intuitive moral judgment, such as it is wrong to torture innocent people for fun. It does not seem that this is a kind of judgment that birds, reptiles, dogs, and even small children can make. If so, this again calls into question Kennett and Fine's thin notion of an intuitive process. In addition, let us consider whether a being who can only make intuitive judgments, such as the judgment that it is wrong to torture innocent people for fun, can have normative agency and whether a judgment that is produced solely by the intuitive process can be a genuine moral judgment. As far as I can tell, it seems both that such a being can have normative agency and that the judgment that it is wrong to torture innocent people for fun can be a genuine moral judgment, even if this judgment is produced solely by the intuitive process. If so, *pace* Kennett and Fine, it is not the case that a being that only has the intuitive capacities cannot be a normative agent; and that judgments generated solely from this kind of intuitive process cannot be genuine moral judgments. In other words, moral judgments generated by intuitions need not be less reliable or truth-tracking than moral judgments generated by reasoning. Shortly, we shall discuss a different way of questioning the reliability of intuitive judgments based on the idea that intuitions are heuristics, that is, some kind of mental rules of thumb.

1.5. Innate Moral Faculty and Moral Judgments

At this point, it is worth discussing a different model of moral judgment, a version of which says that both emotions and reasoning take place after a moral judgment has already been made. As we shall see, neuroscientific results have also been employed to support such a model of moral judgment. Drawing on Noam Chomsky's influential research program in generative linguistics, John Mikhail, Marc Hauser, and their colleagues argue that human beings are endowed with an innate moral faculty.[5] In particular, just as the mind may be equipped with a universal set of principles or "grammar" that enables any normal developing human being in different cultures unconsciously to generate and comprehend a limitless range of well-formed sentences in his or her native language, Mikhail et al. argue that our mind may also be equipped with a universal "moral" grammar that enables each of us in different cultures unconsciously and automatically to evaluate a limitless variety of actions and to generate moral evaluations such as right and wrong. For instance, our mind may have domain-general cognitive mechanisms that generate representations of actions based on variables such as agent, intention, belief, action, receiver, consequence, and moral evaluation. Some complex, possibly domain-specific, cognitive mechanism, that is, the moral faculty, would then combine these representations to generate moral judgments such as "impermissible," "permissible," and "obligatory." There could be at least two versions of how the moral faculty works (Hauser et al. 2008). On a strong version, the moral faculty would directly produce a moral judgment. This version would imply that emotions and reasoning do not cause the initial moral judgment, but rather are caused by the initial judgment. On a weak version, there is an appraisal system that analyzes the causes and consequences of actions, leading to an emotion or process of deliberate reasoning or both, which then produces a moral judgment.

Why think that such a moral faculty exists? An argument in favor of such a moral faculty is the argument from poverty of moral stimulus, according to which the manner by which children acquire their moral capacities suggests that at least some of the core attributes for our moral faculty are innate; that is, they are largely determined by the inherent, biological structure of the mind (Mikhail 2007, 144). As Susan Dwyer explains,

> Absent a detailed account of how children extrapolate distinctly moral rules from the barrage of parental imperatives and evaluations, the appeal to explicit moral instruction will not provide anything like a satisfactory explanation of the emergence of mature moral competence. What we have here is a set of complex, articulated abilities that (i) emerge over time in an environment that is impoverished with respect to the content and scope of their mature manifestations, and (ii) appear to develop across the species. (1999, 173)

Mikhail offers a variety of evidence for the existence of a moral faculty. For instance, he points to studies, which we discussed above, that show that three- to four-year-old children can make the moral/conventional distinction. Also, Mikhail notes that every natural language seems to have words to express basic deontic concepts such as obligatory, permissible, and forbidden; and that prohibitions of murder, rape, and other types of aggression appear to be universal or nearly so, as do legal distinctions based on causation, intention, and voluntary behavior. More pertinently, Mikhail cites Moll et al.'s brain-imaging results as evidence that there is a fairly consistent network of brain regions involved in moral cognition (Mikhail 2007, 143). Lastly, both Mikhail and Hauser argue that surveys using trolley dilemmas show that people make rapid, intuitive moral judgments regarding these cases, and that their judgments appear to be widely shared among demographically diverse populations. According to Mikhail, "The length, complexity and abstract nature of these computations, along with their rapid, intuitive and at least partially inaccessible character lends support to the hypothesis that they depend on innate, domain-specific algorithms" (2007, 148).

To assess whether there is an innate moral faculty, recall that there are at least two versions of how the moral faculty might work. On the weak version, there is an appraisal system that analyzes the causes and consequences of actions, leading to an emotion or process of deliberate reasoning, or both, which then produces a moral judgment. On the strong version, the moral faculty produces a moral judgment, and emotions and reasoning are caused by the judgment. It seems that most people would accept the weak version. That is, most people would accept that in order to make a moral judgment, one first needs to analyze the action at issue, and that to do so there needs to be some kind of biological system that can represent and analyze the causes and consequences of the action. Hence, in his critique of the universal moral grammar model of moral judgment, Ron Mallon states, "I am inclined to agree . . . that there must be action appraisals that are upstream of moral judgment and that the capacity for such appraisals may well be substantially innate" (2008, 145–146). Likewise, Jesse Prinz, who, as we shall see, is critical of the universal moral grammar model, says, "I think Hauser et al. are absolutely right that moral judgment typically requires action analysis, but they are wrong to deny that other theories leave this out. One cannot make a moral judgment about an event without first categorizing that event" (2008, 161). If so, the issue is whether the strong version is true.

According to Prinz, the strong version of the universal moral grammar model must be false, because emotions can be inputs of moral judgments (2008, 161; this volume). However, while all can agree that emotions can amplify the intensity of moral judgments, it may be open to Mikhail and others to question whether emotions can generate moral judgments (Pizarro et al. 2011; Decety and Cacioppo 2012). In response to such a line of argument, Prinz has argued that there is evidence that emotions can shift moral judgments from positive to negative, which suggests that emotions can generate moral judgments (Seidel and Prinz 2013). Be that as it may, recall a point made earlier against Haidt's social intuitionist model that reasoning can at least sometimes disrupt the automatic process of judgment formation by an upfront, conscious control. For instance, one can override one's implicit biases that favor members of one's in-group; and one can produce a judgment that is in accordance with one's explicit preference for moral impartiality. This suggests that reasoning can sometimes be inputs of moral judgments, which would (also) challenge the strong version of the universal moral grammar model, according to which reasoning could not be inputs of moral judgments. If so, there are good reasons to believe that the strong version is too strong. This said, there may be conceptual space for a hybrid version of the universal moral grammar model, according to which moral judgments are sometimes produced by the innate moral faculty alone and sometimes by other cognitive processes such as reasoning and possibly emotions. As we have said, intuitive moral judgments are not the product of the reasoning process. Suppose further that the intuitive process and the emotional process are distinct cognitive processes. If so, arguably, a case can be made that the intuitive processes are part of a certain innate moral faculty that can produce (intuitive) moral judgments without the inputs of reasoning or emotions.

Whether this is plausible or not, what is true is that more work needs to be done to distinguish the intuitive process from reasoning and emotions and to identify the neural correlates of the intuitive process.

I.6. Neuroscience and Normative Ethics

As noted at the outset, there is an ongoing debate regarding whether consequentialism or nonconsequentialism, that is, deontology, is the correct moral theory. To repeat, consequentialism holds that what we ought to do is maximize the best consequences. Deontology, on the other hand, holds that sometimes other things besides consequences, such as fairness, intentions, and so on, can matter in determining what we ought to do. A way to draw out the difference between the two theories is through the use of trolley dilemmas. For instance, consider again

> **Switch:** a runaway trolley is headed toward five people who will be killed. One can hit a switch that will turn the trolley onto another set of tracks where another person sits and where the trolley will kill this person instead of the five.

> **Footbridge:** as before a runaway trolley is threatening to kill five people. One is standing next to a large man on a footbridge, and one can push the large man off the bridge. The large man will die, but his body will stop the trolley from reaching the five people, thereby saving the five.

As we have seen, people tend to think that it is permissible to hit the switch in Switch but impermissible to push the large man in Footbridge. Deontology appears to be able to capture these judgments through something like the Doctrine of Double Effect (DDE), which distinguishes between intending harm and merely foreseeing harm. There is no standard formulation of the DDE.[6] According to one interpretation of it, there is a moral constraint on acting with the intention of doing harm, even when the harm will be used as a means to a greater good (see Kamm 2007, 93, for this formulation). However, it is permissible to act with the intention of employing neutral or good means to promote a greater good, even though one foresees the same harmful side effects, if (*a*) the good is proportionate to the harm, and (*b*) there is no better way to achieve this good. On the DDE, it would be permissible to hit the switch because one merely foresees the death of the one on the sidetrack but one does not intend the person to be hit as a means to saving the five other innocent people. In contrast, it would not be permissible to push the large man, because one intends the large man to be hit by the trolley as a means to stopping the trolley from hitting the five. Consequentialism (at least of the simpler kind, such as act consequentialism), on the other hand, appears unable to capture these judgments. On consequentialism, it would be permissible both to hit the switch and to push the large man off the footbridge, because in both cases the consequences appear to be the same, that is, either one dies or five die.

However, Judith Jarvis Thomson has famously challenged the DDE using a version of the following trolley dilemma (Thomson 1985):

Loop: A runaway trolley is headed toward five innocent people who are on the track and who will be killed unless something is done. Abigail can push a button, which will redirect the trolley onto a second track, where there is an innocent bystander. The runaway trolley would be stopped by hitting the innocent bystander, thereby saving the five but killing the innocent bystander. The second track loops back toward the five people. Hence, if it were not the case that the trolley would hit the innocent bystander and grind to a halt, the trolley would go around and kill the five people.[7]

In Loop, hitting the innocent bystander is causally required to stop the trolley and to save the five other innocent people. According to Thomson, redirecting the trolley therefore seems to involve intending to hit the innocent bystander in order to save the five other innocent people. Given this, the DDE should forbid redirecting the trolley in Loop. However, Thomson argues that intuitively it seems permissible to redirect the trolley in Loop, just like Switch. As Thomson asks, what difference can an extra bit of track make? Since the DDE appears to prohibit an action that Thomson suggests we find intuitively permissible, she argues that we should give up the DDE.

Greene has pointed to Loop in his research in order to suggest that deontology does not have an upper hand over consequentialism with respect to explaining trolley dilemmas and to suggest that the debate between deontology and consequentialism remains unsettled (see, e.g., Greene et al. 2001). Whether Loop serves as a clear counterexample to the DDE is up for debate. Frances Kamm (2007), for example, agrees with Thomson that it is permissible to redirect the trolley in Loop, but she argues that what she calls the Doctrine of Triple Effect (DTE) can explain the permissibility of doing so. Liao et al. (2011), on the other hand, argue that judgments about Loop vary according to the order in which the case is considered and that this undermines the supposed evidential status of our judgments about Loop. In any case, what is novel about Greene's research program is that he believes that evidence from neuroscience can be used to advance this debate between consequentialism and deontology by supporting the idea that deontological judgments are unreliable or not truth-tracking, while consequentialist judgments are reliable or truth-tracking.

As we have seen, Greene gave subjects moral dilemmas, including trolley dilemmas such as Switch and Footbridge, and he found that emotional regions of the brain were more active when subjects made "characteristically deontological judgments," for example, judging that it was not appropriate to push the large man off the footbridge in Footbridge. In contrast, Greene found that when people made "characteristically consequentialist judgments," for example, judging that it was appropriate to push the large man off the footbridge, cognitive regions of the brain were activated. When he examined the brain activity of the subjects who made characteristically consequentialist judgments, he found that they showed more activity in parts of the brain associated with cognitive control than those who made characteristically deontological judgments.

Greene's (2008) striking claim is that these results suggest that deontological judgments are not produced by reasoning; instead, they are triggered by the "up close and personal" features of the cases, for example, the act of pushing the large man off the footbridge. Greene argues that from an evolutionary perspective, it is understandable why subjects would react to "up close and personal" features of the cases. As he explains, "up close and personal" violence is evolutionarily ancient and predates our recently evolved human capacities for complex abstract reasoning. Given this, Greene claims that "it should come as no surprise if we have innate responses to personal violence that are powerful but rather primitive. That is, we might expect humans to have negative emotional responses to certain basic forms of interpersonal violence" (2008, 43). However, so argues Greene, ethically speaking, the "up close and personal" factor is a "contingent, nonmoral feature of our evolutionary history" and is morally irrelevant (70). Given this, since deontological, affective intuitive judgments are responding to this morally irrelevant factor, we have a reason to discount our deontological judgments. In contrast, Greene claims that consequentialist judgments are "less emotional and more 'cognitive'" (63). Accordingly, Greene believes that consequentialist judgments are more reliable or truth-tracking.

Some philosophers have quickly endorsed Greene's idea that neuroscience can be used to question the reliability of deontological judgments. For instance, Peter Singer writes, "If . . . Greene is right to suggest that our intuitive responses are due to differences in the emotional pull of situations that involve bringing about someone's death in a close-up, personal way, and bringing about the same person's death in a way that is at a distance, and less personal, why should we believe that there is anything that justifies these responses?" (2005, 347). Following Greene, Singer proceeds to claim that deontological judgments are "the biological residue of our evolutionary history" and that therefore we should not regard them as having normative force, while consequentialist judgments are the product of reasoning and are therefore not "the outcome of our evolutionary past" (347).

Other philosophers are, however, skeptical that Greene's neuroscientific findings have this kind of normative implication. In particular, Selim Berker argues that Greene faces a dilemma: either his attempts to derive normative implications from the neuroscientific results rely on bad inferences; or else they appeal to substantive normative intuitions that render the neuroscientific results irrelevant to the argument.[8] To establish the first horn of the dilemma, Berker identifies three arguments that Greene could be making. According to what Berker calls the "emotions bad, reasoning good" argument, Greene could be arguing that

P.   Deontological intuitions are driven by emotions, whereas consequentialist intuitions involve abstract reasoning.

C. So deontological intuitions, unlike consequentialist intuitions, do not have any genuine normative force.

Berker argues that this is not a good argument because, among other things, we need a reason for thinking that intuitions based on emotions are less likely to be reliable than those based in reasoning, and this argument alone does not supply such a reason (2009, 316). Next, Berker proposes that Greene could be putting forward the argument from heuristics:

P1. Deontological intuitions are driven by emotions, whereas consequentialist intuitions involve abstract reasoning.

P2. In other domains, emotional processes tend to involve fast-and-frugal (and hence unreliable) heuristics.

C1. So, in the moral domain, the emotional processes that drive deontological intuitions involve fast-and-frugal (and hence unreliable) heuristics.

C2. So deontological intuitions, unlike consequentialist intuitions, are unreliable.

Berker argues that this is also not a good argument because, among other things, when something is a heuristic, usually we have a good grasp of what the right and wrong answers in the relevant domain are. However, so argues Berker, it is not a settled matter what the right and wrong answers in the moral domain are. Given this, it seems problematic to hold that emotional processes in the moral domain consist in heuristics.

Finally, according to what Berker calls the argument from evolutionary history, Greene could be arguing that

P. Our emotion-driven deontological intuitions are evolutionary byproducts that were adapted to handle an environment we no longer find ourselves in.

C. So deontological intuitions, unlike consequentialist intuitions, do not have any genuine normative force.

Berker argues that consequentialist intuitions are just as much a product of evolution as deontological intuitions are, and therefore "an appeal to evolutionary history gives us no reason to privilege consequentialist intuitions over deontological ones" (2009, 319).

To establish the second horn of the dilemma, Berker argues that Greene is appealing to substantive normative intuitions that render Greene's neuroscientific results irrelevant. According to Berker, Greene, most charitably interpreted, is arguing that deontological judgments are responding to factors that are morally irrelevant, namely, up-close-and-personal harm, and that, therefore, deontological judgments should not be trusted. However, suppose that up-close-and-personal harm were a morally irrelevant factor.

According to Berker, this is a substantive intuition that one derives from the armchair; Greene's neuroscientific results appear to play no role in one's having this substantive intuition. As Berker elaborates,

> The "emotion-based" nature of deontological intuitions has no ultimate bearing on the argument's cogency. . . . Issues about the evolutionary history of our dispositions to have deontological and consequentialist intuitions are also irrelevant to the argument's cogency. Even the claim that these two sets of intuitions stem from separate faculties is irrelevant to the argument's cogency. (The argument would be just as plausible if it turned out that only one faculty was responding to two different sorts of factors.) (2009, 326)

Hence, Berker concludes that, once Greene's argument turns on whether deontological or consequentialist judgments are responding to morally irrelevant factors, "we end up factoring out . . . any contribution that the psychological processes underlying those judgments might make to our evaluation of the judgments in question" (326).

Let me offer five thoughts regarding Greene's attempt to use neuroscience to call into question the reliability of deontological judgments, some of which are supportive of Greene's project, while others are critical. First, as far as I am aware, all the interlocutors here, including Greene, would agree that in order to generate normative conclusions from certain empirical research, normative premises are needed. For instance, all would agree that the following argument is incomplete:

P1. Deontological judgments are driven by emotions.
C: Therefore, deontological judgments are unreliable.

To complete the argument, all would agree that an additional normative premise such as the following is needed:

P1. Deontological judgments are driven by emotions.
P2. Judgments that are driven by emotions are unreliable.
C: Therefore, deontological judgments are unreliable.

Second, it seems clear that it would be too strong to claim that evidence from neuroscience is necessary to generate normative conclusions. Consider Greene's claim that deontological judgments are unreliable. Philosophers made this point before the advent of brain-imaging studies. For instance, Singer (1997) has long argued that we should question deontological intuitions such as the thought that we should save a nearby drowning child but that we have no comparable obligation to save a faraway sick and starving child. Given this, it is unlikely that neuroscientists such as Greene are claiming that evidence from neuroscience is necessary to generate normative conclusions.

Third, a more plausible interpretation of Greene is that he is claiming that evidence from neuroscience can advance existing debates by tipping the balance in favor of one theory over another theory. This of course raises the question of how evidence from neuroscience can accomplish this feat. One possibility is to use evidence from neuroscience as part of an *epistemic debunking argument* (see also Kahane, this volume). To see what an epistemic debunking argument is, consider two ways to challenge a claim. One way is to challenge the first-order reasons given for a claim. For instance, suppose that you and a friend are debating about whether Lebron James or Kobe Bryant is the better basketball player. Suppose that your friend argues that Lebron is the better player because he has better individual stats than Kobe. You might respond that this does not therefore show that Lebron is the better player by pointing out that Kobe has won more NBA championships. In doing so, you would be suggesting that your friend has overlooked some crucial first-order evidence that is needed to determine whether Lebron or Kobe is the better basketball player.

Another way to challenge a claim is to point out that the claim may be the result of some kind of performance error in one's thinking/reasoning ability, error that is not the result of having inadequate or mistaken first-order evidence. Performance errors might include partiality, clouded emotions, mistaken heuristics, and so on (see, e.g., Sinnott-Armstrong 2006; Liao 2008). For instance, suppose that your friend and Lebron James are both from Cleveland, Ohio. Suppose you suspect that your friend may be driven by partiality when she claims that Lebron is the better player. You might point out to your friend that she and Lebron are both from Cleveland in order to raise the possibility that she may be driven by partiality, as a means to call into question your friend's claim that Lebron is the better basketball player. In this case, you would be making a kind of epistemic debunking argument against your friend's claim. The argument would be something like this:

Q1.   The claim that Lebron James is the better player may be driven by partiality.
Q2.   Claims that are based on partiality are unreliable.
 C: Therefore, the claim that Lebron James is the better player may be unreliable.

Notice that epistemic debunking arguments do not directly challenge an individual's first-order evidence. For instance, when you point out to your friend that both she and Lebron are from Cleveland, you are not questioning her first-order evidence; for example, you are not arguing that the stats that she has produced to support her claim that Lebron is the better player are incorrect. In addition, notice that an epistemic debunking argument does not show that a particular claim is false. At best, it shows that the claim may be unreliable and therefore one may not be justified in believing in the claim. For instance, by pointing out to your friend that both she and Lebron are from Cleveland, you do not thereby show that your friend's claim that Lebron is the better player is false. You have only raised the concern that your friend's claim may be unreliable and that she may not be justified in believing in this claim.

Using evidence from empirical research as part of an epistemic debunking argument is ubiquitous. For instance, research on implicit bias has been used to raise questions about hiring decisions. People on hiring committees typically believe that they are evaluating dossiers fairly and impartially. Empirical research has shown, however, that people tend to favor males over females, whites over nonwhites, and so on, when making hiring decisions, even though they believe that they are making fair and impartial evaluations. For instance, in one study, academic psychologists evaluated a curriculum vitae randomly assigned a male or a female name. Both male and female participants gave the male applicant better evaluations for teaching, research, and service experience and were more likely to recommend hiring the male than the female applicant (Steinpreis et al. 1999). In another study, randomly assigning different names to resumes showed that job applicants with "white-sounding names" were more likely to be interviewed for open positions than were equally qualified applicants with "African American–sounding names" (Bertrand and Mullainathan 2004). Moreover, when symphony orchestras adopted "blind" auditions by using a screen to conceal candidates' identities, the hiring of women musicians increased (Goldin and Rouse 2000). Using evidence from such empirical research, one can put forward the following debunking argument to raise questions about hiring decisions.

R1. Some hiring decisions involving minority groups are driven by implicit biases.
R2. Judgments that are driven by implicit biases are unreliable.
C: Therefore, some hiring decisions involving minority groups are unreliable.

In a similar vein, evidence from neuroscience can also be used as part of an epistemic debunking argument. Indeed, it seems that Greene's argument against deontological judgments can be put in this form:

S1. Deontological judgments are the product of affect-laden intuitive processes.
S2. Judgments that are the product of affect-laden intuitive processes are unreliable.
C: Therefore, deontological judgments are unreliable.

Hence, at least in theory, Greene's neuroscientific evidence could advance existing debates by being part of an epistemic debunking argument.

Fourth, suppose that Greene is making a kind of epistemic debunking argument. How good is Greene's debunking argument? Let us consider each premise in turn. Consider

S1. Deontological judgments are the product of affect-laden, intuitive processes.

As noted earlier, Greene gave subjects various impersonal and personal moral dilemmas, including trolley dilemmas such as Switch and Footbridge. Finding that emotional regions of the brain were more active when subjects made "characteristically deontological judgments," for example, judging that it was not appropriate to push the large man off the footbridge in Footbridge, Greene argues that these results suggest that the "up close and personal" features of the cases, for example, the act of pushing the large man off the footbridge, trigger negative emotional responses that produce the deontological judgments. Let us accept that at least some deontological judgments are intuitive judgments. Let us also accept that Greene has shown that some deontological judgments are correlated with affect-laden responses. Has Greene shown that deontological judgments are the product of such affect-laden responses? It is not clear that he has. To see this, we can modify Footbridge so that it does not involve up-close-and-personal harm at all. Consider the following:

> **Push:** A runaway trolley is headed toward five innocent people who are on the track and who will be killed unless something is done. Brandon can push a button, which will activate a moveable platform that will move an innocent bystander in front of the trolley. The runaway trolley will be stopped by hitting the innocent bystander, thereby saving the five but killing the innocent bystander.[9]

In this case, there is no up-close-and-personal harm. Nor does Push involve what Greene now calls "personal force," which is present when "the force that directly impacts the victim is generated by the agent's muscles" (Greene et al. 2009, 364). Indeed, to save the five, Brandon merely has to push a button. Given this, Push should not trigger the kind of affect-laden responses that Greene has in mind. Nevertheless, Liao et al. found that most people still judge that it is impermissible for Brandon to push the button in Push, just like Footbridge (Liao et al. 2011). This suggests that affect-laden responses are not necessary to produce deontological judgments. In fact, it is compatible with Greene's findings that something else is producing these deontological judgments and that the negative emotional responses merely amplify these judgments (see, e.g., Pizarro et al. 2011). In other words, the negative emotional responses can cause a subject to judge a wrongful action to be even more wrong. For instance, killing someone with a gun and killing someone with a hammer are both wrong, but people may judge the latter action to be more wrong, given their negative emotional responses to this way of being killed. In any case, examples like Push call into question Greene's claim that deontological judgments are the product of affect-laden responses.

Next, let us consider

S2. Judgments that are the product of affect-laden, intuitive processes are unreliable.

To support this premise, Greene appeals to the literature on heuristics and biases, according to which intuitions are heuristics, that is, some kind of mental rules of thumb.[10] A number of people in this literature, including Greene, then question the reliability of intuitions by pointing out the tendency of heuristics to be inaccurate. For example, Kahneman and Tversky—pioneers of the program on heuristics and biases—famously argue that intuitions are heuristics and that heuristics can lead even the experts astray (Kahneman and Frederick 2005; Kahneman et al. 1982). Likewise, inspired by the heuristics and biases program, Cass Sunstein too proclaims that "moral heuristics exist and indeed are omnipresent. We should not treat the underlying moral intuitions as fixed points for analysis, rather than as unreliable and potentially erroneous" (2005, 531). Similarly, Greene (this volume) also endorses this picture of moral intuitions, according to which moral intuitions tend to be inaccurate, whereas moral reasoning tends to be accurate. Greene offers the following analogy based on digital single-lens reflex (DSLR) cameras. DSLR cameras have an automatic mode and a manual mode. The automatic mode employs heuristics that are efficient but not very flexible. The manual mode is flexible but not efficient. According to Greene, the automatic mode is better suited for familiar problems, whereas the manual mode is better suited for unfamiliar problems. Greene then argues that moral intuitions that produce characteristically deontological judgments are like the automatic mode. They are heuristics that may have operated well for familiar problems in our evolutionary past. But these heuristics are not well suited to handle the kind of unfamiliar problems that we face today. In contrast, moral reasoning that produces characteristically consequentialist judgments is like the manual mode. It is flexible and can be adapted to solve the kind of problems that we face today.

In response to this proposal that intuitions are heuristics and are therefore unreliable, some people accept that intuitions are heuristics but argue that heuristics can be fairly reliable in certain circumstances. For instance, Gerd Gigerenzer takes this approach (Gigerenzer and Todd 1999; Gigerenzer 2008) and argues that "what intuitionist theories could gain from the science of heuristics is to explicate intuition in terms of fast and frugal heuristics" (2008, 9). Equating intuitions with fast, automatic, and affect-laden processing, but not necessarily with heuristics, James Woodward and John Allman argue that moral intuitions are part of a larger set of social intuitions that guide us through complex, highly uncertain, and rapidly changing social interactions, and that they can sometimes play a legitimate role in moral decision-making.[11]

As we have seen from Berker, another possible response to this proposal that intuitions are heuristics and are therefore unreliable is to distinguish between nonmoral and moral intuitions and to argue that moral intuitions may not be heuristics, because unlike the use of heuristics in nonmoral domains, where we have a good grasp of what the right and wrong answers are, it is up for debate what the right and wrong answers in the moral domain are. Berker's point notwithstanding, Walter Sinnott-Armstrong, Liane Young, and Fiery Cushman have argued that moral intuitions are heuristics (Sinnott-Armstrong et al. 2010, 250). Also, if deontological judgments are the product of general, affect-laden, intuitive processes that have been found to be unreliable in nonmoral domains, it might be thought that this is sufficient to call into question the reliability of deontological judgments, whether or not one knows the right answers in the moral domain. Arguably, this is the point of an epistemic debunking argument. For instance, pointing out that your friend may be exhibiting partiality may be sufficient to call into question the reliability of your friend's claim that Lebron is the better basketball player, whether or not you know that Lebron James is the better basketball player. Later on, I shall consider a third way of responding to the proposal that intuitions are heuristics and are therefore unreliable, namely, by questioning whether intuitions—moral and nonmoral—are heuristics at all (see Liao, this volume).

Fifth and last point. As we have seen, Greene believes that the neuroimaging results support the idea that deontological judgments are not reliable, while consequentialist, utilitarian judgments are reliable. However, taking Greene's methodology and findings at face value, one might ask whether the neuroimaging results call into question the reliability of utilitarian judgments. To see this, recall that several research groups found that patients with ventromedial brain damages also tended to express utilitarian judgments. For instance, Koenigs et al. (2007) and Ciaramelli et al. (2007) both found that VMPFC patients were more likely than a control population to make utilitarian decisions in trolley dilemmas. In addition, studies that induced positive emotions in subjects also elicited utilitarian judgments. For instance, Valdesolo and DeSteno (2006) found that subjects who watched five minutes of comedy were more willing to sacrifice the large stranger in Footbridge. Greene interprets these results as lending support to his dual-processing theory on the ground that if people tended to disapprove of the utilitarian choice in personal moral dilemmas such as Footbridge as a result of negative social emotional responses, then modulating the emotional responses should affect people's choices, which these studies appear to have found (Greene 2015). However, there is an alternative way of interpreting these results, one that calls into question the reliability of utilitarian judgments. The alternative explanation is that the utilitarian choice is driven by a decreased aversion to harming others and by deficits in social processing. To support this alternative explanation, recall that VMPFC patients are known to be poor reasoners outside lab settings. Given this, it seems that the fact that these VMPFC patients also tended to make utilitarian judgments should cause one to question the reliability of utilitarian judgments. Also, Valdesolo and DeSteno's study is compatible with the idea that utilitarian judgments are driven, not by reasoning at all, but by a different kind of emotional reaction, namely, lightheartedness.

In fact, in a different study, Koenigs and Tranel (2007) found that VMPFC patients did not lack emotions; instead they experienced increased presence of different emotions. As Koenigs and Tranel write, VMPFC patients "tend to exhibit exaggerated anger, irritability, emotional outbursts, and tantrums, particularly in social situations involving frustration or provocation" (2007, 5). Moreover, numerous recent studies have found that subjects with psychopathic tendencies and decreased levels of empathy were more likely to make the utilitarian choice (Bartels and Pizarro 2011; Conway and Gawronski

2013; Gao and Tang 2013; Gleichgerrcht et al. 2013; Glenn et al. 2010; Koenigs et al. 2012; Young et al. 2012). For instance, Bartels and Pizarro found that participants who indicated greater endorsement of utilitarian solutions had higher scores on measures of psychopathy, Machiavellianism, and life meaninglessness (Bartels and Pizarro 2011). Also, Côté et al. (2013) found that reduced empathy can explain why upper-class participants were more likely to make the utilitarian choice in Footbridge than lower-class participants. Lastly, Greene's dual-processing theory implies that decreased higher-order functioning such as executive functioning should lead to decreased utilitarian preference, while decreased emotions should lead to increased utilitarian preference. Duke and Bègue hypothesized that since alcohol impairs both social cognition, that is, empathy, and higher-order executive functioning, alcohol can be used to test whether utilitarian response is the result of increased deliberative reasoning or the result of decreased aversion to harming others (Duke and Bègue 2015). Indeed, they found that participants' blood alcohol concentrations were positively correlated with utilitarian preferences. According to Duke and Bègue, this suggests that impaired social cognition rather than intact deliberative reasoning predicts utilitarian responses in trolley dilemmas. Taking these studies together, and assuming the validity of Greene's general methodology, a case can be made that neuroimaging results call into question the reliability of utilitarian judgments.

I.7. The Structure of the Volume

This volume is the first to take stock of fifteen years of research of this fast-growing field of moral neuroscience. It contains eleven essays and three replies, all but one of which are original, and it brings together many of the leading international scientists in the neuroscientific study of morality, many prominent international scholars in philosophical ethics and moral psychology, and several promising scholars earlier in their careers whose work will shape the field in future. The volume is divided into four parts: first, on emotions versus reason; second, on deontology versus consequentialism; third, on new methods of moral neuroscience; and fourth, on philosophical lessons. The first two parts build on the two debates discussed earlier, namely, the debate concerning whether moral judgments are the product of reasoning or emotions, and the debate regarding Greene's claim that neuroscientific evidence supports the idea that consequentialist judgments are more reliable and truth-tracking than nonconsequentialist judgments. The third part presents the latest findings from leading neuroscientists on the study of moral judgments. The fourth part offers new ways of drawing philosophical lessons from the scientific data. In each part, I have sought chapters that display a broad range of views, including both established positions and new insights.

In the first part, on emotions versus reason, Jesse Prinz argues that neuroimaging studies leave much uncertainty about the relationship between morality and emotion, but, nevertheless, the preponderance of empirical evidence can be used to support a traditional kind of sentimentalist theory of moral judgment. In the spirit of rationalism, Jeanette Kennett and Philip Gerrans defend a more significant role for reasoning in moral judgment than Jonathan Haidt (or Jesse Prinz) allows by arguing that the capacity for diachronic agency is essential for moral deliberation. James Woodward proposes instead that recent developments in neuroscience undercut the idea that there is a sharp contrast between emotion and cognition when we make moral judgments, and he explores the implications of this view for interpreting various experimental results regarding moral decision-making and for "rationalist" projects in moral philosophy generally.

In the second part, on deontology versus consequentialism, Joshua Greene provides his latest statement on how current neuroscientific research supports his dual-process theory of moral judgment and his normative claim that the reliability of deontological judgments should be questioned. Assessing Greene's latest statement, Julia Driver proposes that the only moral theories that are susceptible to Greene's epistemic debunking argument are simpler, intuitionist moral theories, and that more robust moral theories, including robust kinds of consequentialism and deontology, are not susceptible to such debunking evidence because, among other things, debunking arguments require certain background theory, and to assume a background theory is to beg the question against the moral theory being challenged. Stephen Darwall argues that Greene's experimental results are compatible with a certain kind of rule consequentialism and that since the dictates of this kind of rule consequentialism are "characteristically deontological," this means that Greene's analysis should not lead us to have more confidence in characteristically consequentialist judgments rather than characteristically deontological judgments. In response to Driver, Greene challenges, among other things, Driver's claim that debunking arguments require a background theory. In response to Darwall, Greene argues that it is not a problem that the dictates of the kind of rule consequentialism that Darwall has in mind are "characteristically deontological," because even his (Greene's) preferred theory, that is, act consequentialism, would endorse both "characteristically deontological" and "characteristically consequentialist" judgments in real-world situations.

In the third part, on new methods of moral neuroscience, James Blair, Soonjo Hwang, Stuart F. White, and Harma Meffert argue that four classes of norms can be distinguished from a neurocognitive perspective: harm-based, disgust-based, social conventions, and justice-based; and that learning the prohibitive power of these norms for behavior relies on relatively independent emotional learning systems. After presenting data suggesting that these emotional learning systems can be selectively impaired, Blair et al. then propose that full moral development requires the integration of mental state information provided by a theory of mind and outcome information provided by the emotion-learning systems. Ricardo de Oliveira-Souza, Roland Zahn, and Jorge Moll review and extend previous attempts to infer the neural underpinnings of morality through the analysis of normal and abnormal moral conduct from a broad neurobiological perspective. They emphasize in particular the importance of the use of lesion method, that is, studying the behavior of brain-damaged patients and determining the site of the damage in a postmortem analysis, in addition to functional neuroimaging techniques. Molly Crockett presents recent findings that investigate how the neuromodulator serotonin influences moral judgment and behavior, and she argues that moral judgments are not fixed, but malleable and contingent on neuromodulator levels and stress. According to Jana Schaich Borg, a remaining frontier of research on morality is to understand how and why humans perform moral and immoral actions, particularly those related to unjustified violence. Schaich Borg argues that a way to accomplish this aim is to incorporate neuroscience research that uses rodent models of negative intersubjectivity. After examining the relationship between negative intersubjectivity and moral action and evaluating rodent models of negative intersubjectivity, Schaich Borg investigates how these rodent models can be used to develop treatments for clinically violent behavior and to deepen our understanding of other types of morally relevant action.

In the fourth and final part, on philosophical lessons, Guy Kahane discusses the issue of whether neuroscientific results can tell us something new about what we ought to do. Kahane argues that scientific claims about moral psychology can in fact give nontrivial support to substantive claims in normative ethics, and he identifies several types of arguments that can validly take us from empirical evidence to novel normative conclusions. However, Kahane also argues that these arguments tend to leave only a peripheral role to neuroscience.

Many philosophers appeal to intuitions as evidence for the truth of philosophical claims. However, what, if anything, gives intuitions their evidentiary status? As we have seen earlier, a number of people, including Kahneman, Tversky, Sunstein, Sinnott-Armstrong et al., and Greene hold that intuitions are heuristics with questionable evidentiary status. S. Matthew Liao argues that intuitions are never heuristics, and he explores the implications of this insight for ongoing research in psychology, philosophy, and neuroscience.

Many neuroscientists, psychologists, and philosophers assume that all moral judgments share some common and distinctive neural basis. For instance, as we have seen earlier, Moll et al. have asserted that "recent functional imaging and clinical evidence indicates that a remarkably consistent network of brain regions is involved in moral cognition" (Moll et al. 2005). Walter Sinnott-Armstrong defends the idea that morality is disunified by arguing that the content of morality, the neural level of morality, and the function of morality all fail to be unified. Sinnott-Armstrong then argues that moral neuroscience should adopt a more fine-grained taxonomic approach that investigates more carefully defined groups of moral judgments.

These sets of issues have been chosen both for their intrinsic interests and because as a whole they give the reader a broad grasp of the different kinds of challenges in the field of moral neuroscience. As we will see, there is a great diversity of positions in both the neuroscientific research and the philosophical analysis and interpretation of this research. The contributions in this volume will demonstrate the breadth and value of this diversity.

Acknowledgments

I would like to thank Walter Sinnott-Armstrong, Carolyn Plunkett, Collin O'Neil, Dan Khokhar, Regina Rini, and Joshua Stein for their very helpful comments on early versions of this introduction.

Notes

1. The terms "reliable" and "truth-tracking" are sometimes used interchangeably in the literature. However, it seems that moral judgments can be reliable without being truth-tracking. To make sure that they are not conflated, I shall mention both terms throughout this chapter.

2. See, though, Aharoni et al. 2012, which challenges the idea that psychopaths cannot make the moral/conventional distinction.

3. Greene has since said the results from the reaction time data in his 2001 paper do not support this claim. However, he argues that his 2008 paper, which found that performing a distracting secondary task significantly decreases reaction time for characteristically utilitarian judgments, but not for characteristically deontological judgments, does support the point he was trying to make with the reaction time data in his 2001 paper. See Greene et al. 2008.

4. For a conceptual account of intuition, see, e.g., Goldman 2007. For a rationalist account, see, e.g., Bealer 2000. For a virtue-based account, see, e.g., Sosa 2007. For a naturalistic account, see, e.g., Kornblith 1998. As far as I can tell, the minimalistic account I have offered in this volume is compatible with these accounts.

5. Mikhail 2007, 2011; Hauser 2006; Chomsky 1988. Rawls first proposed this linguistic analogy in *A Theory of Justice* (1971). See also Harman 1999; Dwyer 1999.

6. Many have cited a passage from Aquinas as the origin of the DDE (T. Aquinas, *Summa Theologiae*, II, ii, q. 64, a. 7).

7. It might be worthwhile stipulating that if the five were not present, the trolley would not go around and hit the one, but would carry on harmlessly down the track.

8. Berker 2009. Berker also points out certain methodological problems with Greene's earlier studies. In response, Greene argues that his subsequent studies have addressed a number of these methodological issues. See, e.g., Greene, this volume.

9. This case is drawn from Liao et al. 2011.

10. For a detailed discussion of whether intuitions are heuristics, see Liao, this volume.

11. Woodward and Allman 2007. For a view similar to Woodward and Allman's, see Railton 2014.

References

Aharoni, Eyal, Walter Sinnott-Armstrong, and Kent A. Kiehl. 2012. "Can Psychopathic Offenders Discern Moral Wrongs? A New Look at the Moral/Conventional Distinction." *Journal of Abnormal Psychology* 121, no. 2: 484–497.

Bartels, Daniel M., and David A. Pizarro. 2011. "The Mismeasure of Morals: Antisocial Personality Traits Predict Utilitarian Responses to Moral Dilemmas." *Cognition* 121, no. 1: 154–161.

Bealer, George. 2000. "A Theory of the A Priori." *Pacific Philosophical Quarterly* 81, no. 1: 1–30.

Bechara, Antoine, Daniel Tranel, Hanna Damasio, and Antonio R. Damasio. 1996. "Failure to Respond Autonomically to Anticipated Future Outcomes Following Damage to Prefrontal Cortex." *Cerebral Cortex* 6, no. 2: 215–225.

Berker, Selim. 2009. "The Normative Insignificance of Neuroscience." *Philosophy and Public Affairs* 4: 293–329.

Bertrand, Marianne, and Sendhil Mullainathan. 2004. "Are Emily and Greg More Employable Than Lakisha and Jamal? A Field Experiment on Labor Market Discrimination." *American Economic Review* 94, no. 4: 991–1013.

Bishop, Michael A., and J. D. Trout. 2005. *Epistemology and the Psychology of Human Judgment.* New York: Oxford University Press.

Blair, R. J. R. 1995. "A Cognitive Developmental Approach to Morality: Investigating the Psychopath." *Cognition* 57, no. 1: 1–29.

Chaiken, Shelly, Roger Giner-Sorolla, and Serena Chen. 1996. "Beyond Accuracy: Defense and Impression Motives in Heuristic and Systematic Information Processing." In *The Psychology of Action: Linking Cognition and Motivation to Behavior,* edited by P. M. Gollwitzer and J. A. Bargh, 553–578. New York: Guilford Press.

Chen, Serena, David Shechter, and Shelly Chaiken. 1996. "Getting at the Truth or Getting Along: Accuracy- versus Impression-Motivated Heuristic and Systematic Processing." *Journal of Personality and Social Psychology* 71, no. 2: 262–275.

Chomsky, Noam. 1988. *Language and Problems of Knowledge.* Cambridge, MA: MIT Press.

Ciaramelli, Elisa, Michela Muccioli, Elisabetta Làdavas, and Giuseppe di Pellegrino. 2007. "Selective Deficit in Personal Moral Judgment Following Damage to Ventromedial Prefrontal Cortex." *Social Cognitive and Affective Neuroscience* 2, no. 2: 84–92.

Conway, Paul, and Bertram Gawronski. 2013. "Deontological and Utilitarian Inclinations in Moral Decision Making: A Process Dissociation Approach." *Journal of Personality and Social Psychology* 104, no. 2: 216–235.

Côté, Stéphane, Paul K. Piff, and Robb Willer. 2013. "For Whom Do the Ends Justify the Means? Social Class and Utilitarian Moral Judgment." *Journal of Personality and Social Psychology* 104, no. 3: 490–503.

Crockett, Molly J., Luke Clark, Marc D. Hauser, and Trevor W. Robbins. 2010. "Serotonin Selectively Influences Moral Judgment and Behavior through Effects on Harm Aversion." *Proceedings of the National Academy of Sciences* 107, no. 40: 17433–17438.

Damasio, Antonio. 1994. *Descartes' Error: Emotion, Reason and the Human Brain.* New York: Grosset/Putnam.

Damasio, Antonio, Daniel Tranel, and Hanna Damasio. 1990. "Individuals with Sociopathic Behavior Caused by Frontal Damage Fail to Respond Autonomically to Social Stimuli." *Behavioural Brain Research* 41, no. 2: 81–94.

Decety, Jean, and Stephanie Cacioppo. 2012. "The Speed of Morality: A High-Density Electrical Neuroimaging Study." *Journal of Neurophysiology* 108, no. 11: 3068–3072.

Duke, Aaron A., and Laurent Bègue. 2015. "The Drunk Utilitarian: Blood Alcohol Concentration Predicts Utilitarian Responses in Moral Dilemmas." *Cognition* 134: 121–127.

Dwyer, Susan. 1999. "Moral Competence." In *Philosophy and Linguistics*, edited by K. Murasugi and R. Stainton, 169–190. Boulder, CO: Westview Press.

Fine, Cordelia. 2006. "Is the Emotional Dog Wagging Its Rational Tail, or Chasing It?" *Philosophical Explorations* 9, no. 1: 83–98.

Foot, Philippa. 1967. "The Problem of Abortion and the Doctrine of Double Effect." *Oxford Review* 5: 5–15.

Gao, Yu, and Simone Tang. 2013. "Psychopathic Personality and Utilitarian Moral Judgment in College Students." *Journal of Criminal Justice* 41, no. 5: 342–349.

Gibbard, Alan. 2008. *Reconciling Our Aims: In Search of Bases for Ethics*. New York: Oxford University Press.

Gigerenzer, Gerd. 2008. "Moral Intuition = Fast and Frugal Heuristics?" In *Moral Psychology*, vol. 2: *The Cognitive Science of Morality: Intuition and Diversity*, edited by Walter Sinnott-Armstrong, 1–26. Cambridge, MA: MIT Press.

Gigerenzer, Gerd, and Peter M. Todd. 1999. *Simple Heuristics That Make Us Smart*. Oxford: Oxford University Press.

Gleichgerrcht, Ezequiel, Teresa Torralva, Alexia Rattazzi, Victoria Marenco, María Roca, and Facundo Manes. 2013. "Selective Impairment of Cognitive Empathy for Moral Judgment in Adults with High Functioning Autism." *Social Cognitive and Affective Neuroscience* 8, no. 7: 780–788.

Glenn, A. L., S. Koleva, R. Iyer, J. Graham, and P. H. Ditto. 2010. "Moral Identity in Psychopathy." *Judgment and Decision Making* 5, no. 7: 497–505.

Goldin, Claudia, and Cecilia Rouse. 2000. "Orchestrating Impartiality: The Impact Of 'Blind' Auditions on Female Musicians." *American Economic Review* 90, no. 4: 715–741.

Goldman, Alvin. 2007. "Philosophical Intuitions: Their Target, Their Source, and Their Epistemic Status." *Grazer Philosophische Studien* 74: 1–25.

Greene, Joshua D. 2008. "The Secret Joke of Kant's Soul." In *Moral Psychology: The Neuroscience of Morality*, edited by Walter Sinnott-Armstrong, 35–79. Cambridge, MA: MIT Press.

Greene, Joshua D. 2015. "The Cognitive Neuroscience of Moral Judgment and Decision Making." In *The Moral Brain: A Multidisciplinary Perspective*, edited by Jean Decety and Thalia Wheatley, 197–220. Cambridge, MA: MIT Press.

Greene, Joshua D., Fiery A. Cushman, Lisa E. Stewart, Kelly Lowenberg, Leigh E. Nystrom, and Jonathan D. Cohen. 2009. "Pushing Moral Buttons: The Interaction between Personal Force and Intention in Moral Judgment." *Cognition* 111, no. 3: 364–371.

Greene, Joshua D., and Jonathan Haidt. 2002. "How (and Where) Does Moral Judgment Work?" *Trends in Cognitive Sciences* 6, no. 12: 517–523.

Greene, Joshua D., Sylvia A. Morelli, Kelly Lowenberg, Leigh E. Nystrom, and Jonathan D. Cohen. 2008. "Cognitive Load Selectively Interferes with Utilitarian Moral Judgment." *Cognition* 107, no. 3: 1144–1154.

Greene, Joshua D., Leigh E. Nystrom, Andrew D. Engell, John M. Darley, and Jonathan D. Cohen. 2004. "The Neural Bases of Cognitive Conflict and Control in Moral Judgment." *Neuron* 44, no. 2: 389–400.

Greene, Joshua D., R. Brian Sommerville, Leigh E. Nystrom, John M. Darley, and Jonathan D. Cohen. 2001. "An Fmri Investigation of Emotional Engagement in Moral Judgment." *Science* 293, no. 5537: 2105–2108.

Haidt, Jonathan. 2001. "The Emotional Dog and Its Rational Tail: A Social Intuitionist Approach to Moral Judgment." *Psychological Review* 108: 814–834.

Haidt, Jonathan. 2003. "The Emotional Dog Does Learn New Tricks: A Reply to Pizarro and Bloom." *Psychological Review* 110: 197–198.

Haidt, Jonathan. 2006. *The Happiness Hypothesis.* London: Arrow Books.

Haidt, Jonathan. 2007. "The New Synthesis in Moral Psychology." *Science* 316: 998–1002.

Haidt, Jonathan. 2008. "Social Intuitionists Reason, in Conversation." In *Moral Psychology,* vol. 2: *The Cognitive Science of Morality: Intuition and Diversity,* edited by Walter Sinnott-Armstrong, 241–254. Cambridge, MA: MIT Press.

Haidt, Jonathan, and Fredrik Bjorklund. 2008. "Social Intuitionists Answer Six Questions about Moral Psychology." In *Moral Psychology,* vol. 2: *The Cognitive Science of Morality: Intuition and Diversity,* edited by Walter Sinnott-Armstrong, 181–218. Cambridge, MA: MIT Press.

Haidt, Jonathan, and Matthew A. Hersh. 2001. "Sexual Morality: The Cultures and Emotions of Conservatives and Liberals." *Journal of Applied Social Psychology* 31, no. 1: 191–221.

Hare, R. M. 1981. *Moral Thinking: Its Methods, Levels and Point.* Oxford: Clarendon Press.

Hare, Robert D. 1991. *The Hare Psychopathy Checklist.* Rev. ed. Toronto: Multi-Health Systems.

Harman, Gilbert, 1999. "Moral Philosophy and Linguistics." In *Proceedings of the 20th World Congress of Philosophy,* vol. 1: *Ethics,* edited by K. Brinkmann, 107–115. Bowling Green, OH: Philosophy Documentation Center.

Hauser, Marc D. 2006. *Moral Minds: How Nature Designed Our Universal Sense of Right and Wrong.* New York: HarperCollins.

Hauser, Marc D., Liane Young, and Fiery Cushman. 2008. "Reviving Rawls's Linguistic Analogy: Operative Principles and the Causal Structure of Moral Actions." In *Moral Psychology: The Neuroscience of Morality,* edited by Walter Sinnott-Armstrong, 107–144. Cambridge, MA: MIT Press.

Hume, David. 1978. *A Treatise of Human Nature.* Edited by L. A. Selby-Bigge and P H. Nidditch. 2nd ed. Oxford: Clarendon Press.

Jones, Karen. 2003. "Emotion, Weakness of Will and the Normative Conception of Agency." In *Philosophy and the Emotions,* edited by Anthony Hatzimoysis, 181–200. Cambridge: Cambridge University Press.

Jones, Karen. 2006. "Metaethics and Emotions Research: A Response to Prinz." *Philosophical Explorations* 9, no. 1: 45–53.

Kahneman, D., and S. Frederick. 2005. "A Model of Heuristic Judgment." In *The Cambridge Handbook of Thinking and Reasoning,* edited by K. J. Holyoak and R. G. Morrison, 267–93. New York: Cambridge University Press.

Kahneman, D., P. Slovic, and A. Tversky. 1982. *Judgement under Uncertainty: Heuristics and Biases.* Cambridge: Cambridge University Press.

Kamm, Frances Myra. 2007. *Intricate Ethics: Rights, Responsibilities, and Permissible Harm.* New York: Oxford University Press.

Kant, Immanuel. 1964. *Groundwork of the Metaphysic of Morals.* Translated by H. J. Paton. New York: Harper & Row.

Kennett, Jeanette, and Cordelia Fine. 2008. "Internalism and the Evidence from Psychopaths and 'Acquired Sociopaths.'" In *Moral Psychology: The Neuroscience of Morality,* edited by Walter Sinnott-Armstrong, 173–190. Cambridge, MA: MIT Press.

Kennett, Jeanette, and Cordelia Fine. 2009. "Will the Real Moral Judgment Please Stand Up?" *Ethical Theory and Moral Practice* 12, no. 1: 77–96.

Kerr, Norbert L., Robert J. MacCoun, and Geoffrey P. Kramer. 1996. "Bias in Judgment: Comparing Individuals and Groups." *Psychological Review* 103, no. 4: 687–719.

Koenigs, Michael, Michael Kruepke, Joshua Zeier, and Joseph P. Newman. 2012. "Utilitarian Moral Judgment in Psychopathy." *Social Cognitive and Affective Neuroscience* 7, no. 6: 708–714.

Koenigs, Michael, and Daniel Tranel. 2007. "Irrational Economic Decision-Making after Ventromedial Prefrontal Damage: Evidence from the Ultimatum Game." *Journal of Neuroscience* 27, no. 4: 951–956.

Koenigs, Michael, Liane Young, Ralph Adolphs, Daniel Tranel, Fiery Cushman, Marc Hauser, and Antonio Damasio. 2007. "Damage to the Prefrontal Cortex Increases Utilitarian Moral Judgements." *Nature* 446, no. 7138: 908–911.

Kohlberg, Lawrence. 1969. "Stage and Sequence: The Cognitive-Developmental Approach to Socialization." In *Handbook of Socialization Theory and Research*, edited by David A. Goslin, 347–480. Chicago: Rand McNally.

Kornblith, Hilary. 1998. "The Role of Intuition in Philosophical Inquiry: An Account with No Unnatural Ingredients." In *Rethinking Intuition: The Psychology of Intuition and Its Role in Philosophical Inquiry*, edited by Michael DePaul and William Ramsey, 129–142. Lanham, MD: Rowman and Littlefield.

Levy, Neil. 2006. "The Wisdom of the Pack." *Philosophical Explorations* 9: 99–103.

Liao, S. Matthew. 2008. "A Defense of Intuitions." *Philosophical Studies* 140, no. 2: 247–262.

Liao, S. Matthew. 2009. "The Loop Case and Kamm's Doctrine of Triple Effect." *Philosophical Studies* 146: 223–231.

Liao, S. Matthew. 2011. "Bias and Reasoning: Haidt's Theory of Moral Judgment." In *New Waves in Ethics*, edited by Thom Brooks, 108–127. New York: Palgrave Macmillan.

Liao, S. Matthew, Alex Wiegmann, Joshua Alexander, and Gerard Vong. 2011. "Putting the Trolley in Order: Experimental Philosophy and the Loop Case." *Philosophical Psychology* 25, no. 5: 661–671.

Lord, Charles G., Lee Ross, and Mark R. Lepper. 1979. "Biased Assimilation and Attitude Polarization: The Effects of Prior Theories on Subsequently Considered Evidence." *Journal of Personality and Social Psychology* 37: 2098–2109.

Mahoney, Michael J. 1977. "Publication Prejudice: An Experimental Study of Confirmatory Bias in the Peer Review System." *Cognitive Therapy and Research* 1: 161–175.

Mallon, Ron. 2008. "Reviving Rawls's Linguistic Analogy Inside and Out." In *Moral Psychology: The Neuroscience of Morality*, edited by Walter Sinnott-Armstrong, 145–156. Cambridge, MA: MIT Press.

Mendez, Mario F, Eric Anderson, and Jill S Shapira. 2005. "An Investigation of Moral Judgement in Frontotemporal Dementia." *Cognitive and Behavioral Neurology* 18, no. 4: 193–197.

Mikhail, John. 2007. "Universal Moral Grammar: Theory, Evidence and the Future." *Trends in Cognitive Sciences* 11, no. 4: 143–152.

Mikhail, John. 2011. *Elements of Moral Cognition: Rawls' Linguistic Analogy and the Cognitive Science of Moral and Legal Judgment.* New York: Cambridge University Press.

Moll, Jorge, Ricardo de Oliveira-Souza, Paul J. Eslinger, Ivanei E. Bramati, Janaina Mourao-Miranda, Pedro A. Andreiulo, and Luiz Pesoa. 2002. "The Neural Correlates of Moral

Sensitivity: A Functional Magnetic Resonance Imaging Investigation of Basic and Moral Emotions." *Journal of Neuroscience* 22: 2730–2736.

Moll, Jorge, Paul J. Eslinger, and Ricardo de Oliveira-Souza. 2001. "Frontopolar and Anterior Temporal Cortex Activation in a Moral Judgment Task: Preliminary Functional MRI Results in Normal Subjects." *Arquivos de Neuro-Psiquiatria* 59, no. 3B: 657–664.

Moll, Jorge, Roland Zahn, Ricardo de Oliveira-Souza, Frank Krueger, and Jordan Grafman. 2005. "The Neural Basis of Human Moral Cognition." *Nature Reviews Neuroscience* 6, no. 10: 799–809.

Nisbett, Richard, and Lee Ross. 1980. *Human Inference: Strategies and Shortcomings of Social Judgment*. Englewood Cliffs, NJ: Prentice Hall.

Otsuka, Michael. 2008. "Double Effect, Triple Effect and the Trolley Problem: Squaring the Circle in Looping Cases." *Utilitas* 20, no. 1: 92–110.

Perkins, Adam M., Ania M. Leonard, Kristin Weaver, Jeffrey A. Dalton, Mitul A. Mehta, Veena Kumari, Steven C. R. Williams, and Ulrich Ettinger. 2013. "A Dose of Ruthlessness: Interpersonal Moral Judgment Is Hardened by the Anti-anxiety Drug Lorazepam." *Journal of Experimental Psychology: General* 142, no. 3: 612–620.

Piaget, Jean. 1932. *The Moral Judgement of the Child*. Translated by Marjorie Gabain. New York: Harcourt Brace Jovanovich.

Pizarro, David, Yoel Inbar, and Chelsea Helion. 2011. "On Disgust and Moral Judgment." *Emotion Review* 3, no. 3: 267–268.

Prinz, Jesse J. 2006. "The Emotional Basis of Moral Judgments." *Philosophical Explorations* 9, no. 1: 29–43.

Prinz, Jesse J. 2008. "Resisting the Linguistic Analogy: A Commentary on Hauser, Young, and Cushman." In *Moral Psychology: The Neuroscience of Morality*, edited by Walter Sinnott-Armstrong, 157–170. Cambridge, MA: MIT Press.

Railton, Peter. 2014. "The Affective Dog and Its Rational Tale: Intuition and Attunement." *Ethics* 124, no. 4: 813–859.

Rawls, John. 1971. *A Theory of Justice*. Oxford: Oxford University Press.

Roskies, Adina. 2002. "Neuroethics for the New Millenium." *Neuron* 35, no. 1: 21–23.

Roskies, Adina. 2003. "Are Ethical Judgments Intrinsically Motivational? Lessons From 'Acquired Sociopathy' [1]." *Philosophical Psychology* 16, no. 1: 51–66.

Roskies, Adina. 2008. "Internalism and the Evidence from Pathology." In *Moral Psychology: The Neuroscience of Morality*, edited by Walter Sinnott-Armstrong, 191–206. Cambridge, MA: MIT Press.

Saltzstein, Herbert D., and Tziporah Kasachkoff. 2004. "Haidt's Moral Intuitionist Theory: A Psychological and Philosophical Critique." *Review of General Psychology* 8: 273–282.

Schnall, Simone, Jonathan Haidt, Gerald L. Clore, and Alexander H. Jordan. 2008. "Disgust as Embodied Moral Judgment." *Personality and Social Psychology Bulletin* 34, no. 8: 1096–1109.

Seidel, Angelika, and Jesse Prinz. 2013. "Mad and Glad: Musically Induced Emotions Have Divergent Impact on Morals." *Motivation and Emotion* 37, no. 3: 629–637.

Singer, Peter. 1997. "Famine, Affluence, and Morality." In *Ethics in Practice*, edited by H. LaFollette, 585–595. Oxford: Blackwell.

Singer, Peter. 2005. "Ethics and Intuitions." *Journal of Ethics* 9: 331–352.

Sinnott-Armstrong, Walter 2006. "Moral Intuitionism Meets Empirical Psychology." In *Metaethics after Moore*, edited by T. Horgan and M. Timmons, 339–365. New York: Oxford University Press.

Sinnott-Armstrong, Walter, Liane Young, and Fiery Cushman. 2010. "Moral Intuitions." In *The Moral Psychology Handbook*, edited by J. Doris, 246–272. Oxford: Oxford University Press.

Smolin, Lee. 2006. *The Trouble with Physics: The Rise of String Theory, the Fall of a Science, and What Comes Next*. London: Allen Lane.

Sosa, Ernest. 2007. *A Virtue Epistemology: Apt Belief and Reflective Knowledge*. Vol. 1. New York: Oxford University Press.

Steinpreis, Rhea E., Katie A. Anders, and Dawn Ritzke. 1999. "The Impact of Gender on the Review of the Curricula Vitae of Job Applicants and Tenure Candidates: A National Empirical Study." *Sex Roles* 41, no. 78: 509–528.

Sunstein, Cass. 2005. "Moral Heuristics." *Behavioral and Brain Sciences* 25: 531–73.

Thomson, Judith Jarvis. 1985. "The Trolley Problem." *Yale Law Journal* 94: 1395–1415.

Trope, Yaacov, and Akiva Liberman. 1996. "Social Hypothesis Testing: Cognitive and Motivational Mechanisms." In *Social Psychology: Handbook of Basic Principles*, edited by E. T. Higgins and A. W. Krugalski, 239–270. New York: Guilford.

Turiel, Elliot. 1983. *The Development of Social Knowledge: Morality and Convention*. Cambridge: Cambridge University Press.

Valdesolo, Piercarlo, and David DeSteno. 2006. "Manipulations of Emotional Context Shape Moral Judgment." *Psychological Science* 17, no. 6: 476–477.

Wheatley, Thalia, and Jonathan Haidt. 2005. "Hypnotic Disgust Makes Moral Judgments More Severe." *Psychological Science* 16, no. 10: 780–784.

Wilson, Timothy, and Nancy Brekke. 1994. "Mental Contamination and Mental Correction: Unwanted Influences on Judgements and Evaluations." *Psychological Bulletin* 116: 117–142.

Woodward, James, and John Allman. 2007. "Moral Intuition: Its Neural Substrates and Normative Significance." *Journal of Physiology-Paris* 101, nos. 4–6: 179–202.

Young, Liane, Joan Albert Camprodon, Marc Hauser, Alvaro Pascual-Leone, and Rebecca Saxe. 2010. "Disruption of the Right Temporoparietal Junction with Transcranial Magnetic Stimulation Reduces the Role of Beliefs in Moral Judgments." *Proceedings of the National Academy of Sciences* 107, no. 15: 6753–6758.

Young, Liane, Fiery Cushman, Marc Hauser, and Rebecca Saxe. 2007. "The Neural Basis of the Interaction between Theory of Mind and Moral Judgment." *Proceedings of the National Academy of Sciences* 104, no. 20: 8235–8240.

Young, Liane, Michael Koenigs, Michael Kruepke, and Joseph P. Newman. 2012. "Psychopathy Increases Perceived Moral Permissibility of Accidents." *Journal of Abnormal Psychology* 121, no. 3: 659–667.

I

Emotions versus Reason

1

Sentimentalism and the Moral Brain

Jesse Prinz

OVER THE LAST dozen years, there has been enormous interest in studying the neural basis of moral judgment. A growing number of researchers believe that the moral brain will lead to insights about the nature of morality. There is an emerging conviction that long-standing debates in psychology and philosophy can be settled, or at least propelled forward, by neuroscience. Much of this conviction centers around the more specific belief that we can make progress on questions about the relationship between moral judgment and emotion. That confidence, however, rests on undue faith in what brain scans can reveal, independent of other sources of evidence, including both behavioral studies and theoretical considerations. When taken on their own, extant neuroimaging studies leave classic debates unsettled, and require other evidence for interpretation. This suggests that, at present, the idea that neuroscience can settle psychological and philosophical debates about moral judgments may have things backward. Instead, psychological and philosophical debates about moral judgment may be needed to settle the meaning of brain scans. This reversal of directionality does not render brain scans uninteresting. The surprising range of hotspots seen in studies of moral judgment need to be decoded. Once decoded in light of other evidence, neuroimaging results can be helpful and informative.

My goal here will be, first, to establish that neuroimaging studies leave much uncertainty about moral judgment and, in particular, about the relationship between morality and emotion. Fortunately, I will argue, behavioral evidence and philosophical argumentation can help settle the questions that scans leave unanswered. This, then, points toward an account of what different brain structures are contributing to moral cognition. Such a mapping can be useful in making progress in this domain.

To spoil the surprise, I will say at the outset that I interpret the preponderance of empirical evidence as supporting a fairly traditional kind of sentimentalist theory of moral judgment. According to this theory, occurrent moral judgments are constituted by emotional states. I will contrast this theory with a range of alternatives and argue for its explanatory superiority. For those who are unconvinced by my arguments, the chapter can be read as a plea for an integrative methodology, and many claims can be accepted without joining my sentimentalist bandwagon. For those less interested in methodology, the chapter can be read as a defense of sentimentalism, which happens to engage neuroscientific research.

1.1. Blinded by Head Lights: The Ambiguity of Imagining

1.1.1. THE ANATOMY OF MORALITY

Since Greene et al.'s seminal (2001) study of moral dilemmas, there have been numerous efforts to identify brain structures involved in moral judgments. Though there is a fair degree of convergence between these studies, the results are often somewhat bewildering. Even within a single study, a variety of brain structures are usually implicated, and it is often far from obvious how to interpret the results. I will not attempt a complete review here. A survey of some of the main findings will suffice to make the point. I will focus on studies that compare moral judgments to nonmoral judgments, though I should mention at the outset that many studies also compare different kinds of moral judgments, and many published reports include both kinds of comparisons. There will be occasion to discuss differing kinds of moral judgments as we move on in the discussion.

Let's begin with Greene et al. (2001). Though their emphasis lies elsewhere, they do compare moral judgments (i.e., choices about the right thing to do in a moral dilemma) with nonmoral judgments (e.g., dilemmas about whether to replace an old TV set or whether to take a bus or a train). The findings suggest that moral dilemmas recruit the following brain structures to a greater degree than nonmoral dilemmas: medial frontal gyrus (including parts of Brodmann areas 9 and 10; the latter is also known as ventromedial prefrontal cortex, or VMPFC), posterior cingulate (BA 31), and the angular gyrus (BA 39) bilaterally. Greene et al. also note increased activation in the superior parietal lobule (BA 7/40), but say little about that in their discussion.

Another seminal study, by Moll et al. (2001), compared judgments of moral wrongness (e.g., "They hanged an innocent person") to judgments of factual wrongness (e.g., "Stones are made of water"). Moral judgments were associated with activity in medial frontal gyrus (BA 9/10), as Greene et al. found, as well as the right angular gyrus (consistent with Greene, but more lateralized). They also report activity in the left precuneus (BA 7, just above the posterior cingulate), the right temporal pole (BA 38), and the right posterior superior temporal sulcus (STS). One year later, Moll, Oliveira-Souza, Bramati, et al. (2002) published a study using a similar design and reported slightly different, but overlapping results. As compared to neutral sentences, moral sentences were associated with increases in parts of the left medial temporal gyrus (BA 10), as well as adjacent medial orbital frontal cortex (OFC, or BA 11).

In another study, Moll, Oliveira-Souza, Eslinger, et al. (2002) presented participants with photographs depicting morally bad behavior. As compared to neutral images, the moral photos were associated with medial frontal and orbital frontal areas again (BA 9/10/11), precuneus, and the STS (including parts of BA 21 and 38), all in the right hemisphere. There was also bilateral activity in middle temporal gyrus (BA 19/22), as well as increases in the amygdala and the midbrain. BA 22 is adjacent to the angular gyrus (BA 39) and portions of the superior parietal lobule (BA 40). The area encompassing all three is sometimes called the temporal partial junction.

Other pioneering results include Heekeren et al.'s (2001) study, which compares morally anomalous to semantically anomalous sentences. The moral condition was associated with activity in the left angular gyrus (BA 39), the left middle temporal gyrus (BA 22), and the temporal pole (BA 38), consistent with other studies, and beyond these structures, bilateral inferior frontal gyrus (BA 45/47), which may reflect the linguistic nature of their task. In a subsequent study with a similar design, Heekeren et al. (2003) found that moral sentences were associated with area 47 again (perhaps a language area), as well as cast of areas familiar from the other moral judgment studies: medial frontal gyrus, STS, and temporal pole.

I will mention work by just one other research group; other findings follow a similar pattern. In one study, Harenski and Hamann (2006) presented participants with morally charged pictures (as in Moll, Oliveira-Souza, Eslinger, et al. 2002) and compared these to either nonmoral emotional pictures or a neutral baseline (deciding whether numbers are odd or even). When compared to the neutral condition, moral images produced greater activation in right medial frontal gyrus (BA 10), left amygdala, and left superior frontal gyrus. The latter area—not a big player in other studies—is associated with executive working memory spatial cognition; this may simply reflect that the neutral condition (classifying odd-even numbers) is highly automatic and nonspatial compared to picture viewing. As compared to nonmoral pictures, moral pictures were associated with greater STS activity as well as activity in the posterior cingulate cortex. Harenski et al. (2010) also conducted a follow-up study, presenting participants with moral and nonmoral images once again. When moral images were compared to nonmoral, some of the usual suspects appeared: medial frontal gyrus and OFC (BA 10/11, right lateralized in this study), angular gyrus (bilaterally), and right posterior cingulate. The OFC and posterior cingulate also increased with severity ratings when participants were asked to rate how bad the depicted violations were.

Though there is considerable overlap between these studies, there is no easy interpretation. Numerous brain areas are implicated in moral judgment, and the functions of these areas are often complex, varied, or poorly understood. Early efforts (e.g., Moll et al. 2001) sought a moral module in the brain, but it is now widely believed that moral cognition supervenes on neural mechanisms that also participate in other capacities (Greene and Haidt 2002). But what are these other capacities, and what can we learn from brain scans about how moral decisions are made? These are the questions with which I will be occupied throughout this chapter, but let me make a preliminary observation here.

Every single neuroimaging study of moral cognition that I know concurs on one point: moral judgments regularly engage brain structures that are associated with emotional processing. I say "regularly" because, while some studies imply that this is always the case, others imply that it is often the case, but not always, as we will see below. Even with those exceptions in mind, we can say that the moral brain looks a lot like the emotional brain: a number of brain areas mentioned in the survey above are frequently implicated in studies that investigate the neural correlates of emotion. These include frontal areas 9, 10, and 11 (Damasio 1994; Vytal and Hamann 2010), posterior cingulate (Madock et al. 2003; Nielen et al. 2009), and the temporal pole (Olsen et al. 2007).

The conclusion that emotions are regularly involved in moral judgment is important, but also extremely vague. Involved in what way? The question is exacerbated by the fact that some of the brain structures that come up in these studies are not thought to be correlates of emotion. The STS, for example, is a frequent player, as are potions of the temporal parietal junction (TPJ). Other studies have found associations between some moral judgments and activity in the dorsolateral prefrontal cortex (DLPFC) (Greene et al. 2001; Borg et al. 2006; Cushman et al. 2011). This is a classic working memory area, which Greene et al. refer to as a cognitive area, in contrast to what they label emotion areas. Thus, the cognitive neuroscience of moral judgment has actually yielded a mixed picture, with emotion areas and nonemotion areas both playing a role. This makes the findings somewhat difficult to interpret.

The challenge of interpreting imaging results becomes more vivid if we ask whether extant findings can be used to show that one prevailing theory of moral judgment is correct and others are false. As we will now see, there are numerous theories in the literature, and it is not clear whether any of the aforementioned can adjudicate between them.

1.1.2. MORAL MODELS

There are many debates about the nature of moral judgment. Some of these have deep philosophical routes and remain hotly contested within contemporary moral psychology. Perhaps the most enduring and fundamental debate concerns the role of emotions. It is universally recognized that emotions often arise when we are thinking about moral issues. For example, when we read about injustice, we find it upsetting. What exactly is the role of these emotions? Are they causes of judgments or effects? Are they involved essentially or eliminably?

Divergent answers to questions like these have animated philosophers for generations. In recent years, psychologists have also weighed in on these debates, and a menu of competing theories has emerged. I will summarize these here (see figure 1.1) and ask whether neuroscientific results can settle which is most plausible.

According to one theory, or, more accurately, one class of theories, when emotions arise in moral decision-making, they are the *outputs* of moral judgment. The idea is that we arise at moral conclusions dispassionately, and then, at least sometimes, emotions follow. Such "emotions as outputs" theories come in a variety of forms. For philosophers,

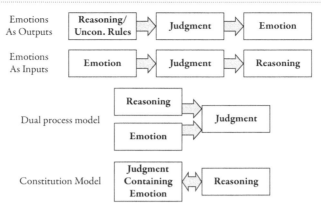

FIGURE I.I Competing models of moral judgment.

the most familiar is a kind of moral rationalism, according to which moral judgments arise at the end of a conscious and deliberate reasoning process. This view is associated with Kant, though this is a mistake, since he actually held that moral judgments often arise as the result of emotions and inclinations. For Kant rational derivation of moral judgments is possible and normatively preferable to emotional induction of moral judgments, but emotional induction does occur.

Within contemporary cognitive science, moral rationalism is not a very popular position. Much more popular is the view that moral judgments are based on the application of unconscious rules (e.g., Cushman et al. 2006; Mikhail 2007; Huebner et al. 2008). For these authors, we determine that something is morally right or wrong by unconsciously analyzing the structure of an event (who did what to whom with what intentions and what outcome) and then assigning a value in accordance with a "moral grammar." Defenders of this approach happily grant that emotions may arise once a moral verdict is reached, but emotions do not play a role in getting to that verdict.

"Emotions as outputs" views contrast sharply with "emotions as inputs," which state that moral judgments arise as the result of emotional states. For example, consider Haidt's (2001) theory, which he calls intuitionism. An intuition, for Haidt is "a conclusion [that] appears suddenly and effortlessly in consciousness, without any awareness by the person of the mental processes that led to the outcome" (181). Haidt considers intuition a form of cognition, but he stresses that intuitions contrast with reasoning. Haidt also suggests that intuitions generally take the form of emotions. His paper is called "The Emotional Dog and Its Rational Tail," implying that intuitions are emotions, and these emotions, rather than reasoning, lead us to our moral judgments. His empirical research on intuitionism has focused on measuring and inducing emotions in the context of moral judgment. Thus, for Haidt, certain forms of conduct cause emotional responses in us, and we use those emotions to arrive at the conclusion that the conduct in question is good or bad. For example, when we think about incest it causes disgust and we infer from this that incest must be bad. Haidt recognizes that we sometimes provide reasons for our moral judgments, but he thinks such reasoning is *post hoc*: emotions lead us to draw moral verdicts and reasoning is used to rationalize those verdicts once they have been drawn.

Emotions as outputs views and emotions as inputs views are sometimes presented as diametrically opposed. There are, however, compromise positions that say emotions can serve as either causes *or* effects. Leading among these are dual-process theories, which say that moral judgments sometimes result from emotions and sometimes result from dispassionate reasoning (Greene et al. 2001; Greene 2008). Greene et al. (2001) make a further claim, which is that emotions are especially likely to be engaged when conduct under consideration involves a direct act of physical aggression against a person, as opposed to a crime where violence is indirect or a mere side-effect of some other action. Greene (2008) also speculates that categorical rules against killing ("deontological" rules) stem from emotional squeamishness about this kind of violence. In contrast, moral decisions based on estimating comparative outcomes ("utilitarian" decision procedures) are driven by reason, rather than emotion, on Greene's story. Other mixed models are also imaginable. For example, some authors suggest that emotions are heuristics for quick moral decision-making, whereas reason can be used when we have time to make decisions more carefully (Sunstein 2005). Greene's dual-process theory can be interpreted as a version of a heuristic view, and I will focus on his account in the discussion below.

The contemporary cognitive science literature often gives the impression that these are the only theoretical options. Indeed, one might think they are exhaustive: emotions are causes or moral judgments, or not causes, or both, depending on the case. But this misses out on a further alternative, which has had many defenders in the history of philosophy. Rather than seeing emotions as causes or effects of moral judgments, one might propose that they are constituent parts. To many ears, this sounds bizarre. Contemporary readers have difficulty imagining what it would mean for an emotion to be part of a judgment. Cognitive science has trained us to think about judgments as something like sentences in a mental language. Judgments are made up of something like words, on this view, so they cannot contain emotions. The linguistic view of judgments is not the only possibility, however. Many prominent figures in the history of philosophy, including rationalists such as Descartes and British empiricists such as Locke and Hume claim that judgments are made up of mental images. For Hume, imagery includes sensory states, such as visual and auditory images, as well as emotions. A judgment can be thought of as a simulation of what it would be like to experience that which the judgment is about. For example, to judge that snow is white might be a visual image of white snow. Such simulations can also include emotions: to judge that sledding is fun, might be a visual-bodily simulation of sledding together with delight. Kant ([1787] 1997) famously argues that such empiricist theories of judgment cannot suffice, since the same image (say white snow) could correspond to many different attitudes other than judgments (e.g., a desire to see white snow). But, in solving this problem, Kant does not conclude that judgments are sentences in the head. Rather, he realizes that what makes a mental state qualify as a judgment has to do with how it is used in thought (cf. Kitcher 1990). If we use an image of white snow in order to draw inferences about snow's color, then we are, in effect, using that image as a judgment. On this view, judgments need not be sentences. They can comprise images, emotions, or anything else, provided those things are used in such a way that they constitute how an agent takes the world to be.

For empiricists like Hume, every word expresses a sensory or emotional idea. "Snow" corresponds to imagery of snow's appearance and feel. "White" corresponds to visual image of whiteness. And so on. In his *Treatise on Human Nature*, Hume raises the question, what ideas in the mind do words like "good" and "bad" express? He didn't think good things or bad things have a characteristic visual appearance. Instead he suggested that "good" and "bad" express emotions (or, in 18th-century vocabulary, sentiments). Indeed, there are many words that seem to express sentiments. "Fun" is one example, and others include: amusing, disgusting, fascinating, confusing, delicious, sexy, and upsetting. When we use such terms, we are expressing how we feel about something. On an empiricist psychology, these words convey an occurrent emotional state. If I bite into a nectarine and say, "This is delicious!" the predicate gives verbal expression to the gustatory pleasure that I am experiencing. By analogy, Hume thought that sentences such as, "that action is bad" express a negative emotion. He didn't say much about what these emotions are (more on that below), but one can imagine various feelings of disapproval or condemnation filling this role: anger, contempt, guilt, and so on.

Hume's view is known as "sentimentalism," and it has had many adherents over the centuries. Modernizing the term, one might describe sentimentalism as a "constitution" view about the relationship between moral judgments and emotions. Emotions are part of what constitutes moral judgments. If one asserts that factory farming is bad, for example, this assertion expresses a judgment that literally contains a negative feeling toward factory farming (factory farming itself might be mentally represented using a complex store of associated imagery, but I will leave that issue to one side). In recent cognitive science, there has been an effort to bring back the empiricist conjecture that all thought uses sensory and affective states as building blocks (e.g., Barsalou 1999; Prinz 2002). That view remains controversial, but here I am only concerned with a more restricted hypothesis: it is both coherent and plausible to suppose that certain concepts, including the examples listed above, are grounded in emotions. The claim that moral concepts are constituted by emotions remains a live possibility, which contemporary cognitive science should include in any menu of competing theories.

We are left, then, with four broad classes of theories: emotions may be outputs of moral judgments or inputs of moral judgments, emotions may play both of these roles depending on the case, or emotions might be constituent parts of moral judgments. The differences between these views are substantive and important. Indeed, they have radically different implications about the nature of morality. Output views tell us there is a nonemotional source of moral judgments. Dual-process theories tell us we can arrive at moral judgments in different ways, and they often imply that the rational route is superior to the emotional route. Input theories describe emotions as intuitions, which are used to support moral judgments, rather than component parts of judgments. Constitution theories are by comparison stronger: if emotions are parts of moral judgments, then one cannot make a moral judgment without having an emotional state. The debates between these competing views are among the most important in moral psychology. They are debates about the very nature of morality, debates about how moral decisions are made, and what it means to be morally competent. The outcome of these debates would have philosophical, scientific, and societal implications.

One might think that extant neuroimaging results can be used to settle which of these very different views is most plausible. Indeed, one might assume this is the main goal of such studies. Why invest in expensive neuroimaging research on morality if not to settle the nature of moral judgments? It is disheartening, therefore, to realize that extant studies make little progress adjudicating between the theories outlined here. Notice that every theory supposes that emotions regularly arise in the context of making moral judgments. Every theory also supposes that non-emotional aspects of cognition are involved (e.g., we can't morally evaluate a bit of conduct without first representing that conduct). Disagreements concern the role and ordering of these components. The problem is that extant studies shed too little light on those questions. They show that "emotion areas" of the brain are active during moral cognition, and they also regularly implicate brain structures that are not presumed to emotion areas. But they tell us little about how these relate. To put it bluntly, every model presented here is consistent with every study cited in the previous subsection.

1.2. Beyond the Brain: Finding the Place of Emotions in Moral Judgment

The fact that extant neuroimaging cannot decide between competing models of moral judgment should not be a cause for despair. Few authors of these studies claim to have provided decisive evidence in favor of any of the theories just surveyed. (For a notable exception, see Greene et al. 2001, whom I will come to in a moment.) Authors of these studies clearly, and rightly, take themselves to be establishing other things, such as the generalization that emotions are involved in moral judgment or, more often these days, that different kinds of moral judgments recruit different resources. At present, the best way to adjudicate between competing theories of moral judgment is to use a combination of behavioral research, some evidence from pathological populations, and attendant philosophical argumentation. I will argue that there are good reasons for rejecting most of the models under consideration. The constitution model, I will argue, enjoys the most support. I will then describe how this model can be used to make sense of imagining results. In other words, I will suggest that a theory of morality can be used to decipher the moral brain, rather than conversely.

1.2.1. EMOTIONS AS OUTPUTS

Let me begin with the view that emotions are outputs of moral judgments, with either reasoning or unconscious dispassionate rules serving as the primary input. Strictly understood, such models predict that moral emotions should not influence our moral judgments. To assume otherwise would be to concede that emotions can be inputs as well as outputs.

Here the evidence is quite clear. Numerous studies have shown that induced emotions can influence our moral judgments. For example, in one early study, Wheatley and Haidt (2005) found that hypnotically induced disgust makes moral judgments more severe. The effect was small, but subsequent work has robustly confirmed the basic effect. Severity of moral judgments increases when disgust is induced by filth, film clips, and memories (Schnall et al. 2008) and well as by bitter beverages (Eskine et al. 2011). It has also been shown that individual differences in disgust sensitivity correlate with more stringent moral attitudes in certain domains (Inbar et al. 2009).

Defenders of output models might counter that emotions can impact all kinds of mental operations even if those operations are not themselves emotional. Perhaps disgust would impair people's performance on math problems, for example. Such a reply misses the point, however. It's not just that disgust impacts moral judgment. It does so in a very particular way. Based on predictions by Rozin et al. (1999), we show that induced disgust increases severity of judgments about crimes against nature, but not crimes against persons (Seidel and Prinz 2013a). We also show that anger has the opposite pattern. In other work, we show that happiness increases positive moral judgments and anger brings them down (Seidel and Prinz 2013b). The pattern of emotional impact is highly specific. Different emotions have distinctive and predictable contributions. They are not noise in the system, but rather a core source of information that people use when expressing their moral attitudes.

There is also a more concessive response available to those who are inclined toward output models. They can grant that emotions increase the intensity of moral judgments, while denying that emotions are the basis of moral judgments (e.g., Pizarro et al. 2011; Decety and Cacioppo 2012; May 2014). I find arguments for this modest view unconvincing. Pizarro et al. suggest that emotions are merely moral amplifiers on the grounds that emotions such as disgust have domain-general effects, making judgments of many kinds more negative. This generality is precisely what I just disputed; new evidence suggests that each moral emotion has highly specific effects. Decety and Cacioppo use high-speed neuroimaging to argue that emotions serve a gain-function, modulating intensity, but not causing moral judgments. Their evidence stems from the fact that brain areas associated with intention attribution come online before areas associated with emotion when making a moral judgment. But this would be predicted by any model: an action must be classified before it is assessed as morally good or bad. Intention attribution is part of that classification process, and it is certainly not sufficient on its own to qualify as a moral judgment (we regularly recognize intentions outside of the moral domain). May is primary bothered by the fact the emotion-induction studies rarely cause judgments to flip from one side of the moral spectrum (e.g., morally permissible) to the other (e.g., morally impermissible). This is an unfortunate artifact of design, since researchers have used valenced vignettes rather than neutral vignettes, so baselines tend to fall on one side of the scale. That said, we have reported results where emotions cause movement across the midpoint of a scale. In Seidel and Prinz (2013b), we show that, on a nine-point scale anchored at "not good" and "extremely good," the mean response to vignettes about helping was 6.9 when we induced happiness and 4.3 when we induced anger. This is stronger than making a neutral vignette negative, which is what May requests; it is a case in which a positive vignette becomes negative! In any case, once defenders of output models grant that emotions can amplify moral judgments, they have rendered their position unstable. Why should emotions have any effect? For output models, this is an ad hoc concession to save the theory, not a principled prediction.

The case against output models can be strengthened by considering the proposed inputs that they envision. Moral rationalists, for instance, say that moral judgments arise through a process of reasoning. This can be challenged both empirically and philosophically. Empirically, it has been shown that people are often very bad at articulating reasons for their moral judgments (Haidt 2001; Hauser et al. 2007). Philosophically, Hume ([1740] 1978) and others have argued that no amount of reasoning can suffice for a moral attitude. By analogy, reasoning alone cannot tell us whether something is funny, delicious, sexy, boring, or annoying. Such affect-laden concepts require prior emotional dispositions. Something is funny only against the background of a certain sense of humor. Importantly, we *can* use reasoning to ascertain whether something is funny *if* a sense of humor is presupposed. If I know you like language play, I can give you reason for thinking you will be amused by Lewis Carroll. If I know you find philosophy boring, I can give you reasons for thinking you will be bored by Alfred North Whitehead. Likewise, if I know you don't like cruelty, I can use reasoning to alter your moral opinion about factory farming. What can't be done, Hume argues, is to arrive at a moral opinion by reason alone (elsewhere I argue against Kant's effort to prove that this is possible; Prinz 2007).

It is not easy to find moral rationalists in the psychology literature, but there is at least one prominent group of researchers who might be classified this way: Turiel (2003) and his collaborators. For Turiel, reasoning can tell us, for example, that an action is harmful or unjust, and, once we see that we will judge that it is wrong. But this conjecture gains plausibility only when we recognize that "harm" and "injustice" are already morally loaded words. Consider "harm." If a teacher intentionally makes a student work hard, or a gym instructor intentionally causes her class to endure exhaustion and muscle pain, we don't call this harm. We are reluctant to use the word in contexts of self-defense, sports (think of boxing), surgery, and other cases where pain is knowingly inflicted by one person on another. Likewise for "injustice." Most distributions in life are not equal. For example, earnings depend on where one lives, what one does, how much one works, how much one produces, and so on. To decide whether unequal division in any of these cases is unjust, one must have moral views about wealth distribution. I don't mean to deny that reasoning is important for making judgments about harm and justice. For example, if we learned that someone harms others for fun, we may become confident that this is a case of moral wrongness. But that itself is not an entailment of reason. Those who do not regard hurting someone for fun as wrong will not come to the same conclusion. Think of societies that have blood sports, for example. To go from "That's a case of hurting for fun" to "That's morally wrong," we need a bridge principle, which says that "hurting for amusement is morally wrong." Turiel has an analysis of what it is to construe something as morally wrong. Morally wrong actions are those that are regarded as serious and independent of authority. He also says that such judgments of moral wrongness are justified by appeals to empathy. But this analysis does little to help the rationalist. Empathy is clearly an emotional construct, and, less obviously, judgments of seriousness may correlate with emotional intensity. There is also evidence that emotions are involved in judging that something is true independent of authority. Blair (1997) has found that judgments of authority independence are diminished in psychopaths, who have emotional deficits, and Nichols (2014) found that induced emotions increase perceived authority independence. This suggests that Turiel's account of moral wrongness is implicitly an emotional account: his operationalization is symptomatic of underlying emotions.

As noted, many psychologists who defend output models are not rationalist. The theory that has usurped rationalism is sometimes called "moral grammar" (Dwyer 1999; Mikhail 2007). The basic idea is that we arrive at moral judgments by applying unconscious rules, like the rules of syntax. These rules are used to assess the underlying structure of an event. For example, we unconsciously assess things like intentions and outcomes: Was this a case of battery? Was the outcome foreseen? Was it a side effect of something else? Evidence for such subtle action assessments comes from research on trolley dilemmas. It turns out that wrongness judgments in trolley cases are graded. Intentionally and directly killing someone (pushing a man in front of a trolley to save five others) is regarded as impermissible, while killing someone as a side effect (diverting a trolley to a side track where it will kill one instead of five) is regarded as permissible, and various cases fall between these options. For example, permissibility judgments fall between the two extremes when people imagine a case where a trolley that was heading for five people is diverted onto a looping track, where it will be stopped by hitting a large man, but would have otherwise continued back onto the main track, killing the five. Moral grammarians think this is evidence of subtle rules, and they think these rules can be applied dispassionately. I think both claims can be challenged.

Intuitions about trolley cases may derive from a simple mental computation, known to be pervasive in human categorization: the use of prototypes. Suppose we have a prototype for "murder"; it may be something like physically aggressing against another person with the explicit intention of taking his or her life. The case where a person pushes someone into the path of a trolley would qualify. But as the elements of the prototype weaken (e.g., if it is not intentional), the category becomes less applicable. Thus, in the case of killing someone as a mere side effect, there is no direct assault on a person and no intention to take a life, merely foreknowledge that a life will be lost. In the case with the looping track, one must intend for a person to die, because that death is a crucial step in stopping the advance of the train. So it is a borderline case of murder. One simple rule is all we need, not a complex moral grammar.

Moreover, even if there were a complex set of action representations, that wouldn't necessarily suffice for making moral judgments. Everyone must agree that we are capable of action perception, and that requires attributions of intentions, outcomes, and so on. So, at one level, the postulation of unconscious rules for parsing actions in uncontroversial. What becomes controversial is the label "moral" and the assumption that certain action representations suffice for judgments of wrongness independent of any emotional attitudes. Indeed, the belief that action representations suffice for moral attitudes is precisely the same as what rationalists claim, minus the supposition that such representations are conscious. Moral grammar is just unconscious rationalism. As such, it has the same weaknesses. There are cases where the same action representation leads to different moral verdicts in different individuals. For example, there is variation in intuitions about trolley cases. These differ depending on gender (Mikhail 2000) and personality (Holtzman 2014), and intuitions also shift with some frontal brain injuries (Koenigs et al. 2007). Presumably actions are parsed the same way but attitudes differ. There is also evidence linking such differences to emotions. Holtzman (2014) found that neuroticism—an emotional construct—correlated with less tolerance in track-diverting cases, and Valdesolo and De Steno (2006) found more tolerance for pushing cases with positive mood induction. Once people have represented the action, they must decide how bad it is, and such findings suggest they do so by consulting their emotions.

I conclude that there is no strong evidence for the view that emotions are merely outputs of moral judgment. People use emotions in arriving at conclusions about moral significance.

1.2.2. THE DUAL-PROCESS MODEL

Given the undeniable evidence that people use emotions in making moral judgments, there is no hope for the view that such judgments always arise from pure reason. There are, however, researchers who think that moral judgments *sometimes* arise from pure reason. These are dual-process views. They claim that we have two ways of arriving at the verdict that something is morally good or bad: an emotional way and a rational way (Greene et al. 2001; Greene 2008). Dual-process views are popular in other domains of psychology. For example, Greenwald and Banaji (1995) explain implicit racism by saying that people who are rationally committed to the view that all ethnicities are equal also harbor emotional biases against members of minority groups. There is a rational high road, on this view, and an emotional low road. The vision suggests a crown of dispassionate and deliberative human intellect perched on a lower animal brain, which works by automatic urges and instincts. Perhaps morality travels both of these pathways.

Or perhaps not. One problem for dual-process theories is already on the table. It is not clear how reasoning can ever suffice for a moral judgment. But there are also problems specific to Greene's proposal. Greene's rational pathway is utilitarian. It basically computes the amount of good or bad that would result from an action and compares this to the good or bad produced by alternative actions. The story is incomplete, of course. We are not told what the good and the bad consist in or how these comparative computations take place. This is an important oversight, because the good and the bad may themselves be affective. The good may be the set of outcomes that the moral deliberator views positively and the bad may be outcomes that are viewed negatively, where the positive and negative are reducible to emotional states. Comparing good and bad could involve weighing conflicting emotions.

Greene is impressed by the fact the utilitarian calculations depend on math, so there is something rational, he thinks, about preferring less bad to more bad. But this is a fragile argument for rationality, given that one could have a weighting scheme where deontological violations were simply weighted as extremely bad. Granted, if one were comparing two outcomes that were equal in every way other than number of lives lost, math alone might settle what to do. But this does not mean that the decision is purely mathematical. The initial assignment of badness value and the belief that it is good to minimize badness are required as well. The credo, "Maximize the good and minimize the bad!" is itself a norm. It is not merely a statement of fact or a deliverance of reason. One could reject the norm (as some Kantians do). Those who embrace it, like Greene, Peter Singer, Jeremy Bentham, and John Stuart Mill, are quite passionate about it. They think it's bad to do otherwise, and they would criticize those who do not follow utilitarianism. It seems then that utilitarian deliberation is not just math, or any other form of pure reason, but is rather a commitment to the moral significance of mathematical outcomes. We need an account of what it is to form such a commitment. Whatever it is, is not merely a matter of reasoning. A plausible suggestion is that forming a moral commitment to utilitarianism is an emotional attitude, a positive feeling toward this normative theory. Or it might turn out that utilitarian convictions are just a consequence of first-order passions. One might feel strongly that one should help people in need. When confronted with opportunities to help one of two groups, where one group has more people in need, a person with the conviction about helping people in need will feel that sense of obligation more intensely when thinking about the larger group. In summary, we could not choose between numerical outcomes if we didn't assign them different values, and the assignment of values may be an emotional matter, either at the first order, or at the level of general principle, or both.

I suspect Greene would agree with this, if pressed. He sometimes concedes that there are emotions behind utilitarianism. They can arise as outputs of utilitarian calculations, of course, and Greene (2007) even admits that they can be inputs. He clarifies, however, that they are not "alarm bells" that cry out "Don't do this!" or "Do this!" but rather calmer passions that can be taken up for consideration and bypassed if reason demands it. On this version of Greene's theory, it is hard to tell whether he thinks moral judgments ever occur without emotional inputs, but he does seem to uphold the view that reason is in the driver's seat in some case. Greene's early defenses of the dual-process model suggest a firm stance on this question. There Greene implies that moral judgments are sometimes reached in a purely rational way, which is to say dispassionately. I don't find the evidence he offers convincing. For example, Greene et al. (2001) report that the emotions are highly active when people reflect on moral dilemmas in which they must consider causing direct intentional harm, as in the case of pushing someone in front of a trolley; and emotions are less active in the track-diverting case, where the dorsolateral prefrontal cortex seems to play a significant role. Does this show that some dilemmas travel the emotion path while others use pure reason? No. The DLPFC is predicable in any case where people begin taking numbers into account, but it doesn't follow that such decisions are dispassionate. As compared to nonmoral dilemmas, Greene et al.'s data suggest that these cases also engage the emotions. Moreover, the subtraction methodology may underestimate the amount of emotionality here. Compare the pushing case to the diverting case. In both a trolley is speeding toward five people, whom the participant in the study would like to help. That desire to help—the conviction that it would be morally good to help five people in need—may be grounded in an emotional state. But the neural correlates of this emotional state are rendered invisible, because saving five people is held constant across the two comparison conditions; it is subtracted away. Instead, we are left with a comparison of pushing someone to his death versus switching a trolley track with fatal consequences, and, unsurprisingly, the former is more emotionally intense than the latter.

Subtraction methodology may also be a factor in other cases where people report moral decision-making in the absence of emotions. In all the fMRI studies that have been published on moral judgment, I have only come across one condition in one study where moral judgment was said to show less emotional response than a control condition. This is a condition in a study by Borg et al. (2006). But their control condition is a scenario in which participants have to imagine a fire encroaching on a precious flower garden—hardly a neutral vignette. The fact that this scenario elicits more emotion than one of the moral scenarios they used is not very surprising. It is also an outlier. The rest of their moral scenarios were more emotional on average than control scenarios, and this has been the pattern in study after study.

With respect to utilitarian intuitions, I would propose the following emotion-based account. I think people tend to make utilitarian judgments in cases where a perceived good (saving five) outweighs a perceived bad (letting one die). Far from being dispassionate, this would be a situation where a strong positive emotion outweighs a weaker negative emotion. This interpretation fits with Greene's data. Positive emotions associated with saving are subtracted from his analysis, but there is evidence for residual, albeit weak, emotionality, which may reflect the wrongness of letting die. The proposal that positive emotions underlie the desire to help enjoys considerable empirical support. There is a big literature linking positive emotion and prosocial behavior (e.g., Isen and Levin 1972; Weyant 1978), and we have done work showing that induced positive emotions lead to increased sense of moral obligation (Seidel and Prinz 2013b). There is also work showing that induced positive emotions greatly increase the likelihood that people will hurt someone in order to save five people in trolley dilemmas (Valdesolo and DeSteno 2006).

Proponents of the dual-process model need evidence that people can make some moral decisions in the absence of emotions, on the basis of reason alone. This interpretation has been suggested in the literature. Koenigs et al. (2007) and Ciaramelli et al. (2007) have shown that people with injuries in the VMPFC are more likely than a control population to make utilitarian decisions in trolley dilemmas. The VMPFC is a hub for emotional coordination, so it does suggest that people moralize without emotions and their moral values align with utilitarianism. But, as the authors of these studies note, VMPFC patients are not lacking in emotions. They are actually highly emotional. The deficit most characteristic of such injuries is a problem with using one emotion to mitigate another. In particular, VMPFC patients do badly on gambling tasks in which the pursuit of valuable playing cards (a positive emotional drive) should be stopped in light of the discovery that those high-value cards are interspersed with even higher losses (a negative emotional cost) (Bechara, Damasio et al. 1994). Thus, the joy of winning cannot be adequately dampened by the sting of losing. This is basically the structure of the pushing case in the set of trolley dilemmas: the joy of saving five is normally arrested by the sting of killing one. The fact that VMPFC patients tend to opt for saving five in such scenarios exactly replicates their gambling performance. This is not an absence of emotions (they are eager to win and take delight in victory), but rather a failure of emotional regulation.

A stronger piece of evidence for dispassionate moralizing comes from a study by Koven (2011). Koven looked at moral reasoning in people who score high in alexithymia, a conditioned characterized by diminished awareness of emotional states. Like VMPFC patients, people with alexithymia make more utilitarian decisions than controls, and, in this case, that looks like a consequence of diminished emotionality. A closer look at the data, however, tells a different story. For one thing, Koven did not find that utilitarian decisions decreased with attention to negative emotions, which is what a dispassionate reasoning account would predict. She did find a negative correlation between utilitarianism and clarity of emotions, but there is a simple explanation for this, which doesn't posit dispassionate reasoning: a person who lacks emotional clarity may have a hard time deciding whether the sting of taking a life is greater than the joy of saving five. The most damning result in the study is that utilitarianism is negatively correlated with three measures of verbal intelligence, suggesting that such decisions do not rely on pure reason. I think the best interpretations of these results are as follows. People with high alexithymia scores have emotions, but their awareness of these emotions is somewhat limited. They have enough awareness to make moral decisions, but can get confused in dilemmas. This is especially likely in cases where, for people without alexithymia, one strong emotion trumps another (the pushing case). In other cases (the diverting case), the negative emotion is weak enough to have little impact. Those with lower verbal intelligence probably have lower working memory capacities as well (verbal encoding helps keep multiple items in mind), so they get more flustered in the high-emotional-conflict cases and choose more or less randomly. Means are not reported in the study, but it is reasonable to assume that any increase in utilitarianism would be driven by fluctuation in scenarios like the pushing case, since other scenarios tend toward utilitarian responses already. A shift in pushing intuitions toward utilitarianism (barring massive reversals, which are not reflected in the correlational data) would be a shift toward chance.

In summary, I think there is no strong evidence for dual-process theories. On both empirical and theoretical grounds, there is no reason to think that we ever make moral judgments without the involvement of emotions.

1.2.3. EMOTIONS AS INPUTS

So far, I have been making a case for the thesis that emotions are not merely outputs of moral judgments, but play a more important role. Emotions are somehow in the driver's seat. This conclusion leaves open various possibilities. In psychology, the most widely discussed view of this kind is Jonathan Haidt's (2001) "intuitionist" model. According to Haidt, moral judgments generally arise as the consequence of "intuitions," which are automatic affective responses. In other work, Haidt makes it clear that these intuitions are emotions, such as anger, guilt, and contempt (e.g., Rozin et al. 1999). The idea is that we experience an emotional response and then, on that basis, settle whether an action under consideration is right or wrong. This is an "emotion as input" model.

Haidt also grants that people offer reasons for their moral conclusions, but he insists that reasoning is normally post hoc: we use reasoning after we have already arrived at a moral verdict. Such reasoning serves to rationalize verdicts that were arrived at nonrationally, which is to say, by way of emotional intuitions. For Haidt, emotions are inputs to moral judgments and reasonings are outputs. Haidt's evidence for this model includes his study on moral dumbfounding in which participants are presented with examples of cannibalism and incest that are designed to disqualify the reasons that people usually give when condemning these behaviors. The incest scenario involves consenting adult siblings who use birth control, and the cannibalism scenario involves a doctor who eats part of an unclaimed cadaver. Most participants continue to insist that incest and cannibalism are wrong even in these cases, but they admit that they cannot provide good reasons. This dogmatic insistence suggests that, in more typical cases, the reasons that people give are actually inert. We stick to these norms whether or not our favorite justifications apply. Haidt also cites his own research on emotion induction to suggest that emotional intuitions can be sufficient for drawing moral conclusions even in the absence of prior reasons. For example, in one study he found that people who were hypnotically induced to feel disgust expressed moral misgivings about a person who was described as exceptionally good (Wheatley and Haidt 2005).

The intuitionist model is very appealing and fits well with the evidence that I have reviewed thus far. On closer examination, however, it may not turn out to be the best way to characterize the relationship between emotions and moral judgments. Ironically, I think Haidt underestimates the role of both emotions and reasoning. Let me take up both of these points, beginning with reasoning.

Haidt says that reasoning in the moral domain is post hoc, and this is a plausible claim in many cases. But why think it is true? There do seem to be cases where reasoning is used to change moral opinions. An oft-cited example is animal rights. Peter Singer's book *Animal Liberation* seems to have persuaded many people to become vegetarians or oppose factory farming. There are also many debates about public policy that seem to play a role in shaping public opinion. Arguments have been given for or against social-ized healthcare, various military actions, and gay marriage. Some of these arguments seem to persuade. To see this, we can conjure up a policy decision that has not yet gotten much public discussion. Suppose we ask about plural marriages and point out that those who support gay marriage should, on pain of inconsistency, also favor the legalization of polygamy. Someone might be persuaded by this or might identify a legitimate difference between the two cases. It seems we must reflect and do intellectual toil to decide, and it is plausible that reasoning would play an important role in arriving at a verdict. Haidt overstates the case when he describes reasoning as post hoc. Indeed, in his dumbfound-ing study, 20 percent of participants actually change their view and say abortion and cannibalism should be permitted in the special cases he describes.

In response, Haidt seems to concede that reasoning can in fact play an active role in leading to a moral verdict. But he says this happens only rarely. Most of the time, reason-ing is inert. This concession and restatement of the position is puzzling. Notice, first, that it is tantamount to endorsing a dual-process model. In some sense, this is no great revelation; Haidt is explicitly committed to dual-process theories, arguing that emotion and reasoning are both core cognitive systems. But Haidt's main narrative focuses on the claim that the reasoning system is usually inert in arriving at moral judgments. But a closer reading reveals that he can (and must) admit that reasoning can influence moral judgment. This is a bit like the moral rationalists who admit that sometimes emotions drive morality. That too, is an admission that the dual-process model is right. Thus, the three views—inputs, outputs, and dual process—collapse into one. To avoid this embar-rassing conclusion and establish that intuitionism is a distinctive view that competes with these alternatives, Haidt insists that the reasoning route is rarely traveled. But what evidence does he have for this statistical claim? It is not even clear what such evidence would look like. Haidt would need some way to keep tabs on how people draw moral conclusions in their daily lives. He would need to have a measure of when reasoning is efficacious as opposed to inert, and a massive reservoir of field data looking at the moral judgments that people actually make. He would also need a varied sample. Perhaps some people (judges? children? political independents?) are very open to reasoned persuasion, while others are not. Haidt offers no evidence to support his conclusion that reasoning is usually inert, and it is unlikely that such evidence is forthcoming (for a similar argument, see Mallon and Nichols 2011, on what they call "the counting problem"). Ironically, Haidt may have done proponents of emotionally based ethics a disservice by implying that their position must somehow oppose reasoning, when, as we will see, this is not the case.

Let's turn now to the charge that Haidt underestimates the role of emotions. As a preliminary, it is important to see that any emotion-as-input model must draw a distinction between emotions and moral judgments. In Haidt's diagram of the model, emotions (or intuitions, which include emotions as the primary example) are one box and judgments are another. These are presented as two stages in a sequence of processing. Emotional intuitions lead to judgments. If emotions are merely inputs, it follows that moral judgments must be something other than emotional states. But what are they? Haidt does not say. Notice that we can't just define moral judgments as sentences, or even sentences in the head. Speakers of different languages may draw the same moral judgment, and the very words that we use to express moral judgments may express non-moral judgments. "That's wrong" can be used to express judgments in many different domains. Instead moral judgments must be the mental states that such words are used to express when considering moral scenarios. We need an account of what these mental states are. Astonishingly, this fundamental question gets very little discussion in the moral psychology literature, and I have not seen any answer in Haidt.

There is also a deeper worry in the vicinity. If moral judgments are some as-yet-undefined output of emotions, then they should be the kind of thing that could occur without emotion. When there is a causal relationship between two things, it should be possible to get the effect without the cause. If emotions cause moral judgments, then there should also be moral judgments caused some other way. Haidt implies as much when he concedes that, on rare occasions, moral judgments are caused by reasoning. But this possibility does not have empirical support. Strikingly, I am not aware of a single demonstration of a moral judgment being made in the absence of emotions. When emotions are measured, during moral cognition, they are found. Moreover, there is evidence that emotional deficiencies lead to corresponding deficits in moral judgment. Blair (1995) has argued that psychopaths do not comprehend moral judgments, and he attributes this to the fact that they have flattened affective states, particularly anger, sadness, fear, and guilt. Some have argued that psychopaths give normal responses on some tests of moral competence, but this has only been established in cases where the moral vignettes deal with familiar kinds of cases, which psychopaths could come to recognize by memorizing attitudes of their healthy peers. The claim that psychopaths do not understand morality hinges on two key findings, which are both noted by Blair: their tendency to treat moral judgments as akin to conventions, and their abnormal patterns of justification, as measured in the moral/conventional test, police reports, and moral development scales. There is also evidence that people with Huntington's disease, which decreases disgust, show patterns of paraphilic behavior, suggesting an acquired indifference to sexual norms (Schmidt and Bonelli 2008). Such evidence is not decisive because it is hard to find complete emotional deficits or uncontroversial measures of moral comprehension, but the findings are suggestive. Absent evidence for moral judgments without emotions, the dissociation predicted by input models like Haidt's remains resoundingly unconfirmed.

In summary, I think Haidt's model underestimates the impact or reasoning and unwittingly implies that moral judgments can occur without emotions. I now want to suggest a model that directly denies the latter entailment.

1.2.4. THE CONSTITUTION MODEL

As noted above, philosophers of the sentimentalist stripe have traditionally postulated an intimate relationship between emotions and moral judgments. They do not say that emotions are inputs to moral judgments. Rather, they say that emotions are constituent parts. To form the judgment that something is morally bad is, at least in part, to have a negative feeling toward that thing. It could be, for example, a state of outrage, disgust, or guilt. These emotions literally constitute the moral attitude. Being outraged at an action literally is a judgment that the action was morally bad.

The constitution model differs from input models in key respects. It does not need to give a separate story of what moral judgments consist in, since it equates moral judgments with emotional attitudes. It owes some details about these attitudes, which I will come to presently, but it doesn't imply that moral judgments are something over and above emotional states. Consequently, the constitution model doesn't predict dissociations between emotions and moral judgments. It predicts that when people make genuine moral judgments, they will be in emotional states. It might of course be that people can mouth the words, "Joy killing is wrong" or some other moral platitude without getting riled up, as when we mention this judgment rather than using it. But even that is empirically dubious. Emotion-priming studies suggest that morally charged words are sufficient for evoking an emotional response even when presented in a word list without any context (see, e.g., Arnell et al. 2007; Chen and Bargh 1999). There seems to be something quite automatic about the emotional responses that arise when we contemplate actions that we regard as morally wrong.

The constitution model faces two prima facie problems, which have led, I think, to its comparative neglect in recent moral psychology. First, one might wonder how an emotional state could qualify as a judgment. As indicated above, I think this concern stems from an overly sentential metaphor for thinking. Since the dawn of cognitive science, computer metaphors have led people to think of thoughts as sentences in the head. But thoughts can also comprise sensations. If you touch a stove and say, "That's hot!" the sentence expresses a feeling of heat joined with a perception of the stove. Likewise, if we taste some wine and say, "That's delicious!" the sentence will express our gustatory pleasure. "That's wrong" can equally be an expression of an emotional state.

A second worry concerns the differentiation of moral judgments and nonmoral emotions. Disgust and anger can arise in nonmoral contexts. So it seems implausible to claim that we are making moral judgments every time we experience these emotions. Here I concur. I think a moral judgment is not just an emotional state, but an emotion that derives from what I call a moral sentiment (Prinz 2007). A sentiment is a standing emotional disposition toward something (e.g., an action type, a trait, a motivation, a person, etc.). A moral sentiment is a disposition that causes us to feel emotions of other-blame (i.e., anger or disgust) when another person performs an action of a certain type (or has a certain trait, etc.), and emotions of self-blame (i.e., guilt or shame) when we ourselves perform that action. A moral judgment is an emotional state that issues from such a bidirectional disposition. Thus, to tell whether a state of disgust is a moral judgment we must know whether it comes from a moral sentiment. That, in turn, depends on whether the object of our disgust would have caused shame if we ourselves have been responsible for it.

Consider some examples. Suppose I experience disgust when I see someone eat insects. Is that a moral judgment? That depends on whether eating insects myself would cause shame. In all likelihood it would not. If I just find insects disgusting, but not immoral to eat, I would feel disgust on eating one, not shame. But suppose I think it is immoral to harm insects. Then I would feel ashamed if I ate one. This disposition to have self-directed emotions of blame can distinguish moral judgments from nonmoral instantiations of the disgust and anger. Conversely, the disposition to experience other-directed blame can be used to determine when guilt and shame are moral. If someone feels ashamed of her grades, or guilty about having survived a tragedy that killed others, these are not necessarily moral responses. To qualify as moral, the person who is ashamed of her grades would also have to feel disgusted by others who get bad grades, and the person who feels survivor guilt would also have to feel angry at other survivals. Without such bidirectional feelings of blame, we do not tend to regard a person's emotions as moral in nature. There is some empirical evidence suggesting that guilt and shame complement anger and disgust in the moral domain, but further evidence would be welcome (Giner-Sorolla and Espinosa 2011). One prediction is that moral vegetarians, as opposed to health vegetarians, would be more likely to report shame if they ate meat.

By postulating that emotions are components of moral judgments rather than mere causes, the constitution model assigns a more central role to emotions than input models. This may be taken to suggest that the constitution model is less capable than input models of accommodating the role of reason in moral judgment. The opposite is the case. Input models insist that emotions, as opposed to reasoning, are the primary source of moral judgment. The constitution model makes no such claim. It is a claim about what emotions are, not how they come about. There are, admittedly, good philosophical arguments for doubting that dispassionate reasoning can bring about a moral judgment if the constitution model is true. Dispassionate reasoning can tell us how things are in the world, but merely factual information can always be regarded with indifference. It is always possible to imagine someone who is completely unmoved by anything that reasoning can reveal—a person who is, for example, indifferent to mass famine. Fortunately, normally developing human beings are not indifferent to such facts. That is because we form (through learning or evolution) strong emotional associations. We come to experience despair when we think about mass famine. Reasoning does not entail despair, but our cultivated concern for human life does. So if reasoning uncovers that a government's policies will lead to mass famine, that will lead us to despair. It will also lead us to outrage, insofar as we blame the government for bringing about a negative consequence. On this picture, reasoning can be an important precursor to a moral conclusion, but not reasoning alone. Reasoning can uncover facts toward which we have prior sentiments.

This picture suggests that reasoning and emotion work together in the moral domain. We have a set of moral sentiments, which are emotional dispositions toward action types, traits, and so on. Then reasoning can be used to tell us whether one of these action types has been instantiated. We are outraged at those who cause intentional harm. If we realize that a government has intentionally caused harm, outrage will ensue. But it may take a lot of reasoned reflection to make this discovery. Likewise, reasoning can tell us that factory farms are cruel, and we have negative sentiments toward cruelty. Reasoning can tell us that the criminal justice system unfairly targets African Americans, and we are outraged by unfairness and disgusted by racism. Such rational derivations allow us to make moral judgments about governments, factory farms, and criminal justice systems. Any theory of moral judgment must allow this. By insisting that reasoning is normally post hoc, Haidt's intuitionist model neglects such important cases and dichotomizes the debate between rationalist and sentimentalist accounts. A sentimentalist who defends the constitution model can reply that reasoning can lead to moral judgments provided reasoning leads us to discover facts about which we have emotional dispositions.

A moral rationalist might want to push a bit further, arguing that reasoning can provide a basis for our emotions. For example, Matthew Liao has suggested (in conversation) that the reason-based recognition of human equality can warrant feelings of disgust when we encounter racial discrimination. Such a view about reasons entailing emotions would be especially plausible on a cognitive view of emotions, according to which emotions are cognitive appraisal judgments. I have argued against such views of emotion elsewhere (Prinz 2004). Here let me just say that, on the noncognitive view I favor, emotions are perceptions of patterned changes in the body, which correspond to behavioral dispositions. Disgust is a perception of the body preparing to reject or expel a noxious substance. Reasons cannot entail emotions, on this view, because no facts about the world entail any practical response. If you notice that your home is on fire, it doesn't follow by entailment that you should try to escape. One could be indifferent one's own death or even welcome it. Rather, we react to a fire precisely because we care about our well-being, and that care is implemented through the emotions that make us run from flames. Likewise, one could believe that all people are equal but be indifferent to racism; for example, one could be indifferent to the fact that people have false beliefs (i.e., beliefs in racial inequality)—indeed, we are not in general disgusted by falsehood. When we are disgusted by racism, we are not drawing a logical inference; rather we are expressing the fact that certain forms of falsehood repel us. Reasoning alone cannot bring us to this state. That requires a good deal of social conditioning, unfortunately. But reasoning can help us identify subtle cases of discrimination, and, thus, reason is a powerful instrument in determining when we will experience our moral passions.

My defense of the constitution model is an argument to the best explanation. The model fits with the psychological evidence and philosophical arguments that I have surveyed here better than competing models. I think it is the most plausible account of moral judgments currently under consideration. Future work may tip the balance in another direction, of course. For now I want to assume the model is right and return to the neuroimaging data. We will see that, with a model in hand, we can begin to make concrete proposals about what different brain structures contribute to moral cognition.

1.3. Labeling Lobes: How Sentimentalism Maps onto the Moral Brain

The constitution model posits the following components in moral cognition. To make a moral judgment, we must first categorize an action. That may involve reasoning, and will normally involve ascertaining certain facts that are important to our moral values, such as whether the action was carried out intentionally. Once we have analyzed the action, our moral sentiments will be accessed. Moral sentiments, recall, are emotional dispositions. If the action is morally significant, these sentiments will generate an actual emotional state. That emotion, bound with the action representation, constitutes the judgments that the action is morally good or bad. Different emotional systems will be recruited depending on what kind of action we are considering and whether it is regarded positively or negatively. If the task requires that we report these judgments, then we must also engage in emotional introspection. We must focus on what we are experiencing. Language centers might also be required to verbally express the verdict, and motor systems might be needed to select a verdict on a computer keyboard or other input device.

All of these components can be mapped onto the moral brain. The other models I reviewed might end up with similar interpretations of imaging results, but there is at least one crucial difference. Only the constitution model posits an identity between moral judgments and emotional states. This raises a somewhat embarrassing question for other models. If moral judgments are not emotional states, what brain structure is their neural correlate? There is no obvious candidate suggested in the literature. We are left wondering where moral judgments reside, with no clear proposal for how to find the answer. The constitution model provides an answer: moral judgments reside in emotion pathways, or, more accurately, in the joint activation of those pathways and brain structures that represent actions.

Let's now return to the neuroanatomy and assign functional significance in light of what we have learned. First, let's consider action representations. Here different brain structures will serve different roles. The TPJ, including the superior parietal sulcus, is a likely key player. This part of the brain has been implicated in theory of mind tasks, and would be especially useful in representing intentional actions. It doesn't follow that we should always expect activity in the TPJ. There may be situations where an action type is so familiar and so obviously wrong that we don't need to reflect much on the intentions of the agents involved. There is evidence the TPJ is actually deactivated in such easy cases (FeldmanHall et al. 2013). Similarly, when moral decisions require close attention to numerical outcomes, we may see activation in lateral frontal areas associated with working memory, such as the dorsolateral prefrontal cortex. But this will not be observed when the action in question is so obviously bad to us that we don't bother to do any math.

Actions about which our moral attitudes are well established may be represented in the part of the brain that forms associations between emotions and events. Two key structures are the ventromedial prefrontal cortex and the OFC, which can be thought of as emotion association areas because they form links between emotions and cognitively represented inputs. Another emotion association area is the temporal pole, which is especially associated with affect-laden imagery (Olson et al. 2007). This structure links visually represented information with emotions. In the language of the constitution model, these can structures are the correlates of our sentiments. They are not the correlates of actual emotional states, but rather play a role in initiating emotions in response to information that has been cognitively, perceptually, or imaginatively presented. As noted in discussing dual-process models, the ventromedial prefrontal cortex may also play a role adjudicating conflicts between sentiments.

What about the emotions themselves? I have argued elsewhere that emotional states are most likely associated with brain structures that are implicated in bodily perception, such as the insula and parts of the cingulate cortex (Prinz 2004). This is borne out by the evidence, and in some cases, different emotions lead to greater involvement of different areas. For example, Lewis et al. (2012) contrasted brain volumes associated with individual differences in emphasis on "individualizing" norms (harm and fairness) as compared to "binding" norms (authority, purity, and in-group loyalty). They found anatomical correlates in the subgenual cingulate and insula respectively. The relationship between insula and purity norms fits with prior literature associating this structure with the experience of disgust and other emotions that involve a visceral phenomenology (Wicker et al. 2003; Critchley et al. 2004). The anterior cingulate has been associated with heart-rate regulation (Critchley et al. 2000) and pain (Rainville 1997), making it a good candidate for high-arousal emotions. The posterior cingulate has been associated with negative emotions as well (e.g., Maddock et al. 2003). It is believed to be a correlate of guilt (Basile et al. 2011). All three of these areas, insula, anterior cingulate, and posterior cingulate, have been associated with anger (Denson et al. 2008). This should remind us that discrete emotions can engage multiple regions, and that different emotions use overlapping brain mechanisms. Such findings are predictable on theories that equate emotions with perceived changes in bodily patterns (Prinz 2004). Many distinct emotions involve cardiovascular changes, changes in posture, and changes in respiration. One should therefore expect similarities at the level of gross anatomy, but subtle differences within regions. Disgust may be the biggest outlier, since its phenomenology engages the digestive system more than other emotions.

It is sometimes said that positive emotions have different correlates than negative emotion. In particular, positive emotional responses are associated with the ventral striatum. I suspect that striatum structures, such as the nucleus accumbens, are actually the seat of positive sentiments (dispositions to feel positive emotions), rather than the positive emotions themselves. The OFC has also been implicated in reward computation, which makes it another candidate substrate for positive sentiments, though it is implicated in negative sentiments as well. Where then are positive emotions? I think they are most likely realized by some of the same brain structures that are implicated in negative emotions, since these register bodily changes that take place in both negative and positive states. For example, Moll et al. (2006) found that charitable giving was associated with the subgenual cingulate.

In addition to these emotion areas, moral cognition judgment must recruit brain areas associated with emotional awareness. One likely structure, and a frequent player in fMRI studies of moral cognition, is Brodmann area 9. This area has been implicated in studies of emotional introspection (Satpute et al. 2012). Some studies also ask people to report their moral judgments, either verbally or through key presses. The obvious candidates are classic language centers and motor areas. These rarely show up in the studies, but they are usually subtracted out because all conditions involve the same kind of response.

This mapping is only a first pass, and many of the brain structures I have mentioned are large and complex, with subnuclei that may each play different roles. The point of this exercise is not to assign a final or precise interpretation to the structures that make up the moral brain. Rather, the goal is to illustrate the value of doing such a mapping with a theory in hand. When we read a list of brain areas at the end of an fMRI study, it is often bewildering. We ultimately want a functional decomposition, which tells us what each of these areas does. We should not rely on neuroscience alone to deliver such a decomposition. Rather behavioral research, philosophical theorizing, and neuroscience should work together.

Practicing cognitive neuroscientists would certainly agree on the importance of functional decomposition. We have moved a long way from the phrenological days, when it was deemed adequate to list hotspots without making a serious effort to understand their functional contribution. It is now standard practice to include brief literature reviews on the structures that show activity during fMRI test conditions. My approach here is meant to be an extension of this practice. The point is that neuroscientists should not just look to other fMRI studies when interpreting their results. They should include behaviorally tested and philosophically grounded theories in their discussions as well. My modest methodological suggestion is to use these other sources of evidence when trying to decipher the moral brain. Many neuroscientists already do this (Joshua Greene is a paradigm case), but the practice has not been consistently or regularly implemented. It is rare, for example, to see extensive citations of behavioral work in imaging papers. That underscores the need for an integrative neuroscience, supported by journals that encourage interdisciplinary papers.

The need for such interdisciplinarity can be pressed by asking what we have learned about moral judgment from imaging that we didn't know from behavior or philosophical argumentation. This is a surprisingly difficult question to answer. Many imaging studies compare different kinds of moral judgments and show that they engage different brain areas, but this is a trivial result if we don't think hard about what those brain areas are in fact doing. Working neuroscientists try to do this, but their interpretations often echo well-known behavioral results rather than leading to new insights. Are there cases where imaging has changed our understanding of the moral mind? Greene might say we learned that deontological judgments are more emotionally grounded than utilitarian judgments. I have disputed this interpretation here, but it illustrates how imaging can be informative—even revelatory. Indeed, once we have mapped the moral brain, every imaging study can be reexamined for potential revelations. For example, suppose it is true that the temporal pole is a structure that maps sensory imagery onto emotions. That would imply that trolley dilemmas that engage this structure are being visualized, even when presented as vignettes. This raises the possibility that features found in imagery are playing a role in driving intuitions, which might lead to a deeper understanding of how those intuitions are formed. We could test this by seeing whether certain trolley intuitions are altered in behavioral paradigms where mental imagery is occupied by a concurrent task. We should seek out such opportunities for back-and-forth research between behavior and brain.

Here I argued that we already have good behavioral and philosophical evidence for a constitution model, according to which moral judgments contain emotions as parts. I then described how this model might be mapped onto the moral brain. This is only a first step in an integrative methodology. Functional maps are tools for brain-based discoveries, which can then guide further behavioral work. At the moment, behavior has had more to teach us about the nature of moral judgment than imaging, but it is easy to imagine a more integrative approach, where different methods are used to confirm, interpret, inform, and inspire each other reciprocally.

Acknowledgments

I am exceedingly grateful to Matthew Liao and an anonymous referee for supremely helpful comments on an earlier draft.

References

Arnell, K. M., K. V. Killman, and D. Fijavz. 2007. "Blinded by Emotion: Target Misses Follow Attention Capture by Arousing Distractors in RSVP." *Emotion* 7: 465–477.

Barsalou, L. 1999. "Perceptual Symbol Systems." *Behavioral and Brain Sciences* 22: 577–609.

Basile, B., F. Mancini, E. Macaluso, C. Caltagirone, R. S. Frackowiak, and M. Bozzali. 2011. "Deontological and Altruistic Guilt: Evidence for Distinct Neurobiological Substrates." *Human Brain Mapping* 32: 229–239.

Bechara, A., A. R. Damasio, H. Damasio, and S. W. Anderson. 1994. "Insensitivity to Future Consequences Following Damage to Human Prefrontal Cortex." *Cognition* 50: 7–15.

Blair, R. J. R. 1995. "A Cognitive Developmental Approach to Mortality: Investigating the Psychopath." *Cognition* 57: 1–29.

Blair, R. J. R. 1997. "Moral Reasoning and the Child with Psychopathic Tendencies." *Personality and Individual Differences* 22: 731–739.

Borg, J. S., C. Hynes, J. Van Horn, S. Grafton, and W. Sinnott-Armstrong. 2006. "Consequences, Action, and Intention as Factors in Moral Judgments: An fMRI Investigation." *Journal of Cognitive Neuroscience* 18: 803–817.

Chen, M., and J. A. Bargh. 1999. "Consequences of Automatic Evaluation: Immediate Behavioral Predispositions to Approach or Avoid the Stimulus." *Personality and Social Psychology Bulletin* 25: 215–224.

Ciaramelli, E., M. Muccioli, E. Ladavas, and G. di Pellegrino. 2007. "Selective Deficit in Personal Moral Judgment Following Damage to Ventromedial Prefrontal Cortex." *Social Cognitive Affective Neuroscience* 2: 84–92.

Critchley, H. D., S. Wiens, P. Rotshtein, A. Ohman, and R. J. Dolan. 2004. "Neural Systems Supporting Interoceptive Awareness." *Nature Neuroscience* 7: 189–195.

Critchley, H. D., D. R. Corfield, M. Chandler, C. J. Mathias, and R. J. Dolan. 2000. "Cerebral Correlates of Peripheral Cardiovascular Arousal: A Functional Neuroimaging Study." *Journal of Physiology* 523: 259–270.

Cushman, F. A., D. Murray, S. Gordon-McKeon, S. Wharton, and J. D. Greene. 2011. "Judgment before Principle: Engagement of the Frontoparietal Control Network in Condemning Harms of Omission." *Social Cognitive and Affective Neuroscience* 7: 888–895.

Cushman, F. A., L. Young, and M. D. Hauser. 2006. "The Role of Conscious Reasoning and Intuitions in Moral Judgment: Testing Three Principles of Harm." *Psychological Science* 17: 1082–1089.

Decety, J., and S. Cacioppo. 2012. "The Speed of Morality: A High-Density Electrical Neuroimaging Study." *Journal of Neurophysiology* 108: 3068–3072.

Damasio, A. 1994. *Descartes' Error.* New York: Penguin.

Denson, T. F., W. C. Pendersen, J. Ronquillo, and A. S. Nandy. 2008. "The Angry Brain: Neural Correlates of Anger, Angry Rumination, and Aggressive Personality." *Journal of Cognitive Neuroscience* 21: 734–744.

Dwyer, S. 1999. "Moral Competence." In *Philosophy and Linguistics*, ed. Kumiko K. Murasugi and R. Stainton, 169–190. Boulder, CO: Westview Press.

Eskine, J. K., A. N. Kacinik, and J. J. Prinz. 2011. "A Bad Taste in the Mouth: Gustatory Disgust Influences Moral Judgment." *Psychological Science* 22: 295–299.

FeldmanHall, O., D. Mobbs, and T. Dalgleish. 2013. "Deconstructing the Brain's Moral Network: Dissociable Functionality between the Temporoparietal Junction and Ventro-Medial Prefrontal Cortex." *Social Cognitive and Affective Neuroscience.* doi:10.1093/scan/nss139.

Giner-Sorolla, R., and P. Espinosa. 2011. "Social Cuing of Guilt by Anger and of Shame by Disgust." *Psychological Science* 22: 49–53.

Greene, J. D. 2007. "The Secret Joke of Kant's Soul." In *Moral Psychology*, vol. 3: *The Neuroscience of Morality: Emotion, Disease, and Development*, ed. W. Sinnott-Armstrong, 35–79. Cambridge: MIT Press.

Greene, J. D., and J. Haidt. 2002. "How (and Where) Does Moral Judgment Work?" *Trends in Cognitive Science* 6: 517–523.

Greene, J. D., R. B. Sommerville, L. E. Nystrom, J. M. Darley, and J. D. Cohen. 2001. "An fMRI Investigation of Emotional Engagement in Moral Judgment." *Science* 293: 2105–2108.

Greenwald, A. G., and M. R. Banaji. 1995. "Implicit Social Cognition: Attitudes, Self-Esteem, and Stereotypes." *Psychological Review* 102: 4–27.

Harenski, C. L., O. Antonenko, M. S. Shane, and K. A. Kiehl. 2010. "A Functional Imaging Investigation of Moral Deliberation and Moral Intuition." *NeuroImage* 49: 2707–2716.

Hauser, M. D., F. A. Cushman, L. Young, R. Jin, and J. M. Mikhail. 2007. "A Dissociation between Moral Judgment and Justification." *Mind and Language* 22: 1–21.

Heekeren, H. R., I. Wartenburger, H. Schmidt, C. Denkler, H. Schwintowski, and A. Villringer. 2001. "The Functional Anatomy of Moral Judgment: An fMRI-Study. *NeuroImage* 136: S417–S417.

Heekeren, H. R., I. Wartenburger, H. Schmidt, H. P. Schwintowski, and A. Villringer. 2003. "An fMRI Study of Simple Ethical Decision-Making." *NeuroReport* 14: 1215–1219.

Holtzman, G. 2014. "Failed Taxonomies, Faulty Heuristics, and False Premises: An Individual Differences Approach to Conceptual Analysis." Ph.D. diss., Department of Philosophy, City University of New York, Graduate Center.

Huebner, B., S. Dwyer, and M. Hauser. 2008. "The Role of Emotion in Moral Psychology." *Trends in Cognitive Science* 13: 1–6.

Hume, D. [1740] 1978. *A Treatise of Human Nature*. Ed. L. A. Selby-Bigge and P. H. Nidditch. Oxford: Oxford University Press.

Inbar, Y., D. A. Pizarro, and P. Bloom. 2009. "Conservatives Are More Easily Disgusted Than Liberals." *Cognition and Emotion* 23: 714–725.

Isen, A. M., and P. F. Levin. 1972. "The Effects of Feeling Good on Helping: Cookies and Kindness." *Journal of Personality and Social Psychology* 21: 384–388.

Kant, I. [1787] 1997 *Critique of Pure Reason*. Trans. P. Guyer and A. Wood. Cambridge: Cambridge University Press.

Kitcher, P. 1990. *Kant's Transcendental Psychology*. New York: Oxford University Press.

Koenigs, M. L., R. Young, D. Adolphs, F. Tranel, M. Cushman, M. Hauser, and A. Damasio. 2007. "Damage to the Prefrontal Cortex Increases Utilitarian Moral Judgements." *Nature* 446: 908–911.

Koven, N. S. 2011. "Specificity of Meta-emotion Effects on Moral Decision-Making." *Emotion* 11: 1255–1261.

Lewis, G. J., R. Kanai, T. C. Bates, and G. Rees. 2012. "Moral Values Are Associated with Individual Differences in Regional Brain Volume." *Journal of Cognitive Neuroscience* 24: 1657–1663.

Maddock, R. J., A. S. Garrett, and M. H. Buonocore. 2003. "Posterior Cingulate Cortex Activation by Emotional Words: fMRI Evidence from a Valence Decision Task." *Human Brain Mapping* 18: 30–41.

Mallon, R., and S. Nichols. 2011. "Dual Processes and Moral Rules." *Emotion Review* 3: 284–285.

May, J. 2014. "Does Disgust Influence Moral Judgment?" *Australasian Journal of Philosophy* 92: 125–141.

Mikhail, J. 2000. "Rawls' Linguistic Analogy: A Study of the 'Generative Grammar' Model of Moral Theory Discussed by John Rawls in *A Theory of Justice*." Ph.D. diss., Department of Philosophy, Cornell University.

Mikhail, J. 2007. "Universal Moral Grammar: Theory, Evidence, and the Future." *Trends in Cognitive Science* 11: 143–152.

Moll, J., P. J. Eslinger, and R. Oliveira-Souza. 2001. "Frontopolar and Anterior Temporal Cortex Activation in a Moral Judgment Task: Preliminary Functional MRI Results in Normal Subjects." *Arquivos de Neuro-Psiquiatria* 59: 657–664.

Moll J., R. Oliveira-Souza, I. E. Bramati, and J. Grafman. 2002. "Functional Networks in Emotional Moral and Nonmoral Social Judgments." *NeuroImage* 16: 696–703.

Moll, J., R. Oliveira-Souza, P. J. Eslinger, I. E. Bramati, J. Mourao-Miranda, P. A. Andreiulo, and L. Pesoa. 2002. "The Neural Correlates of Moral Sensitivity: A Functional Magnetic Resonance Imaging Investigation of Basic and Moral Emotions." *Journal of Neuroscience* 22: 2730–2736.

Moll, J., F. Kreuger, R. Zahn, M. Pardini, R. Oliveira-Souza, and J. Grafman. 2006. "Human Front-Mesolimbic Networks Guide Decisions about Charitable Donation." *PNAS* 103: 15623–15629.

Nichols, S. 2014. "Process Debunking and Ethics." *Ethics* 124: 727–749.

Nielen, M. M. A., D. J. Heslenfeld, K. Heinen, J. W. Van Strien, M. P. Witter, C. Jonker, and D. J. Veltman. 2009. "Distinct Brain Systems Underlie the Processing of Valence and Arousal of Affective Pictures." *Brain and Cognition* 71: 387–396.

Olson, I., A. Plotzker, and Y. Ezzyat. 2007. "The Enigmatic Temporal Pole: A Review of Findings on Social and Emotional Processing." *Brain* 130: 1718–1731.

Pizarro, D., Y. Inbar, and C. Helion. 2011. "On Disgust and Moral Judgment." *Emotion Review* 3: 267–268.

Prinz, J. J. 2002. *Furnishing the Mind*. Cambridge: MIT Press.

Prinz, J. J. 2004. *Gut Reactions*. New York: Oxford University Press.

Prinz, J. J. 2007. *The Emotional Construction of Morals*. New York: Oxford University Press.

Rainville, P., G. H. Duncan, D. D. Price, B. Carrier, and M. C. Bushnell. 1997. "Pain Affect Encoded in Human Anterior Cingulate but Not Somatosensory Cortex." *Science* 277: 968–970.

Rozin, P., L. Lowery, S. Imada, and J. Haidt. 1999. "The CAD Triad Hypothesis: A Mapping between Three Moral Emotions (Contempt, Anger, Disgust) and Three Moral Codes (Community, Autonomy, Divinity)." *Journal of Personality and Social Psychology* 76: 574–586.

Satpute, A. B., J. Shu, J. Weber, M. Roy, and K. Ochsner. 2013. "The Functional Neural Architecture of Self-Reports of Affective Experience." *Biological Psychiatry* 73: 631–638.

Schmidt, E. Z., and R. M. Bonelli. 2008. "Sexuality in Huntington's Disease." *Wiener Medizinischen Wochenschrift* 158: 84–90.

Schnall, S., J. Haidt, G. L. Clore, and A. H. Jordan. 2008. "Disgust as Embodied Moral Judgment." *Personality and Social Psychology Bulletin* 34: 1096–1109.

Seidel, A., and J. Prinz 2013a. "Sound Morality." *Cognition* 127: 1–5.

Seidel, A., and J. Prinz. 2013b. "Mad and Glad: Musically Induced Emotions Have Divergent Impact on Morals." *Motivation and Emotion* 37: 629–637.

Sunstein, C. 2005. "Moral Heuristics." *Behavioral and Brain Sciences* 28: 531–573.

Turiel, E. 1983. *The Development of Social Knowledge: Morality and Convention.* Cambridge: Cambridge University Press.

Valdesolo, P., and D. DeSteno. 2006. "Manipulations of Emotional Context Shape Moral Judgment." *Psychological Science* 17: 476–477.

Vytal, K., and S. Hamann. 2010. "Neuroimaging Support for Discrete Neural Correlates of Basic Emotions: A Voxel-Based Meta-analysis." *Journal of Cognitive Neuroscience* 12: 2864–2885.

Weyant, M. J. 1978. "Effects of Mood States, Costs, and Benefits on Helping." *Journal of Personality and Social Psychology* 36: 1169–1176.

Wheatley, T., and J. Haidt. 2005. "Hypnotic Disgust Makes Moral Judgments More Severe." *Psychological Science* 16: 780–784.

Wicker, B., C. Keysers, J. Plailly, J. P. Royet, V. Gallese, and G. Rizzolatti. 2003. "Both of Us Disgusted in My Insula: The Common Neural Basis of Seeing and Feeling Disgust." *Neuron* 40: 655–664.

The Rationalist Delusion?

A POST HOC INVESTIGATION

Jeanette Kennett and Philip Gerrans

2.1. Introduction

According to Jonathan Haidt (2012, 17), moral rationalists believe that "reasoning is the most important and reliable way to attain moral knowledge." He argues that this belief is a delusion that expresses a persistent faith in reason that ignores the well-known facts about the flaws and limits of reasoning. Those well-known flaws are described in a large literature on motivated irrationality, confirmation bias, the primacy of intuitive over reflective judgment, and the pervasive influence of social context on decision-making.

These flaws carry over to the moral domain. When we make moral judgments, says Haidt, we do not reason according to canonical norms but express affectively based intuitions. Haidt argues that a range of experimental results suggest that people's moral competence does not consist in the ability to *reason* on the basis of evidence and argument but to *persuade* by engaging evolved affective responses.[1] "We do moral reasoning not to reconstruct the actual reasons why *we ourselves* came to a judgment; we reason to find the best possible reasons why *somebody else ought to join us* in our judgment." (45–46) Haidt's argument has two essential strands that we do not dispute. (1) Experimental results show that moral judgments often express emotional responses. (2) Moral deliberation is essentially a practical/social process, not a theoretical one. Moral reasoning is for *social doing*, as Haidt puts it.

It follows that the cognitive processes engaged by everyday moral deliberation will most often be those that evolved to manage social cooperation and conflict, rather than cognitive processes such as logical inference or probability theory that test propositions for correctness and consistency. Haidt argues that "reasoning matters, particularly because reasons do sometimes influence other people, but *most of the action in moral psychology is in the intuitions*" (80). Once those intuitions are elicited, the role of reasoning is ex post facto, to find emotionally inflected evidence in support of the intuitive judgment rather than to canvass the full range of potentially relevant disconfirming evidence. Once the intuitive judgment has been supported in this way, the role of reason becomes rhetorical: to persuade others or oneself to accept the decision. When reason plays this instrumental, persuasive role, consensus, prestige, and the support of allies, rather than truth, become the goal of argument. The delusion that afflicts rationalists ensures their inability to escape the cycle of motivated reasoning and see our moral practices for what they are.

Like Haidt, we put practical and social concerns at the heart of morality, but, unlike him, we argue that the well-known facts about the flaws and limits of reasoning do not undermine the idea that people's moral decision-making is underpinned by processes that are "broadly rational" (Bayne and Pacherie 2004).[2] We thus offer an account that is in the spirit of rationalism in emphasizing rational justification, but which accommodates Haidt's critique of overly abstract theorizing as a basis for everyday moral practice.

In doing so we interpret the psychological and neuroscientific evidence quite differently than Haidt. We think a capacity for diachronic agency is essential to moral deliberation, but that this capacity is obscured by several aspects of Haidt's account. The first is the emphasis on synchronic judgments in hypothetical scenarios rather than protracted, socially embedded deliberation. The second is the dual-process framework Haidt relies upon. The third is the all-or-nothing contrast between theoretical rationality and affective processing. These three contrasts make it seem as if moral decisions can only depend on intuitive processes *or* abstract reasoning. Rationalists thus look to be forced into adopting an empirically implausible and unappealing position. However, once the diachronic aspects of agency, cognition, and practical deliberation are highlighted, we can see moral reasoning in broadly rationalist terms as involving a socially reinforced disposition to greater impartiality and wide reflective equilibrium.

2.2. Dual Processing, Mental Time Travel, and Moral Judgment

The contexts in which Haidt and others investigate moral judgment place artificial temporal and informational restrictions on the decision process. Not surprisingly, they tend to trigger so-called system 1 processes, designed to operate semiautomatically and instantaneously. Moreover, the dual-process model of moral cognition inherits a defect of other dual-process models. Namely, it holds that moral cognition is the product either of system 1 or of system 2, where system 2 is conceived of as effortful or abstract reasoning. However, the mind has more resources than encapsulated automated processes and abstract reasoning, and it tends to deploy them as needed in different contexts.

We draw attention to the recent trend in cognitive neuroscience to treat the mind as a hierarchically organized system that uses models of its world (including the social world and the agent considered as part of the world) to make and revise predictions about particular domains, including the moral. The basic idea is that cognitive systems try to reduce error signals produced by mismatches between expectations and outcomes. Most errors are corrected semiautomatically. Others are referred upward until they surface as conscious experiences or thoughts that require attentive, deliberate responses.

Higher levels of cognitive control are activated by signals of discrepancy or error that cannot be resolved at lower levels. Anomalous experiences in effect represent problems that cannot be solved at lower levels by perceptual and sensory systems. Higher levels of executive control then are engaged to resolve the problem (Fletcher and Frith 2009; Clark 2012).

The first stage of problem-solving is to provide an autobiographical context for the experience: to rehearse scenarios in which such experiences have or could occur as a way of gathering information relevant to responding. The so-called default mode network (or DMN) is essentially a simulation system that evolved to provide these kinds of actual and possible contexts for experiences. This simulatory capacity employed in the service of planning is now baptised mental time travel to capture the fact that it allows us to escape the stimulus-bound present, review the past, and preview the future by projecting ourselves into different scenarios ("re-experiencing the past and pre-experiencing the future"). As we have argued elsewhere (Gerrans and Kennett 2010), this capacity for mental time travel is essential to moral agency and decision-making.

To illustrate: When my smile of greeting is met by a frown, I have some initial automatic responses mediated by system 1 responses to prediction error (my expression, posture, and vocalization will change almost instantaneously), but I can also respond at much higher levels. I can wonder why my friend seems upset, mentally rehearse previous interactions with her, and make inferences about the role of background circumstances. I can talk to her and, directly or indirectly, discover why she is upset with me. This interaction between automatic and higher-level controlled response is the stuff of social and, we would say, moral, life. Not all such problems are solved immediately. Some, like many real moral problems, are insoluble, and deliberation only produces a "least worst" option. In such cases deliberation, in the sense of rehearsing options and outcomes, may never cease, precisely because the mind never settles into an equilibrium that stops signals of discrepancy.

Someone who puts a disabled child into care, for example, may be making a rational and entirely permissible decision, but it is unlikely that moral thinking simply stops once the decision is made, precisely because the different cognitive and emotional processes that operate at different time scales involved cannot all be reconciled. A parent in this situation may never stop rehearsing alternatives or leave behind emotional feelings that inform decision-making. Not only that, but a crucial dimension to the deliberative process is provided by the ability to imagine the future of all concerned by the decision. We are not saying, of course, that such rehearsals always lead to the right decision, just that a multiple choice test on Survey Monkey or in an fMRI machine may not engage all aspects of moral deliberation in the wild—a point we will take up in more detail later.

The DMN is essentially a mechanism for constructing the elements of personal narratives: stories and scenarios that make experience intelligible in terms of goals and motives. As Pace-Schott describes it, the DMN is the substrate of a capacity "to represent reality in the form of narrative—a 'story-telling' instinct or module" (Pace-Schott 2013; See also Christoff et al. 2009). Thus we can picture the DMN as a mechanism that provides a necessary subjective perspective on experiences, locating them in personally or socially compelling narratives. The same information can also be represented neutrally and impartially as pure description or theoretical explanation, but such representations are processed by different cognitive systems. The processes that accomplish these forms of representation are baptised *decontextualized* processes by cognitive psychologists.[3]

In fact there is evidence that the DMN needs to be *deactivated* for these kinds of *decontextualized* cognitive processes. Subjects (including delusional subjects) who have hypeactive or hyperassociative DMNs perform poorly at tasks that require decontextualization, such as symbolic reasoning and memory tasks (Broyd et al. 2009; Whitfield-Gabrieli et al. 2011). A crucial hub of decontextualized processing is the right dorsolateral prefrontal cortex.

This suggests that Haidt may well be correct that moral decision-making naturally proceeds by way of affectively scaffolded intuition to subjective narrative, which may then be mobilized to persuade others. But it also suggests two other things: (1) that this is in fact a rational way to proceed since it accesses hierarchically organized cognitive processing; (2) that in a normal mind the process does not necessarily stop there.

2.3. Wide Reflective Equilibrium

If moral rationalists insist that moral deliberation requires the application of theoretical reasoning to test the truth of propositions, rather than the application of practical reason underpinned by affective processing to solve social and personal problems, then rationalists have indeed mischaracterized everyday moral judgment. But should rationalism about morality be committed to this view? Rationalists about logic, probability, and decision theory certainly should endorse this view of their enterprise since those projects are essentially instances of theoretical reasoning under idealized conditions.

However, rationalism about morality can be characterized in a different way. We see it as the disposition to take an increasingly impartial perspective in order to put our starting intuitions into wide reflective equilibrium. Reflective equilibrium "is the endpoint of a deliberative process in which we reflect on and revise our beliefs about an area of inquiry, moral or non-moral" (Daniels 2011). It does not follow that the endpoint of the process must be a single, ultimate truth, a perfectly consistent set of propositions, or that it achieves a "view from nowhere" on the problem. Nor does it follow that the deliberative process consists of logical proof or hypothesis testing (even if it is useful for psychologists to reconstruct the process that way).

Haidt notes that other people are often best placed to point out flaws in our reasoning and to provide evidence and reasons for alternative positions. We agree. The model of wide reflective equilibrium (Rawls 1971; Daniels 1979) endorsed by many rationalists assumes something like this interaction between intuitions, argument, evidence, and principle. The process of WRE is fundamentally interactive. Further, it proceeds on the assumption that the social process that aims to reach equilibrium is governed by certain norms.

When moral deliberation is directed at practical problems with the aim of securing agreement about policies and actions, the agents involved must be able to make some assumptions about each other and the norms governing the process. The social process of reaching agreement must be at least partially governed by norms of reason, or the resolution of practical problems will rely on coercion or force.

First, as Haidt says, conversational participants offer their best reasons in order to convince their interlocutor to share their views.[4] But this must assume that the other is at least somewhat responsive to good reasons and is engaging in the conversation in good faith.[5] Pettit and Smith (1996) argue that "insofar as people converse, not just about theoretical questions but also about practical matters—about what it is right or wrong, good or bad, rational or irrational, sensible or stupid, to do in a given situation—we think they are more or less bound to treat one another—and of course themselves—as satisfying [certain rational norms] . . . . The pair of you balk at the conversational discrepancy and seek out ways to resolve your evaluative difference" (436). If someone was not disposed or not able to change her views in the light of reasons and evidence that emerge in what Pettit and Smith call the conversational stance, we could not engage with her from within that stance.

It is not enough, however, to offer our best reasons to persuade others. We must also be at least somewhat disposed ourselves to respond to reasons and evidence; otherwise the practical point of moral deliberation and reasoning can't be realized. Of course we don't always reason well. But as Haidt acknowledges, we can do so when we are faced with social demands for accuracy and accountability. Both of these demands are consistent with a move to greater impartiality and the rational goal of wide reflective equilibrium. It is rational to ask an expert, seek an intuitive explanation from a friend, check the facts, imaginatively rehearse alternative outcomes. These are strategies that may fall short of idealized rationality but indicate the disposition to evaluate the adequacy of one's intuitive solution to a practical problem. To be irrational, a person has to lack the disposition to *recognize, understand,* or *employ* sound inferential procedures under favorable conditions. Lapses or partial failures due to time constraints or emotional or social pressure are matters of rational *performance*, not *competence*.

Rationality does require that the participant in reflective equilibrium be able to engage in open-ended inquiry, which acknowledges that her starting point is partial and local, and that she aspire to a more impartial perspective on events. *One* way to attain such a perspective would be to reframe the issue in entirely theoretical terms: as a problem of discovering or applying a universal principle that subsumes a current case. However, this is not the only way to rationally evaluate one's intuitions. A disposition to impartiality is not quite the same thing as a disposition to reframe practical questions as abstract, theoretical ones. In fact, Haidt's characterization of the Piagetian explanation of moral development seems ungenerous here. For Piaget abstraction is not a goal in itself: an endpoint of moral development. Rather, abstraction is a tool for impartiality. The child who can leave her own subjective perspective behind is better equipped to take other's interests into account. And, as Piaget rightly noted, cognitive development, which includes mastery of progressively more abstract concepts, helps the child attain an impartial perspective on her own actions.

We are not sure how Haidt would respond to our proposal to conceive of rationality as the disposition to seek moral reflective equilibrium. Perhaps he might find it overly intellectualistic or abstract. It is an objection sometimes made against reflective equilibrium theories that the impartiality they require abstracts too far from the social and subjective to make them useful as characterizations of real-world deliberation.

Like the rationalist, Haidt conceives of moral reasoning as conscious and effortful, but he denies that people reason about morality in the way that rationalists claim is required. In particular Haidt argues that moral reasoning does not aim at getting the right answer, though he acknowledges that the processes of reasoning may, in the right circumstances, lead us to the truth, as well as to better solutions to practical problems. This suggests that his rejection of moral rationalism is based upon a version of rationalism that casts moral reasoning as a purely theoretical enterprise. Such an approach would connect poorly at best with those processes that regulate social life and would tend to support his claim that rationalist accounts of morality are a delusion.[6]

On our view, however, to be rational is not necessarily to apply canonical rules of reasoning. On our view to be "rational" in the practical sense is to have a disposition to resolve conflict within oneself or between people by accessing higher levels of representation. The highest, most impersonal level of representation is theoretical rationality, but this fact does not place theoretical reasoning on the other side of a cognitive divide from practical deliberation. Hugo Mercier and Dan Sperber (2011) make the point this way. Imagine two people arguing about the quickest way to a destination. Given their preferences and histories, they may have an intractable disagreement about whether tram or bus is the fastest journey from the airport to the city center. The way to resolve the problem is to look at a map and a timetable—in other words, to represent the problem impersonally, using information not drawn from subjective experience. This does not change the problem from practical to theoretical. Rather it shifts to a more *decontextualized form* of representation. The shift is (rationally) required *because*, as Haidt puts it, "Moral thinking is for social doing."

Decontextualization can take many forms and come in degrees. The obvious form for cognitive psychologists is the use of symbolic logic, the purest and most abstract form of decontextualization. However, this type of abstract cognition is a rare cognitive achievement for humans. Even Panglossians (as Keith Stanovich calls them) about human reasoning do not require that humans always reason according to the rules of logic. Rather humans count as minimally rational to the extent that they can detect inconsistency and have the disposition to resolve it by reference to higher levels of cognitive processing. There are many levels of processing between intuitive belief and formal logic or decision theory. Personal or social narrative, expertise, imaginative simulation, and informal reasoning are all examples. Not only that, but all of these options can be situated in an argumentative or social context in which the aim is to *transcend the individual perspective* in order to resolve intra- or interpersonal conflicts between intuitive personal beliefs.

The point is not that Haidt is wrong to think that there are reflexive processes that produce intuitive moral responses and more abstract and effortful reasoning processes that often deliver different outputs. However, his contrast between the intuitive elephant and the rational rider is too coarse. It suggests that the only options for dealing with intra- or interpersonal conflict between intuitions are (1) the manipulation of intuitions by "affective engineering" or (2) theoretical reasoning, which translates the intuitions into hypotheses to be verified and compared using canonical procedures of reasoning. In fact the mind is constantly involved in conflict monitoring and resolution at all levels. One important source of high-level monitoring is other people. Another is mental simulation of possible situations in order to sample some emotional consequences of future decisions. Abstract reasoning is one of many higher levels of processing that can provide a necessary form of impartiality, allowing us to escape the stimulus-bound present.

Mercier and Sperber's example can easily be translated into the moral realm, as seen in our earlier example. Family members may disagree about the way to cope with a child's disability. They may have different emotionally scaffolded intuitions about the best solution, which lead to conflict. It does not seem to us that the only options here for the family are to try to persuade by manipulating each other's automatic emotional responses or to treat the issue as a question in decision theory, or as the rote application of a universal principle, leaving behind the families' emotional history and possible futures.

Surely one option might be to acknowledge that each person has a different perspective on the issue and that a more impartial perspective might help. At the very least the family might consult specialist physicians and carers before making a joint decision. To do otherwise would be irrational. To try to be impartial in this way is the essence of practical rationality. It does not follow, of course, that everyone can attain the "view from nowhere" or that this is needed. Nor does it follow that the attempt to be impartial will deliver consensus. It may show that suboptimal compromises are the best that can be achieved. The point is merely that the disposition to transcend the purely subjective present is the beginning of practical moral deliberation, and that the ordinary processes we have described as one way to realize this disposition count as rational.

2.4. Post Hoc Reasoning and Rationalist Accounts of Agency

For rationalists, moral judgments are not distinct from moral decision-making; they are essentially concerned with identifying reasons for action that will structure what the agent does. As such they are exercises of agency. Indeed Christine Korsgaard claims that it is "from the standpoint of practical reason that moral thought and moral concepts . . . are generated" (1992, 132). We have claimed that a moral agent needs to be able to conceive of herself as temporally extended entity as a necessary condition of practical moral reflection and decision-making. Moral reasoning is not a purely synchronic process; if it were, it must rely on either intuitive processes or the application of learned rules to a situation. But as is apparent from our discussion, many moral decisions, particularly complex decisions, take time. Deciding whether or not to end a marriage, to put one's demented parent into a nursing home, or to become a whistleblower engages memory, prospection, and imagination. Moreover, because we see ourselves as diachronic agents and our choices as interconnected, events that occur now or new evidence that becomes available may also prompt reflection on past choices and behavior, leading to reinterpretation of the past, and rational revision of relevant judgments and principles.

Yet in contrast to such everyday diachronic moral reasoning, experimental work on moral judgment imposes forced-choice, synchronic judgments on subjects. Subjects are asked to render instant verdicts on what are often highly emotive and unusual scenarios. As argued elsewhere (Kennett 2011, 2012) the setup of these tasks does not allow us to draw conclusions about the rationality or otherwise of everyday moral judgment. First, when a quick decision is needed, intuition unsurprisingly dominates. Second, there is evidence from Haidt's own work on moral dumbfounding that subjects may not believe the scenarios as presented. This is the case with Haidt's sibling incest scenario, in which it is specified that no harm befalls the siblings from their decision to have sex. Haidt tells us that his subjects continued to argue "that Julie and Mark will be hurt . . . even though the story makes it clear that no harm befell them" (2001, 814). This is taken by Haidt to be further evidence of post hoc rationalization, but it might just as well be evidence of the difficulty experienced by subjects in imaginatively occupying the scenarios provided and making sense of the protagonists' choices.

Third, it is also important to note that moral reasoning and judgment often takes place in conditions of uncertainty, and this offers a marked contrast to experimental circumstances where outcomes are specified and counterfactual reasoning is ruled out. So a real Mark and Julie could not be sure that their decision to have sex would have no untoward consequences, and the doubts expressed by subjects may reflect this uncertainty.

Fourth, the experimental data do not measure the effect of reflection over time on moral judgment, which may counter the dominance of intuition. A question that experimentalists have barely begun to address is what would happen if people had more time to think. On the one hand, Haidt appears to dismiss the notion that moral reasoning may take time to produce an effect. "I used a computer program to force some people to answer quickly, before they had time to think, and I forced other people to wait 10 seconds before offering their judgment. Surely that manipulation would weaken or strengthen moral reasoning and shift the balance of power ... but it didn't" (39). However, he also cites Paxton et al. (2012), who tested participants on the sibling incest scenario used by Haidt and then provided them with either a good or weak argument to justify the siblings' decision. Haidt notes:

> People who were forced to reflect on the weak argument still ended up condemning Julie and Mark—slightly more than people who got to answer immediately. But people who were forced to reflect on the good argument for two minutes actually did become substantially more tolerant toward Julie and Mark's decision to have sex. (63)

If two minutes' reflection makes a difference in the quality of responses to an artificial scenario in the lab, it is likely that important and difficult real-life moral decisions, such as the decision either to put one's demented parent in a nursing home or to take care of her oneself, require time to adequately establish and respond to relevant considerations and resolve disagreements with affected others about what should be done.

It is in recognition of this important dimension of moral decision-making that we have offered a qualified defense of the rational credentials of post hoc reasoning interpreted as a move toward the achievement of wide reflective equilibrium. Some post hoc reasoning is indeed confabulation and rationalization. But some is not. Just because the reasons motivating our decisions are not always immediately accessible to us does not mean no such reasons exist, a point with which Haidt would surely agree. Karen Jones (2006) argues that ordinary subjects tacitly take their intuitive moral responses to be *tracking* reasons that, once articulated, would justify their moral judgments. That they cannot presently "put their finger" on the reason may not rationally compel them to the view that no such reason exists. That is what a post hoc examination of our gut reactions and the situation that prompted them might seek to establish. If this is right, post hoc reasoning is not mere lawyering. Where post hoc reasoning involves a move to more impartial consideration of the situation, by considering times other than the present or by considering perspectives other than one's own, as well as consulting sources of authority in an attempt to resolve inter- and intrapersonal discrepancies, the resulting judgment or decision will count as broadly rational.

2.5. Conclusion

What is a moral judgment? Haidt and others who adopt a dual-process model of cognition see moral judgment as largely automatic—the product of tacit affective processes, and partially encapsulated from explicit reasoning. Explicit reasoning is directed to the task of ex post facto justification and persuasion, which may if successful generate new intuitions and extinguish others. Interestingly, Haidt and Bjorklund (2008) distinguish between moral *judgments*, which are "about whether *another person* did something right versus wrong" (243; our emphasis) and moral *decision-making*, and they stipulate that their social intuitionist model describes the phenomenology and causal processes of (third personal) moral judgment only. They argue that moral judgment is functionally distinct from moral decision-making and suggest that it is shaped by different selection pressures. As they see it, moral judgment and moral decision-making differ insofar as, in the former, there is very little at stake for the self. "We can make a hundred judgments each day and experience them as little more than a few words of praise or blame, linked to flashes of feeling, that dart through consciousness. But moral . . . decisions are different: they have real consequences for the self and others" (243). They concede that moral decisions must take into account many factors besides the initial intuitive response.

Haidt and Bjorklund here appear to divorce moral judgment from moral agency. If we accept this distinction, then moral judgment so described is not the result of rational processes.[7] But the more interesting question and the one we have focused on here is whether the rationality of moral *decision-making* is similarly called into question by the range of experimental and other evidence cited by Haidt. If we focus on the full range of processes involved in moral decision-making, it is not so clear that rationalism is undermined. Initial moral judgment—the quick affective flashes resulting in intuitive judgments of approval and disapproval that are picked up in moral judgment research—then becomes just one input to moral decision-making, subject to moderation by social and rational pressures consistent with a broadly rationalist perspective.

We have suggested that moral judgment is like judgment in general: it engages cognitive processes according to the degree of cognitive disequilibrium produced by a problem. Very roughly, the mind will try to solve the problem rapidly and automatically; then it will build a subjective autobiographical context for the potential solutions, engaging with others as appropriate in argument and discussion to try to reach ever-wider levels of equilibrium. The court of last resort is abstract reasoning according to canonical principles. Perhaps Haidt is right that some philosophers have placed too much emphasis on the supreme court of judgment in explaining morality, but it does not follow that decisions made at any lower level of cognition count against the notion that moral reasoning and decision-making in a social context are rightly subject to rational pressures to adopt the kinds of impartiality required for wide reflective equilibrium.

Notes

1. Haidt says (in comments on this essay) that persuasion is only part of moral competence. The competent moral *agent* sees things quickly and automatically in the right way. But it would seem that competence in moral *reasoning* on his account is largely cashed out in terms of competence in persuasion of others and successful self-presentation.

2. Bayne and Pacherie introduced the term "broadly rational" to cover cases in which people reason, without making a serious error, on the basis of experience to conclusions that are irrational measured against prescriptive standards. That is to say that were the person to assess all the available evidence and competing hypotheses from a (relatively) impartial standpoint, the person would reach a different conclusion. In other words they are suggesting that even quite serious confirmation biases would not render a person irrational.

3. Decontextualization is not itself a specific form of inference such as logical reasoning or hypothesis confirmation, reading maps or graphs, but a *necessary precondition* for such forms of context-independent cognition. This is why the neural correlates of decontextualized processes can be activated in a wide range of tasks, from working memory to goal recalibration or abstract symbol manipulation. What these tasks have in common is they require the subject to represent information in a context-free way. Decontextualization requires activation in specific (dorsolateral) neural structures, which are the last to develop, phylogenetically and ontogenetically, and the most cognitively expensive to deploy. The interesting fact about the anticorrelation between DMN and the structures that enable decontextualization is not that the DMN is a default state, but that it is a default state of a system *specialized for representing the world from the subject's perspective*. Decontextualized processes are *aperspectival*.

4. In some contexts our aim might not be to persuade opponents but to rally the troops on our own side. That is not the context focused on here.

5. To be sure, we may often have no particular grounds for optimism that reason will prevail. But we offer our reasons nonetheless. This is particularly the case when opposing moral views are deeply entrenched, as in much of political discourse. But most moral deliberation is, as Paul Bloom says, and our examples illustrate, about "the problems of everyday life" (Bloom 2014), where some rational norms are necessarily employed in order to resolve practical conflicts and maintain social harmony. Utter intransigence in the face of the evidence is not a particularly good strategy.

6. While Haidt may be descriptively correct—as a matter of psychological fact, most people might only be concerned with rallying the troops and getting allies in the post hoc reasoning process, and so their deployment of their reasoning skills has this purpose—nevertheless it is more rational to seek WRE with others and in one's own case, and that requires being responsive to impartial considerations and to the facts as we know them. And it appears that this is perfectly possible for us, even if more or less difficult on occasion, and even though it is not always required because conflicts are resolved at an earlier level in a way that counts as broadly rational. Moral rationalism as we conceive it *recommends* resolving disputes and inconsistencies by these increasingly impartial processes. We do not here address rationalist approaches to conceptual questions about morality.

7. The restriction of the scope of the social intuitionist model to third-personal moral judgment would appear to limit both its interest and its explanatory power. It is surprising that first-personal moral judgments, those concerning what *I* have done or should do, are excluded, although they would ordinarily be considered to be primary instances of moral judgment and are particularly salient to moral decision-making. However, Haidt's more recent elucidation of his view focuses on social doing. Such a focus, we think, allows and requires the kinds of rational processes we describe here.

References

Bayne, T., and E. Pacherie. 2004. "Bottom-Up or Top-Down? Campbell's Rationalist Account of Monothematic Delusions." *Philosophy, Psychiatry and Psychology*, 11, no. 1: 1–12.

Bloom, P. 2014. "The War on Reason." *The Atlantic.* http://www.theatlantic.com/magazine/archive/2014/03/the-war-on-reason/357561/.

Broyd, S. J., C. Demanuele, S. Debener, S. K. Helps, C. J., James, and E. J. Sonuga-Barke. 2009. "Default-Mode Brain Dysfunction in Mental Disorders: A Systematic Review." *Neuroscience and Biobehavioral Reviews* 33, no. 3: 279–296.

Christoff, K., A. M. Gordon, J. Smallwood, R. Smith, and J. W. Schooler. 2009. "Experience Sampling during fMRI Reveals Default Network and Executive System Contributions to Mind Wandering." *Proceedings of the National Academy of Sciences USA* 106, no. 21: 8719–8724.

Clark, A. 2012. "Dreaming the Whole Cat: Generative Models, Predictive Processing, and the Enactivist Conception of Perceptual Experience." *Mind* 121, no. 483: 753–771.

Daniels, N. 1979. "Wide Reflective Equilibrium and Theory Acceptance in Ethics." *Journal of Philosophy* 76, no. 5: 256–282.

Daniels, N. 2011. "Reflective Equilibrium." In *Stanford Encyclopedia of Philosophy*, edited by Edward N. Zalta. Winter 2013 ed.

Fletcher, P., and C. Frith. 2009. "Perceiving Is Believing: A Bayesian Approach to Explaining the Positive Symptoms of Schizophrenia." *Nature Neuroscience* 10, no. 16: 48–58.

Gerrans, P., and J. Kennett. 2010. "Neurosentimentalism and Moral Agency." *Mind* 119, no. 475: 585–614.

Haidt, J. 2012. *The Righteous Mind: Why Good People Are Divided by Politics and Religion.* New York: Pantheon.

Haidt, J., and F. Bjorklund. 2008. "Social Intuitionists Reason, in Conversation." In *Moral Psychology*, vol. 2: *The Cognitive Science of Morality: Intuition and Diversity*, edited by W. Sinnott-Armstrong, 241–254. Cambridge, MA: MIT Press.

Haidt J. 2001. "The Emotional Dog and its Rational Tail: A Social Intuitionist Approach to Moral Judgment." *Psychological Review* 108, no. 4: 814–834.

Jones, K. 2006. "Metaethics and Emotions Research: A Response to Prinz." *Philosophical Explorations* 9, no. 1: 45–54.

Kennett, J. 2011. "Imagining Reasons." *Southern Journal of Philosophy* 49, issue supplement s1: 181–192.

Kennett, J. 2012. "Living with One's Choices: Moral Judgment in Vivo." In *Emotions, Imagination and Moral Reasoning*, edited by C. Mackenzie and R. Langdon, 257–278. New York: Psychology Press.

Korsgaard, C. 2002. "Internalism and the Sources of Normativity." In *Constructions of Practical Reason: Interviews on Moral and Political Philosophy*, edited by H. Pauer-Studer, 49–69. Stanford CA: Stanford University Press.

Mercier, H., and D. Sperber. 2011. "Why Do Humans Reason? Arguments for an Argumentative Theory." *Behavioral and Brain Sciences* 34, no. 2: 57–74.

Pace-Schott, E. 2013. "Dreaming as a Story-Telling Instinct." *Frontiers in Psychology* 4. Front. Psychol., 02 April 2013 | http://dx.doi.org/10.3389/fpsyg.2013.00159.

Paxton, J., L. Ungar, and J. Greene. 2012. "Reflection and Reasoning in Moral Judgment." *Cognitive Science* 36, no. 1: 163–177.

Pettit, P., and J. Smith. 1996. "Freedom in Belief and Desire." *Journal of Philosophy* 93, no. 9: 429–449.

Rawls, J. 1971. *A Theory of Justice*. Cambridge, MA: Harvard University Press.

Whitfield-Gabrieli, S., J. M. Moran, A. Nieto-Castanon, C. Triantafyllou, R. Saxe, and J. D. Gabrieli. 2011. "Associations and Dissociations between Default and Self-Reference Networks in the Human Brain." *NeuroImage* 55, no. 1: 225–232.

3

Emotion versus Cognition in Moral Decision-Making

A DUBIOUS DICHOTOMY

James Woodward

3.1. Introduction

My goal in this chapter is to explore some issues having to do with the contrast between "emotion" and "cognition" and the ways in which these figure in moral judgment and decision-making. I begin by sketching a view that I call the *rationalist dichotomy* (RD) position. This assumes a sharp dividing line between human "cognitive" (rational, conceptual) capacities and capacities labeled as "emotional" or affective and valorizes the former at the expense of the latter. I will then suggest that current understanding of how the brain works and of the functions of neural areas commonly described as "emotional" undermines the RD position and instead suggests an alternative picture, which I will call the *integrative nondichotomy* (IND) view. According to the IND view, emotion and cognition are not sharply distinct, and emotional processing, properly understood, plays (and ought to play, on virtually any plausible normative theory, including utilitarianism) a central role in moral judgment. The implications of the IND view for the interpretation of various experimental results regarding moral decision-making and for "rationalist" projects in moral philosophy more generally will then be explored.

The rationalist dichotomy position. The RD view has been very influential, both historically and in recent theorizing, and both among those adopting naturalistic approaches to moral judgment (e.g., Greene et al. 2004) and among those adopting less naturalistic and more aprioristic treatments (e.g., Parfit 2011). The RD view sometimes takes a "scientific" form but more commonly (among moral philosophers) takes a form that assumes the superiority of reason but is noncommittal about neurobiological and evolutionary details. In its "scientific" form RD is commonly framed in terms of the assumption that our reasoning abilities are "modern" in evolutionary terms (perhaps unique to human beings), highly sophisticated in terms of the information processing they carry out, and flexible in terms of their ability to respond optimally to a wide range of circumstances. By contrast, "emotion" is claimed to be produced by structures that are ancient in evolutionary terms (perhaps the product of the "reptilian" part of the triune brain, as Paul MacLean [1990] notoriously claimed), "primitive" in terms of the information processing they can accomplish, and inflexible and stereotyped in operation, often encoding responses that are genetically fixed and relatively unmodifiable. On this view, emotions are sometimes heuristically useful as "alarm bells" that alert us to events in our environment that impinge on our welfare, as when we have a fear response to a snake. However, precisely because they are primitive, inflexible, and insensitive to many relevant considerations, emotions are likely to lead us astray when we need to make complex or sophisticated decisions. Although, as noted above, the positions of many contemporary moral philosophers differ from the views just described in making no specific claims about the neural structures involved in cognitive or emotional processing, they nonetheless hold to the basic commitments of the RD position—in particular, its positive assessment of the involvement of reasoning in moral decision-making and its negative assessment of the effects of emotion. Strikingly, these RD commitments are shared both by many philosophers sympathetic to utilitarianism (Greene, Singer, Parfit) and by many philosophers favoring alternatives to utilitarianism (Kamm [1993]), many contemporary neo-Kantians, and, on many interpretations, Kant himself. These commitments provide one of the main motivations for the adoption of some variety of moral rationalism, according to which the source of moral requirements is found in "reason," conceived as something distinct from and independent of "emotion."

The neural structures generally described as involved in "emotional" processing include ventromedial prefrontal cortex, orbital frontal cortex (which I will generally classify together as VMPFC/OFC), anterior cingulate cortex (ACC), insula, amygdala, and other structures like the ventral striatum involved in reward processing. If we are to assess RD claims about the generally negative impact of emotion on moral judgment and decision-making, we need to understand what these areas *do* in the brain. What, if anything, do these structures contribute to decision-making, moral and otherwise? To what features of an organism's environment or of the organism itself (e.g., other neural structures) are these structures responsive? If one were to somehow remove their contribution to decision-making, replacing them with contributions commonly described as purely cognitive or "reason based," what would be the likely upshot? Would this lead to normatively better decisions by some plausible standard? Is it even possible for neurotypical subjects to systematically do this?

The integrative nondichotomist position. In contrast to the RD view, I will argue for a very different account of the contribution to judgment and decision-making of the "emotional" structures mentioned above. On the IND account, which I believe is better supported by current brain research, these structures (and especially structures like the OFC/VMPFC) engage in complex, sophisticated information processing and computation. What they compute are *values* or *rewards* associated with distal stimuli and with actions directed to those stimuli. The structures under discussion are highly flexible and capable of sophisticated forms of learning, particularly in social contexts, which are often informationally very complex. Contrary to what is sometimes thought, these structures have *not* been retained in relatively unmodified form from our nonhuman ancestors. Instead, they have continued to change under the distinctive selection pressures to which human beings have been exposed, and as a consequence are importantly different, both anatomically and functionally, from homologous structures in nonhuman primates. They are used in information-processing tasks that in some respects are importantly different from those for which they are used in other animals. The result is that humans have emotional responses that differ in important respects from those of other animals, including other primates.

An illustrative example is provided by the human insula. In nonhuman mammals (e.g., rats), this structure is involved, among other things, in assessment of taste and food intake that is potentially harmful (generating literal "disgust" reactions), as well as the monitoring of interior bodily states. In human beings, this structure is involved in (it has been co-opted or reused for) a wide variety of other tasks, including empathetic identification, decisions regarding charitable donations, affective response to pain in self and in others, reactions to perceived unfairness in economic interactions, and assessments of risk. Needless to say, not all of these activities are engaged in by rats—and when humans engage in these activities, it is not by making use of a rat insula overlaid by more sophisticated "purely cognitive" control structures. The distinctive functions of the human insula are supported by distinct anatomical structures (cf. Allman et al. 2010).

The alternative picture of the role of neural structures involved in "emotional" processing that I will defend has a number of consequences that should be of interest to moral philosophers and philosophers of mind/psychology. First and most fundamentally, it suggests that we should be skeptical of the idea that reason and emotion are sharply distinct and mutually exclusive categories. Second (and relatedly), we should skeptical of attempts to ground morality purely in "reason," conceived as something distinct from "emotion." Third, there is no reason to suppose that *in general* the quality of judgment and decision-making (in either moral or nonmoral domains) would be improved to the extent that emotional processing plays no role in such decisions. This is not to deny, of course, that involvement of particular emotions in some decisions can detract from the goodness of those decisions. For example, decisions made in intense rage are often not good decisions, either morally or prudentially. However, this observation obviously does not imply that judgment and decision-making would be improved if completely uninfluenced by the emotion-processing structures mentioned above. My view is that the general question "Does the involvement of emotion enhance or undermine the quality of decision-making?" rests on (or strongly suggests) a mistaken empirical presupposition—that evaluative judgment and decision-making among neu-rotypical subjects could be typically carried out without the involvement of emotional processing, the only question being whether this would be a good or bad thing. Since, on my view, judgment and decision-making, both in the moral domain and elsewhere, usually involve emotional processing (see below for the qualification intended by "usu-ally"), I believe that the real issue is not *whether* emotion should be involved but rather *how* it should be involved. Thus, insofar as questions about the impact of emotion on decision-making have determinate answers, a better approach is to ask more specific and nuanced questions: for example, for a particular kind of decision, made under such and such conditions, does the involvement of this particular sort of emotion improve or de-tract from judgment?

Before turning to details of my argument, however, several additional clarificatory com-ments are in order. First, the claims that follow are intended as *empirical* and *causal* claims about the operation of certain neural structures and their influence on moral judgment and decision-making, rather than as semantic or conceptual claims about, for example, how emotion enters into the "meaning" of moral judgments (as when it is claimed that moral judgment "essentially involves" the expression of emotion). The sorts of claims I will be defending are claims like (1.1) "Insula activation causally influences judgments about the appropriateness of contributing to charity," rather than claims like (1.2) "When someone says stealing is wrong, what is meant is that the speaker is expressing a strong negative emo-tional response (or a certain pattern of insula activation in response) to stealing."

Second, in what follows, I sometimes claim that certain decisions are normatively superior to others, either prudentially or normatively. Since my intention in this chap-ter is not to defend any particular global normative theory but rather simply to explore how various neural structures influence moral decision-making, some explanation of the bases for these claims about normative superiority is in order. In an attempt to mini-mize reliance on question-begging normative assumptions, I have followed a strategy of appealing to standards that are regarded as uncontroversial by most people and are en-dorsed by many different normative approaches. For example, VMPFC patients system-atically make choices with effects like the following: they result in large financial losses, unemployment, and alienation of friends, family, and coworkers. Identifying such deci-sions as prudentially defective does require normative assumptions, but these assump-tions are not usually taken to be controversial. Similarly, subjects who donate money to charity in experiments described below show greater activation in neural areas identified as involving "emotional" processing, in comparison with nondonors. Common-sense moral judgment, as well as most moral theories, whether utilitarian or deontological, regards donations to charity as sometimes morally praiseworthy or at least not morally inferior to decisions not to donate. I assume such standards in what follows rather than arguing for them.[1]

I should also emphasize that these assessments of decisions as normatively superior or inferior involves appeal to standards that are *independent* of any valuation of the neural processes leading to these decisions. In other words, I do not assume that decisions involving some particular level of cognitive or emotional processing are, for that reason alone, inferior or superior to other decisions. In my view, normatively inferior decisions can result both from processes in which so-called cognitive factors dominate and from those in which so-called emotional factors dominate, although it is also true (and consistent with this) that damage to areas like the VMPFC/OFC tends to lead to consistently inferior prudential decisions.

3.2. The Basic Picture

I first sketch the basic picture I will defend and then turn to details. I see the structures mentioned above as involved in emotional processing (VMPFC/OFC and so on) as all having the function of processing information about positive and negative reinforcers, or, as they are also described in the neurobiological literature, "rewards" and "punishers."[2] The current understanding is that these structures *compute* (literally—see below) *values* (for the organism) associated with reinforcers and actions undertaken to provide reinforcers. *Primary reinforcers* are reinforcers that are such that a person does not have to learn that they are rewarding, because, for example, this is specified genetically. Thus sweet-tasting stimuli are for most people automatically experienced as rewarding. Primary reinforcers include stimuli producing specific sensory states but also very likely include stimuli associated with more general and abstract rewards. For example, many human beings experience certain kinds of cooperative or mutually beneficial social interactions as intrinsically rewarding and social isolation or rejection as punishing. In many cases, this is probably something that does not need to be learned. This preference for prosocial interactions emerges very early in human development, prior to the acquisition of language and sophisticated reasoning abilities, and seems to be one of many features distinguishing us from other primates, such as chimpanzees, who do not seem to have the sorts of affective processing that lead them to value cooperative interactions in the way that humans often do.[3] The view taken here is thus that the value humans attach to cooperation and prosocial interactions is not just a matter of our being smarter or more rational than chimpanzees or better calculators of long-term self-interest, but also reflects a difference in the emotions we experience and what we care about.

Organisms like ourselves who are able to act flexibly require a great deal more than just a genetic specification of primary reinforcers. In particular, organisms capable of behavioral flexibility must be able to *learn* about *secondary reinforcers*—stimuli or objects that are predictive of the arrival of primary reinforcers, but often only imperfectly or probabilistically. For example, assuming that sweetness signals the presence of a substance that is biologically valuable, an organism must learn that certain foodstuffs will taste sweet and that others are foul-tasting. This involves a process by which the reward value that attaches to the primary reinforcer also comes to be associated with stimuli that are predictive of it, so that reward circuitry also becomes activated when, say, ripe blueberries are present because these are predictive of sweetness. In fact, the *same* reward circuitry and processing that are activated by primary reinforcers are also activated by secondary reinforcers or the expectation that they will occur. In human beings, reward learning and processing are sufficiently flexible that all sorts of stimuli may acquire the status of secondary reinforcers through learning. For example, monetary reward, although of no intrinsic biological significance, activates the same reward-processing circuitry that is involved in responding to more "biological" stimuli like pleasing tastes. A similar point holds for many socially and morally relevant stimuli. Thus choices to give to charity, as well as decisions to behave cooperatively in prisoner's dilemmas, activate the same neural circuitry as is active when subjects experience rewards connected to sensory gratification. One important consequence is that there appears to be nothing in the brain corresponding to a "moral module" and no neural structures specifically devoted only to moral judgment or the processing of moral values.

As mentioned above, in many ecologically realistic circumstances secondary reinforcers are associated only probabilistically with the arrival of primary reinforcers. This is particularly true of the social environment, in which, for example, we may have (at best) probabilistic information about how others are likely to behave toward us. For this reason, the structures involved in reward processing might be expected to be—and in fact are—highly sensitive to probabilistic information relevant to the arrival of reinforcers. In particular, there is evidence that structures like the insula and VMPFC/OFC integrate information about reward value with relevant probabilistic information—indeed, these structures seem to compute features such as the expected value of reward or reward variance (Quartz 2009). Structures like the VMPFC/OFC are also involved in rapidly adjusting estimates of expected reward value as the probability distributions governing rewards change, as in reversal learning, when previously rewarding outcomes become punishing and vice versa. Again, this role is particularly important in social contexts—for example, when your previous friend suddenly becomes your enemy or vice versa. In addition, some neural structures involved in emotional processing and valuation such as the amygdala are sensitive to (among many other things) the presence of *uncertainty*, as opposed to *risk*. In situations involving risk, one does not know the outcomes of one's choices with certainty but does know the probability distribution governing those outcomes. By contrast, in situations involving uncertainty one does not know the probability distribution governing the outcomes resulting from one's actions, as would be the case if one were required to bet on a coin toss without knowing anything about the bias of the coin. Human beings (and presumably other animals as well) treat risk very differently from uncertainty, as evidenced by such phenomena as the Ellsberg paradox. In particular, they tend to be very averse to uncertainty—averse in the sense that they try to avoid choices involving uncertainty if possible and, when these are unavoidable, often choose very conservatively in such cases, employing worst-case or maximin, rather than expected utility, reasoning.

These features of human emotional response involving risk and uncertainty figure importantly in moral and political theorizing: compare Rawls's characterization of his original position, which conceives of the parties as choosing under conditions of uncertainty, with Harsanyi's characterization, which treats this situation as involving only risk. Because the Rawlsian parties choose under conditions of uncertainty, it seems (given our aversion to uncertainty) intuitive or psychologically natural to suppose, as Rawls claims, that they will employ conservative, maximin reasoning. By contrast, because, as Harsanyi conceives of matters, his parties face a situation of risk, his claim that they will employ expected utility reasoning in that situation and thus be led to some form of utilitarianism also seems plausible. In effect, Rawls's treatment trades on the difference between the neural processing underlying risk and uncertainty and the way that the latter affects evaluation—this is one of many cases in which features of human neural processing involving "emotion" affect which moral principles we find appealing or intuitive. The sensitivity of many of the structures involved in emotional processing to complex and changing probability information is one reason why it is appropriate to think of these as involved in sophisticated and flexible information processing, rather than myopic, stereotyped responses.

One important way in which the values associated with secondary reinforcers are learned involves *reinforcement learning*. Put abstractly, a system involved in such learning produces signals—call them P—that predict the arrival of some rewarding stimulus S′ (sweet taste) on the basis of some other stimulus S (the sight of ripe berries). The system detects whether S′ in fact arrives (and is rewarding) and then compares this with what was predicted by P. The discrepancy between these two (between actual and predicted reward) yields a reward prediction error. This error is combined with the original prediction P to yield a new updated prediction P′ of the reward value expected on the basis of S, which is then again compared with the actual reward. The process is iterated until the prediction error approaches zero. As I note below, reward prediction error signals of this sort (with the right normative characteristics) have been found in a number of the structures involved in emotional processing, including the insula, amygdala, and VMPFC/OFC, which is one reason why it seems appropriate to think of these structures as involved in learning.

As noted above, many commentators (particularly those influenced by RD views) think of emotions as associated with relatively fixed and stereotyped responses to environmental conditions that are unaffected by learning and experience. It should be obvious from my discussion above that this is a misconception: one of the advantages of having "emotional" structures that compute and represent values is that this greatly enhances behavioral flexibility and normatively appropriate modification of behavior as a result of learning. Having the capacity to compute value assessments that reflect input from a variety of sources and to then use this information to guide judgment and action allows organisms to move beyond fixed input/output patterns of response (cf. Rolls 2005).

All of this has been very abstract, and the reader may well wonder what it has to do with moral judgment and decision-making. More detailed examples will be discussed below, but to illustrate what I take the connection to be, consider the following generic example, which is a composite loosely based on a study of reports of autobiographical memories from ordinary subjects assembled by Jessica Escobedo at Caltech.[4] These include reports by subjects of things that they had done that they regarded as wrong or discreditable in their lives. The reports fell into a number of different categories, but one not uncommon set conformed to the following pattern: The subject S, often an adolescent, chose some course of action A, either not thinking at all about its impact on a second person or being willing to discount this impact because S anticipated other benefits from doing A or because S underestimated its cost for the second person. For example, in one report, the subject, call her Sally, avoided going to the fair with her best friend so that she could go with another group of girls who were more popular. Sally then became aware that her best friend felt hurt and distressed as a consequence of this action, and this in turn led Sally to feel distressed, guilty, and ashamed—that is, to have aversive feelings about having done A that outweighed whatever benefits she obtained from A. Sally reported that these feelings were far worse than she expected. She described herself as having been "taught a lesson" by this experience and resolved not to do anything similar in the future.

This is an example of one-shot learning, rather than the more gradual learning that might take place in the presence of a probabilistic relationship and a less strongly aversive reinforcer, but in other respects it seems to conform to the pattern described above. Initially, Sally predicts certain benefits and certain costs from choosing A, but she is wrong about them: the actual consequences of A are more aversive and less rewarding than predicted, and this leads her to avoid A-like actions in the future. In at least this sense, Sally made a mistake or fell into an error in her choice of A—an error about how rewarding or punishing A would be to her—and she learned in the sense that she altered her valuation of A-like actions so that this valuation better reflected the rewarding and punishing features of the action for her. Put slightly differently, Sally learned in the sense that she acquired new and more accurate information about the reward value (for her) of A. It is these notions of "information," "learning," "mistake," "error," and so on that I have in mind when I describe structures like the VMPFC/OFC as engaged in learning about reward value and involved in error correction.

More systematic studies of moral learning show that episodes of the sort just described are common (although they are certainly not the only form of moral learning—see below). In his research on young children, Martin Hoffman (2001) describes a process, which he calls "induction," which works in roughly the following way: A child engages in what an adult would regard as a moral transgression (Mary hits Harry, causing him to cry). The adult then draws Mary's attention to Harry's reaction and says something like, "How would you like it if Harry did that to you?," thus (in many cases) creating or strengthening ("inducing") an empathetic response in Mary and an averse reaction to what she has done. Hoffman claims, as an empirical matter, that induction is much more effective than other measures (such as punishing Mary without further explanation) in altering behavior and in getting children to voluntarily conform to moral requirements. James Blair (Blair et al. 2005) in his studies of psychopaths claims that normal human adults and children possess what he calls a "violence inhibition mechanism" that, at least in many circumstances, produces an aversive response when they cause harm to others; this leads them to learn to avoid harm-causing activities. This mechanism is impaired in psychopaths, with the result that they do not learn to avoid behavior that harms others.

I recognize that many philosophers will wish to resist the suggestion that Sally (or the children described by Hoffman) have undergone "moral learning" or the like. They may wish to claim, for example, that Sally has learned only that (2.1) actions of kind A are aversive or punishing for her; and this is very different from learning that (2.2) A was morally wrong. I fully agree that (2.1) is different from (2.2), and nothing in my discussion, either here or subsequently, is meant to imply otherwise. As I see the example, Sally learns (2.2), and part of the causal explanation for why she learns (2.2) is the occurrence of (2.1) and the processing underlying it. The claim that the process described above causally influences Sally's judgment that she behaved wrongly does not require that we commit ourselves to the idea that her moral judgment involves "nothing but" her having an emotionally aversive reaction when she learns of the impact of her behavior on her friend. Fortunately for our purposes, as we shall see below, these causal claims by themselves suggest important consequences for moral psychology and moral theory— we don't need to supplement them with unnecessary "nothing but" claims.

The moral learning present in Sally's case represents just one possibility, although a particularly important one. Human beings engage in many other forms of moral learning—they can learn not just from experiencing the consequences of their own actions, as Sally does, but also from moral instruction (often in the form of stories and illustrations) in which they learn to have adverse or favorable reactions to various sort of behavior without actually engaging in that behavior. But these cases too seem to involve the same sorts of emotional-processing and reward structures.

3.3. The Role of the Orbital Frontal and Ventromedial Prefrontal Cortex

As noted above, many different neural structures are involved in emotional processing and the computation of reward value. Among such structures, the OFC/VMPFC plays a particularly important role. Following many others (e.g., Rolls 2005), I take the OFC/VMPFC to contain a final, common, integrated value signal that is computed via some variant of the reward-learning process described above from inputs provided by other neural structures, where these depend on the nature of the decision problem faced. Some of these inputs come from structures like the amygdala and insula that are often described as involved in "emotional" processing, including processing of information having to do with the emotional states of others (so-called hot theory of mind). Other inputs come from structures like the right temporo-parietal junction (RTPJ) and posterior superior temporal cortex (pSTC), often regarded as involved in more "cognitive" or "cooler" theory of mind tasks such as the ascription of beliefs and intentions to others. For example, in a charitable-giving task described below, willingness to give is correlated with activity in the OFC/VMPFC, and this signal is in turn modulated by input from other areas, including both the pSTC and the insula. The former is thought to be involved in processing information about the desires and intentions of recipients, and the latter is involved in empathetic identification. In addition, input that modulates value signals in the OFC/VMPFC can also come from what are often taken to be paradigmatic "cognitive control" structures like the dorsolateral prefrontal cortex (DLPFC) (structures taken by Greene and others to be fundamentally different from "emotional" structures). Although there is some uncertainty about whether there is an independent "value signal" originating in DLPFC (or whether instead DLPFC merely modulates signals in the VMPFC/OFC), the weight of opinion at present seems to be that *all* rewarding and punishing stimuli, as well as their combined or integrated significance, are eventually represented in some way in the OFC/VMPFC. It is thus assumed that these structures have the function of combining reward signals concerning quite different stimuli into a "common currency" that guides comparison and choice among different alternatives, as when an animal must choose between continuing to exploit a food source and a mating opportunity. Such a common currency is thought to be required if decision-makers are to choose in a minimally consistent way, avoiding, for example, intransitive preferences. (Damage to the VMPFC/OFC produces, among many other pathologies, violations of transitivity [Schoenbaum et al. 2011].) Moreover, as one would expect from the characteristics needed if such a signal is to guide all-things-considered judgment and decision in situations in which probabilities attach to outcomes, it does not merely represent that some stimulus or outcome is valued more or less than another but instead represents something more like reward magnitude—in other words, the signal has a "cardinal-like," rather than merely ordinal, character, which makes possible the representation of quantities like expected reward.

As is well known from cases like that of Phineas Gage or EVR (Anderson et al. 1999), OFC/VMPFC patients suffer from many pathologies in choice and decision-making, apparent both in laboratory contexts and in real life. The best characterization of these incapacities are a matter of ongoing disagreement, but they include choices that are highly imprudent, failure to learn from mistakes, problems in emotional regulation, and failure to conform to ordinary norms of social behavior. A recent review (Schoenbaum et al. 2011) takes the fundamental impairment to be a failure to learn about the valuations of expected outcomes,[5] which is very much in line with the account I have advocated, but in any event such patients are profoundly disabled and require institutionalization.

Several other features of the OFC/VMPFC are worth emphasizing. First, not only are there extensive projections forward from structures like the amygdala and insula to the

OFC/VMPFC, there are also backward projections from the OFC/VMPFC to these structures. These allow the OFC/VMPFC to influence and modulate these structures, rather than just serving as receivers to which they broadcast. Acquisition/learning of normatively appropriate responses in structures like the amygdala is thought to depend on appropriate modulatory input from structures like the OFC/VMPFC—for example, according to one prominent theory (Blair et al. 2005), psychopathy is associated with deficiencies in VMPFC/amygdala connections, leading to failure to develop aversive responses to harm inflicted on others. In general, during the process of normal maturation, from childhood to adulthood, functional connectivity between the VMPFC/OFC and other structures like the amygdala and insula increases (Decety et al. 2011).

Given the evidence just reported about the role of a common set of structures involved in the representation of the values of stimuli as food and money, a very natural expectation is that these same structures should also be involved in moral evaluation and the representation of moral value. This is exactly what is reported in a number of recent papers. In an fMRI experiment investigating brain regions involved in charitable giving (Hare et al. 2010), subjects were given an amount of money that they could donate to charities. Subjects were imaged in both a forced-giving task, in which they were required to make donations, and a "free choice" task, in which they made their own decisions about donations. In the latter task, but not the former, a value signal was present in the VMPFC/OFC that correlated with amount donated, suggesting that this signal computed the value to the subject of making a donation. This signal in the VMPFC/OFC was found in turn to be modulated by areas known to be involved in social cognition, in this case anterior insula and posterior superior temporal cortex. The pSTC is thought to be involved in shifting attention to another's perspective and to contain an updating signal in contexts in which the optimal choice involves detecting the intentions of others (Behrens et al. 2008; Hampton et al. 2008). Both regions have been found in other studies to be active in tasks involving altruistic giving. The general picture is thus again one in which a value signal computed in the "emotional area" OFC reflects input from other areas, and in a way that seems normatively appropriate, both in the sense that charitable giving itself is sometimes normatively appropriate and in the sense that it seems normatively appropriate that areas involved in empathy and social cognition and perspective taking should influence decisions about charitable donations. This is because appropriate charitable giving requires awareness of which choices will benefit others, and these areas process such information.

Given these empirical results, should we think of the VMPFC/OFC (or for that matter, the insula and amygdala) as "cognitive" or as "emotional" areas? In some important respects, much of the activity in these areas seems to be cognition-like or representational, or at least to be involved in "information processing." First, these areas are involved in calculation, computation, and learning, and these are activities that are often thought of as "cognitive." In addition, signals in the VMPFC/OFC, as well as in structures like the insula, are representational in the sense of representing quantities like expected reward and reward variance. Moreover, valuations associated with this area are attached to representations of objects and situations computed in occipital and temporal areas that are relatively cognitively complex and in some cases rather abstract—for example, to a subject's representation of "snake" (evaluated as dangerous) or "offer received in an ultimatum game" (evaluated as unfair and exploitive). Notions of error and misrepresentation also often seem applicable to activities in these areas, sometimes in very straightforward ways. For example, areas like the insula can misrepresent experiences or evaluations of other subjects affected by one's actions, in the sense of failing to accurately represent pain experienced by others. More generally, these areas can also misrepresent in the sense of failing to accurately represent the bearing or significance of various environmental stimuli for the subject or whether they should be regarded as sources of concern. For example, a harmless snake may be evaluated as dangerous and, in the vignette described above Sally initially misrepresented the valuation that she would come to attach to her experience of her friend's hurt feelings. Finally, as emphasized above, structures like the VMPFC/OFC combine inputs from many different sources, including those usually regarded as cognitive, such as the pSTC, which also may make it seem appropriate to think of the VMPFC/OFC as "cognitive."

On the other hand, if one associates "reasoning" or "cognition" with deliberate effortful inference involving the conscious manipulation of proposition-like mental structures of the sort carried out in logic and mathematics, including the use of complex combinations of these structures, then because the information processing carried out in structures like the VMPFC typically does not involve this sort of conscious inference, labels like "cognition" and "reasoning" seem misleading. In addition, the processing in the VMPFC appears to be dedicated and specialized in the sense that it is quantities like expected reward and so on that are computed—there is no suggestion that this machinery might be used for other sorts of abstract reasoning. This assessment is reinforced when one considers that there is independent evidence that logical and mathematical reasoning is generally carried out in areas like the dorsolateral prefrontal cortex that are distinct from the areas standardly associated with emotional processing. Characterization of areas like the VMPFC as involving "reasoning" will also be misleading if one also associates reasoning with the absence of affect or if one thinks of one of the roles of reasoning as the suppression of emotion or its replacement with other sorts of "purely rational" motivations.

These considerations suggest that invoking a dichotomy between cognition and emotion (= noncognitive) and then arguing about on which side of this dichotomy the activity of structures like the VMPFC/OFC should be placed is probably not a fruitful way of proceeding. If by "emotional" we mean structures that are affective, involved in evaluation (appraisal of what ought to be the case) and in motivation, then structures like the VMPFC/OFC are indeed involved in "emotional" processing, but this does not mean that they are nonrepresentational, impervious to influence from learning or by cognitive structures, or passive in the sense of not involved in modulation and control of other neural structures. Processing in such structures seems to involve an intermixture of elements we associate with information processing and affect.

Whether or not this skepticism about the emotion/cognition dichotomy is correct, it definitely seems wrong to think of the role of the insula in the charitable donation experiment as merely a "distractor" or alarm bell that, unless suitably controlled, would undermine the superior decisions that would otherwise be made by purely "cognitive" processing. Judged by both deontological and utilitarian standards, the normatively superior decisions in this experiment will at least sometimes involve donating to charity rather than keeping all of the money for oneself. Moreover, willingness to do this, as we have seen, is correlated with and apparently causally influenced by the level of insula activation. Thus, assuming the above standard for what is normatively appropriate in charitable giving, subjects whose choices are *not* influenced by their "emotional" insulas make normatively inferior decisions, in comparison with those who are so influenced.[6]

3.4. Greene on Deontological versus Utilitarian Decision-Making

With this as background, I want now to turn to some very interesting and influential papers by Joshua Greene on the neural structures involved in moral judgment.[7] In Greene et al. 2004, subjects were presented with a series of moral dilemmas designed to elicit choices that were either more "utilitarian" or more "deontological." Greene et al. found greater activation in the VMPFC among deontological (as opposed to utilitarian) decision-makers and more activation in DLPFC among utilitarian as opposed to deontological decision-makers. On the basis of their identification of the VMPFC as an "emotional" area and the DLPFC as "cognitive," Greene et al. concluded that deontological decisions were differentially associated with emotional processing and utilitarian decisions with more cognitive processing. In a similar vein, reports from several sources (e.g., Koenings et al. 2007) that patients with lesions to the VMPFC make more utilitarian decisions were taken to show that utilitarian decisions rely less or not at all on emotional processing, again on the basis of the claim that the VMPFC is an emotional area. Following the RD position outlined in section 3.1, Greene et al. also hold that greater involvement of "cognitive" processing generally leads to normatively superior decisions. They thus conclude that these results about neural processing provide support for the superiority of utilitarianism as a normative doctrine, a claim that has also been endorsed by Singer (2005).

A more recent paper by Shenhav and Greene (2010) complicates these claims in an interesting way. These authors presented subjects with hypothetical choices involving rescuing groups of people of different sizes with different probabilities of success. They found what they describe as

a BOLD [blood oxygen level dependent] signal in VMPFC/MOFC correlated with the "expected moral value" of decision options—the interaction between the value of various outcomes and probability. This is consistent with the hypothesis that this region supports the integration of positive and negative reward signals into a more abstract representation of value, a kind of decision "currency." (671)

They add, "Our results suggest that an individual's sensitivity to lives saved/lost in the context of moral judgment is in part determined by the same mechanisms that determine the individual's sensitivity to the probability of losses and to overall reward in the context of economic decision-making" (673). Thus, their results fit very nicely with the ideas described in earlier sections of this chapter, according to which the OFC/VMPFC contains an overall, integrated signal that represents moral values, as well as other kinds of value, and which takes account of information about probabilities.

As so far described, the results from this paper say nothing about distinctively utilitarian moral decision-making. In fact, Shenhav and Greene found a value signal in OFC/VMPFC among decision-makers who have what they consider to be a utilitarian orientation, but they also found such a signal among more deontological decision-makers. This is exactly what one should expect if, as argued above, the OFC/VMPFC is involved in the representation of value for *all* those who make judgments or decisions, whether utilitarian or deontological. Of course, this value representation will differ in detail in utilitarian and nonutilitarian decision-makers, since these subjects do, after all, make different decisions, with this difference presumably reflecting differences in input from other neural structures, but both the results from Shenhav and Greene and those described in earlier sections suggest that this will not be a matter of the deontologically inclined making use of an entirely different system or mechanism of value representation and computation than those who make utilitarian judgments. This has an important consequence: if the VMPFC/OFC has a role in *all* decision-making, then it appears that one can't argue for the moral superiority of utilitarianism over deontology merely on the grounds that the "emotional" VMPFC/OFC is involved only in the latter.

Is there nonetheless some basis for retaining the idea that utilitarian decision-making has a distinctive neural signature? As I understand them, Shenhav and Greene remain committed to the idea that utilitarian decision-making disproportionately involves "cognitive" processing, although they now identify the OFC as involved in such processing (whereas previously Greene regarded it as an "emotional" area). They write:

We found that increased activity in bilateral lateral OFC . . . was associated with more frequent endorsement of utilitarian trade-offs. According to Greene et al.'s dual-process theory of moral judgment . . ., utilitarian judgments are driven primarily by controlled cognitive processes, which may compete with countervailing emotional responses. These results are broadly consistent with this dual-process theory, given the implication of lateral OFC in reducing the influence of emotional distracters on judgments (regulating pain and negative emotions, [favoring delayed rewards over more immediate ones], inhibiting socially inappropriate behaviors), and more generally controlling the influence of emotional responses that interfere with the pursuit of more distal goals. (673)

Noting that Greene had previously suggested that utilitarian judgment was associated with increased activity in the DLPFC (a "cognitive" area) rather than the OFC, Shenhav and Greene go on to suggest that the DLPFC may be associated with effortful cognitive control of emotions, while the OFC may be involved in more "implicit modulation of affective representations," adding that this is "consistent with the aforementioned literature implicating the lateral OFC in performing a gating or weighing function as opposed to the overriding of a prepotent response" (674).

Let me make what I hope are some constructive suggestions about this, which may or may not accord with Greene's current views. First, the change in classification of the OFC (or OFC/VMPFC) from "emotional" to "cognitive" seems to me to support the misgivings expressed earlier about the clarity and usefulness of this distinction. Second, phrases like "inhibition," "reducing the influence of emotional distractors," and "modulation" suggest a range of different pictures concerning the relation between the VMPFC/OFC and the input that it regulates. It is important to be clear about which of these pictures is most appropriate. It seems fairly clear both from Shenhav and Greene's paper and from the other results reported in section 3.3 that it is misguided to think of the role of the VMPFC/OFC as one of entirely removing or suppressing the influence of "emotional" or affective factors on decision-making, allowing only purely cognitive or rational factors to be operative. Assuming one thinks of structures like the amygdala and insula as engaged in emotional processing, then a picture according to which information from these sources is integrated or synthesized with information from other sources by the VMPFC/OFC when judgment and decision-making are functioning in normatively appropriate ways seems more correct than a model in which emotional influences are excised from decision-making, either by the VMPFC/OFC or by other structures. This is not at all to deny that judgment and decision in which the VMPFC/OFC exercises top-down control or regulation are often normatively superior to judgments and decisions in which these structures are not playing this role—if nothing else, this is suggested by the poor quality of decision-making in subjects in which these structures are damaged. But it does suggest that this normative superiority, when present, is not just a matter of "cognition" inhibiting "emotion." Rather than thinking of the activity of the VMPFC/OFC as "cognitive" simply on the grounds that it involves regulation of emotion, it seems to me more natural (echoing the arguments of section 3.3) to think of these structures as neither exclusively cognitive nor exclusively emotional, but rather as combining elements of both.

I can expand on this point and also on the role of effortful "cognitive control" involving structures like the DLPFC in decision-making by comparing Shenhav and Greene's experiment to two very interesting papers by Hare et al. (2009, 2011) on dietary choice. In the experiments reported by Hare et al. (2009), self-described dieters were scanned while asked to rate foodstuffs for health and tastiness separately. For each subject, a reference item was selected that was neutral for both taste and health, and subjects were then presented with choices between various food items and these neutral items. Subjects who were self-controllers (that is, subjects who chose healthy items) were found to make their decisions on the basis of both health and taste and exhibited activity in the VMPFC that reflected the integrated influence of both health and taste considerations, as expressed in the earlier ratings. By contrast, signals in the VMPFC of non-self-controllers reflected the influence only of taste evaluations. The crucial difference was that in the self-control group, VMPFC activity was modulated by the DLPFC, generally thought of as a more cognitive area, which is consistent with a large body of independent evidence implicating the DLPFC in "cognitive control." At least in these experiments, however, there was no evidence for a "value signal" within the DLPFC; instead the DLPFC influenced or modulated evaluation of food items, by influencing the value signal within the VMPFC.

The second paper confirmed and extended this picture, showing that when individuals made healthy choices and exercised self-control, the value signal in the VMPFC was modulated by the DLPFC in such a way that greater value was attached to healthier foods in comparison with tasty foods.

Suppose, for the sake of argument, that, as Greene claims, increased activity in areas associated with "effortful" cognitive or executive control like the DLPFC (in addition to "gating" activity on the part of the VMPFC/OFC) is characteristic of utilitarian decision-makers. Focusing for the moment just on the role of the DLPFC, if what goes on among such "utilitarian" subjects is like what goes on among subjects who exercise dietary self-control, perhaps what one should expect is the following: in both deontological and utilitarian subjects, a value signal associated with choice and judgment will be present in the VMPFC/OFC, which is just what Shenhav and Greene found. However, (continuing this line of thought) for utilitarian (as opposed to deontological) subjects, there will be more activity in the DLPFC and perhaps other cognitive areas that will operate so as to modulate this value signal. Put differently, if one wants to continue to think of the VMPFC/OFC as an "emotional" area, then the difference between deontological and utilitarian subjects will not be, as some of the language in Greene's earlier papers perhaps suggested, that the former rely solely on input from emotional areas and the latter solely on input from cognitive areas, but rather that both rely on valuation signals in the VMPFC in judgment and decision-making, but, in the case of utilitarian decision-makers, in contrast to deontological decision-makers, this emotional input will in addition be more influenced by processing in areas associated with cognition and executive control. I will add that if, as I have already suggested, the "emotional" and "cognitive" labels are not terribly helpful in this context, it might be even better to put matters in terms of a contrast between valuation that includes but is not limited to areas associated with executive control and working memory versus valuation not involving those areas, or involving them to a lesser degree (but perhaps involving other areas to a greater degree—see below). Going further, one might also suggest, in contrast to a standard "dual process" picture in which there are two "systems," asymmetrically related, in which one has the role of inhibiting or correcting mistakes made by the other, it may be more appropriate to think in terms of ongoing reciprocal interaction and feedback, involving a number of "systems" rather than just two. Consistently with all this, one might still retain the idea that greater involvement of systems associated with cognitive control, like the DLPFC and whatever else one might want to include in this category, typically leads to normatively superior decisions and that in virtue of such involvement, these decisions tend to be "utilitarian," thus yielding an argument for utilitarianism as a normative theory along broadly the same lines that Greene has endorsed before.

I put this forward as a way of framing or reframing Greene's views—as a friendly amendment (or perhaps a description of what he now thinks). I want now, however, to raise some questions about the resulting picture: First, note that given the overall argument above, it is not clear why one should expect to see areas involved in cognitive control *only* when there is "utilitarian" choice. An alternative, and in many ways more natural, assumption is that higher levels of "cognitive control" are required whenever a subject successfully suppresses and acts against a strong initial adverse reaction to some course of action, whether this action is recommended by utilitarianism of not.[8] As an extreme (but real) case, consider those fanatical Nazis who described themselves as feeling empathy for their victims and revulsion at killing them but who self-consciously set out to suppress these feelings in favor of what they took to be their duty to conform to Nazi doctrine, acting out of what some commentators have described as a sort of perverted or distorted Kantianism that prescribed duty's for sake. One might conjecture that these Nazis had rather high levels of activity in the DLPFC and other cognitive control areas as they struggled against their feelings of humanity, but their choices were not "utilitarian" either in the sense that they conformed to what utilitarianism understood as a normative doctrine requires or in the sense that they were attempting to decide on the basis of utilitarian considerations.

A less extreme case, conceivably subject to experimental investigation, might involve someone who is committed to conforming to some requirement regulating diet or religious observance and is tempted, for either self-interested or nonreligious other-regarding reasons, not to follow this requirement (e.g., perhaps helping someone in need would involve violating this requirement). If Rangel's diet experiment is any guide, successful resistance to the temptation to violate the requirement would involve activity in the DLPFC and other areas associated with cognitive control, including perhaps the VMPFC/OFC, even though successful resistance may not (and often will not) be recommended by utilitarianism, or based on explicit utilitarian calculation, or, from the point of view of many of us, normatively appealing.

One possible response concedes the possibility just described but contends it is not the ecologically most common or usual situation. That is, it might be suggested that most often, although admittedly not always, when people exert strong executive/cognitive control, they are reasoning in a utilitarian way, and, conversely, when people engage in utilitarian reasoning, they tend to make use of areas involved in such control. Because such involvement tends to improve the normative quality of decision-making, decisions based on utilitarian reasoning may be expected to be normatively superior.

This leads to another set of issues. As is perhaps obvious, I have been using "utilitarian decision-making" in a way that is ambiguous: it might mean (4.1) "decision coinciding with the recommendations of correctly applied utilitarian principles," or it might mean (4.2) "decision made via deliberate explicit utilitarian calculation that attempts to take account of all benefits and costs." The argument associating involvement of the VMPFC/OFC and the DLPFC with "utilitarian decisions" seems most naturally understood as an argument that associates these areas with effortful, explicit utilitarian deliberation about costs and benefits—with decisions that are utilitarian in sense (4.2) above. It is an old idea that if one wishes to produce outcomes that are best in the sense of conforming to what is recommended by utilitarian moral theory (decisions that are utilitarian in sense 4.1 above), the best strategy in many cases may not be to try to engage in explicit utilitarian calculation (sense 4.2). It may be that Greene is assuming the opposite—that judgments involving explicit utilitarian calculation are likely to produce superior outcomes by utilitarian standards. Perhaps this is right, but it is not obviously right, even if one is a utilitarian.

There is another point to be made about the notion of "utilitarian judgment" in sense (4.1) above: The judgments described as utilitarian in the empirical literature on moral decision-making reflect a very particular (and arguably controversial) conception of what utilitarianism requires. Roughly speaking, this conception involves a commitment to what I have elsewhere called "parametric" as opposed to "strategic" utilitarianism (Woodward and Allman 2007). The difference between these two conceptions may be illustrated by Williams's example in which Jim, an explorer in the jungle, is told by Pedro that he will shoot ten villagers unless Jim shoots one (in my version of the story I stipulate that this one is distinct from the ten). One sort of utilitarian analysis (the parametric sort) takes this to a very simple decision problem. There are two possibilities: (1) One person will die if Jim shoots, (2) ten if he does not. The consequences under (1) are better than the consequences under (2); therefore utilitarianism recommends Jim should shoot. With this understanding of utilitarianism, a subject who judges that Jim should not shoot is regarded as making a "deontological" judgment.

I described this utilitarian analysis as "parametric" because it takes the decision problem faced by Jim to have a very simple transparent structure characterized by a few fixed and stable parameters that, moreover, Jim knows for certain: it is assumed, for example, that Jim can take Pedro at his word, so that the relevant probabilities are all either zero or one, and that the only relevant considerations are the number of lives saved under each course of action. In effect, the parametric utilitarian treats the dilemma Jim faces as a simple arithmetic problem. A more "strategic" utilitarian analysis would take into account considerations such as the following: What is the probability that Pedro will act as he claims, rather than, say, killing the ten after Jim kills the one? Is there even a well-defined, knowable probability here, or is the situation faced by Jim characterized by extreme uncertainty, in the sense described in section 3.2, with the result that there is no basis for any expected utility calculation of the sort utilitarians advocate performing? What protections do the villagers have against Pedro after Jim kills the one and leaves, with Pedro remaining? More generally, what are Pedro's plans and intentions in making this offer? Does he see some advantage in involving Jim in the killing? Does he intend some form of blackmail? A discrediting of Jim so that he will not be a credible witness? Would Jim be more effective in saving lives if he were to refuse to participate in the killing and go on to publicize Pedro's behavior to the outside world? What other indirect effects might follow from Jim's participation (or not) in the killing?

When these additional considerations are taken into account, it is no longer so obvious that the action recommended by "utilitarianism" is for Jim to the kill the one, rather than refusing, as at least some versions of deontology would require. In any case, I take it that it is the choice conforming to the recommendations of the strategic rather than the parametric analysis that is required by utilitarianism, since a consistent utilitarian must take into account all available information about the expected effects of his choices, as a properly performed strategic analysis will do.

Similar points can be made about many of the other standard "utilitarianism versus deontology" dilemmas in the philosophical literature—pushing the big guy in front of the trolley, using the organs of one patient to save the lives of five others, and so on. In some of these cases, a strategic form of utilitarianism might recommend the same course of action as standard versions of "deontology."

Several consequences follow from this observation. First, it is not obvious that judgments regarding such dilemmas are measures of whether subjects are "utilitarian" as opposed to "deontological," rather than measures of whether subjects are parametric as opposed to strategic utilitarians. Second, consider the information that strategic as opposed to parametric utilitarians consider. This includes (4.3) theory-of-mind information about the intentions, beliefs, desires and plans of the various actors in a situation, (4.4) related to these, dynamic or strategic considerations about how the situation may evolve over time (how Pedro will respond to Jim's choice, what choices will be available to Jim in the light of that response), and (4.5) information about probabilities and the presence of uncertainty. As noted above, so-called emotional areas are heavily involved in processing all of these kinds of information. Since, as argued above, utilitarians *ought* to take such information into account, this provides further reasons for thinking that, given a commitment to utilitarianism, the involvement of such areas in moral judgment and decision-making can sometimes lead to normatively superior results. It also provides additional reasons to be skeptical of the claim that it is a mark of utilitarian decision-making per se that it does not involve such areas or involves them only minimally.[9]

3.5. Moral Rationalism

There is more that might be said about this line of thought, but rather than succumbing to the temptation for further exploration, I want to step back and use some of the experimental results I have been describing to raise some more general questions about the role of "reason" and "emotion" in moral judgment and decision-making. As I noted in the introduction, a very striking feature of great deal of contemporary moral philosophy (at least to an outsider like me) is its strongly rationalist flavor. For the purposes of this chapter, "moral rationalism" can be taken to be the conjunction of two claims: (5.1) moral claims are the sorts of claims that can be true or false, in (as adherents of this doctrine say), "a mind-independent way," and (5.2) true moral claims can be "grasped" or recognized as such just through the operation of "reason"—this recognition does not require "emotional" processing. In this respect, the recognition of such truths is, according to moral rationalists, very much like the recognition of mathematical truth. Just as (it is supposed) emotion or affect has no role (either causally in learning or in justification) to play in judgments about mathematical truths, similarly for moral judgment.

Many contemporary deontologists and many contemporary utilitarians seem committed to moral rationalism: both groups favor analogies between, on the one hand, moral judgment and the processes leading to moral judgment and, on the other, judgments about mathematical truth and the processes underlying the recognition of such truths. Such analogies occur throughout Parfit's book (2011) and in the work of deontologists like Kamm, who writes as follows about intuitive responses to hypothetical moral dilemmas:

> The responses to cases with which I am concerned are not emotional responses but judgments about the permissibility or impermissibility of certain acts.... These judgments are not guaranteed to be correct [but] if they are, they should fall into the realm of *a priori* truths. They are not like racist judgments that one race is superior to another. The reason is that the racist is claiming to have "intuitions" about empirical matters and this is as inappropriate as having intuitions about the number of the planets or the chemical structure of water. Intuitions are appropriate to ethics because ours is an a priori, not an empirical investigation. (1993, 8)

I will have nothing directly to say about the rationalist claim (5.1) concerning the truth-aptness of moral claims, but I want to suggest that the rationalist claim (5.2) about the processes involved in moral judgment does not fit very well with the empirical facts described in this chapter. Think of the Hare et al. imaging study of dieters. The picture of valuation and decision-making that emerges from this and other studies described above might loosely be described as having both Kantian and Humean aspects. Following Kant, it appears there is an aspect of the self (involving the DLPFC and other "cognitive" structures) associated with our reasoning abilities that can stand back from, assess, and attempt to influence more immediate desires (e.g., for tasty food). We can have such desires for immediate sensory reward and yet fail to endorse them or act on them. We can also use structures like the DLPFC to alter our evaluation of immediate rewards relative to more distant goals like health. Contrary to Hume's famous remark that "reason is, and ought only to be the slave of the passions, and can never pretend to any other office than to serve and obey them," if we associate "reason" with the DLPFC, it looks as though reason is *not* confined to merely assessing various strategies for realizing goals given to us by a preference or valuational structure that is fixed and independent of our reasoning abilities. Instead, reason can influence or modulate that structure. Yet at the same time—here the underlying picture looks more Humean— the way in which "reason" exerts this influence is by modulating an affect-laden value signal that reflects input from other sources (including "emotional" areas) outside of the DLPFC. (If it is part of Humeanism that something affective or connotative must be present for evaluative judgment or decision or action to occur at least "normally" (see below), and the presence of a value signal in VMPFC/OFC corresponds to this affective element, then this strand of Humeanism seems vindicated.) As noted above, at least in the experiments described by Hare et al. (2009, 2011), the DLPFC does not have its own value signal that somehow supplants or replaces the signal in the VMPFC, so that the DLPFC generates, as it were, purely reason-based valuations. Instead the DLPFC modulates evaluative signals that are influenced by other, "emotional" input as well. Moreover, even if, as some claim, the DLPFC generates its own value signal, it remains the case that this signal is apparently integrated with value signals from other neural structures that are known to be involved in "emotional" processing.

Suppose we understand the notion of "reason" narrowly, as having to do with the sorts of abilities involved in logical or mathematical reasoning and "moral rationalism" to be the view that considerations supplied by reason, so understood, can by themselves generate moral requirements. Then, as far as the experimental results described above go, they do not seem to provide support for a picture according to which claim (5.2) (above) in moral rationalism describes the process by which people typically come to hold the moral evaluations that they do. That is, when people make moral judgments or hold moral values, these are, as an empirical matter, not typically generated by or grounded in just their reasoning capacities, acting, so to speak, on their own. Instead, other structures that are affective or emotional also play central causal roles in moral judgment and valuing, just as they do in other sorts of valuation. As far as their casual genesis goes, in normal cases, involving intact brains, our values result from the interaction and integration of the output of these structures with the influence of other structures that we tend to think of as more cognitive or reason-based.

One possible response to this is to concede these causal claims, but to hold that they do not in any way undermine moral rationalism. Recall that, as formulated above, moral rationalism holds only that moral truths "can be" grasped as such by reason, not that this is the way they are typically recognized. Thus (it might be argued), the acceptability of moral rationalism turns on whether moral requirements, correct moral judgments and evaluations, and so on, are *derivable* from considerations supplied by reason, understood as above. It may be true, as an empirical matter, that most people are not caused to make the moral judgments they make solely as result of their contemplation of considerations rooted in reason, construed narrowly, but as long as such judgments, insofar as they are correct, follow from such considerations, that is enough to vindicate moral rationalism.

An obvious problem with this response is that the different theorists who claim to be able to ground moral requirements in derivations from principles supported by reason alone reach very different, indeed inconsistent conclusions about those requirements. Some hold that some form of utilitarianism is uniquely favored by reason, others that one or another form of deontology is. Each purported derivation convinces, at best, a minority of discussants. Everyone else regards the derivation as unsound. This is very unlike the situation that holds for valid arguments in logic and mathematics.

The ideas advanced in this chapter provide a simple and plausible explanation for this state of affairs. Reason, narrowly conceived, is too weak—too lacking in substantive content—to supply sound derivations of substantive moral requirements of the sort required. This is why no one has been able to produce them. The additional processing that is at work in generating the moral judgments we make is supplied by the "emotional" structures discussed in this chapter. When we leave these out of the picture, not enough remains (just in "reason" itself) to generate, either causally or as a matter of logic, the content of our moral judgments.

For some this will be bleak conclusion. That we possess the emotional/evaluative processing structures we do is obviously a contingent matter—these structures are shaped by natural selection and, as I have emphasized, are apparently in some respects specific to human beings. So what seems to follow is something like this: moral and other values are values *for us* or values in relation to the sort of creatures we are, rather than values that are "objective" in the sense of being values for all rational creatures or mattering independently of the emotional processing to which human beings as a species are susceptible.

For both reasons of space and competence, I will not try to discuss this conclusion in any detail, confining myself to just a few remarks. First, and most fundamentally, one might wonder why "ethics for us" is not ethics enough (for us, that is). Our emotional/evaluative capacities are, as I have emphasized, plastic and influenced by learning, but it is not as though we can collectively simply excise them or replace them with something totally different. Whatever contingency in moral evaluation is present simply as a result of our possession of these structures may not reflect alternative possibilities actually available to neurologically normal subjects. So why should we be concerned about them? Even if it is true that highly intelligent social insects or chimpanzees would find very different moral requirements appealing (see below for more on this possibility), why should this matter to human beings, who cannot simply assume the affective and motivational capacities of these creatures?

Second, a number of influential moral and political philosophers are sympathetic to the idea that the derivation of substantive moral conclusions requires a notion of reason or reasoning that is thicker or more contentful than the thin notion described above. For example, one might think of the notion of what is "reasonable" as this occurs in Rawls and Scanlon as embodying such a thicker notion. From the perspective adopted in this chapter, one might attempt to flesh out the additional content possessed by this thicker notion of the "reasonable" in terms of the role played by emotional and affective structures and their interaction with other more cognitive structures. It is this additional content that would allow us to say such things as the following: "Although it may not be contrary to reason, narrowly conceived, to prefer the destruction of the rest of the world to the pricking of my finger, it is certainly unreasonable to have such a preference, and others could reasonably reject my acting on such a preference." Here part of the content of "reasonable" would be supplied by the prosocial emotions and affect that are the output of structures like the VMPFC/OFC, and so on. One consequence of making use of this thicker, more affect-laden notion of reason in moral argument may be that one is also forced to recognize that our possession of it is the result of various biological contingencies. However, wishing that matters were otherwise is not an argument that they *are* otherwise.

As I noted above, the suggestion that our moral commitments reflect features of our emotional processing is presumably troubling to some in part because it seems to raise the possibility of a group of creatures who are as rational and intelligent as human beings with respect to activities like logic and mathematics but very different emotionally. For example, we may be tempted to imagine a population of primates with the emotional/affective/motivational capacities of chimpanzees who are nonetheless as intelligent as humans. Although "rational," they may be (because of their emotional capacities and the valuations to which this leads) far less cooperative than we are, much more hierarchical, disinclined to treat one another as equals except when it is in their self-interest to do so, and so on. This seems to raise the troubling question of whether, in view of these differences, we should think of this population as subject to very different moral requirements from those that we think govern human populations. We might also find it tempting to ask whether, in view of their shared rationality, this population would discover and come to regard as binding a set of moral requirements similar to those we endorse, despite their affective differences, as some optimistic moral rationalists might suppose. (And we might also ask whether they would be subject to these requirements even if, because of their affective differences, they were rarely motivated to conform to them.)

I think this thought experiment rests on a very problematic assumption—that cognitive/rational abilities can evolve independently of emotional/affective/motivational capacities. In my view, we are as smart as we are at logic and related activities in part *because* of the emotional/affective differences that separate us from chimps and that make possible for us forms of social life and interaction that are unavailable to chimps.

And those different emotional capacities would not have been useful to us or favored by natural selection if we were not also able to use them in conjunction with cognitive capacities that differentiate us from chimps. In short, there is every reason to suppose that the emotional processing subserved by structures like the VMPFC/OFC coevolve with capacities associated with structures like the DLPFC. I certainly don't claim that it follows that creatures with cognitive capacities like ours would automatically also possess emotional/affective processing just like ours, but I do claim that such creatures are unlikely to have the emotional lives of chimps, honeybees or, for that matter, human psychopaths—such creatures will instead possess forms or emotional processing or valuation that lead to some degree of cooperation and concern for others.[10]

3.6. Internalism versus Externalism

Let me now turn to some additional issues having to do with "internalism." Philosophers like to debate whether moral judgment (or perhaps "sincere" moral judgment) is "intrinsically motivating." If the account I have been defending is on the right track, the following picture seems correct. If we confine attention to neurotypical subjects, then, as we have seen, moral judgment is (at least often or usually) causally influenced by a value signal in the OFC/VMPFC—this is true both for subjects who make deontological and subjects who make utilitarian choices. People can of course make moral judgments in circumstances in which there is no opportunity to undertake actions associated with those judgments, but when action or behavior is possible, these value signals also typically causally influence choice of action. Thus, as a matter of empirical fact, in neurotypicals the evaluations that causally influence moral judgment often also causally influence choice of action, when there is opportunity for the latter. This empirical fact apparently holds whether or not it is also true that it is a conceptual or semantic truth that sincere moral judgment *always* motivates or influences action.

Some recent work on internalism and related issues has focused on the implications of various special or atypical populations (psychopaths, patients with VMPFC damage, autistics, etc.) with compromised processing in emotional areas for these issues (see, e.g., Roskies 2003). Suppose, for example, we come to believe that psychopaths can make genuine moral judgments or can recognize that some actions are morally wrong without being motivated at all to act in accord with these judgments. Would this show that internalism is mistaken? If, on the other hand, we decide that psychopaths cannot make genuine moral judgments because they do not engage in the emotional processing that typically accompanies this in neurotypicals, does this provide support for internalism or undercut moral rationalism?

I think that my remarks above can help cast some light on these questions. At the risk of oversimplifying, I take the general picture of these special populations that is emerging to be the following (cf. Glenn et al. 2009; Koenigs et al. 2007; Young et al. 2010, 2012). Psychopaths, VMPFC patients, and autistics can use sentences expressing moral judgments like "Stealing is wrong" in ways that show normal linguistic competence. For some range of cases, such subjects will also make judgments that are not very different from the judgments made by neurotypicals—they will agree or at least say they agree that stealing is wrong. Nonetheless, subjects in these special populations tend to differ from judgments made by neurotypicals in more subtle ways, with the nature of the difference depending on the character of the impairments in the different special populations. For example, VMPFC patients have been found to differ from neurotypicals in their judgments of the wrongfulness of actions that involve *attempts* to produce harm and, as noted above, they also tend to make different (more "utilitarian") judgments with respect to certain moral dilemmas such as the trolley problem. Psychopaths judge nonintentional harms more leniently than normals. In contrast to neurotypicals, high-functioning autistics are reported to not reliably judge accidental and attempted harms as morally different. To the extent that such subjects have impaired functioning in the OFC/VMPFC or in structures like the amygdala that provide input to these, we can conclude (quite independently of any differences in the content of their judgments) that it must be the case that the causal pathways leading to their moral judgments are different from or are functioning differently from those employed by neurotypical subjects. It is presumably these differences that lead to the subtle differences in judgment described above. Thus one possibility—arguably a natural conjecture—is that although subjects in special populations are sometimes able to produce moral judgments that are similar to those produced by neurotypicals, they do this by making use of processing that is quite different from that employed by neurotypicals. (See Glenn et al. 2009 for a similar suggestion.) For example, someone with impaired or abnormal processing in structures like the OFC/VMPFC might nonetheless have been able to learn a set of moral rules or maxims that are generally accepted in her society—that it is wrong to steal, kill, and so on. These might be committed to memory and then be deployed to answer moral judgment questions through the activity of structures like the DLPFC without any involvement of emotional structures. This may result in judgments that exhibit considerable overlap with those made in more normal ways by neurotypicals for some range of cases, while differing in more subtle ways in tasks that require deployment of structures like the OFC/VMPFC (such as trolley problems). To the extent that such subjects make moral judgments without making use of structures like the OFC/VMPFC, it seems entirely possible that there may be no associated motivation to act or at least a weaker or different motivation than in neurotypicals.

Philosophers who are sympathetic to the idea that moral judgments must, for conceptual or semantic reasons, be motivating or involve emotional processing are often tempted to suppose that moral judgments of psychopaths and other special population subjects are not "genuine" or "sincere" moral judgments because they lack the elements of normal processing just described. This move strikes me as question-begging (or at least unfruitful) in the absence of some independent characterization of what makes a moral judgment real or sincere. On the other side, philosophers sympathetic to rationalism and externalism sometimes take the apparent possibility of moral judgment in special populations to show that there is no intrinsic or essential connection between moral judgment and motivation. Whatever one thinks of this last claim, it is important that it not lead us to overlook the causal connection between emotional processing, valuation, judgment, and motivation that *is* usually present in neurotypicals. In other words, when construed not as a universally true conceptual/semantic claim, but rather as an empirical claim about what is usual in neurotypical populations, internalism has much to recommend it. Moreover, if the conjectures advanced above are correct, it also seems to follow that the moral judgments endorsed by special populations are to a substantial extent parasitic on the judgments of neurotypicals in the sense that those in the special populations learn to make these judgments by mimicking those of surrounding neurotypicals. If this is correct, there is no reason to suppose a population consisting entirely of psychopaths without any contact with neurotypicals would acquire on its own tendencies to moral judgment that even loosely resemble those of neurotypicals.

So far I have neglected an issue that may seem central to debates about internalism and moral rationalism. This has to with the significance of differences, not between human beings and other species, or between neurotypicals and special populations, but *among* neurotypicals in emotional processing and evaluative assessment. Both casual observation and more careful empirical observation support the claim that neurotypical humans vary considerably in emotional/evaluative response, particularly in the moral sphere. Some people are very empathetic and find helping others rewarding (at least for some others), other people much less so. Does it follow that, for example, the extent to which moral requirements are binding on people (or the extent to which they have "reasons" to conform to such requirements) depends on the extent to which their affective processing is such that they value acting in conformity to these requirements?

In my view, nothing I have said above requires a positive answer to this question. Although the matter deserves more discussion than I can give it here, my view, very roughly, is that it is generic facts about human emotional processing and valuation, characteristic of us as a species, rather than individual differences, that are regulative when it comes to moral requirements and reasons. For example, in many situations in which outcomes would be improved by cooperation, very substantial numbers of people (although far from all) find cooperation and reciprocation rewarding and nonreciprocation sufficiently adverse that they are willing to punish free-riders. When cooperation would provide goods (evaluated as such by nearly all those affected) that would not otherwise be provided, these facts about the emotional response and evaluation underlie our willingness to require cooperation from those who do not find cooperation rewarding in itself—a requirement that we may be willing to enforce with sanctions. Moral requirements have to do, after all, with regulating our common lives together, and there are very obvious considerations (having to do, e.g., with incentives) for not allowing people to evade those requirements simply because they say, even truthfully, that their preferences and emotions are such that they do not value conforming to them. So while some particular person, Jones, can be subject to a requirement (and have a reason) to help others even if he does not feel like doing so, in my view it would be a mistake to conclude from this observation that recognition of this moral requirement is completely independent of *any* emotionally mediated evaluation that is widely shared by human beings.

3.7. Conclusion

I have argued that areas commonly identified as involved in emotional processing play a central role in moral judgment in neurotypical human beings because such areas contribute causally to the construction of moral evaluations. The moral judgments that humans find appealing or compelling or intuitive reflect features of the operation of such areas, and this is so whether the judgments in question are "utilitarian" or "deontological." It is because of the involvement of these areas in moral judgment that attempts to derive moral requirements from "reason," conceived as something totally distinct from anything affective and just involving the kind of processing that is operative when humans work on logic and mathematics, are likely to be unsuccessful. The way forward is not to look for moral requirements that are binding on all rational creatures just in virtue of their rationality but rather to recognize that moral requirements that we find appealing and that are suitable for regulating our lives will reflect facts about our affective and motivational commitments, as well as our capacities for reasoning.

Acknowledgments

Thanks to Ralph Adolphs, Josh Greene, Antonio Rangel, and Kyle Stanford for helpful discussions.

Notes

1. In addition to the considerations described in this paragraph, other possible bases for non-question-begging normative judgments to which I sometimes appeal below include consistency (e.g., choices violating formal constraints like transitivity are regarded as normatively defective) and whether a decision fails to take account of considerations that are regarded as relevant by virtually all competing normative theories. The general problem of how to identify non-question-begging constraints for the normative assessment of moral judgments in the absence of any generally accepted moral theory is an important and difficult one that deserves more attention from philosophers.

2. The following remarks are heavily influenced by Rolls 2005, as well as by the other papers cited below.

3. For details, see, e.g., Hamann et al. 2011 and Decety et al. 2011. As argued below, this is one reason why the rationalist project of deriving moral requirements humans find compelling from "reason" alone, independently of features of specifically human emotional processing, seems unlikely to succeed.

4. For some details about this database, see Escobedo and Adolphs 2010.

5. These authors explicitly deny (and provide evidence against the claim) that the primary role of OFC is to inhibit inappropriate responses, as suggested in the Shenhav and Greene (2010) paper discussed below, or to flexibly encode associative information.

6. Of course, it might be responded that such subjects are irrational (or "nonrational"), since their choices are influenced by "emotion," and that even in the absence of any influence from emotional areas like the insula, subjects who are "rational" would be led just through the exercise of their reason to donate large amounts to charity (perhaps on the grounds that reason tells me that it would be "irrational" to give any particular preference to myself over any other sentient creature in the universe or some such). If this is understood as an empirical claim and "rational" subjects are understood as those showing a high level of activity in cognitive areas like the DLPFC, then this response predicts that subjects with such high levels of cognitive activity and no activity in emotional areas like the insula will make large charitable donations—a claim for which, as far as I know, there is no evidence. If the claim is understood as an a priori or conceptual one (in effect building a willingness to donate into the definition of "rationality"), then one faces the problem that subjects with a high level of activity in what are thought to be "cognitive" areas still may not be rational according to this definition.

7. Although I express some skepticism below about several of Greene's claims, I want to say explicitly that, probably more than any other researcher, he has played a central role in developing and driving forward the whole area of investigation of the neural structures underlying moral judgment. Disagreement with him is a measure of the extent to which his ideas have established the agenda and framework for discussion in this area.

8. Another way of putting this point is that the dilemmas employed by Greene are those in which the "utilitarian" choices require actions that for most people require suppression of some strong adverse reaction to the course chosen. The issue is whether neural activity observed in connection with such choices reflect this fact, rather than distinctively utilitarian content of the choices. For some similar concerns, see Kahane 2012.

9. It seems to me that a similar conclusion also follows for most plausible nonutilitarian moral theories. This is because most plausible moral theories will require decision-makers to be guided by accurate information about how their actions affect others, how others are likely to respond to one's choices, and so on. (Of course different theories may disagree about how such information is relevant.) As long as it is acknowledged that such information is often morally relevant in some way, it will be normatively better to take such information into account than to ignore it. This in turn requires the involvement of neural areas involved in processing such information, including "emotional" areas.

Let me add that some readers may find it tempting to take this consideration to vindicate the suggestion that greater involvement of "cognition" leads to better moral decisions on the grounds that taking into account more rather than less information automatically amounts to a greater involvement of cognition. I regard this as not so much wrong as unilluminating: on this suggestion, all of the emotional processing areas discussed in this chapter are doing "cognitive" processing simply in virtue of doing information processing. "Cognition" has been *defined* in such a way that it no longer contrasts with emotion and indeed so that pretty much anything the brain does is "cognitive." The view vindicated is thus not the RD view or the views expressed in Greene 2004.

10. A referee asks whether I am claiming that it somehow conveniently works out that our emotional apparatus has been molded by natural selection in such a way that we make moral judgments that are "correct" by some standard entirely independent of that apparatus. This is not what I am claiming; my talk of "ethics for us" is meant to suggest there is no such independent standard.

References

Allman, J., N. Tetreault, A. Hakeem, K. Manaye, K. Semendeferi, J. Erwin, S. Park, V. Goubert, and P. Hof. 2010. "The von Economo Neurons in Frontoinsular and Anterior cingulate Cortex in Great Apes and Humans." *Brain Structure and Function* 214: 495–517.

Allman, J., K. Watson, N. Tetreault, and A. Hakeem, 2005. "Intuition and Autism: A Possible Role for Von Economo Neurons." *Trends in Cognitive Science* 9: 367–373.

Anderson, S., A. Bechara, H. Damasio, D. Tranel, and A. R. Damasio. 1999. "Impairment of Social and Moral Behavior Related to Early Damage in Human Prefrontal Cortex." *Nature Neuroscience* 2: 1032–1037.

Behrens, T., L. Hunt, M. Woolrich, M. Rushworth. 2008. "Associative Learning of Social Value." *Nature* 456: 245–249.

Blair, J., D. Mitchell, and K. Blair. 2005. *The Psychopath: Emotion and the Brain.* Oxford: Blackwell.

Decety, J., K. Michalska, and K. Kinzler. 2012. "The Contribution of Emotion and Cognition to Moral Sensitivity: A Neurodevelopmental Study." *Cerebral Cortex* 22: 209–220.

Escobedo, J., and R. Adophs. 2010. "Becoming a Better Person: Temporal Remoteness Biases Autobiographical Memories for Moral Events." *Emotion* 10: 511–518.

Glenn, A., A. Raine, R. Schug, L. Young, and M. Hauser. 2009. "Increased DLPFC Activity during Moral Decision-making in Psychopathy." *Molecular Psychiatry* 14: 909–911.

Greene, J., L. Nystrom, A. Engell, J. Darley, and J. Cohen. 2004. "The Neural Bases of Cognitive Conflict and Control in Moral Judgment." *Neuron* 44, 389–400.

Hamann, K., F. Warneken, J. Greenberg, and M. Tomasello. 2011. "Collaboration Encourages Equal Sharing in Children but Not Chimpanzees." *Nature* 476: 328–331.

Hampton, A., P. Bossaerts, J. O'Doherty. 2008. "Neural Correlates of Mentalizing-related Computations during Strategic Interactions in Humans." *Proceedings of the National Academy of Sciences* 105: 6741–6746.

Hare, T., C. Camerer, and A. Rangel. 2009. "Self-Control in Decision-Making Involves Modulation of the vmPFC Valuation System." *Science* 324: 646–648.

Hare, T., C. Camerer, D. Knoepfle, J. O'Doherty, and A. Rangel. 2010. "Value Computations in Ventral Medial Prefrontal Cortex during Charitable Decision Making Incorporate Input from Regions Involved in Social Cognition." *Journal of Neuroscience* 30: 583–590.

Hare, T., J. Malmaud, and A. Rangel. 2011. "Focusing Attention on the Health Aspects of Food Changes Value Signals in the vmPFC and Improves Dietary Choice." *Journal of Neuroscience* 31: 11077–11087.

Hoffman, M. 2001. *Empathy and Moral Development: Implications for Caring and Justice.* Cambridge: Cambridge University Press.

Kahane, G. 2012. "On the Wrong Track: Process and Content in Moral Psychology." *Mind and Language* 27: 519–545.

Kamm, F. 1993. *Morality, Mortality.* Vol. 1: Death and Whom to Save from It. New York: Oxford University Press.

Koenigs, M., L. Young, R. Adolphs, D. Tranel, F. Cushman, M. Hauser, and A. Damasio. 2007. "Damage to the Prefrontal Cortex Increases Utilitarian Moral Judgements." *Nature* 446, no. 7138: 908–911.

Maclean, P. 1990. *The Triune Brain in Evolution: Role in Paleocerebral Functions.* New York: Plenum Press.

Parfit. D. 2011. *On What Matters.* Oxford: Oxford University Press.

Quartz, S. 2009. "Reason, Emotion, and Decision-Making: Risk and Reward Computation with Feeling." *Trends in Cognitive Sciences* 13, no. 5: 209–215.

Rolls, E. 2005. *Emotion Explained.* Oxford: Oxford University Press.

Roskies, A. 2003. "Are Ethical Judgments Intrinsically Motivational? Lessons from Acquired Sociopathy." *Philosophical Psychology* 16: 51–66.

Scanlon, T. 1998. *What We Owe to Each Other.* Cambridge, MA: Harvard University Press.

Schoenbaum, G., M. Roesch, T. Stalnaker, and Y. Takahashi. 2011. "Orbital Frontal Cortex and Outcome Expectancies: Optimizing Behavior and Sensory Perception." In *Neurobiology of Sensation and Reward*, edited by J. Gottfried, 329–350. Boca Raton, FL: Taylor and Francis.

Shenhav, A., and J. Greene. 2010. "Moral Judgments Recruit Domain-General Valuation Mechanisms to Integrate Representations of Probability and Magnitude." *Neuron* 67: 667–677.

Singer, P. 2005. "Ethics and Intuitions." *Journal of Ethics* 9: 331–352.

Woodward, J., and J. Allman. 2007. "Moral Intuition: Its Neural Substrates and Normative Significance." *Journal of Physiology–Paris* 101: 179–202.

Young, L., A. Bechara, D. Tranel, H. Damasio, M. Hauser, and A. Damasio. 2010. "Damage to Ventromedial Prefrontal Cortex Impairs Judgment of Harmful Intent." *Neuron* 65: 845–851.

Young, L., M. Koenigs, M. Kruepke, and J. Newman. 2012. "Psychopathy Increases Perceived Moral Permissibility of Accidents." *Journal of Abnormal Psychology* 121: 659–667.

II

Deontology versus Consequentialism

4

Beyond Point-and-Shoot Morality

WHY COGNITIVE (NEURO)SCIENCE MATTERS FOR ETHICS

Joshua D. Greene

THE COGNITIVE SCIENCE of ethics is booming, thanks in no small part to philosophers (Sinnott-Armstrong 2007; Doris 2010). Nevertheless, many philosophers wonder whether this, or any, empirical research could have implications for foundational questions in normative ethics. In this chapter I will explain why cognitive science matters for ethics. More specifically, I will defend the following thesis:[1]

> Science can advance ethics by revealing the hidden inner workings of our moral judgments, especially the ones we make intuitively. Once those inner workings are revealed, we may have less confidence in some of our judgments and the ethical theories that are (explicitly or implicitly) based on them.

In section 41, I will describe our brains as *dual-process* systems and introduce the *camera analogy*, the organizing metaphor of this chapter and a central idea in my book (Greene 2013). In section 4.2, I will describe and present evidence for the dual-process theory of moral judgment. In section 4.3, I will describe related experimental research examining influences on our moral intuitions. In sections 4.4 and 4.5, I'll describe two routes by which cognitive science can have implications for ethics, and with no illicit is/ought border crossings. I call these routes *direct* and *indirect*. In section 4.6, I'll explain why a deeper understanding of moral psychology favors certain forms of consequentialism. I will then close with a few words about the bright future of ethics as an interdisciplinary enterprise.

4.1. The Dual-Process Brain

I own a digital SLR camera that, like many others, operates in two complementary modes. First, it has a variety of point-and-shoot automatic settings that are optimized for typical photographic situations ("portrait," "action," "landscape," etc.). I use these most of the time. Occasionally, I get ambitious and put the camera in manual mode, which allows me to adjust all of the camera's settings by hand.

This dual-mode design exemplifies an elegant solution to a ubiquitous design problem, namely, the trade-off between *efficiency* and *flexibility*. The automatic settings are highly efficient, but not very flexible, and the reverse is true of the manual mode. Put them together, however, and you get the best of both worlds, provided that you know when to use each mode.

The human brain has the same general design (Kahneman 2003). First, we humans have a variety of automatic settings—reflexes and intuitions that guide our behavior, many of which are emotional. We may be conscious of such emotional responses, but we are generally not conscious of the processes that trigger them. We rely on our automatic settings most of the time, and they generally serve us well (Bargh and Chartrand 1999).

Our brains also have a manual mode. It is a general-purpose reasoning system, specialized for enabling behaviors that serve long(er)-term goals, that is, goals that are not automatically activated by current environmental stimuli or endogenous somatic states (Miller and Cohen 2001). The operations of this system are typically conscious, experienced as voluntary, and often experienced as effortful. Our manual mode allows us to formulate behavioral plans based on detailed and explicit knowledge of the situations we face, along with explicit general knowledge about the world and how it works. Manual mode allows us to guide our behavior using explicit rules and to think explicitly about how the world works. In short, manual mode thinking is the kind of thinking that we think of as "thinking."[2]

The way our brains handle the efficiency/flexibility trade-off is nicely illustrated by our navigation of the familiar tension between *now* and *later*. We have automatic settings that urge us to consume or acquire valuable resources, such as calorie-rich food and money, whenever they are available. This is very efficient because it is generally adaptive to acquire valuable resources. At the same time, we humans have the capacity to think explicitly about whether our long-term goals are served by immediate consumption/acquisition, along with the capacity to regulate our behavior accordingly. In other words, we can delay gratification, choosing, for example, a slimmer waistline in three months over chocolate cake right now. This is a dual-process phenomenon. If, for example, our manual mode capacity is occupied by a distracting memory task, our automatic settings gain the advantage, and we are more likely to choose chocolate cake over fruit salad (Shiv and Fedorikhin 2002).

Recent brain-imaging studies reveal the underlying neural dynamics (McClure et al. 2004). Brain regions such as the ventral striatum and the ventromedial prefrontal cortex

(VMPFC) produce the automatic response favoring *now* and enable this response to influence behavior. Other brain regions, most notably the dorsolateral prefrontal cortex (DLPFC), enable the controlled response that sometimes favors *later*, depending on the situational details. We see the dual-process brain at work in other domains, for example, in the cognitive control of negative reactions to members of racial out-groups and sad scenes (Cunningham et al. 2004; Ochsner et al. 2002). In these cases, among others, the amygdala, an ancient mammalian brain structure with direct connections to the VMPFC, plays a critical role in automatic responding, while the DLPFC plays a central role in coordinating manual mode thinking and responding.

Before moving on, it's worth highlighting three ways in which the camera analogy may mislead. First, while a camera must be in one mode or another, the waking human brain's automatic settings are always on. Second, a camera's dual modes can function independently of each other, but in animals there is an asymmetrical dependence. One can have automatic settings without a manual mode, as in most animals, but not the reverse. Finally, automatic settings need not be "innate" or "hardwired." They can be acquired or modified through cultural learning (as in prejudicial responses to racial out-groups) and through individual experiences (as in classical conditioning).

4.2. Dual-Process Morality

4.2.1. THE DUAL-PROCESS THEORY OF MORAL JUDGMENT

According to the dual-process theory of moral judgment (henceforth "dual-process theory") (Greene et al. 2001; Greene et al. 2004; Greene et al. 2008; Greene 2007), moral psychology looks much like the rest of judgment and decision-making. Moral judgment is influenced by both automatic emotional responses (automatic settings) and controlled, conscious reasoning (manual mode). Moreover, these processes are enabled by the usual cast of neural characters in their characteristic roles. These tenets of the dual-process theory should be relatively unsurprising and uncontroversial. The more interesting, and correspondingly controversial, tenet of the dual-process theory is this:

> *The Central Tension Principle*: Characteristically deontological judgments are preferentially supported by automatic emotional responses, while characteristically consequentialist judgments are preferentially supported by conscious reasoning and allied processes of cognitive control.

The name of this principle reflects a more general idea, which is that the central tension in ethics between deontology and consequentialism is a manifestation of the central tension in cognitive design between efficiency and flexibility.

Some terminological clarification is in order. My use of "deontological" and "consequentialist" is not entirely consistent with standard philosophical usage, necessitating my use of the technical qualifier "characteristically." This has been a source of some confusion.[3] I define "characteristically deontological" judgments as ones that are naturally justified in deontological terms (in terms of rights, duties, etc.) and that are more difficult to justify in consequentialist terms, such as judgments against killing one person to save five others. I define "characteristically consequentialist" judgments as ones that are naturally justified in consequentialist terms (i.e., by impartial cost-benefit reasoning) and that are more difficult to justify in deontological terms because they conflict with our sense of people's rights, duties, and so on. Approving of killing one to save five is a characteristically consequentialist judgment. (Note that I will sometimes drop the qualifier "characteristically" in the interest of brevity, using instead an asterisk [*] to indicate that the qualifier still applies.)

Two further points about these terms: First, they imply nothing a priori about the psychology behind a given judgment, and therefore nothing about the judge's *reasons*. Such psychological facts are to be ascertained empirically. Second, making "characteristically consequentialist" and "characteristically deontological" judgments requires no explicit or implicit commitment to consequentialist or deontological theories. For example, card-carrying deontologists, and people who carry no theoretical cards, can make characteristically consequentialist judgments. Mutatis mutandis for consequentialists.

My nonstandard use of these terms will strike some as perverse, but there is a method to this madness. The dual-process theory aims to characterize the moral-philosophical tendencies of distinct cognitive systems.[4] This endeavor is complicated by the fact that these systems do not correspond precisely to distinct ethical schools as designated by contemporary ethicists. This is largely because sophisticated consequentialist and deontological theories are designed to capture the outputs of multiple cognitive systems (cf. "climbing the mountain from different sides") (Parfit 2011). Nevertheless, if I'm right, the psychological *essence* of deontology lies with the automatic settings, and the psychological *essence* of consequentialism lies with manual mode. To articulate and test this idea we need to modify both our vocabulary and corresponding concepts. To get sophisticated about moral psychology we must *temporarily* get unsophisticated about philosophical terminology. Please bear with me.

4.2.2. EVIDENCE

The dual-process theory was inspired by the trolley problem, with which I assume most readers are familiar (Foot 1967; Thomson 1985). For present purposes, the two key dilemmas are the Switch (also known as Bystander) and Footbridge cases. Very briefly for the uninitiated: In the Switch case, one can hit a switch that will turn a runaway trolley away from five people and onto one. In the Footbridge case one can push one person off a footbridge and into the path of a runaway trolley, saving five further down the track. People tend to give characteristically consequentialist responses to the Switch case ("Yes, it's permissible to hit the switch to save more lives") and characteristically deontological responses to the Footbridge case ("No, it's impermissible to push to save more lives").

Our first neuroimaging experiment compared "personal" moral dilemmas such as the Footbridge dilemma to "impersonal" moral dilemmas such as the Switch dilemma (Greene et al. 2001). Our hypothesis, based on the dual-process theory, was that the former would preferentially engage brain regions associated with emotion, while the latter would preferentially engage brain regions associated with controlled cognition. This is indeed what we found. The "personal" dilemmas elicited relatively greater activity in a large swath of the medial prefrontal cortex, including parts of the VMPFC, and a subsequent analysis with more data showed the same effect in the amygdala (Greene et al. 2004). Similar effects were observed in other brain regions previously associated with emotion. In contrast, the "impersonal" dilemmas elicited relatively greater activity in the DLPFC and allied brain regions. Such results were specifically predicted by the dual-process theory and thus lend it some support.[5]

Now, over a decade later, the dual-process theory is supported by a large and diverse body of evidence. We'll begin with evidence concerning the role of emotional intuition in characteristically deontological judgment—or, alternatively, characteristically non-consequentialist judgment (Koenigs et al. 2007). (Unless otherwise specified, the results below are based on [or driven by] responses to one or more "high-conflict" personal dilemmas.)

Patients with frontotemporal dementia, which typically involves emotional blunting, are about three times as likely as control subjects to give consequentialist* responses to the Footbridge case. (Mendez et al. 2005)

Patients with damage to the VMPFC are about five times as likely as others to give consequentialist* responses.[6] A research team in Italy produced similar results. A follow-up study shows that consequentialist* judgments are associated with absent skin-conductance responses (SCRs, which indicate affective arousal) in VMPFC patients and reduced SCRs in healthy subjects. (Moretto et al. 2010)

VMPFC patients give more consequentialist* responses to dilemmas in which familial duties are pitted against consequentialist* considerations (e.g., turning a trolley onto one's sister to save others). (Thomas et al. 2011)

People who exhibit greater physiological reactivity (constriction of peripheral blood vessels) to performing a stressful arithmetic task give less consequentialist* responses. (Cushman et al. 2012)

Low-anxiety psychopaths (known for their social-emotional deficits) are more likely than healthy people to give consequentialist* responses. (Koenigs et al. 2012)

People who are more empathetic, or induced to be more empathetic, give more deontological* responses.[7]

Individuals high in psychopathy exhibit lower amygdala responses and higher DLPFC responses to "personal" dilemmas. (Glenn, Raine, and Schug 2009; Glenn, Raine, Schug, and Hauser 2009)

Thinking about death reduces consequentialist* judgment. (Trémolière et al. 2012)

Individuals with deficits in emotional awareness (due to alexithymia) make more consequentialist* judgments. (Koven et al. 2011)

Amygdala activity correlates positively with ratings of negative emotion in response to Footbridge-like cases and correlates negatively with consequentialist* judgments. (Shenhav and Greene 2014)

Citalopram—a selective serotonin uptake inhibitor (SSRI) that, in the short term, increases emotional reactivity through its influence on the amygdala and VMPFC, among other regions—reduces consequentialist* responses. (Crockett 2010)

Inducing mirth (the positive emotion associated with humor, here thought to counteract negative emotional responses) increases consequentialist* responses. (Valdesolo and DeSteno 2006; Strohminger et al. 2011)

Visual thinking is generally more emotionally evocative than verbal thinking, and individuals with more visual cognitive styles tend to give less consequentialist* responses. Likewise, interfering with visual thinking (but not verbal thinking) makes judgments more consequentialist*. (Amit and Greene 2012)

Other evidence links characteristically consequentialist judgment to controlled cognition.

Consequentialist* judgment is associated with increased DLPFC activity within individuals (Greene et al. 2004) and across individuals. (Wharton 2011; Cushman et al., n.d.)

Performing a distracting secondary task (i.e., being under cognitive load) reduces consequentialist* responses (Trémolière et al. 2012; Conway and Gawronski 2013) or slows consequentialist* responses, while having no effect on deontological* responses. (Greene et al. 2009)

Removing time pressure and encouraging deliberation increases consequentialist* responses. (Suter and Hertwig 2011)

The experience of successfully solving tricky math problems (ones that require one to question one's intuitions) makes people subsequently more likely to give consequentialist* responses. Individuals who solve more tricky math problems tend to give more consequentialist* responses to a higher-stakes version of the Footbridge case, independent of whether they solved math problems first. (Paxton et al. 2012)

Individuals who generally favor effortful thinking over intuitive thinking are more likely to give consequentialist* responses. (Bartels 2008; see also Conway and Bertram Gawronski 2013; Moore et al. 2008)

People are invariably conscious of the consequentialist rationale for making consequentialist* judgments, but lack conscious access to the causes of their deontological* patterns of judgment (approving of some consequentialist* trade-offs but not others). People often question or rewrite dilemmas' assumptions so as to produce a coherent consequentialist justification for disapproval. (Cushman et al. 2006; Hauser et al. 2007)

That's a lot of evidence. All of it comes from trolleyology, but that's no reason to dismiss it. We philosophers have puzzled over trolley dilemmas for decades because they capture a central—if not *the* central—tension in normative ethics, and the myriad scientific results these dilemmas have generated implies that they tap something deep—revealing the hidden tectonics of the moral mind (Cushman and Greene 2012). That said, there is evidence for the dual-process theory beyond trolleyology:

Negative emotional responses predict characteristically nonconsequentialist disapproval of harmless moral transgressions, including disapproval that is characteristically deontological (e.g., disapproval of breaking a promise without negative consequences). (Haidt et al. 1993; Wheatley and Haidt 2005)

Several experiments indicate that consequentialist considerations play a minimal role in people's judgments about punishment, though people readily appeal to consequentialist considerations when asked to explicitly justify punishments.[8] Instead, punishment judgments follow a pattern consistent with retributivism, a distinctively nonconsequentialist, and specifically Kantian, philosophy of punishment. Punishment appears to be driven primarily by automatic negative emotional responses, and people who are more punitive tend to rely less on controlled cognition. (Sargent 2004)

People's judgments and decisions about helping behavior follow a nonconsequentialist* pattern and tend to be driven by automatic processes. (Small and Loewenstein 2003; Kogut and Ritov 2005; Slovic 2007)

Public health professionals (for whom the patient is the society at large) make more consequentialist* judgments than doctors and ordinary people in response to medical dilemmas. (Ransohoff 2011; Ransohoff et al., n.d.)

In sum, the dual-process theory is supported by an exceptionally wide range of convergent and complementary evidence from many independent researchers.[9] No one piece of evidence is definitive, and each piece, taken in isolation, is open to alternative interpretations. But no theory of which I am aware comes anywhere close to explaining this body of evidence better than the dual-process theory, which explicitly predicted most of these results in advance and predicts (in the timeless sense) all of them.[10]

4.2.3. COUNTEREVIDENCE?

Is there any positive evidence against the dual-process theory? Kahane et al. hypothesize that consequentialist judgments have so far been associated with controlled cognition simply because research has, so far, focused on cases in which consequentialist* judgments happen to be supported by controlled cognition (Kahane 2012). If you look elsewhere, they say, you'll find characteristically deontological judgments preferentially supported by controlled cognition.

I once speculated about the possibility of finding such cases:

> This [dual-process theory] also makes sense of certain deontological anomalies. . . . Consider, for example, Kant's infamous claim that it would be wrong to lie to a would-be murderer in order to protect a friend who has taken refuge in one's home. . . . Kant sticks to his theory and rejects the intuitive response. (He "bites the bullet," as philosophers say.) But what is interesting about this bit of Kantian ethics is that it's something of an embarrassment to contemporary Kantians, who are very keen to explain how Kant somehow misapplied his own theory in this case. . . . If you want to know which bits of Kant contemporary Kantians will reject, follow the emotions. (Greene 2007, 66)

This suggests a more general formula for generating counterintuitive deontological* judgments: Find a moral rule that reasonable adults rarely hold as absolute ("Don't lie") and then pit that rule against a serious harm that we are intuitively inclined to avoid and that we have consequentialist reason to avoid. This is precisely the strategy adopted by Kahane et al., who examine cases of "white lies" (Should you devastate your friend by telling him what his mean-spirited uncle really thought of him?), and "imprudent autonomy" (Should you buy an alcoholic beggar booze instead of food because that's what he really wants?), and so on. Kahane et al. conducted an fMRI experiment using dilemmas such as these, along with standard Footbridge-like dilemmas. They predicted that deontological* judgments in response to their new dilemmas would show signs of preferentially engaging controlled cognition, providing evidence that these deontological* judgments are counterintuitive, contrary to the dual-process theory and the Central Tension Principle, more specifically.

My collaborators and I did not find Kahane et al.'s fMRI and reaction time data convincing, but we wondered whether they might be right about some of their cases.[11] With this in mind, Joe Paxton, Tommaso Bruni, and I (2014) conducted a more definitive behavioral test using one of our standard dilemmas (also used by Kahane et al.) and one of Kahane et al.'s "white lie" dilemmas. We used the "tricky math problems" technique, mentioned above. As expected, subjects who distrusted their intuitions on the tricky math problems were more likely to give consequentialist* responses to our standard case. And, most critically, subjects who distrusted their faulty intuitions on the math problems also gave more consequentialist* responses to Kahane et al.'s "white lie" dilemma—exactly what the original dual-process theory predicts, and exactly the opposite of what Kahane et al.'s theory predicts. Given that this dilemma was engineered to be a counterexample to the Central Tension Principle and the dual-process theory, it's hard to imagine this theory's receiving more striking confirmation. That said, I've no doubt that, somewhere, an exception to the dual-process theory's predicted pattern will be found. The point, however, is not that the dual-process theory predicts every case perfectly, but rather that it captures the general shape of philosophical moral psychology.

At this point, having read a short summary of the evidence supporting the dual-process theory, you may or may not be inclined to accept it as true, or approximately true. Nevertheless, for the remainder of this chapter, I will assume that it's correct, in order to explore its implications.

4.3. What Pushes Our Moral Buttons?

We have automatic emotional responses that support characteristically deontological judgments. But what triggers these emotional responses? What, for example, is it about pushing the man off the footbridge that makes us feel that it's wrong? Experiments are answering this question, among others.

It seems that there are two key factors that explain why most people say yes to the Switch case and "no" to the Footbridge case (henceforth, the *switch-footbridge* effect). The first is whether the victim is harmed as a means or as a side effect (Mikhail 2000; Cushman et al. 2006), a factor that has long been cited by ethicists as relevant here and elsewhere (Foot 1967). The second has to do with the "personalness" of the harm (Royzman and Baron 2002; Cushman et al. 2006; Waldmann and Dieterich 2007; Moore et al. 2008). I and my collaborators have conducted a set of experiments (Greene et al. 2009) showing that these two factors interact to produce the switch-footbridge effect.[12] (I use term "interact" in the technical statistical sense, meaning that the influence of one factor is influenced by the presence/absence of another factor, as in an interaction between medications.) Here I will focus on the personalness factor because it is the most normatively relevant. We'll return to the means/side effect factor in section 4.6.

The action in Footbridge involves the application of *personal force*. That is, the agent directly impacts the victim with the force of his/her muscles. The effect of personal force is revealed by examining four footbridge variations. In the Footbridge Pole version, the agent pushes the victim with a pole. In the Footbridge Switch version, the agent drops the victim onto the tracks through a switch-operated trapdoor, while standing near the victim on the footbridge. In the remote Footbridge version, the switch is located elsewhere, away from the victim. We asked separate groups of subjects to judge whether the action proposed is morally acceptable. The proportions of subjects responding yes to these cases are as follows:

A. Standard Footbridge: 31 percent yes
B. Footbridge Pole: 33 percent yes
C. Footbridge Switch: 59 percent yes
D. Remote Footbridge: 63 percent yes

The results for the first two cases do not differ significantly. That is, there is no evidence for an effect of physical contact per se. Likewise, comparing the last two cases, there is no evidence for an effect of spatial distance per se. However, the difference between the first two cases and the last two, the difference between pushing and hitting a switch, is highly significant, doubling the number of yes responses. (At this point, you may already feel a normative tingle in your extremities. That's normal.)

I'll briefly mention a parallel line of research, led by Jay Musen (Musen 2010; Musen and Greene, n.d.), related to Peter Singer's (1972) famous drowning child dilemma. It seems monstrously wrong to allow a child to drown in a shallow pond because one is concerned about muddying up one's clothes. And yet it seems to most people morally acceptable, if not morally ideal, to spend one's disposable income on luxuries for oneself, even if that money could be used to save the lives of desperately needy people. Why do we say both of these things? Evidence from Musen's experiments suggests that our judgments are highly sensitive to *mere spatial distance*. This effect is nicely illustrated by contrasting two cases, which we'll call Near and Far.[13]

In the Near case, you are vacationing in a developing country that has been hit by a devastating typhoon. You are safe and well supplied in your temporary home on a coastal mountainside, but many people along the coast are dying. A relief effort led by an international organization is underway, and you can help by donating money. A relatively modest donation can save a life, and no money will go to waste. Are you morally obliged to donate?

In the Far case it's your friend, rather than you, who is there. Your friend uses a smartphone to capture audio and video from the scene, transmitting these to you live over the Internet, while you sit comfortably at home. You can also donate to the relief effort over the Internet. In other words, you know everything your friend knows, see and hear everything your friend sees and hears, and you are in just as good a position to help. The only difference is that your friend is physically near while you are physically far.[14] It seems that this difference dramatically affects people's judgments.[15] (Tingle?)[16]

4.4. Moral Implications: The Direct Route

It's time to explain and vindicate these *oughty* tingles, induced by purely *is-ish* experimental findings. I will do this with no is/ought sleight of hand.

Such experiments identify factors to which our moral judgments are sensitive. This information may be combined with independent normative assumptions concerning the kinds of things to which our judgments ought to be sensitive.[17] This combination can lead us to new, substantive moral conclusions. In other words, scientific information can allow us to trade in difficult "ought" questions for easier "ought" questions, and thus advance ethics.

For example, suppose we want to know whether capital juries make good judgments—a normative question that is, at the outset, open.[18] Next we get a bit of disturbing scientific information: Capital juries are sensitive to race. May we now say that capital juries, at least sometimes, make bad decisions? Not yet. For that we need an additional, nonscientific normative assumption, stating that the judgments of capital juries ought not be sensitive to race. However, if we're willing to make this assumption, we may now draw a new and substantive moral conclusion: Capital juries, at least sometimes, make bad decisions.

As this example illustrates, we can reach interesting normative conclusions by combining interesting scientific facts with uninteresting normative assumptions. However obvious this may seem, some mistakenly assume that empirically based normative arguments are empty or question-begging if they rely on nonempirical normative assumptions.[19] The above example suggests a more general principle: An empirically driven normative argument is non-question-begging if the normative assumptions it requires are less interesting (i.e., less controversial) than its normative conclusion. I am not claiming one can derive a moral "ought" from nothing but a scientific "is." Rather, my point is that moral psychology matters for ethics, that it is "normatively significant." Moral psychology matters, not because it can generate interesting normative conclusions all by itself, but because it can play an essential role in generating interesting normative conclusions.

A natural objection to this example is that the work done by the science, while not insignificant, is *normatively* insignificant. The science does not challenge anyone's values. Instead, it simply alerts us to an application of the values we already have.[20] With this objection in mind, let's consider a second example, the case of consensual adult incest. Ought we condemn all incestuous behavior? This is a difficult "ought" question, at least for some people, and any answer one gives will be controversial. Suppose we learn (as we likely have already) that the inclination to condemn incest of all kinds is based on an emotional response whose function is to avoid producing offspring with genetic diseases (Lieberman 2007). As before, we need to answer a second, easier "ought" question before reaching a new moral destination: Ought we rely on such emotional responses in cases in which there is no special concern about genetic diseases? For example, we might imagine a brother-sister pair, Joe and Jane, who were separated in early childhood and who later met and fell in love (see Weathers 2008). We might imagine that they become aware of their biological relation, but nonetheless choose to remain together, taking major precautions (e.g., vasectomy) to ensure that they are no more likely than typical couples to produce children with genetic diseases. With Joe and Jane in mind, we might make the following normative assumption: If our inclination to condemn Joe and Jane's behavior depends on an emotional response that makes their behavior seem wrong, and this emotional response evolved to prevent birth defects, and birth defects are not a special issue in their case, and we have no additional reason to condemn their behavior, then we ought not condemn their behavior.[21] Having made this assumption, and having learned something from science, we may now conclude that we ought not condemn all incestuous behavior—an interesting normative conclusion. This example—a classic *debunking* explanation—is notable because it genuinely challenges some people's moral values. Indeed, such arguments can change people's minds, if you give them enough time to think (Paxton et al. 2014).

We're now ready to make good on our tingles. Here, our initial, difficult "ought" question in this: Do people make good moral judgments when confronted with moral dilemmas? Next, science tells us that people's judgments are, at least sometimes, sensitive to things like mere personal force and mere spatial proximity. Next we face an easier "ought" question: Ought people's moral judgments be sensitive to such things? We all answer no, of course.

(Perhaps you're tempted to withhold your negation because personal force and spatial proximity may be reliable correlates of things that matter morally, such as the presence of harmful violence and binding social relationships. You should resist this temptation, bearing in mind the word "mere." The question is this: Were a friend to call you from a footbridge seeking moral advice, would you say, "Well, that depends . . . Will you be pushing or using a switch?" If questions such as this, including similar questions concerning mere spatial distance, are not on your list of relevant moral questions, then you, too, should say no.)

And thus we've earned an interesting normative conclusion: People, at least sometimes, do not make good moral judgments in response to moral dilemmas, for they are inappropriately sensitive to mere personal force and mere spatial distance. And thus we've shown that interesting scientific facts about moral psychology can, when combined with relatively uninteresting normative assumptions, lead us to relatively interesting normative conclusions. That's progress, powered by science.

Limited progress, however. We've seen how one can get a substantively new "ought" by combining an old "ought" with a new "is," but, still, one might hope for more. The above argument tells us that *something* is wrong with *some people*'s judgments, but it doesn't tell us *what* or *who* is wrong (see also Kumar and Campbell 2012). (Are we oversensitive to personal force in response to Footbridge, or undersensitive in response to Switch?) Thus, we could use a more general theory that tells us when our judgments are likely to go astray.

4.5. Moral Implications: The Indirect Route

According to the dual-process theory, some moral judgments are driven by automatic emotional responses, analogous to a camera's automatic settings. Other judgments are made in manual mode, based on the controlled, conscious application of moral principles. So, what's better, automatic settings or manual mode?

Some readers seem to think that I think that emotion-based moral judgments are categorically bad.[22] I do not hold this view (see Greene 2007, 66–72). Rather, I believe, as suggested by the camera analogy, that automatic settings and manual mode are respectively better and worse at different things. Automatic settings are efficient, but inflexible, while manual mode is flexible, but inefficient.

So when is it better to rely on automatic settings? Automatic settings can function well only when they have been shaped by *trial-and-error experience*. This may be the experience of our biological ancestors, as reflected in, for example, a genetic predisposition to fear snakes. Our automatic settings may be shaped by the experience of our cultural "ancestors," as reflected in a fear of guns, despite one's having never been harmed by one. Finally, our automatic settings are shaped by our own trial and error, as when one learns to fear hot stoves by touching them. These three mechanisms—genetic transmission, cultural transmission, and learning from personal experience—are the only mechanisms known to endow human automatic cognitive processes with the information they need to function well. For one of our automatic settings to function well, its design must be informed by *someone's* trial-and-error experience. Any other way, and it's a *cognitive miracle*.

(Note that being informed by trial-and-error experience is a necessary, but not sufficient, condition for good function. In addition to this, the selection mechanism that classifies trials as successful or unsuccessful must employ an evaluative standard that is consistent with the standard we employ in calling a disposition "good" or "bad." For example, some behaviors, such as aggression toward vulnerable out-groups, may be good from a biological/genetic point of view, but not from ours.)

Let us define *unfamiliar** problems as ones with which we have inadequate evolutionary, cultural, or personal experience. (Here, too, an asterisk indicates the specified technical meaning.) Driving a car is, at first, unfamiliar*. Our hunter-gatherer ancestors didn't drive, and cultural familiarity with driving is inadequate to produce skilled driving. And, of course, personal experience with driving is exactly what new drivers lack. Thus, learning to drive requires manual mode—effortful processing involving the conscious application of rules. If one could drive like an experienced driver from the outset, that would be a cognitive miracle.

Likewise, *it would be a cognitive miracle if we had reliably good moral instincts about unfamiliar* moral problems*. This suggests the following more general principle:

The No Cognitive Miracles Principle: When we are dealing with unfamiliar* moral problems, we ought to rely less on automatic settings (automatic emotional responses) and more on manual mode (conscious, controlled reasoning), lest we bank on cognitive miracles.

This principle is powerful because it, when combined with empirical knowledge of moral psychology, offers moral guidance while presupposing nothing about what is morally good or bad. A corollary of the NCMP is that we should expect certain pathological individuals—VMPFC patients? psychopaths? alexithymics?—to make better decisions than healthy people in some cases. (This is why such individuals are no embarrassment to the view I will defend in the next section.)[23]

Wielding the NCMP requires us to know (or make educated guesses about) two things: (1) which of our candidate judgments are preferentially supported by automatic settings versus manual mode, and (2) which of the moral problems we face are unfamiliar*. We'll consider each of these epistemic demands in turn.

Knowledge of which judgments are preferentially supported by automatic settings versus manual mode is precisely the kind of knowledge supplied by the research outlined in section 4.2 in support of the dual-process theory. And thus, with the No Cognitive Miracles Principle before us, we are finally positioned to appreciate the (indirect) normative significance of this research: If we believe that we ought to rely on automatic settings versus manual mode to different extents in different situations, and if cognitive science can tell us when we are relying on automatic settings versus manual mode, then cognitive science gives us normatively significant information—information that can nudge us, if not propel us, toward new and interesting normative conclusions.

It's worth pausing here to correct a common misunderstanding. Some are under the mistaken impression that *neuroscience* plays a special, essential role in my normative arguments (see Berker 2009). It doesn't. Neuroscience is simply one source of evidence concerning which judgments are preferentially supported by automatic settings versus manual mode. I've not claimed that one can derive moral "oughts" from scientific facts alone (see above); nor have I claimed that neuroscientific facts possess some special normative power. This view is a straw man.

Once again, to apply the No Cognitive Miracles Principle we must determine which of the problems we face are unfamiliar*. We can make educated guesses about unfamiliarity* in two ways. First, moral problems that arise from recent cultural developments, most notably the rise of modern technology and the intersection of disparate cultures, are especially likely to be unfamiliar*. (Think climate change, global terrorism, global poverty, bioethics, etc.)[24] As it happens, I strongly suspect that the Footbridge dilemma is unfamiliar*, a bizarre case in which an act of personal violence against an innocent person is the one and only way to promote a much greater good.[25]

Second, and perhaps more practically, we can use *disagreement* as a proxy for lack of familiarity*. If two parties have a practical moral disagreement—a disagreement about *what* to do, not about *why* to do it—it's probably because they have conflicting intuitions.[26] This means that, from a moral perspective, if not from a biological perspective, at least one party's automatic settings are going astray (assuming that both parties have adequate access to the relevant nonmoral facts).[27] Absent a reliable method for determining whose automatic settings are misfiring, both parties should distrust their intuitions. Thus, I propose that we distrust our automatic settings, and rely more heavily on manual mode, whenever we have practical moral disagreements that do not appear to be based on disagreements over nonmoral facts. (And, for that matter, I make the same recommendation for when we think that our disagreements *are* over nonmoral facts.)

I've said that we should not rely on our automatic settings when we're dealing with unfamiliar* problems. Two clarifications concerning the meaning of "rely": First, not relying on automatic settings doesn't mean assuming that the answers given by one's automatic settings are always wrong. This misguided policy is like that of a dieter who never eats because he's always hungry. Second, not relying on automatic settings doesn't mean discounting one's judgments when and only when one's automatic settings are actively engaged. Automatic settings can fail by being overactive (e.g., fearing a life-saving injection) or underactive (e.g., not fearing the subway's third rail). Relying on our automatic settings means allowing our judgments to follow their *ups and downs*.

On the one hand, the normative significance of dual-process moral psychology, by way of the NCMP, flies in the face of is/ought orthodoxy. On the other hand, our conclusion here shouldn't be too hard for most ethicists to embrace. The idea that we should apply manual mode thinking to complex, controversial moral problems sounds more like a want ad for ethicists than a sheriff's "Wanted" sign. Things get a bit stickier, however, when we combine the NCMP with what we're learning about the cognitive underpinnings of competing moral philosophies.

4.6. Tilting toward Consequentialism

We should distrust our automatic settings and rely more on manual mode when attempting to resolve practical moral disagreements. So far, so palatable. But where does this lead? I believe it favors consequentialist approaches to moral problem-solving, ones aimed solely at promoting good consequences, rather than deontological approaches aimed at figuring out who has which rights and duties, where these are regarded as constraints on the promotion of good consequences. More specifically, I believe that reliance on manual mode favors act consequentialism at the level of first principles and something resembling rule consequentialism in everyday practice (see Hare 1981). As private individuals, we should nearly always respect the conventional moral rules, but in establishing those rules (as voters and policymakers) we should aim simply for the best long-term consequences. (For present purposes I will leave aside questions concerning the metaethical status of these claims.)

Why consequentialism? Recall from section 4.2:

The Central Tension Principle: Characteristically deontological judgments are preferentially supported by automatic emotional responses, while characteristically consequentialist judgments are preferentially supported by conscious reasoning and allied processes of cognitive control.

Thus, shifting into manual mode means shifting toward consequentialism. Satisfied? Maybe not.

Why, you might ask, must manual mode thinking be consequentialist? Do not others—Kant, for example—engage in *moral reasoning*? It may seem that I've made a giant, unwarranted leap from empirical facts about the psychology behind ordinary people's "characteristically" deontological judgments to claims about the psychology behind sophisticated philosophical theories.

There's no denying that Kant et al. do plenty of work in manual mode. The critical question is: What are they doing in manual mode? I hypothesize that they are not, *for the most part*, actually engaged in moral reasoning.[28] By this I mean that they are not using reasoning to *figure out* what's right or wrong. Instead, their reasoning serves primarily to justify and organize their preexisting intuitive conclusions about what's right or wrong. In other words, what looks like moral rationalism is actually moral *rationalization* (cf. Haidt 2001).

I've called this the Secret Joke of Kant's Soul (2007), which is colorfully illustrated by Kant's views on masturbation. Kant, being an uptight eighteenth-century Prussian, is uncomfortable with masturbation, but he's not content simply to voice his distaste. He wants to *prove from first principles* that masturbation is immoral, and he's got a pretty clever idea about how to do it: masturbation is wrong because it involves *using oneself as a means*. We today find this bit or rationalization amusing because we no longer share Kant's sexual repression, but if I'm right, this passage is in fact representative of his general approach to ethics. Nietzsche agrees.

> *Kant's Joke*: Kant wanted to prove in a way that would dumbfound the common man that the common man was right: that was the secret joke of this soul. He wrote against the scholars in favor of the popular prejudice, but for scholars and not for popularity. (1974, 205–6)

If Nietzsche is right, this Kantian style of rationalizing goes well beyond the ethics of masturbation. A standard method—if not *the* standard method—for identifying the principles that define our rights and duties is rather like Kant's method in the above passage. One discerns, intuitively, the presence of rights and duties in particular cases, and then one searches for principles that might explain why those rights and duties are indeed present. I call this process *intuition chasing*, conforming general principles to specific judgments that (mostly) follow the ups and downs of intuition. The opposite of intuition chasing is *bullet biting*, conforming judgments to principles, despite the ups and downs of intuition.

A nice empirical illustration of intuition chasing and its pitfalls comes from an experiment by Eric Schwitzgebel and Fiery Cushman (2012). They presented both ordinary people and philosophers with cases like Footbridge (harm as means, with personal force) and cases like Switch (harm as side effect, without personal force). We'll call these *footbridgesque* and *switchy* cases, respectively. Because these sets of cases straddle the means / side effect distinction, one may appeal to the doctrine of double effect (DDE) to justify treating them differently.

This experiment leverages people's tendency to shift around their judgments depending on the *order* in which cases are presented. This order effect is explicitly predicted by the dual-process theory as follows: Suppose you get Footbridge first. Your automatic emotional response is no, and you go with it. Next comes Switch. Here the emotional response is minimal, leaving the decision to manual mode. Your manual mode thinking is naturally drawn toward the characteristically consequentialist response, but here it has a further problem. You just said that it's wrong to trade one life for five in the Footbridge case, and you're not confident that there is a morally relevant difference between the Switch and Footbridge cases. In an effort to be consistent, you judge that it's also wrong to hit the switch. That is, you give the same response to both cases, which is not the pattern of judgment encouraged (though not required) by the DDE.

What happens when Switch comes first? Here, once again, the emotional response is minimal, allowing manual mode to hold sway. Manual mode is drawn to the characteristically consequentialist response, and in this case there is no consistency-based reason to say otherwise. Thus, you endorse hitting the switch. Next comes Footbridge. The automatic setting kicks in, and the action feels terribly, horribly wrong. Manual mode recognizes the consequentialist rationale for pushing, along with the consistency-based rationale for endorsing pushing, but your automatic emotional response tells you that you simply cannot endorse such a horrific act. Thus, you say no to pushing. This response pattern—yes to Switch, no to Footbridge—*is* the one encouraged by the DDE.

To summarize, if you get Switch first, your pattern of judgment is more likely to conform to the DDE. This happens because it's a lot easier to say no to something that feels okay than to say yes to something that feels horribly wrong. In other words, saying no to Switch involves biting a bullet, but it's a *rubber* bullet—easy to bite because it's actually a manual mode consequentialist* judgment that is jettisoned. To say yes to Footbridge is to bite a *metal* bullet—much harder. The desire for consistency is sufficient to motivate biting a rubber bullet, but not a metal bullet—hence the order effect.

Results: Both ordinary people and professional ethicists exhibited the predicted order effect, and, remarkably, to the same extent. Later, Schwitzgebel and Cushman asked their participants whether they endorse (the critical bit of) the DDE. For the nonphilosophers, the ordering of the dilemmas had no effect on their endorsement of the DDE. However, the ethicists were about 50 percent more likely to endorse the DDE if they got the switchy cases first.

Let us return to the motivating problem at hand, comparing lay moral psychology to professional moral psychology: Deontological philosophers, for understandable reasons, don't want to be lumped in with lay moralists, who are undoubtedly much less thoughtful. Schwitzgebel and Cushman's results help explain what's right about this complaint, while also speaking to its limitations. Their experiment shows that philosophers *are* different from lay moralists and that they do indeed think harder. Both groups' judgments were affected by their intuitions, and both groups made a manual mode effort to be consistent. However, only professional philosophers felt compelled to adjust their theoretical commitments to make them consistent with the judgments they'd made. In other words, the folk are happy to let "popular prejudice" be "popular prejudice," but philosophers are motivated to translate that popular prejudice into principle. This is indeed a manual mode activity, but it's not one that is likely to free philosophers from the ups and downs of their automatic settings. On the contrary, it codifies those ups and downs.

I suspect that many readers will be tempted to draw a different lesson from this experiment, which is simply that some philosophers ought to have their licenses revoked. Suppose that's correct. Where *exactly* did our errant colleagues go wrong? The most popular answer, I think, will be this: The philosophers who said no to the switchy cases following their no to the footbridgesque cases messed up. Instead of being "consistent" by saying no to both, they should have recognized that these cases differ in ways that *justify* treating them differently. In other words, they were too quick to bite a bullet, albeit a rubber one (but see Thomson 2008).

Let's see where this leads. What critical difference did the errant ethicists miss? By design, the switchy and footbridgesque cases differ in two ways, in the presence of personal force and in the causation of harm as a means versus a side effect. We've agreed that personal force is morally irrelevant, which leaves the means / side effect factor, or perhaps a more subtle variant thereof. The accusation, then, is that the errant philosophers failed to remember the DDE. (Revoke their licenses!) But why *should* they have invoked the DDE? Wherein lies its justificatory power? It's been on the books for a long time, which gives it a dusty air of authority. But how did it get on the books? It seems that the DDE was codified because it was observed that certain intuitive patterns in moral judgment could be *summarized* by a set of principles now known as the DDE. We may infer this (inductively, not deductively) from the finding that lay moralists the world over make judgments consistent with the DDE while having no clue that they are doing so.[29] This suggests, in other words, that the doctrine doesn't justify the judgments. Instead, *the judgments justify the doctrine* (Cushman and Greene 2011; see also Cushman et al. 2012). This evidence suggests that the justification for the DDE ultimately comes from nothing beyond the automatic settings that produce the pattern of judgment that it summarizes.[30] (And if I'm right, the DDE is actually just a byproduct of a morally irrelevant cognitive limitation; Greene 2013, 211–40.) Indeed, the DDE's lack of independent authority is evident in the willingness of philosophers to abandon it when it fails to get the intuitively right answers. The DDE famously choked on the Loop case, for example, prompting a hunt for a better principle (Thomson 1985). But what is "better?" "Better" just means "better able to summarize our intuitive judgments." Thus, to chide our colleagues for failing to invoke the DDE (or one of its more sophisticated successors) is simply to chide them for not abiding by the dictates of their—our—mysterious automatic settings.

I've said that characteristically deontological judgments are used to justify deontological principles, rather than the other way around, but that's a bit too strong. What intuition chasing aims for is *reflective equilibrium*, harmony between intuition and principle (Rawls 1971). This means that some intuitive judgments will be jettisoned to achieve a better fit with principle. In other words, even intuition chasers do some bullet biting. While this is undoubtedly true, I doubt it's enough to save intuition chasing from the unreliability of intuition. Suppose that a scientist unwittingly crafts a theory based on unreliable data. In so doing, he ignores some outliers, data points that don't fit with his theory. He's then informed that the data are unreliable. "Indeed!" he says. "Just as I suspected!" The reflective equilibrator's analogous hope is that the judgments he's jettisoned through the equilibration process, the outliers, are the bad ones. I think that's too optimistic. We may think that we're biting the right bullets, when in fact we're just biting the *soft* bullets, the ones that are least emotionally offensive.

Let us consider this pitfall in its proper trolleyological context. What should a deontologically minded trolleyologist make of the personal force effect and the doubts it raises about our intuitions? I'll take this as an opportunity to respond to some remarks by Frances Kamm (2009). Here is Kamm's response to the first iteration of the "personalness" hypothesis from my 2001 research article:

> However, objections have been raised to this type of "personal versus impersonal factors" explanations of intuitions . . . the Lazy Susan Case is a counterexample to this explanation. In this case, five people are on one side of a lazy Susan turntable and the only way to save them from a trolley headed at them is to manually push the lazy Susan. However, if we do this, we will ram the lazy Susan into a bystander. In this case, a new threat (the lazy Susan) and something up close and personal is done to the bystander (pushing a lazy Susan into him). . . . Intuitively, even a nonconsequentialist might agree it is permissible to act in such cases. Cases like the Lazy Susan Case led me to say that "nonconsequentialists are not squeamish, they are downstreamish," in the sense that they are willing to "up close" personally harm someone when (very roughly) the person's being killed is causally downstream from the good of the five being saved.

Kamm's response highlights the importance of doing the empirical work, as it's all but impossible to know our minds from the armchair. As it happens, Kamm's intuition about the Lazy Susan case and others like it is widely shared.[31] But it's also the case that people—Kamm included, perhaps—are *both* "squeamish" and "downstreamish." As noted in section 4.3, such factors *interact*. In the Lazy Susan case and others like it, the effect of "squeamishness" disappears because the person is killed as a downstream side effect. But when the harmful event is upstream, as in the footbridge variations, the effect of personal force (a kind of "squeamishness") emerges. Once again, most people say yes to Footbridge Switch, but no to Footbridge Pole and Footbridge. Kamm anticipates this contrast:

> What if it were possible to press a switch that opens a trapdoor under the man on the bridge . . .? Regardless of what fMRIs of the general population indicate, moral philosophers who object to pushing the man over the bridge would respond in the same way to this "impersonal" way of getting the man off the bridge.

Indeed, no self-respecting philosopher would explicitly give different answers to these two cases. But are we then licensed to ignore the experimental research, confident that our philosophical reflections will jettison any bad intuitions and corresponding judgments? Not so fast. We dare not give different answers to these two cases, but which single answer should we give? Kamm's answer is clear: We should say that it's wrong to act in both cases. But why? The psychological explanation is now familiar: We say no to both cases because saying yes to Footbridge (metal bullet) feels worse than saying "no" to remote Footbridge (rubber bullet). Thus, what appears to be a case of experts making better judgments than the folk (avoiding the pitfalls of untutored intuition through careful reflection) may in fact be a case of experts outfolking the folk (making the not-so-hard choices necessary to protect our strongest untutored intuitions from inconsistency). To put the point another way, unless you're prepared to say yes to the Footbridge case, your automatic settings are still running the show, and any manual adjustments that you're willing to make are at their behest.

But, so what if our emotions are leading us around? Perhaps they're leading us to the right places (with a few bumps along the way). Kamm's hope is that some other distinction, a more sophisticated variation on the DDE perhaps, will save the day. But this just puts us back where we were in condemning the "errant" philosophers in Schwitzgebel and Cushman's experiment. The DDE and its more subtle successors have no independent justification. The most that can be said for them is that they appeal to factors that are not obviously morally irrelevant (unlike personal force). As noted above, I suspect that the means/side effect distinction will seem irrelevant once we understand why we're sensitive to it. We can wait and see if I'm right, but we can't be indifferent to the outcome of this research, or assume its conclusion.

The upshot of the foregoing discussion is this: Ethicists need to worry about their intuitions, and not just the ones that they're willing to dump in order to save the ones they really want to keep. We can't assume that our manual mode thinking will scrub away the blemishes of moral intuition if we're relying on our moral intuitions to tell us where to scrub.

The next step is to agree, but to insist that this is a problem for everyone, consequentialists and deontologists alike. In the end, don't we all just have our intuitions? No. Not in the same way. Act consequentialism is not intuition chasing. An act consequentialist's judgment may be *consistent* with the dictates of automatic settings, and in that sense there are "consequentialist intuitions," but an act consequentialist's judgment never *depends* on them. An act consequentialist can know what she thinks about a case without knowing anything other than the answer to this question: Which choice produces better consequences? Act consequentialism is WYSIWYG: What You See Is What You Get. It doesn't rely on mysterious automatic settings, and thus its soul has no secrets.

But doesn't act consequentialism ultimately depend on some kind of intuition? After all, where do act consequentialists get their ideas about which consequences are worth promoting or preventing? Here Sidgwick is helpful in distinguishing among what he calls "perceptual," "dogmatic," and "philosophical" intuitions (see Brink 2014; Sidgwick 1907, 97–102). If Sidgwick is correct, consequentialism (and utilitarianism, more specifically) does ultimately depend on "intuition," that is, on an affectively based evaluative premise. But intuition enters consequentialist theory at a very high level ("philosophical" intuition), and not as a reaction to particular actions ("perceptual" intuition) or action types ("dogmatic" intuition). This is consistent with the psychological evidence, for example, the fact that VMPFC patients, who cannot react emotionally to particular actions, tend to make characteristically consequentialist judgments. That act consequentialism is based on a "philosophical" intuition, rather than on "perceptual" or "dogmatic" ones, doesn't imply that it's correct, but it does shield it from the objection that it's is too tightly yoked to the ups and downs of unreliable automatic settings.

Let's suppose, then, that we've forsaken all intuition chasing. Why favor act consequentialism? Aren't there better alternatives? First, let's note that act consequentialism is a pretty good place to start. The idea that we should try to make things overall better makes moral sense to everyone. The objection to act consequentialism is not that it's based on a generally bad idea, but that it's too imperialistic, that it fails to leave room for other legitimate values, both moral and self-interested. Like other act consequentialists, I believe that act consequentialism, properly understood, does surprisingly well in the real world, and that its failures "in principle" are really failures to comport with intuitions that are not worth chasing. But I will not offer a positive defense of act consequentialism here (see Greene 2013). For now, my point is simply that act consequentialism should get points for not chasing intuitions and that some of its competitors (including some forms of consequentialism) should lose points for doing so. Note that the present argument also casts doubt on theories that, rather than chasing intuitions with codifying principles, simply allow our intuitions roam free. Likewise, it casts doubt on theories that purport to derive from first principles, but that are in fact intuition chasing—that is, theories that are actually attempts to get from first principles *to the intuitively right answers* rather than attempts to get from first principles to wherever those principles happen to lead. (And, if you're like me, you suspect that this covers most, if not all, of act consequentialism's competition.)

4.7. Conclusion

A great philosopher who despised the likes of me once wrote, "It is not profitable for us at present to do moral philosophy; that should be laid aside at any rate until we have an adequate philosophy of psychology, in which we are conspicuously lacking" (Anscombe 1958, 1). I think Professor Anscombe went too far. I don't regret the last half-century of ethics. Nor do I share her vision for our enterprise. But she did have a point. There's a lot going on beneath the hood of morality, and we ignore the details at our peril.

Our brains, like all complex functional systems, face a trade-off between efficiency and flexibility. To promote efficiency, our brains have point-and-shoot automatic settings in the form of intuitive emotional responses. These are marvelous, but nonetheless limited in what they can do. In particular, we should not expect them to perform well in the face of peculiarly modern problems, ones with which we have inadequate genetic, cultural, and individual experience. Many of the most important moral problems we face may be of this kind. For example, it's only very recently that ordinary people have routinely had the opportunity to save the lives of distant strangers by making modest material sacrifices. Our automatic settings tell us that our exercise of this privilege is generally morally optional. Should we trust them? (Singer 2009, 2005).

Philosophy happens in manual mode, and this gives us a choice about what to do with our reasoning capabilities. We can use them, as William James said, to "rearrange our prejudices." Alternatively, we can use our capacity for moral and scientific reasoning to transcend our prejudices. Today's ethicists undoubtedly do both, but we could do more of the latter and less of the former.

In the last half-century, ethics has gone in two different directions. Some ethicists have gotten very sophisticated about moral theory, devising principles that aspire to comport with both consequentialist thinking and incompatible moral intuitions. Others have given up on action-guiding moral theory altogether, and with it the hope of offering the world specific answers to specific moral questions. I don't think we should abandon this ambition. But if I'm right, the way forward is not through the construction of increasingly sophisticated moral theories. Instead, we must get sophisticated about moral *data*. We need to understand the structure, origins, and limitations of our intuitive moral thinking, the better to know when our moral instincts are on target, and when they are giving us the right answers to the wrong questions (see also Stich 2006).

Is this a new approach to ethics, or just a natural extension of current practice? It's a bit of both. On the one hand, this approach may be seen as nothing more than a further widening of our reflective equilibrium. Along with our "considered judgments" and organizing principles, we must add to the mix a scientific understanding of the psychological and biological processes that have produced them. (Call this *double-wide* reflective equilibrium.)[32] I regard this as a natural extension of current practice, and one consistent with philosophy's historical commitment to active empiricism.

Nevertheless, from a professional perspective, what I am proposing may sound rather radical. Today, ethicists are not expected to know anything in particular about how the mind actually works, and are trained to dismiss anyone who laments this practice as confused about the relationship between "is" and "ought." I suggest that, in the future, we ethicists will require a detailed knowledge of moral psychology, and the more actively we participate in the generation of such knowledge, the better off we'll be. To do moral philosophy well we must understand the strengths and limitations of the tools we bring to our job. Why would anyone think otherwise?

Acknowledgments

Many thanks to John Mikhail, Henry Richardson, and other participants in the symposium "Experiment and Intuition in Ethics" held at Georgetown University, April 2011. Thanks to James Weinstein and other participants at the "Origins of Morality" conference, Arizona State University, November, 2010. Thanks to Tommaso Bruni, John Doris, Steven Frankland, Geoff Holtzman, Dylan Murray, and Joe Paxton for comments on this manuscript.

Notes

1. This chapter is reprinted from Joshua D. Greene, "Beyond Point-and-Shoot Morality: Why Cognitive (Neuro)Science Matters for Ethics." *Ethics* 124, no. 4: 695–726. © 2014 by The University of Chicago Press.

2. One might ask, what, exactly, is "dual" in dual-process theories? Is it types of processing? Types of cognitive systems? Different brain regions? Different kinds of outputs? The answer is "all of the above," but the core difference, in my view, concerns the type of processing. As Turing taught us, dual-process psychology can be implemented or simulated on a computer using a single processing system occupying a single physical location and using one set of computational principles (at low levels, at least). But, as it happens, that's not how it generally works in the brain. Instead, distinct neural systems typically engage in distinct types of processing in distinct locations. Likewise, cognitive outputs typically reflect the kinds of processing that produced them. As a result, a brain injury can alter behavior because it causes damage to a particular location, which houses a particular cognitive system, which processes information in a particular way, and which therefore tends to push behavior in a particular direction. Of course, not all dual-process dissociations are so clean, but sometimes they are. See Gazzaniga et al. 2008.

3. Several authors disregard the "characteristically" qualifier (Greene 2007), insisting that the judgments I call "consequentialist" must (*a*) reflect a full commitment to consequentialism and (*b*) be inconsistent with alternative normative theories (Kahane and Shackel 2010; Kamm 2009).

4. Here I'm referring to the Central Tension Principle and the more general idea that different moral philosophies may be supported to different extents by the outputs of different cognitive systems.

5. There has been much confusion about what this experiment shows and what it was intended to show. It was designed to test the dual-process theory, though not the Central Tension Principle specifically. Some critics have conflated the dual-process theory with the theory implicit in the 2001 personal/impersonal distinction; see Greene 2009. Others have assumed that the 2001 experiment was intended to test the specific version of the personal/impersonal distinction that it used, and then faulted it for failing to do so adequately; see Kamm 2009; Berker 2009; and also Mikhail 2011. The testing and refining of the personal/impersonal distinction was accomplished by later experiments, discussed in section 4.3 (Greene et al. 2009).

The looseness of the personal/impersonal comparison in the 2001 experiment did not prevent it from supporting the dual-process theory, but it did impose limitations. Subsequent studies have overcome these limitations by (*a*) focusing primarily or exclusively on "personal" dilemmas similar to Footbridge, and (*b*) examining factors that cause or correlate with people's *judgments*, rather than effects of different stimuli (personal vs. impersonal). These studies typically use one or more "impersonal" dilemmas, but only to establish the specificity of the main result, generated using one or more "personal" dilemmas.

Some have wondered why the 2001 experiment asked subjects to classify actions as "appropriate" or "inappropriate." This was done to keep the response prompt constant across moral and nonmoral trials. Subjects were explicitly instructed to judge based on moral considerations where applicable.

6. Koenigs et al. 2007. Guy Kahane and Nicholas Shackel (2008, author reply, E5–E6) criticized the Koenigs et al. study for employing dilemmas in which the utilitarian judgment is not, according to Kahane and Shackel and other philosophers surveyed, truly (i.e., uniquely) utilitarian. Koenigs et al. replied by analyzing the data from only those dilemmas approved by Kahane and Shackel and produced the same results.

7. Conway and Gawronski 2013. This very clever study used the "process dissociation" method to separate utilitarian* and deontological* components. This required a modified set of dilemmas.

8. See Carlsmith et al. 2002; see further evidence and discussion in Greene 2007, 2013.

9. Unfortunately, some philosophers have been given a different impression by Berker's discussion (2009) of the evidence supporting the dual-process theory, primarily in sections 2 and 3 of his article. I have documented Berker's various errors, misleading statements, and misleading omissions in a set of notes that I prepared for a 2010 meeting. These notes are available on my web page (https://static1.squarespace.com/static/54763f79e4b0c4e55ffb000c/t/54cb945ae4b001aedee69e81/1422627930781/notes-on-berker.pdf) or by request. Berker's errors include multiple false statements about statistical analyses and experimental confounds. More generally, he presents a misleading picture of the evidence supporting the dual-process theory by ignoring and/or erroneously dismissing most of the then-available evidence. For more details concerning these and other problems with Berker's article, readers are encouraged to consult the aforementioned online document.

10. It's worth noting that the experiments described above did not use philosophers as subjects, and they have focused on responses to specific cases rather than abstract principles. For this reason, one might wonder whether these results have any bearing on the psychology behind familiar philosophical theories. As I will explain in section 4.4, I believe that the psychology of philosophers is, in some important ways, different from that of ordinary moralists, but that

studies of ordinary people's judgments in response to specific cases can also illuminate the psychology behind familiar philosophical theories.

11. They found no effect of "counterintuitive" deontological* judgment in the DLPFC, the signature of controlled cognition, previously observed in association with consequentialist* judgment (Greene et al. 2004; Cushman et al., n.d.). For the "white lie"–like dilemmas, the deontological* judgments took slightly longer than the consequentialist* judgments and were rated as more difficult, consistent with Kahane et al.'s conclusions (Greene et al. 2004). However, these "counterintuitive" deontological* judgments were actually *faster* than the intuitive deontological* judgments in the Footbridge-like cases and were rated as no more difficult than them. This is not consistent with their theory.

12. Other factors contribute to the switch-footbridge effect but these two factors account for much, if not most, of it.

13. These cases borrow from Unger 1996.

14. Is this the *only* difference? Strictly speaking, no. For example, in *far*, but not in *near*, you get your information over the Internet. What matters for present purposes is whether there are other differences that are plausibly regarded as morally relevant. More on this shortly.

15. Further details are withheld so as not to preempt the scientific publication of these results.

16. For further normative tingles, see Paharia et al. 2009. See also Nichols and Knobe 2007.

17. Such assumptions are, ideally, shared by both philosophers and nonphilosophers, but this may vary from case to case.

18. I am here and elsewhere in this chapter remaining metaethically agnostic and therefore leaving it open as to what counts as a "good" judgment. "Good" judgments may be true, or may simply be good according to some other set of evaluative criteria.

19. For example, Berker (2009, 326) claims that nonempirical normative assumptions "do all the work" in the above arguments, rendering the science "normatively insignificant." That is not true. Normative assumptions do some work, but empirical evidence does essential work as well.

20. Thanks to Thomas M. Scanlon on this point.

21. For example, we do not believe that their behavior will damage them or others psychologically, promote immoral behavior more generally, and so on. One might object that this "no additional reason" clause is what's doing "all the work" in this argument. I disagree. This clause simply closes off alternative escape routes, forcing a confrontation between the emotional response that is driving the judgment and the empirically based debunking argument that challenges it.

22. See Kamm 2009; and Woodward and Allman 2007. Woodward and Allman, by pressing me on this point, have helped me articulate my view more clearly.

23. See Bartels and Pizarro 2011. These authors argue against utilitarianism as a normative theory on the grounds that antisocial personality traits predict utilitarian responses to standard dilemmas. However, it is unlikely that such individuals are especially concerned with maximizing happiness. Rather, it is more likely that they are especially unconcerned with causing harm to innocent people. In other words, they are really "undeontological" rather than utilitarian. More recent research using "process dissociation" supports this interpretation by dissociating these two components. See Conway and Gawronski 2013.

24. Such problems undoubtedly share features with familiar* problems, but this need not prevent us from identifying some problems as essentially unfamiliar*.

25. I suspect that the Switch case is an unfamiliarity* double negative, with unfamiliar* impersonal violence unfamiliarly* promoting the greater good.

26. Haidt 2001. Haidt argues that moral controversies are primarily driven by conflicting moral intuitions.

27. Doris and Plakias 2007. These authors argue many moral disagreements are not simply disagreements over nonmoral facts.

28. See below on biting "rubber bullets," which involves genuine reasoning. Kant, however, bites at least one metal bullet (see section 4.2).

29. Hauser et al. 2007. The alternative explanation—far less likely, in my opinion—is that ordinary people, including young children, make judgments consistent with the DDE due to unacknowledged philosophical influences (Pellizzoni et al. 2010).

30. One might note that it's been in use for a long time (see Mikhail 2014)—true, but so have a lot of other moral and legal practices that few readers would defend.

31. Eighty percent approval (unpublished data). See also the Obstacle Collide case in Greene et al. 2009.

32. The problem with reflective equilibrating is its susceptibility to the influence of inflexible automatic settings. If these ill effects can be neutralized with scientific self-knowledge, then reflective equilibrating is fine.

References

Amit, Elinor, and Joshua D. Greene. 2012. "You See, the Ends Don't Justify the Means: Visual Imagery and Moral Judgment." *Psychological Science* 23: 861–868.

Anscombe, G. E. M. 1958. "Modern Moral Philosophy." *Philosophy* 33: 1–19.

Sinnott-Armstrong, Walter, ed. 2007. *Moral Psychology.* 3 vols. Cambridge, MA: MIT Press.

Bargh John A., and Tanya L. Chartrand. 1999. "The Unbearable Automaticity of Being." *American Psychologist* 54: 462–479.

Bartels, Daniel M. 2008. "Principled Moral Sentiment and the Flexibility of Moral Judgment and Decision Making." *Cognition* 108: 381–417.

Bartels, Daniel M., and David A. Pizarro. 2011. "The Mismeasure of Morals: Antisocial Personality Traits Predict Utilitarian Responses to Moral Dilemmas." *Cognition* 121: 154–161.

Berker, Selim. 2009. "The Normative Insignificance of Neuroscience." *Philosophy and Public Affairs* 37: 293–329.

Brink, David O. 2014. "Principles and Intuitions in Ethics: Historical and Contemporary Perspectives." *Ethics* 124: 665–694.

Carlsmith, Kevin M., John M. Darley, and Paul Robinson II. 2002. "Why Do We Punish? Deterrence and Just Deserts as Motives for Punishment." *Journal of Personality and Social Psychology* 83: 284–299.

Ciaramelli, Elisa, Michela Muccioli, Elisabetta Làdavas, and Giuseppe di Pellegrino. 2007. "Selective Deficit in Personal Moral Judgment Following Damage to Ventromedial Prefrontal Cortex." *Social, Cognitive, and Affective Neuroscience* 2: 84–92.

Conway, Paul, and Bertram Gawronski. 2013. "Deontological and Utilitarian Inclinations in Moral Decision Making: A Process Dissociation Approach." *Journal of Personality and Social Psychology* 104: 216–235.

Crockett, Molly J. 2010. "Serotonin Selectively Influences Moral Judgment and Behavior through Effects on Harm Aversion." *Proceedings of the National Academy of Sciences USA* 107: 17433–17438.

Cunningham, William A., Marcia K. Johnson, Carol L. Raye, J. Chris Gatenby, John C. Gore, and Mahzarin R. Banaji. 2004. "Separable Neural Components in the Processing of Black and White Faces." *Psychological Science* 15: 806–813.

Cushman, Fiery A., Kurt Gray, Allison Gaffey, and Wendy Berry Mendes. 2012. "Simulating Murder: The Aversion to Harmful Action." *Emotion* 12: 2–7.

Cushman, Fiery A., and Joshua D. Greene. 2012. "Finding Faults: How Moral Dilemmas Illuminate Cognitive Structure." *Social Neuroscience* 7: 269–279.

Cushman, Fiery A., and Joshua D. Greene. 2011. "The Philosopher in the Theater." In *The Social Psychology of Morality*, edited by Mario Mikulincer and Philip R. Shaver, 33–50. Washington, DC: APA Press.

Cushman, Fiery A., Dylan Murray, Shauna Gordon-McKeon, Sophie Wharton, and Joshua D. Greene. 2012. "Judgment before Principle: Engagement of the Frontoparietal Control Network in Condemning Harms of Omission." *Social, Cognitive, and Affective Neuroscience* 7: 888–895.

Cushman, Fiery A., Sophie R. Wharton, and Joshua D. Greene. N.d. "Distinct Neural Processes Underlying Decisions to Help versus Decisions to Avoid Doing Harm." Manuscript in preparation.

Cushman, Fiery A., Liane Young, and Marc Hauser. 2006. "The Role of Conscious Reasoning and Intuition in Moral Judgment: Testing Three Principles of Harm." *Psychological Science* 17: 1082–1089.

Doris, John M., ed. 2010. *The Moral Psychology Handbook*. Oxford: Oxford University Press.

Doris, John M., and Alexandra Plakias. 2007. "How to Argue about Disagreement: Evaluative Diversity and Moral Realism." In *Moral Psychology*, vol. 2: *The Cognitive Science of Morality*, edited by Walter Sinnott-Armstrong, 303–331. Cambridge, MA: MIT Press.

Foot, Phillipa. 1967. "The Problem of Abortion and the Doctrine of Double Effect." *Oxford Review* 5: 5–15.

Gazzaniga, Michael, Richard B. Ivry, and George R. Mangun. 2008. *Cognitive Neuroscience: The Biology of the Mind*. 3rd ed. New York: Norton.

Glenn, Andrea L., Adrian Raine, and R. A. Schug. 2009. "The Neural Correlates of Moral Decision-Making in Psychopathy." *Journal of Molecular Psychiatry* 14: 5–6.

Glenn, Andrea L., Adrian Raine, R. A. Schug, and Marc D. Hauser. 2009. "Increased DLPFC Activity during Moral Decision-Making in Psychopathy." *Journal of Molecular Psychiatry* 14: 909–911.

Greene, Joshua D. 2007. "The Secret Joke of Kant's Soul." In *Moral Psychology*, vol. 3: *The Neuroscience of Morality: Emotion, Disease, and Development*, edited by Walter Sinnott-Armstrong, 35–79. Cambridge, MA: MIT Press.

Greene, Joshua D. 2009. "Dual-Process Morality and the Personal/Impersonal Distinction: A Reply to Mcguire, Langdon, Coltheart, and Mackenzie." *Journal of Experimental Social Psychology* 45: 581–584.

Greene, Joshua D. 2013. Moral Tribes: Emotion, Reason, and the Gap between Us and Them. New York: Penguin.

Greene, Joshua D., Fiery A. Cushman, Lisa E. Stewart, Kelly Lowenberg, Leigh E. Nystrom, and Jonathan D. Cohen. 2009. "Pushing Moral Buttons: The Interaction between Personal Force and Intention in Moral Judgment." *Cognition* 111: 364–371.

Greene, Joshua D., Sylvia A. Morelli, Kelly Lowenberg, Leigh E. Nystrom, and Jonathan D. Cohen. 2008. "Cognitive Load Selectively Interferes with Utilitarian Moral Judgment." *Cognition* 107: 1144–1154.

Greene, Joshua D., Leigh E. Nystrom, Andrew D. Engell, John M. Darley, and Jonathan D. Cohen. 2004. "The Neural Bases of Cognitive Conflict and Control in Moral Judgment." *Neuron* 44: 389–400.

Greene, Joshua D., R. Brian Sommerville, Leigh E. Nystrom, John M. Darley, and Jonathan D. Cohen. 2001. "An fMRI Investigation of Emotional Engagement in Moral Judgment." *Science* 293: 2105–2108.

Haidt, Jonathan. 2001. "The Emotional Dog and Its Rational Tail: A Social Intuitionist Approach to Moral Judgment." *Psychological Review* 108: 814–834.

Haidt, Jonathan, Silvia Helena Koller, and Maria G. Dias. 1993. "Affect, Culture, and Morality, or Is It Wrong to Eat Your Dog?" *Journal of Personality and Social Psychology* 65: 613–628.

Hare, Richard. 1981. *Moral Thinking: Its Levels, Method, and Point* (Oxford: Oxford University Press.

Hauser, Marc, Fiery Cushman, Liane Young, R. Kang-Xing Jin, and John Mikhail. 2007. "A Dissociation between Moral Judgments and Justifications." *Mind and Language* 22: 1–21.

Kahane, Guy, and Nicholas Shackel. 2008. "Do Abnormal Responses Show Utilitarian Bias?" *Nature* 452: E5.

Kahane, Guy, and Nicholas Shackel. 2010. "Methodological Issues in the Neuroscience of Moral Judgment." *Mind and Language* 25: 561–582.

Kahane, Guy, Katja Wiech, Nicholas Shackel, Miguel Farias, Julian Savulescu, and Irene Tracey. 2012. "The Neural Basis of Intuitive and Counterintuitive Moral Judgment." *Social, Cognitive and Affective Neuroscience* 7: 393–402.

Kahneman, Daniel. 2003. "A Perspective on Judgment and Choice: Mapping Bounded Rationality." *American Psychologist* 58: 697–720.

Kamm, Frances M. 2009. "Neuroscience and Moral Reasoning: A Note on Recent Research." *Philosophy and Public Affairs* 37: 330–345.

Koenigs, Michael, Michael Kruepke, Joshua Zeier, and Joseph P. Newman. 2012. "Utilitarian Moral Judgment in Psychopathy." *Social, Cognitive, and Affective Neuroscience* 7: 708–714.

Koenigs, Michael, Liane Young, Ralph Adolphs, Daniel Tranel, Fiery A. Cushman, Marc D. Hauser, and Antonio Damasio. 2007. "Damage to the Prefrontal Cortex Increases Utilitarian Moral Judgements." *Nature* 446: 908–911.

Kogut, Tehila, and Ilana Ritov. 2005. "The Singularity Effect of Identified Victims in Separate and Joint Evaluations." *Organizational Behavior and Human Decision Processes* 97: 106–116.

Koven, Nancy S., Luke Clark, Marc D. Hauser, and Trevor W. Robbins. 2011. "Specificity of Meta-emotion Effects on Moral Decision-Making." *Emotion* 11: 1255–1261.

Kumar, Victor, and Richmond Campbell. 2012. "On the Normative Significance of Experimental Moral Psychology." *Philosophical Psychology* 25: 311–330.

Lieberman, Debra, John Tooby, and Leda Cosmides. 2007. "The Architecture of Human Kin-Detection." *Nature* 445: 727–731.

McClure, Samuel M., David I. Laibson, George Loewenstein, and Jonathan D. Cohen. 2004. "Separate Neural Systems Value Immediate and Delayed Monetary Rewards." *Science* 306: 503–507.

Mendez, Mario F., Eric Anderson, and Jill S. Shapira. 2005. "An Investigation of Moral Judgment in Frontotemporal Dementia." *Cognitive and Behavioral Neurology* 18: 193–197.

Mikhail, John. 2000. "Rawls' Linguistic Analogy: A Study of the 'Generative Grammar' Model of Moral Theory Described by John Rawls in *A Theory of Justice*." PhD diss., Cornell University.

Mikhail, John. 2011. "Emotion, Neuroscience, and Law: A Comment on Darwin and Greene." *Emotion Review* 3: 293–295.

Mikhail, John. 2014. "Any Animal Whatever? Harmful Battery and Its Elements as Building Blocks of Moral Cognition." *Ethics* 124: 750–786.

Miller, Earl K., and Jonathan D. Cohen. 2001. "An Integrative Theory of Prefrontal Cortex Function." *Annual Review of Neuroscience* 24: 167–202.

Moore, Adam M., Brian A. Clark, and Michael J. Cane. 2008. "Who Shalt Not Kill? Individual Differences in Working Memory Capacity, Executive Control, and Moral Judgment." *Psychological Science* 19: 549–557.

Moretto, Giovanna, Elisabetta Làdavas, Flavia Mattioli, and Giuseppe di Pellegrino. 2010. "A Psychophysiological Investigation of Moral Judgment after Ventromedial Prefrontal Damage." *Journal of Cognitive Neuroscience* 22: 1888–1899.

Musen, Jay D. 2010. "The Moral Psychology of Obligations to Help Those in Need." Honors thesis, Department of Psychology, Harvard University.

Musen, Jay D., and Joshua Greene. N.d. "Mere Spatial Distance Weakens Perceived Moral Obligations to Help Those in Desperate Need." Manuscript in preparation.

Nietzsche, Friedrich. [1882] 1974. *The Gay Science*. Translated by Kaufmann. New York: Random House.

Nichols, Shaun, and Joshua Knobe. 2007. "Moral Responsibility and Determinism: The Cognitive Science of Folk Intuitions." *Noûs* 41: 663–685.

Ochsner, Kevin N., Silvia A. Bunge, James J. Gross, and John D. E. Gabrieli. 2002. "Rethinking Feelings: An fMRI Study of the Cognitive Regulation of Emotion." *Journal of Cognitive Neuroscience* 14: 1215–1229.

Paharia, Neeru, Karim S. Kassam, Joshua D. Greene, and Max H. Bazerman. 2009. "Dirty Work, Clean Hands: The Moral Psychology of Indirect Agency." *Organizational Behavior and Human Decision Processes* 109: 134–141.

Parfit, Derek. 2011. *On What Matters*. New York: Oxford University Press.

Paxton, Joseph M., Leo Ungar, and Joshua D. Greene. 2012. "Reflection and Reasoning in Moral Judgment." *Cognitive Science* 36: 163–177.

Paxton, Joseph M., Tommaso Bruni, and Joshua D. Greene. 2014. "Are 'Counter-intuitive' Deontological Judgments Really Counter-intuitive? An Empirical Reply to Kahane et al." *Social, Cognitive, and Affective Neuroscience* 9, no. 9: 1368–1371.

Pellizzoni, Sandra, Michael Siegal, and Luca Surian. 2010. "The Contact Principle and Utilitarian Moral Judgments in Young Children." *Developmental Science* 13: 265–270.

Ransohoff, Katherine J. 2011. "Patients on the Trolley Track: The Moral Cognition of Medical Practitioners and Public Health Professionals." Honors thesis, Department of Psychology, Harvard University.

Ransohoff, Katherine J., Daniel Wikler, and Joshua D. Greene. N.d. "Patients on the Trolley Track: The Moral Cognition of Medical Practitioners and Public Health Professionals." Manuscript in preparation.

Rawls, John. 1971. *A Theory of Justice.* Cambridge, MA: Harvard University Press.

Royzman, Edward B., and Jonathan Baron. 2002. "The Preference for Indirect Harm." *Social Justice Research* 15: 165–184.

Sargent, Michael J. 2004. "Less Thought, More Punishment: Need for Cognition Predicts Support for Punitive Responses to Crime." *Personality and Social Psychology Bulletin* 30: 1485–1493.

Schwitzgebel, Eric, and Fiery A. Cushman. 2012. "Expertise in Moral Reasoning? Order Effects on Moral Judgment in Professional Philosophers and Nonphilosophers." *Mind and Language* 27: 135–153.

Shenhav, Amitai S., and Joshua D. Greene. 2014. "Integrative Moral Judgment: Dissociating the Roles of the Amygdala and the Ventromedial Prefrontal Cortex." *Journal of Neuroscience* 34: 4741–4749.

Shiv, Baba, and Alexander Fedorikhin. 2002. "Spontaneous versus Controlled Influences of Stimulus-Based Affect on Choice Behavior." *Organizational Behavior and Human Decision Processes* 87: 342–370.

Sidgwick, Henry. 1907. *The Methods of Ethics.* 7th ed. London: Macmillan.

Singer, Peter. 1972. "Famine, Affluence and Morality." *Philosophy and Public Affairs* 1: 229–243.

Singer, Peter. 2005. "Ethics and Intuitions." *Journal of Ethics* 9: 331–352.

Singer, Peter. 2009. *The Life You Can Save: Acting Now to End World Poverty.* New York: Random House.

Slovic, Paul. 2007. "'If I Look at the Mass I Will Never Act': Psychic Numbing and Genocide." *Judgment and Decision Making* 2: 79–95.

Small, Deborah A., and George Loewenstein. 2003. "Helping a Victim or Helping the Victim." *Journal of Risk and Uncertainty* 26: 5–16.

Stich, Stephen. 2006. "Is Morality an Elegant Machine or a Kludge?" *Journal of Cognition and Culture* 6: 181–189.

Strohminger, Nina, Richard L. Lewis, and David E. Meyer. 2011. "Divergent Effects of Different Positive Emotions on Moral Judgment." *Cognition* 119: 295–300.

Suter, Renata S., and Ralph Hertwig. 2011. "Time and Moral Judgment." *Cognition* 119: 454–458.

Thomas, Bradley C., Katie E. Croft, and Daniel Tranel. 2011. "Harming Kin to Save Strangers: Further Evidence for Abnormally Utilitarian Moral Judgments after Ventromedial Prefrontal Damage." *Journal of Cognitive Neuroscience* 23: 2186–2196.

Thomson, Judith Jarvis. 1985. "The Trolley Problem." *Yale Law Journal* 94: 1395–1415.

Thomson, Judith Jarvis. 2008. "Turning the Trolley." *Philosophy and Public Affairs* 36: 359–374.

Trémolière, Bastien, Wim De Neys, and Jean-François Bonnefon. 2012. "Mortality Salience and Morality: Thinking about Death Makes People Less Utilitarian." *Cognition* 124: 379–384.

Unger, Peter K. 1996. *Living High and Letting Die: Our Illusion of Innocence.* New York: Oxford University Press.

Valdesolo, Piercarlo, and David DeSteno. 2006. "Manipulations of Emotional Context Shape Moral Judgment." *Psychological Science* 17: 476–477.

Waldmann, Michael R., and Jorn H. Dieterich. 2007. "Throwing a Bomb on a Person versus Throwing a Person on a Bomb: Intervention Myopia in Moral Intuitions." *Psychological Science* 18: 247–245.

Weathers, Helen. 2008. "How We Fell in Love, by the Brother and Sister Who Grew Up Apart and Met in Their 20s." *MailOnline.com*, February 17.

Wharton, Sophie R. 2011. "Thou Shalt versus Thou Shalt Not: The Neural Processes Underlying Decisions to Help versus Decisions to Avoid Doing Harm." Honors thesis, Department of Psychology, Harvard University.

Wheatley, Thalia, and Jonathan Haidt. 2005. "Hypnotic Disgust Makes Moral Judgments More Severe." *Psychological Science* 16: 780–784.

Woodward, James, and John Allman. 2007. "Moral Intuition: Its Neural Substrates and Normative Significance." *Journal of Physiology–Paris* 101: 179–202.

5

The Limits of the Dual-Process View

Julia Driver

EMPIRICAL MORAL PSYCHOLOGY in recent years has set off a reappraisal of traditional normative ethical theories. Joshua Greene's work, which investigates the underpinnings of our moral intuitions, has been at the center of this reappraisal. Greene notes
that we think about moral issues in two very distinct ways—via a quick and dirty response, and via careful deliberation. This is the dual-process view. As Greene describes it:

> First, we humans have a variety of automatic settings—reflexes and intuitions that
> guide our behavior, many of which are emotional. We may be conscious of such
> emotional responses, but we are generally not conscious of the processes that trig-
> ger them. We rely on our automatic settings most of the time, and they generally
> serve us well.
>
> Our brains also have a manual mode. It is a general-purpose reasoning system,
> specialized for enabling behaviors that serve long(er)-term goals, that is, goals that
> are not automatically activated by current environmental stimuli or endogenous
> somatic states. The operations of this system are typically conscious, experienced
> as voluntary, and often experienced as effortful. Our manual mode allows us to for-
> mulate behavioral plans based on detailed and explicit knowledge of the situations
> we face, along with explicit general knowledge about the world and how it works.
> Manual mode allows us to guide our behavior using explicit rules and to think
> explicitly about how the world works. In short, manual mode thinking is the kind
> of thinking that we think of as "thinking." (Greene, this volume)

Greene uses the helpful analogy to an SLR camera, with its automatic and manual modes
of operation. A typical design problem, he notes, is making the best trade-off between
efficiency and flexibility. It doesn't pay to invest a lot of thought into routine matters, but

it does often pay to invest the resources necessary to conscious thought and conscious deliberation in difficult or unusual matters. The human brain makes the same trade-off, and when it comes to moral matters we often make decisions or judgments about what is permissible or impermissible on the basis of quick, emotional responses. These responses might not withstand careful scrutiny in odd or unusual circumstances, however.

This is relevant to normative ethics on Greene's view, because the emotional responses to dilemma situations that come up in the normative ethics literature seem to be broadly "Kantian," whereas the thoughtful responses seem to broadly "utilitarian." I don't think that the empirical research settles the normative question, and I also don't think that it is *relevant* to that question except in one way—some theoretical approaches, such as some forms of normative intuitionism, seem to give great weight to intuitive responses, perhaps too much weight. If that is the case (and I imagine that such intuitionists would disagree), then Greene's, and others', research offers a kind of debunking of such intuitions. The debunking needs to be developed, however. In this chapter one of my goals is to fill out this argument, using Greene's work, and also show that sophisticated versions of such theories as utilitarianism offer ways of counteranalyzing some of Greene's data. I imagine that similar strategies could be adopted by a Kantian who would also want to offer an account of moral evaluation that is more nuanced than some of the "straw man" versions of Kant that are commonly critiqued. Thus, while I agree with Greene that act consequentialism is the right theory, I don't think that empirical evidence establishes that.

5.1. Debunking the Normative Intuitionist

Normative intuitionism is contrasted with metaethical intuitionism in the following way: metaethical intuitionism is an epistemological view about how we can know anything about morality, given that moral properties are nonnatural and causally inert. Intuitionists of this sort hold that moral principles are self-evident, usually drawing on an analogy with mathematical principles. Normative intuitionism, on the other hand, holds that the correct principles of normative ethics, both those that guide action and those that provide a standard for act evaluation, can be directly extracted from intuitive responses to concrete cases. By "directly" I mean "without theoretical mediation." Normative intuitionists think that our intuitions about concrete cases sometimes *track* what is morally true. They track the truth and don't simply, accidentally, reflect the truth. But normative intuitionists are open to the possibility that our intuitions may need correction, since they recognize that various biases and prejudices can distort judgment. Most actual normative intuitionists writing today are deontologists, contrasting their approach to consequentialism, though the approach can be adopted by other theorists as well. It is just that, generally, theories (such as consequentialism) need to defend themselves against counterintuitive implications.

One worry that Greene has about these approaches is that they aren't sensitive to empirical data that indicate that our intuitions just are not very reliable. The strategy of starting out by treating verdicts about cases as givens from which we try to generate accommodating principles is assuming a kind of epistemic privilege to those cases.

Attempts at debunking normative intuitionism take a variety of forms, but the basic idea is that appeal to intuitions about concrete cases is unlikely to lead us to correct conclusions about the content of normative principles. Some of this skepticism was generated long before the contemporary appeals to empirical moral psychology.

For example, the method of contrasting cases provides at least prima facie evidence that something is amiss with some of our intuitions about concrete cases. Consider, for example, the following two cases, part of the classic literature on the "trolley problem":

In the Switch case, one can hit a switch that will turn a runaway trolley away from five people and onto one. In the Footbridge case one can push one person off a footbridge and into the path of a runaway trolley, saving five further down the track. People tend to give characteristically consequentialist responses to the Switch case ("Yes, it's permissible to hit the switch to save more lives") and characteristically deontological responses to the Footbridge case ("No, it's impermissible to push to save more lives"). (Greene, this volume)

Why the discrepancy, when the cases seem structurally similar—that is, in both it is necessary, in order to save five persons, that one sacrifice one person? Consequentialists have argued that it is permissible to sacrifice one, even in the Footbridge case, but that our intuitions are not to be trusted because normally pushing someone off a footbridge indicates a desire to kill absent a desire to save lives. Another theorist could argue that it is wrong to sacrifice one, even in the Switch case, but that our intuitions are not to be trusted because normally acting on benevolent intentions will not require us to so dramatically undermine the autonomy of an innocent person. Because the intuitions can seemingly be explained away in this manner, consequentialists, for example, argue we need to appeal to more general theoretical commitments such as very fundamental norms of rationality to adjudicate between cases. If two cases are structurally the same and yet we get different intuitive normative verdicts for those cases, then we do need to look at how the problems have been framed and what sorts of normatively irrelevant or insignificant factors might be influencing those intuitions. Work in moral psychology, such as Greene's, offers us more of the materials by which we can understand the various factors that influence our intuitions. It *is* interesting that harm as the result of personal contact is intuitively worse than harm that is the result of more distant causal forces. It *is* very interesting that we seem to shift our views when we carefully think about why we hold them. I think that this literature has much to offer our understanding of how human beings engage in a normative review of their own reactions, emotions, and judgments. But this doesn't establish the correctness of the values they actually use to engage in that normative review. Empirical moral psychology can help us understand the sorts of things that we respond to psychologically, as human beings, given how we evolved (e.g., as social creatures) and the culture we happen to live in. But we need independent standards in making evaluations. The normative intuitionist is in the awkward position of, methodologically anyway, taking on board the intuitions and just trying to accommodate them in their presentation of a principle that is supposed to inform us about what is permissible or impermissible. The intuitions may be revisable—for example, cases may be underspecified in various ways, and fleshing them out removes the problematic contrast, or they may simply be rejected as displaying a kind of bias that the principle that has been settled upon does not allow. But there is great weight on accommodating intuitions nevertheless. Thus, for example, a first pass at accommodating both of the intuitions in Switch and Footbridge is to say that there is a morally relevant difference between the two since Footbridge involves using another as a means, whereas in Switch one isn't actually using another as a means, even if one is causing that person's death without that person's consent. But this first pass has well-known problems. In Loop trolley cases most people think it is permissible to kill one to save five, even though the killing *does* involve using another as a means (Thomson 1985). Thus, to accommodate the intuitions about permissible killing in different sorts of trolley scenarios, even more emendations and changes need to be made. One can predict that a principle to accommodate intuitions about a wide variety of permissible sacrifices will become extremely complicated. Critics of this methodology have long suspected that the resulting principles are merely *covering* principles. This is, I take it, at the heart of Greene's worry at the end of his chapter in this volume, where he notes that normative intuitionists are really just summarizing their own "intuitive patterns in moral judgment." The problem with covering principles is that they don't have the authority of normative principles. A covering principle with respect to intuitions simply, in principle form, tells us what people tend to think about a given phenomenon.

So, given what they are covering, the candidate principles don't seem to be the right sort of principle from which we can even *extract* a plausible standard of evaluation, one that gets at the core of what makes sacrificing one to save others morally wrong. That is, we can't extract such a standard without making a very hefty assumption that our intuitions about concrete cases both track the truth very reliably and do so in such a way that offers a kind of insight into the norms that we are somehow responsive to in our intuitive judgments. What seems far more likely is that the principles we get really only tell us about our intuitions, not the truth.

Again, Greene's work helps us to see in more detail and with more precision why such skepticism is warranted. Proximity factors, personal factors, matter very much in our intuitive responses, and yet they seem morally irrelevant. In order to see why certain factors in cases are morally irrelevant *between* cases, however, we need to have an independent standard. While I agree that consequentialism provides the correct standard, the standard itself is not established by appeal to how we engage in practical deliberation or to how we come to form moral evaluations under abnormal circumstances that require "conscious cognitive control." I turn to this issue in the next section.

5.2. Consequentialism and Intuition Chasing

Part of Greene's endorsement of consequentialism traces back to the view that making the world a better place is a very compelling moral ideal. Indeed, many enemies of consequentialism have pointed this out—though their view is that this does not withstand scrutiny. That's because making the world a better place, where that is understood impartially, from the "God's eye" point of view would come at the expense of particular individuals whose rights would be violated in pursuit of the greater good.[1]

But Greene's case for consequentialism doesn't rest solely on this observation. Recall that he also notes that when making a decision that is emotional we are on *automatic*, so to speak—and *that* default is characteristically deontological. There is a great deal of reluctance, of negative emotion, associated with actually pushing someone off a bridge to his death, even if the death was necessary to save others. Pulling a switch is less emotional. Greene proposes the following based on his data:

> *The Central Tension Principle*: Characteristically deontological judgments are preferentially supported by automatic emotional responses, while characteristically consequentialist judgments are preferentially supported by conscious reasoning and allied processes of cognitive control. (Greene, this volume)

Many writers have pointed out counterexamples to both the claim about consequentialist reasoning and the claim about Kantian reasoning. Guy Kahane (2012) has pointed out that one can easily come up with cases where the deontological verdict requires controlled cognition. However, one difficulty in philosophically critiquing Greene's claim here is that he does not see himself as providing necessary, sufficient, or necessary and sufficient conditions for moral judgment. After defending his view against criticisms by Kahane et al., he notes "I've no doubt that, somewhere, an exception to the dual-process theory's predicted pattern will be found. The point, however, is not that the dual-process theory predicts every case perfectly, but rather that it captures the general shape of philosophical moral psychology" (Greene, this volume). This means that the view is not refuted by counterexample. One would need to show that, for example, deliberation *tended* to be less reliable than our gut emotional reactions in deciding moral issues, and that is not something one can do with a single counterinstance, or even a set of such cases.

However, there is at least one related issue that can be explored, and which was raised in the first section: if deliberation *tends* to be more reliable, by what standard do we judge the reliability? R. Eugene Bales wrote a classic article in the consequentialism literature in which he noted that both the proponents and critics of utilitarianism (utilitarianism is a type of consequentialist theory) have tended to conflate two distinct issues—the issue of what the correct decision procedure, or way to go about making decisions, is for the utilitarian, and the issue of what the correct standard is for utilitarian moral evaluation.

> My claim is that a proposed ethical theory—and I have act-utilitarianism in mind—*could* provide a correct account of right-making characteristics *without* spelling out a procedure which, if followed, would crank out in practice a correct and immediately helpful answer. (Bales 1971, 261)

This basic idea has been used by consequentialists to argue that even though promoting the good is the right thing to do, it may also be the case that *trying* to promote the good leads to suboptimal outcomes. Perhaps the attempts are self-defeating, for example (see Railton 1984).

Thus, the standard used to evaluate actions, and so on, and the decision procedures a theory may or may not recommend are not the same at all. Another example: it could well turn out that the best way, on consequentialist grounds, for deciding moral issues makes no direct appeal *at all* to consequences. Perhaps if we all acted on "Love thy neighbor as thyself" we would all end up maximizing the good, generating the best consequences. What is distinctively consequentialist is the standard used for evaluation—whether we are evaluating actions, motives, or the states of mind involved in practical deliberation. It would be an interesting empirical issue if acting on expected utility, where that's understood, let's say, in terms of the good the agent is consciously trying to promote, actually *did* produce the best outcomes. I frankly would be surprised if it turned out to even *tend* to lead to the best outcomes. Of course, the standard itself could be "maximizes expected (rather than actual) utility." But this simply means—on most plausible versions of this account—that the beliefs of the agent, along with the desires (or value assignments) she *ought* to have—determine the rightness of the act in question.[2] It does not require that the agent consciously deliberate about promoting the good, or doing her best, or anything along those lines. It may turn out, as an interesting empirical fact, that if we do consciously try to figure out how to do our best, we will—but then again, maybe not.

Things are even more complicated when we note that actions are not the only things we morally evaluate. We also evaluate an agent's motives, intentions, and character—indeed, pretty much anything relating to agency. Thus we can along consequentialist lines hold perfectly consistently that an agent acted wrongly, but out of a good character (perhaps he couldn't bring himself to kill an innocent baby who was being used as a human shield by an evil dictator, and this is due to a trait he had, a strong reluctance to kill the innocent); or an agent acted rightly, but out of a bad character (he did manage to kill the evil dictator precisely because he did not regard the death of an innocent child to be something to worry about). Thus, perhaps the *unusual* thing the agent is called upon to do is so emotionally wrought—such as killing an innocent child—that she cannot bring herself to do it, even though she is convinced it is the right thing to do under the circumstances. When viewed through the lens of character, her emotions are good. It is good to be the sort of person who finds it emotionally horrific to kill an innocent person. Why is it good? There are many answers one can give to this question. And certainly one of them appeals to a consequentialist standard: people with such traits act better, overall; they tend to act in ways conducive to happiness. Thus, simply pointing out that emotions can interfere with right action is not enough to condemn them on consequentialist grounds. Further, if she could bring herself to do it, against her emotional responses, we would also hold that she probably ought to also feel very bad about it. That is also part, arguably, of having the good character. We don't just make moral judgments and perform morally loaded actions; we also think about those judgments and actions; we engage in a *normative review* of what we do. And the content of that normative review is relevant to understanding whether a person has a good character, and that in turn is evaluable using a consequentialist standard. It is doubtful, for example, that psychopaths engage in the right sort of normative review.

Many other critics of Greene's work have noted that there is a risk here of begging the question in favor of utilitarianism or consequentialism by assuming that deliberation gets the better answer in unusual cases. Writers such as Frances Kamm (2009) have also noted that an independent, non-question-begging standard needs to be appealed to. The content of the deliberation and the standard itself must be kept distinct. Maybe people, in general—as opposed to the fully informed rational agent—are just really bad at deliberating. In fact, there seems to be a lot of empirical evidence that this is so when we look at non-moral-judgment research.

Greene notes in the chapter that we need "independent normative assumptions concerning the kinds of things to which our judgments ought to be sensitive," in contrast to information on what they are in fact sensitive to. However, he seems to regard the normative assumptions as uninteresting or uncontroversial. He gives the example of a norm used in the legal system: it is uncontroversial that juries ought not to be sensitive to issues of race when reaching a verdict in a capital case. He does consider a more difficult case, that of consensual adult incest; but this simply shows something uncontroversial to most normative ethicists, that is, that our intuitions about concrete cases can be debunked. But in the debunking itself we appeal to an independent standard of what we ought to care about and what we ought to find morally compelling. When we answer the question "Ought people's moral judgments be sensitive to such things?" (proximity, personal force, etc.) with a no, we are appealing to an independent understanding of what is morally significant in itself. Maybe this is what Greene means when he mentions reliance on an "old ought" in his argument. But he is more ambitious at the end of the chapter. Because it would be a miracle if our instincts gave us good, reliable responses, he holds, we should rely more on conscious, controlled reasoning. This is the upshot of the No Cognitive Miracle principle: "When we are dealing with unfamiliar* [unfamiliar* = "characteristically unfamiliar"] moral problems, we ought to rely less on automatic settings (automatic emotional responses) and more on manual mode (conscious, controlled reasoning), lest we bank on cognitive miracles." However, there are two issues to raise with respect to this consideration. One is that this ignores another avenue by which some of our instincts might develop. For example, one could hold that some of our instincts in moral matters arise via habituation, through, perhaps, initially relying on controlled reasoning, but abandoning that reasoning after the habit has been developed. This would not show up on brain scans. The second is that the miracle argument is much too broad for Greene's purposes: Might it also be considered a miracle that our considered moral judgments track the truth? If not, why not? There is a line of argument in the metaethics literature that holds that it would be a miracle if—even given the existence of moral truths—our capacities had evolved to track those truths about value or even be able to pick up on them reliably. This would hold not only for intuitive reactions, but also for considered judgments about what has value. Instead, we should expect our capacities to have evolved to pick up on features that promote survival (see Joyce 2001; Street 2006). This line of argument is controversial, and it is not my intention to endorse it, but simply to point out that if Greene relies on it in the case of intuitive judgments, it is not clear that the same could not be said for the considered judgments as well.

Greene believes that No Cognitive Miracle and Central Tension support "consequentialist approaches to moral problem-solving" (this volume). Again, it is not clear whether he thinks we should explicitly think in consequentialist terms when approaching a moral problem, or whether the right answer is determined by a consequentialist (rather than some other) standard. His view should be clarified on this issue. But the most surprising claim he makes is that Kantians, unlike consequentialists, while in manual mode aren't engaged in moral reasoning but instead engaged in rationalization—that is, they are engaged in post hoc justification of entrenched intuitions or positions. This is what Greene terms "intuition chasing," and it is a charge that, even if it were true, doesn't affect whether or not the theory being appealed to is true or false. Indeed, I suspect that many philosophers are guilty of this. In critiquing the practice we need to distinguish two (at least) very different issues. Consider the question: "Why does A hold view v?" There are at least two different ways to answer this meaningfully—one is by providing a purely causal story: A believes v because A's parents raised A in such a way that belief in v would be quite natural. Another provides a justificatory story: A believes v because A accepts reasons x, y, and z in support of v (or discounts considerations against v). We *further* need to distinguish these two issues from whether or not the view just is justified, independently of what A happens to believe.

Someone engaged in rationalization may have come to hold his views via arational, or even irrational, causal processes. But this is orthogonal to whether or not the view is in fact true (and thus justified objectively), which in turn is distinct from the issue of whether A is justified in holding v. Kant, the person, was wrong about masturbation, but this does not condemn Kant's theory. Indeed, many Kantians would hold that the tools required to criticize Kant's view on masturbation are provided by the theory itself.

5.3. Conclusion

Greene's work, as well as the work of others engaged in empirical moral psychology, is deservedly influential in detailing the factors that influence our intuitive moral judgments. It is interesting and inventive, and a great pleasure to read and engage with. However, I remain skeptical of its deeper normative implications.

Acknowledgment

I would like to thank S. Matthew Liao for his very helpful comments on an earlier draft.

Notes

1. For example, Judith Thomson believes it is by appeal to rights that we can understand where utilitarianism, and consequentialism more generally, goes wrong.

2. This is basically Frank Jackson's approach (1991). If one does not idealize the agent's value commitments, one is committed to the view that an agent acts rightly even in cases of truly perverse value commitments.

References

Bales, R. Eugene. 1971. "Act-Utilitarianism: Account of Right-Making Characteristics or Decision-Making Procedure?" *American Philosophical Quarterly* 8: 257–265.

Jackson, Frank. 1991. "Decision-Theoretic Consequentialism and the Nearest-and-Dearest Objection." *Ethics* 101: 461–482.

Joyce, Richard. 2001. *The Myth of Morality.* New York: Cambridge University Press.

Kahane, Guy. 2012. "On the Wrong Track: Process and Content in Moral Psychology." *Mind and Language* 27: 519–545.

Kamm, Frances. 2009. "Neuroscience and Moral Reasoning: A Note on Recent Research." *Philosophy and Public Affairs* 37: 330–345.

Railton, Peter. 1984. "Alienation, Consequentialism, and the Demands of Morality." *Philosophy and Public Affairs* 13: 134–171.

Street, Sharon. 2006. "A Darwinian Dilemma for Realist Theories of Value." *Philosophical Studies* 127: 109–166.

Thomson, Judith Jarvis. 1985. "The Trolley Problem," *Yale Law Journal* 94: 1395–1415.

6

Getting Moral Wrongness into the Picture

Stephen Darwall

JOSHUA GREENE ARGUES that "science can advance ethics,"[1] if not directly, getting ought out of is, at least indirectly. Discovering what happens in our brains when we make moral judgments can, he thinks, show that we should be less inclined to maintain some judgments and moral theories related to them, than others. In what follows, we can simply stipulate, as lawyers say, to the experimental results Greene presents and to the general dual-processing model of the brain they illustrate. What we want to know is this: What can we conclude from these about which moral judgments are true or which we should most confidently maintain?

Greene's thesis—that when the "inner workings" of our moral judgments are revealed, "we may have less confidence in some of our judgments and the ethical theories that are (explicitly or implicitly) based on them"—is uncontroversial if "may" means "might." Even if "may" means something normative, like "may reasonably" or "should," there are certainly instances where everyone should agree. To take one kind of case Greene cites, when we learn that juries in capital cases are responding to defendants' race, then, given what we know about implicit racial bias, we should have less confidence in their judgments. A second example comes from Schwitzgebel and Cushman's (forthcoming) experiments on the order in which the trolley cases are considered. Subjects who first judge that it is wrong to stop the trolley by pushing a person off a footbridge are likelier to judge subsequently that it is also wrong to stop the trolley by switching it to a sidetrack, if that kills one person as a side effect. And vice versa, those who first judge that it is morally permissible to switch are also likelier to judge subsequently that is not wrong to stop the trolley by pushing someone off the footbridge. Here again, experimental evidence shows that we need to be aware of contextual features in considering how confident we should be in moral judgments.

So let us also agree at the outset that experimental findings can have relevance for moral epistemology and that there are cases where we can learn from experimental psychology and neuroscience about which moral judgments, made under which circumstances, we should be suspicious of.

Greene's metaphor for the brain is a point-and-shoot camera with automatic settings and a manual mode; both trade off efficiency and automaticity with flexibility and intentional control. Like point-and-shoot cameras, the human brain is the seat of automatic processes, including emotional, action-guiding intuitions, as well as "a general-purpose reasoning system," which can be used intentionally to enable "behaviors that serve long(er)-term goals, that is, goals that are not automatically activated by current environmental stimuli or endogenous somatic states."

More specifically, Greene advances a "dual-process theory of moral judgment." It should be relatively uncontroversial, as he notes, that human moral judgment is influenced by both "automatic emotional responses" and "controlled conscious reasoning." The more controversial core of Greene's dual-process theory of moral judgment is the following:

> *The Central Tension Principle [CTP]*: Characteristically deontological judgments are preferentially supported by automatic emotional responses, while characteristically consequentialist judgments are preferentially supported by conscious reasoning and allied processes of cognitive control.

The CTP must be interpreted with some care. Greene emphasizes that "characteristically" deontological and consequentialist judgments need carry no "explicit or implicit commitment to consequentialist or deontological theories," at least in the first instance. Rather, a judgment is "characteristically consequentialist" if it is more "naturally justified" in consequentialist terms (act consequentialist, as it turns out; more on this later) and is more difficult to justify in deontological terms ("because they conflict with our sense of people's rights, duties, and so on"). And vice versa for "characteristically deontological" judgments. They are "naturally justified" in deontological rather than (act) consequentialist terms. We should also note that in classifying moral judgments by how they are more naturally justified, Greene means to be abstracting from any "judge's *reasons*" for her judgments. Why people judge as they do is an empirical question that is to be answered experimentally.

The CTP says, then, that moral judgments that are more naturally justified in deontological terms are "preferentially supported by automatic emotional responses," whereas those that are more naturally justified in consequentialist terms are "preferentially supported by conscious reasoning." We might question what is meant by "preferential support," but we can proceed well enough if we understand Greene to mean that characteristically deontological and consequentialist judgments are likelier to be accompanied by (and arguably to result from) automatic emotional responses and conscious reasoning, respectively.[2] This is what seems to drive his argument.

Now ultimately Greene's aim is to argue that the fact that characteristically deontological judgments are frequently tied to, and perhaps the product of, automatic emotional responses should lead us to have less confidence in them than in consequentialist judgments. But Greene does not mean to debunk automatic moral emotional response and intuition-guided action completely. To the contrary, he takes the point-and-shoot analogy seriously, holding that more automatic settings also have their role. As we shall see, however, he nonetheless maintains that none of this should incline us to think that the judgments our responses and intuitions lead us to make are actually true. According to Greene's reading of the experimental results, the judgments whose truth we should be more confident of are steadfastly act utilitarian.

However, Greene makes a general point about when we should rely on automatic intuitive responses that I cannot see deontologists should disagree with in principle. He calls "unfamiliar*" (unfamiliar* meaning "characteristically unfamiliar") situations those "with which we have inadequate evolutionary, cultural, or personal experience." He then states

> *The No Cognitive Miracles Principle [NCMP]*: When we are dealing with unfamiliar* moral problems, we ought to rely less on automatic settings (automatic emotional responses) and more on manual mode (conscious, controlled reasoning), lest we bank on cognitive miracles.

Since unfamiliar* situations are those of which we have "inadequate" experience of various kinds, NCMP is virtually analytic. But even if we define "unfamiliar*" in nonnormative terms as situations with which we have "less" experience, there is no reason a deontologist should be wary of NCMP, so long, that is, as it is interpreted to mean that we ought to rely less on automatic settings (and more on conscious reasoning) *than we otherwise (justifiably) would.* Who can possibly disagree with the proposition that as we become more familiar with and learn more about the objects of moral evaluation, or have more historically extended reflection with the same information and experience, we should give our intuitive responses greater weight.

Even if we interpret NCMP to say that in unfamiliar* situations, we should rely less on intuition *than on conscious reasoning*, a deontologist can agree, depending on how we understand "conscious reasoning." To take an obvious example, analyzing situations with various formulations of the Categorical Imperative is surely conscious reasoning if anything is (as Greene agrees), and Kantians tend to *believe*, at least, that these analyses will eventuate in *some* characteristically deontological judgments, for example, that it is wrong to push a person off a footbridge to stop a trolley, even if this will save five lives.

This last point may not bother Greene much, since his target is less theory-wielding Kantians than those who come to deontological theories, not, as Kant does, from more general philosophical reflection, but from intuitions about cases. If Kant is an intuitionist of any sort, he is a "philosophical intuitionist," in Sidgwick's terms. Any reliance on intuition comes at a "very high level," to use Greene's phrase, about, say, the equal dignity of persons that makes it wrong ever to treat persons as means only, rather than as ends in themselves, and not concerning the wrongness of act types (dogmatic intuitionism) or specific act tokens (perceptual intuitionism). Greene accepts the Sidgwickian point that a consequentialist cannot, and should not wish to, escape relying on intuition at this level. Indeed, he says that if Sidgwick is right, act consequentialism is based on "an affectively based evaluative premise."

Again, I am prepared to stipulate that the experimental evidence supports the CTP. What is at issue is whether these scientific results "can advance ethics" as Greene proposes, whether, that is, they tend to support characteristically consequentialist over deontological judgments. I shall argue that this is not the case.

We should be clear that what Greene means by "characteristically consequentialist" judgments are judgments that are supported by *act consequentialism*. And we should note, first, that act consequentialism is a theory of *moral right and wrong*. It is not itself a theory of the good, even of what would be desirable or good from the moral point of view, although it of course presupposes such a theory. Nor is it a theory of what would be advisable to do from the moral point of view. It is a theory of what a person morally ought to do in the sense that it would be morally *wrong* for her to do otherwise. More specifically, it is the view that, in any situation, agents are morally *required* to do (one of) the action(s), of those available, that would have the best consequences. So it assumes a theory of the (impartial) goodness of outcomes and holds that morally right actions are those whose outcomes are at least as good as any other action that was available to the agent in the circumstances.

It is important to bear in mind, therefore, that consequentialist theories like act consequentialism necessarily make use of two distinct ethical concepts: the concept of good, of course, but also that of the right. So far as they pronounce only on what makes outcomes better or worse, considered impartially (or perhaps even morally), they take no stand on what is at issue with their deontological critics, namely, in W. D. Ross's phrase, "What makes right acts right?" (Ross 1930, 16). Act consequentialists maintain that the only features that are relevant to the rightness and wrongness of acts are their consequences, whereas their deontological critics hold that while these features are of course relevant, there are other relevant features also, such as whether the act violates a promise or someone's right, treats someone as a means only, aims directly at injury and harm, and so on.

So we need to keep in mind that the specific *kind* of ethical issue that Greene is arguing that the CTP can give us insight into is a *deontic* rather than an *evaluative* moral issue. It is the issue of what makes actions morally right and wrong. Greene's description of his experimental setup bears this out. He describes the issue that subjects are presented with in the trolley problems as which actions are "permissible" or "morally acceptable." This is clearly a deontic question. It is not the question of which outcomes would be better, or even of which action would be most advisable in light of the outcomes. It is the question of which actions would be morally right or wrong.

Presently, I shall be arguing that deontic moral concepts—the interdefinable notions of (1) moral right, requirement, and obligation, (2) moral permissibility or acceptability, and (3) moral wrong (the morally unacceptable or impermissible)—have features that distinguish them from other ethical concepts, including evaluative ones, and that these features bear on what lessons we should draw from the CTP. To anticipate, my claim will be that the notions of moral right and wrong are tied conceptually to the idea of moral responsibility or *accountability*, and therefore to the distinctive attitudes through which we hold ourselves and others answerable—"reactive attitudes," as P. F. Strawson called them—such as guilt, resentment, and moral blame (Strawson 1968; see also Darwall 2006, 2013a, 2013b). It will follow that to make deontic moral judgments and "get moral wrongness into the picture," we have to judge whether a given action is of a type that would justify attitudes like blame and guilt, so long as the agent were to perform the action without excuse. And although this normative issue is surely different from whether we do blame, resent, or feel guilty about the action in fact, what is at issue is nonetheless reasons for these distinctive attitudes.

Greene notes that "low-anxiety psychopaths" and individuals with damage to the ventromedial prefrontal cortex are likelier to make characteristically consequentialist than deontological judgments. Remarkably, he claims that "we should expect certain pathological individuals," including VMPFC patients and psychopaths, "to make better decisions than healthy people" in unfamiliar* cases like Footbridge and Switch and have greater confidence in their judgments of moral right and wrong. So much, he thinks, follows from the NCMP, according to which, in unfamiliar* cases, we should trust conscious reasoning more. Owing to the NCMP, the fact that the judgments of psychopaths and those with "social-emotional deficits" are likelier to be consequentialist than deontological is "no embarrassment" to consequentialism. I read Greene as implying, in fact, that this experimental evidence actually *supports* consequentialism.

Now above I conceded the NCMP. But all the NCMP says is that in unfamiliar* cases we should rely on conscious reasoning more and automatic emotion-laden intuitions less. This could just mean that we should balance these differently in unfamiliar* cases, even if we sometimes (properly) end up relying more on intuition than on conscious reasoning. But even if we were to accept that in unfamiliar* cases we should always rely more on conscious reasoning than on emotion-laden intuition, this would not necessarily vindicate taking the judgments of psychopaths as evidence for the truth of consequentialism. Even if we should look to conscious reasoning in such cases, it does not follow that we should look to consequentialist reasoning or restrict ourselves to forms of reasoning of which psychopaths are capable.

As I mentioned earlier, there are certainly forms of reasoning that nonconsequentialist moral theorists have taken to support deontological rather than "characteristically consequentialist" judgments. For all we know, there may be valid forms of moral reasoning that psychopaths and others with VMPFC deficits are incapable of engaging in. If, for example, psychopaths either lack or have a diminished capacity for guilt, and if, as I shall argue, deontic moral concepts are related to reactive attitudes conceptually, then they will lack attitudes that are relevant to the distinctive kind of reasoning that is relevant to the issues of moral right and wrong that divide deontologists and consequentialists. Although they have no diminished capacity to judge whether the consequences of various courses of action are better or worse, they may be unable to think properly about what makes actions morally right or wrong.

In *The Second-Person Standpoint*, I argue that reasoning about moral right and wrong must ultimately proceed from a second-person standpoint, since one is considering what standards people can legitimately be *held* to. Agents who lack the capacity for guilt may lack the second-personal capacity for holding themselves to deontic moral standards and perhaps, therefore, the capacity to reason well about moral right and wrong, that is, the standards to which moral agents can reasonably be held.

Before I lay out this conceptual argument, I would like to clarify further the precise ethical claims that, according to Greene, his experimental results support. There are various possible consequentialist theories of moral right, and although they all reckon the right in relation to consequences in some way, there are important differences between them. Compare just two of these: *act consequentialism* (AC) and what we can call *acceptance rule consequentialism* (ARC).

Act consequentialism (AC): An agent A in circumstance C is morally obligated to perform actions that, of those available to her, would have the best consequences.

Acceptance rule consequentialism (ARC): An agent A in circumstance C is morally obligated to perform an action of which it is true that the general acceptance of a rule requiring that action would have better consequences than would the general acceptance of any other rule for circumstances like C.

There are, of course, other forms of AC, for example, that agents are morally required to do whatever action would yield the highest expected value (taking account of their probability estimates or subjective credences), or whatever action would yield the highest expected value on the available evidence, and so on. There are also other forms of rule consequentialism than ARC, for example, where moral right and wrong depend on the consequences of a deontic moral rule being generally followed, rather than its being encoded in social common sense, as ARC proposes.

I pick the contrast of AC with ARC because it is especially relevant for focusing in on Greene's claim. Greene accepts, recall, that there is a role for automatic emotional-intuitive settings in the moral life. This is actually common ground to AC and ARC. Consequentialists of all stripes can agree that there is significant benefit in what Greene calls "conventional moral rules" being deontological, requiring individuals, for example, to keep their promises or not to make use of bystanders by pushing them off footbridges, even when these acts would have better consequences. And they can all agree that these benefits are likelier to be greater if these deontological rules are encoded in emotion-laden, intuitive common sense, for example, through the intuition that it is wrong to violate these rules, that feeling guilt is justified if one does violate them without excuse, and so on.

The issue between AC and ARC is the relevance of the agreed benefits of deontological rule-based, emotion-tinged common intuitions to which actions *really are morally right and wrong*. That is, when the deontological intuitions that are beneficial for people to have conflict with (act) consequentialist judgments about the relevant cases, which should we have "confidence" in, in the sense of believing they *are actually true*? Greene clearly sides with AC here. As he notes, he embraces deontological emotional defaults in the way that R. M. Hare did in *Moral Thinking*, namely, as a good thing to guide us for normal purposes, but not as having any bearing on what actually makes right acts right (Hare 1981). Hare held that AC gives, in every case, the correct answer to which actions really are morally right and why, even if we often do better to navigate with intuitive defaults that conflict with this, and so apparently does Greene.

It is important to notice that the deontological judgments that AC and ARC can both accept that it is good for people to be generally disposed to make are "characteristically deontological" judgments rather than "characteristically consequentialist" judgments, since they are "naturally justified," not by the consequences of *actions available in the circumstances* but in other terms. AC holds that, even though it is good that we be disposed to make these deontological judgments, that helpful disposition should not give us (theorists) any confidence that these judgments are actually true. According to act utilitarians like Hare, the truth conditions of judgments of moral right are always act consequentialist, regardless of what it is best that people generally think and feel. This is what makes AC a potentially "esoteric" morality, in the term of its greatest proponent, Henry Sidgwick, and leads one of its most prominent critics, Bernard Williams, to calls it a "government house" doctrine—something that theorists should believe but not widely broadcast (Williams 1985, 120–122).

Unlike AC, ARC holds that what makes acts right and wrong is *not* acts' consequences, but the consequences of the social acceptance of rules that would require or prohibit the acts in the relevant circumstances. So the judgments that ARC counts as true and holds we should have confidence in will be "characteristically deontological" rather than "characteristically consequentialist" judgments. ARC will of course hold, like AC, that which rules we should accept *to guide action and moral criticism* are themselves justified by the consequences of accepting them. But the deontic judgments of moral right that accepting these rules will incline us to make will not be consequentialist. Those judgments will be "characteristically deontological." And though AC holds that we should have no confidence in these judgments as true, ARC holds that the fact that it is beneficial for us to be disposed to make these judgments is precisely what makes them true.

I have gone into these matters in some detail for two reasons: first, to clarify the form of consequentialism that Greene is claiming his experimental results support, namely, AC, and second, to introduce a different form of consequentialism, ARC, that I will suggest is better tailored to the features of deontic moral concepts like moral right and wrong that I shall presently discuss. If moral obligations are what we are *accountable* to one another and ourselves for doing, then it is contrary to their nature to be kept esoteric; they must not lose their justification by being encoded in moral common sense.

Note first that nothing in Greene's results tells in favor of AC as opposed to ARC. Proponents of both need face no embarrassment by the CTP. Indeed, both can applaud the fact that characteristically deontological judgments are preferentially supported by "automatic emotional responses" that come with the acceptance of moral rules. Nor will either take these emotional intuitive responses at face value. Even the proponent of ARC will hold that we should have confidence in the judgments they incline subjects to make only if they reflect the acceptance of optimal rules. The CTP surely does not support AC as opposed to ARC.[3]

I hold no brief for ARC. However, I do believe that there are conceptual features of deontic moral concepts like right and wrong that make ARC a far more plausible consequentialist theory of right than AC. By this I do not mean just that ARC is better supported by *moral* intuitions. Defenders of AC agree about that, as, of course, does Greene. A central point of his chapter, indeed, is to debunk such support as "intuition chasing." My point, rather, is that ARC responds better than AC to *conceptual* features of the right that are inconsistent with the truth about right and wrong being "esoteric." After laying these out, I will give a striking example that illustrates how theses conceptual points matter. I will illustrate how they operate in Derek Parfit's turn from defending AC in *Reasons and Persons* to supporting ARC in *On What Matters*. In *OWM*, Parfit holds that the main idea underlying at least one version of AC "may be better regarded, not as a moral view" at all, but "as being, like Rational Egoism, an external rival to morality" (Parfit 2011, 1:168).

In *The Second-Person Standpoint* and a number of papers since, I argue that the concepts of moral obligation, right, wrong—deontic moral concepts—are tied to accountability conceptually. What it is wrong for us not to do is, as a conceptual matter, what we would warrantably be held accountable for doing through Strawsonian reactive attitudes like resentment, guilt, and moral blame, so long, that is, as we acted without excuse (Darwall 2006, 2013a, 2013b).[4] Moral obligations are actions that are blameworthy if we fail to perform them without excuse. There is thus a conceptual connection between deontic concepts and blameworthiness. The point is not that the concept of being wrong is the same as the concept of the blameworthy. An action can be wrong without being blameworthy if the agent has an excuse. Rather, the point is that it is a conceptual truth that if an action is wrong, then it is of a kind that is blameworthy unless the agent has an excuse. Deontic moral concepts are thus inextricably tied to those of blameworthiness and excuse, and vice versa.

This means that there is a conceptual difference between deontic concepts and evaluative concepts like the good. The idea of moral obligation differs also from the idea of there being good, or even most reason to do something from the moral point of view. (This is a point on which Parfit is especially clear [2011, 1:150–174].) Consider a case where a great good can be accomplished only at great cost to the agent—say rescuing someone from a burning building. We can coherently think that the costs to the agent make not attempting the rescue morally permissible although attempting it might remain morally better (if the risks are not so great as to make the rescue foolhardy). In other words, it seems perfectly coherent to think that such a rescue would *be supererogatory*: a better thing to do from the moral point of view, but not morally wrong not to do. But if we think supererogation is so much as a coherent possibility, then we cannot think that being morally obligatory is just being most recommended by moral reasons, or that acting wrongly simply involves going against such reasons. If that were true, supererogation would not be a coherent possibility.

What is morally required is what morality *demands*. So if we think that it would be unreasonable to demand that people assume a given risk for a given impersonal gain, then we can coherently think that morality does not demand it, and therefore that it would not be morally obligatory. This makes perfect sense, if moral obligation is tied to blameworthiness in the way I have proposed. As Strawson (1968) pointed out, reactive attitudes like guilt and moral blame implicitly make a demand of their objects. Strawson argued that because this is so, we have these attitudes from a distinctively "interpersonal," or what I call a "second-personal," standpoint (Strawson 1968, 77; Darwall 2006). Reactive attitudes like blame implicitly address demands to their objects and bid for their addressees' recognition of the authority to make the demand. Unlike other critical attitudes like contempt, reactive attitudes like blame and guilt hold their objects *answerable*—they come with an RSVP, an implicit claim on the addressee to hold himself accountable and acknowledge the authority to make the demand they address (Darwall 2006, 2013a, 2013b).

If deontic moral notions are tied to justified reactive attitudes and accountability conceptually, then it is easy to see why their justification cannot depend on remaining esoteric. When we hold people accountable with reactive attitudes like moral blame, we presuppose that the (deontic) standards we are holding them to are accessible to blamer and blamed alike. I can hardly intelligibly hold someone answerable for complying with a standard that is not accessible to him, indeed, to both of us in common. To have confidence in a judgment of moral right, therefore, is to be committed to it as a common standard to which we hold ourselves and one another accountable.

For this reason, ARC is a more plausible consequentialist theory of right than AC, not just on intuitive moral grounds, but also on conceptual grounds. If to be morally wrong is to be contrary to standards we should accept for holding ourselves and one another accountable in common, then any space between what these standards or rules require and what morality requires vanishes. The idea of an esoteric standard of moral right ends up being an oxymoron in a way that esoteric standards of goods or excellences of various other kinds need not be.

As I read Parfit in *On What Matters*, it is at least partly an appreciation of these conceptual features of deontic moral concepts that has led him from being a vigorous, indeed preeminent, defender of AC in *Reasons and Persons* to now arguing for ARC as one prong of his "Triple Theory" (along with Kantian contractualism and Scanlonian contractualism) (Parfit 2011; Darwall 2014). Parfit now holds that deontic moral notions differ conceptually from evaluative notions like those of goods of various kinds (whether personal or impartial). Although Parfit says that the idea of moral wrong is "indefinable," he nonetheless evidently accepts that it is conceptually linked to what he calls "blameworthiness" and "reactive attitude" senses of deontic notions in a way that other evaluative notions are not. For example, when he argues that Sidgwick's act-consequentialist principle of universal benevolence may be better regarded as an "external rival to morality" than as a rival theory of moral right, he adds:

> When Sidgwick claims that he *ought* not to prefer his own lesser good [to greater impartial good], he does not seem to mean that such a preference would be blameworthy . . . or that such an act would give him reasons for remorse and give others reasons for indignation. (1:168)

In other words, Sidgwick's "ought" is better regarded, not as the deontic "ought" of moral obligation, right, and wrong, but as having some other "reason-implying sense," for example, of what there is most impartial reason to prefer or do. So it is ill suited to being interpreted as a deontic moral doctrine like AC.

As I said above, Greene's results provide no support for AC as a theory of moral right. Defenders of ARC have no more problems accepting the CTP than do defenders of AC. When, however, we include the conceptual matters we have just been considering, the situation looks far dimmer for AC than for ARC.

Again, my point has not been to defend ARC. I am simply trying to challenge Greene's claim that the CTP should lead us to have less confidence in characteristically deontological rather than characteristically consequentialist judgments. In my view, as I argue in *Second-Person Standpoint*, the conceptual connection between moral right and wrong and accountability makes a theory that is grounded in a conception of *mutual accountability*, like contractualism, an especially attractive theory of right. However, the judgments that ARC entails are no less characteristically deontological in Greene's terms than are those that are entailed by contractualist moral theories. Characteristically consequentialist judgments, by contrast, are those that would be entailed by AC. I hope it is now obvious why Greene's experimental results, including the CTP, should not lead us to have more confidence in characteristically consequentialist rather than characteristically deontological judgments.

Notes

1. All quotations from Greene are from his chapter in this volume.

2. Even here, we might ask, "Likelier than what" (i.e., "preferentially supported" over what)? Is the idea that consequentialist judgments are likelier to result from conscious reasoning than from automatic emotional processes, and vice versa for characteristically deontological judgments? Or that automatic emotional processes are likelier to result in characteristically deontological than in characteristically consequentialist judgments, and vice versa for conscious reasoning? I will take Greene to mean the former.

3. A similar point is made in Woodward and Allman 2007. I am indebted to S. Matthew Liao for this reference.

4. This claim is by no means original with me. In chapter 5 of *Utilitarianism*, Mill (1998) writes that "we do not call anything wrong unless we mean to imply that a person ought to be punished in some way or other for doing it; if not by law, by the opinion of his fellow creatures; if not by opinion, by the reproaches of his own conscience." Otherwise, he says, we do not think it "a case of moral obligation." Note also that Mill seems much more attracted to ARC than AC in chapter 5.

References

Darwall, Stephen. 2006. *The Second-Person Standpoint: Morality, Respect, and Accountability*. Cambridge, MA: Harvard University Press.

Darwall, Stephen. 2013a. *Morality, Authority, and Law: Essays in Second-Personal Ethics I*. Oxford: Oxford University Press.

Darwall, Stephen. 2013b. *Honor, History, and Relationship: Essays in Second-Personal Ethics II*. Oxford: Oxford University Press.

Darwall, Stephen. 2014. "Agreement Matters: Critical Notice of Derek Parfit, *On What Matters*." *Philosophical Review* 123: 79–105.

Parfit, Derek. 1984. *Reasons and Persons*. Oxford: Clarendon Press.

Parfit, Derek. 2011. *On What Matters*. Edited by Samuel Scheffler. 2 vols. Oxford: Oxford University Press.

Ross, W. D. 1930. *The Right and the Good*. Oxford: Oxford University Press.

Schwitzgebel, E., and F. A. Cushman. Forthcoming. "Expertise in Moral Reasoning? Order Effects on Moral Judgment in Professional Philosophers and Non-philosophers." *Mind and Language*.

Strawson, P. F. 1968. "Freedom and Resentment." In *Studies in the Philosophy of Thought and Action*. London: Oxford University Press.

Williams, Bernard. 1985. *Ethics and the Limits of Philosophy*. Cambridge, MA: Harvard University Press.

Woodward, James, and John Allman. 2007. "Moral Intuition: Its Neural Substrates and Normative Significance." *Journal of Physiology–Paris* 101: 179–202,

7

Reply to Driver and Darwall

Joshua D. Greene

BOTH JULIA DRIVER and Stephen Darwall pose important and challenging questions, and I appreciate the opportunity to respond to their ideas. I'll begin with Driver's comments. If I understand her correctly, her main argument may be summarized as follows:

> Moral psychology is a useful tool for what one might call "microdebunking," raising doubts about specific moral judgments. But moral psychology can do little for "macroscopic" moral theorizing, aimed at evaluating whole moral theories. This is because microdebunking requires having a moral theory already in place. Psychology can tell us how moral judgment works and, more specifically, identify features to which our intuitive moral judgments are sensitive or insensitive. But this information is morally inert without further judgments concerning what is morally relevant, concerning the features to which our judgments *ought* to be sensitive. These further judgments, produced through a process that may be called "normative review," require having an independent moral theory. Thus, the only moral theories that can be challenged by empirical microdebunking are thoroughly intuitionist theories, ones that merely "cover" sets of intuitive judgments, and therefore lack the internal resources needed to distinguish between relevant and irrelevant moral influences. More robust theories, by contrast, can't be challenged by microdebunking because microdebunking requires a background theory, and to assume a background theory is to beg the question against whatever moral theory is being challenged.

The above argument concerns what I've called the *direct* route by which empirical research can have normative implications. Driver makes a parallel argument about what

I called the *indirect* route, which I will discuss shortly. Driver's argument hinges on the assumption that microdebunking presupposes a moral theory. I disagree with this assumption and believe that microdebunking is powerful precisely because this assumption is false.

Consider, once again, our findings concerning the effect of *personal force* (roughly, pushing vs. hitting a switch) on our intuitive moral judgments (Greene et al. 2009). As a consequentialist, I believe that the use of personal force in causing harm is (in itself) morally irrelevant. But, critically, one hardly needs to be a consequentialist to hold this opinion. When I tell people that the subjects we tested were twice as likely to approve of sacrificing the man on the footbridge if he's dropped through a switch-operated trapdoor (the Footbridge Switch case), rather than pushed (original Footbridge), the most common response is laughter. People laugh, not because they are committed to consequentialism or some other moral theory, but because they believe, as a matter of moral common sense, that the moral permissibility of a lethal act does not depend on whether it involves a switch-operated trapdoor. Understanding how our judgments work (e.g., with sensitivity to personal force) can lead us to question our judgments. And this "us" can be a very general "us," with no special theoretical commitments. Thus, if microdebunking ends up challenging a dearly held moral theory, one can't defend that theory on the grounds that the challenger is simply begging the question. The defense can't be, "You're just saying that because you're a committed consequentialist." Instead, the defense will have to be, "You're just saying that because you're a reasonable person."

We've established, then, that empirical microdebunking can operate without begging any general theoretical questions. But can a vigorous program of microdebunking add up to more than a collection of microconclusions? Can it have broad implications for moral theory? I believe that it can.

Let's begin with my favored moral philosophy, deep pragmatism,[1] better known by its ugly and misleading conventional name, utilitarianism. (Throughout this reply I will use the terms "utilitarianism" and "consequentialism" interchangeably, even though the former is a special case of the latter.) There are some common-sense judgments that fit rather well with utilitarianism, such as the judgment that it's permissible to turn a trolley away from five and onto one. And there are common-sense judgments that are relatively difficult to square with utilitarianism, such as the judgment that it's impermissible to push the man off the footbridge, even if it's guaranteed to produce good overall consequences. Suppose that when we examine the psychology behind such antiutilitarian judgments, we always find some kind of moral undersensitivity or oversensitivity at work. Such a result (for now, hypothetical) would provide strong support for utilitarianism over its theoretical rivals.

However, the "over" in "oversensitive" and the "under" in "undersensitive" are normative modifiers. How can we use them without begging our questions? Let's suppose, as suggested above, that the normative commitments underwriting these modifiers are very widely held and not distinctively utilitarian. In other words, suppose that the over-/

undersensitivities in question are like our sensitivity to personal force, a response tendency that is incompatible with the common-sense notion that the physical mechanisms of harm are not in themselves morally relevant. If it turns out that all of the intuitive challenges to utilitarianism (cases in which utilitarianism seems to get the wrong answer) are cases in which our judgment appears to be sensitive to something generally regarded as irrelevant, or insensitive to something generally regarded as relevant, that would certainly provide some support for utilitarianism over its theoretical rivals. And, critically, the argument behind this theoretical shift would not be question-begging. Such an argument would not be defending utilitarianism by assuming utilitarianism. Rather, it would be defending utilitarianism through a combination of new scientific knowledge ("Your judgment, unbeknownst to you, is influenced by personal force") and unremarkable moral common sense ("The implication of personal force is morally irrelevant").

To engage in this kind of scientifically powered debunking is to seek what I have called *double-wide reflective equilibrium.* In addition to our "considered judgments" about particular cases and our organizing theoretical principles, we add our increasingly sophisticated understanding of moral psychology. As illustrated above, psychological science can (legitimately) cause us to reconsider some of our "considered judgments" about specific cases. And there is no reason to assume that this microdebunking can only have "micro" effects. With enough scientifically motivated revision of our "considered judgments" we may reach new "macro" philosophical conclusions. In any case, it's certainly too early to assume that this cannot happen. As explained in *Moral Tribes*, I believe that an empirically informed case for deep pragmatism/utilitarianism is already taking shape.

Before moving on, I want to consider an objection that I've already addressed, but that warrants more detailed consideration: How can we determine whether a dubious moral tendency counts for or against a particular considered judgment (and, by extension, for or against a moral theory that is supported/challenged by that judgment)? Consider, once again, the case of personal force. We agree, I'll assume, that the use of personal force is, in itself, morally irrelevant. But does that mean that the typical response to the Footbridge case (that it's wrong to push) is oversensitive to personal force? Or does it mean that the typical response to the Footbridge Switch case (that it's permissible to open the trapdoor with the switch) is corrupted by the absence of personal force? If one simply examines these two cases in isolation and without an understanding of the underlying psychology, it may be impossible to tell. But further empirical investigation across many cases and at multiple levels of analysis may shed further light.

Fiery Cushman has argued that our sensitivity to personal force is the product of "model free" learning, whereby certain action types acquire positive or negative valences as a result of their past consequences (Cushman 2013; see also Crockett 2013). Critically, once an action type has acquired a valence through model-free learning, the valence is applied to new instances *independent of their known consequences.* In other words, the valence is attached to "the act itself." This is the type of learning that makes you absentmindedly drive to work when you're supposed to be going elsewhere and that impels rats to press levers that deliver food when they are no longer hungry (Dickinson et al. 1995). By contrast, characteristically utilitarian judgments appear to be products of "model based" learning and reasoning. They follow from a rapidly learned, context-specific cause-and-effect model ("Given what I know about this specific situation, performing this action will save more lives") combined with a very general preference for producing good consequences.

Knowing all this gives us insight into which judgments are likely to be normatively distorted. If Cushman and I are correct,[2] these judgments are produced by qualitatively different systems with characteristic strengths and weaknesses. Critically, these strengths and weaknesses can be characterized as such without making any controversial moral assumptions. For example, if you think that an action's expected consequences are at least *relevant* to determining its moral quality (not a very controversial assumption), then you should be wary of relying too heavily on emotional responses that completely ignore information about the present action's expected consequences.

This brings me to the second part of Driver's objection, aimed at what I have called the *indirect* route by which psychology can have normative implications. Here, I argue that psychology can tell us about the kind of process by which a judgment is reached and also offer general guidance concerning which kinds of thought processes are likely to yield good judgments in which situations. More specifically, I've argued that judgments driven by automatic processes are less likely to be reliable in what I have called "unfamiliar*" situations, ones with which we have relatively little genetic, cultural, or individual experience. Combine this with my empirical claim that deontological judgments tend to be driven by automatic responses, and we conclude that we should be wary of our deontological judgments in unfamiliar* situations, at least insofar as they conflict with the competing aim of producing good consequences.

The crux of Driver's objection is, once again, that my argument in favor of utilitarianism is question-begging. She asks: "If deliberation *tends* to be more reliable, by what standard do we judge the reliability?" As in the case of the direct route, this argument's strength lies in its lack of contentious assumptions. Automatic responses are, by their very nature, bound to be unreliable in unfamiliar* situations. And this is true *regardless of the standard we apply for determining reliability.* Take, once again, the case of driving a car. As I've said, it would be a *cognitive miracle* if one could drive well the first time behind the wheel. This is because humans have no genetic experience with driving, because cultural familiarity with driving offers insufficient experience, and because new drivers by definition lack personal experience with driving. And, critically, it would be a cognitive miracle if one were to drive well as a total novice *regardless of what one means by "well."* "Well" could mean deftly darting through heavy traffic, like a seasoned racecar driver. Or "well" could mean driving slowly and cautiously, like my mother. But either way, driving "well" from the outset would be a cognitive miracle. Of course, if by driving "well" you mean crashing immediately into a tree, then all bets are off. But within the range of plausible conceptions of good driving, we can say with confidence that new drivers cannot drive well based on automatic responses (intuition) and must instead rely on explicit, controlled decision-making.

In the same way, we can say with confidence that we are generally unlikely to make good intuitive judgments about unfamiliar* moral problems, and we can say this *regardless of what we mean by "good."* Moreover, if we can say on independent grounds that characteristically deontological judgments tend to be driven by automatic emotional intuitions (emotional valences produced through model-free learning?), then we can say that our characteristically deontological judgments are unlikely to serve us well in unfamiliar* situations. It may be a challenge to decide what exactly counts as unfamiliar*, but we are not without a clue. For example, a case in which committing an act of personal violence (such as pushing an innocent person off a footbridge) is guaranteed to yield the best available consequences is clearly not representative of the human experience. What's more, I have offered a general heuristic for deciding when to distrust our moral intuitions, one that allows us to sidestep questions about which situations are and are not familiar*: If two groups ("tribes" in my parlance) have a moral disagreement, and that disagreement is fueled by incompatible moral intuitions, then both groups should distrust their moral intuitions because we know that at least one group's intuitions are unreliable. And if, as an empirical matter of fact, characteristically deontological judgments reflect our automatic responses, then we should eschew characteristically deontological arguments when we are attempting to resolve intertribal disagreements. Once again, this argument presupposes no moral theory, utilitarian or otherwise, and therein lies its power.

With this in mind, I can respond to some of Driver's objections more directly. Responding to my claim that it would be a cognitive miracle if we were to have reliable intuitions about unfamiliar* moral problems, she writes:

> This ignores another avenue by which some of our instincts might develop. For example, one could hold that some of our instincts in moral matters arise via habituation, through, perhaps, initially relying on controlled reasoning, but abandoning that reasoning after the habit has been developed. (Driver, this volume)

Far from ignoring such a possibility, this is precisely the kind of learning process that Cushman and I have in mind, a process that may involve some tough decisions involving controlled reasoning. Suppose, for example, that we learn from years of playground experience that intentionally pushing people is bad. Now, as adults, when we encounter such familiar* cases of intentional pushing, our condemnation is automatic. However, this automatic response, while good, is not completely reliable. The problem is that there are also unfamiliar* cases of pushing, such as cases in which the pushing is guaranteed to lead to good consequences overall. The more general point is this: No matter how sophisticated our moral intuitions are, no matter how much learning they have incorporated, there will always be unfamiliar* cases for which they are unprepared. Understanding these psychological dynamics is important for moral theorists wrestling with trolley dilemmas, but it's also important decision-makers facing real-world problems such a physician-assisted suicide, where action types that are generally bad may have good consequences.

Driver continues:

> The second [problem] is that the miracle argument is much too broad for Greene's purposes: Might it also be considered a miracle that our considered moral judgments track the truth?

No—at least not if my understanding of cognitive evolution is correct. In general—although not always—it's adaptive to have true beliefs. If there's a tiger or source of clean water hidden over there, it's good to know it. We can acquire true beliefs automatically if our situation is familiar*, but not all situations are familiar*. This, I believe, is why evolution endowed us—primates who thrive in a uniquely broad range of environments—with a highly flexible, general-purpose reasoning system, analogous to the "manual mode" of a digital SLR camera. The purpose of such a system is to extract and apply useful knowledge in unfamiliar* situations. Of course, there's no guarantee that our "manual mode" thinking will lead us to true beliefs or good decisions in unfamiliar* situations, but it's by no means a miracle when they do.

Finally, I would like to address a further question raised by Driver. She distinguishes between consequentialism as a *normative standard* and consequentialism as a *decision procedure*. She asks whether I am defending it as one, or the other, or both. The answer is both, first as a normative standard, and secondarily as a decision procedure to be applied in some situations. In *Moral Tribes* I argue that deep pragmatism (utilitarianism, properly understood and wisely applied) is our best bet for a global "metamorality," a higher-order normative standard that adjudicates among competing tribal values and interests, just as a single tribe's value system adjudicates among the competing values and interests of its individual members. I do not claim that deep pragmatism is the moral truth, only that it's our most promising metamorality.

If we adopt utilitarianism as our preferred normative standard, we then face a further question: How should we think about moral problems? In other words, what should our *decision procedure* be? As Driver and others have noted, utilitarianism as a normative standard need not favor the adoption of a utilitarian decision procedure, whereby one explicitly attempts to maximize happiness. Concerning the merits of utilitarianism as a decision procedure, I've reached a specific conclusion based on my empirical analyses of moral decision problems and moral psychology: When we are dealing with everyday moral problems, which are primarily about the tension between self-interest and concern for others ("Me vs. Us"), we should rely on our moral intuitions and not attempt to add up costs and benefits. For example, one should not decide whether to shoplift by attempting to estimate its expected effects on aggregate happiness. Instead, one should simply refrain from shoplifting as a matter of intuitive moral common sense. However, when we are dealing with controversial moral issues, matters over which moral tribes disagree ("Us vs. Them"), then we should not rely on our moral intuitions and should instead rely on controlled "manual mode" thinking. More specifically, we should be deep pragmatists who aim explicitly to make the world as happy as possible, based on the best available evidence concerning the likely effects of our actions.

Darwall's argument, if I understand it correctly goes like this:

> According to Greene, moral psychology combined with plausible normative assumptions supports act consequentialism (AC) and judgments that are "characteristically consequentialist." Act consequentialism is a moral theory, a theory of right and wrong. As a conceptual matter, if an act is wrong, it is appropriate to hold one publicly accountable for committing that act. This means that esoteric moral theories (aka self-effacing theories) are incoherent. Esoteric theories favor the adoption of operative moral principles (ones used to hold people accountable) that are different from the theory's actual principles. However, if a theory's actual principles should not be used to hold people publicly accountable, then that theory is not in fact a moral theory. Thus, AC is not truly a moral theory. A consequentialist alternative to AC is acceptance rule consequentialism (ARC), a form of rule consequentialism. According to ARC, actions are to be evaluated based on their consistency with the set of rules that, if widely accepted, would produce the best consequences. ARC is a proper moral theory because it is not esoteric. What's more, ARC is compatible with Greene's psychological analysis. However, the dictates of ARC are "characteristically deontological." Thus Greene's analysis does not in any general way favor judgments that are "characteristically consequentialist" over judgments that are "characteristically deontological."

This is an interesting argument. In the end, I disagree with Darwall on multiple counts, but our disagreements are more subtle and less stark than one might think. I'll begin with the first part of Darwall's argument, according to which AC is disqualified from moral theoryhood.

To begin, I agree that AC has an esoteric element, but I deny that this disqualifies it from public service. The conception of utilitarianism (the version of AC in question) as a "government house" philosophy implies that it is *interpersonally* esoteric: The "elites" in the government house adopt AC, but discourage "the masses" from adopting it, for fear that they would behave badly, by AC's own accounting. If "the masses" cannot use AC as their normative standard, then there is indeed a very real sense in which AC is not a proper moral theory. But I deny that AC must be *interpersonally* esoteric, and thus affirm AC's suitability for public service.

Whether AC must be interpersonally esoteric is largely an empirical question about what happens when people in the real world adopt AC as their normative standard.

I agree with Darwall that AC is unfit for directly guiding everyday moral behavior, but this does not entail that AC must be interpersonally esoteric. Instead, it may be *intrapersonally* esoteric. Instead of having different classes of people with different operative moral philosophies (the "elites" and "the masses"), all people may coherently operate under AC at some times and under more conventional deontic moral norms at other times. That is, people may operate in "masses mode" most of the time, relying on what I have called our "automatic settings," but on occasion operate in "elite mode," applying consequentialist principles in what I have called "manual mode." Or, to put the point in Hare's (1981) terms, our moral thinking may operate on different *levels* at different times. For example, one can have a strong emotional commitment to honesty in one's everyday life, but also recognize that dishonesty is sometimes morally permissible, even obligatory, when the costs of honesty (impartially assessed) clearly outweigh the benefits.

The idea that AC, applied in light of human psychology, naturally leads to a multilevel philosophy is not new. It's present in Mill and Hare, and Darwall is well aware of this. Nevertheless, Darwall's attempt to disqualify AC from public service seems to ignore this possibility. He writes:

> If deontic moral notions are tied to justified reactive attitudes and accountability conceptually, then it is easy to see why their justification cannot depend on remaining esoteric. . . . I can hardly intelligibly hold someone answerable for complying with a standard that is not accessible to him, indeed, to both of us in common. . . . The idea of an esoteric standard of moral right ends up being an oxymoron.

This charge, that AC is "oxymoronic," holds only if it is *interpersonally* esoteric, such that the masses lack access to the foundational moral standards upheld by the enlightened elites. But there is nothing oxymoronic about AC as an *intrapersonally* esoteric standard. We can apply conventional deontic standards in everyday moral situations (e.g., when passing judgment on the student who "forgot" to attach his term paper to his eleventh-hour email) while reserving explicit evaluation under AC for more difficult cases (e.g., when passing judgment on Edward Snowden, the hero and/or villain who leaked government documents revealing massive covert surveillance of ordinary citizens). In short, AC can be "esoteric" in the sense that it's generally unfit for direct application in everyday life, but not "esoteric" in the sense that its status as the ultimate moral standard must remain a secret.

The devastating conclusion that I just avoided is that AC is not even a moral theory. As it happens, this is not a conclusion that I feel compelled to resist. In fact, I have to a large extent already embraced it. As Darwall says, it might make more sense to think of AC as a theory of "what there is most impartial reason to prefer or do." That sounds pretty good to me.

Recall that I've characterized utilitarianism, not as a morality, but as a *metamorality*. My claim is *not* that utilitarianism is a good guide to everyday moral life, but rather a good normative standard for dealing with difficult cases, especially cases in which members of different "tribes" have reached incompatible moral conclusions based on their respective "automatic settings." I won't go so far as to say that utilitarianism is not a moral standard. Unlike, say, rational egoism, it embodies an impartial perspective, which is, in my opinion, a central moral ideal. Nevertheless, if you insist that utilitarianism is not a real moral standard because it's not an everyday moral standard, that's fine with me. What matters is that it's a metamoral standard.

Moving on to the second part of Darwall's argument, he denies that psychological research generally favors "characteristically consequentialist" judgments over "characteristically deontological" ones. I agree. But my aim is not to provide a general defense of "characteristically consequentialist" judgments over "characteristically deontological" ones. Instead, my aim is to defend utilitarianism as a metamorality, and utilitarianism does not entail a general rejection of "characteristically deontological" conclusions, nor a general acceptance of "characteristically consequentialist" conclusions. If that sounds strange, it's probably because your attention is focused on unrealistic hypothetical philosophical dilemmas instead of real-world moral problems. As Mill argued, everyday deontic judgments have great utilitarian value, and in nonobvious ways (Bentham and Mill 2004). Wise utilitarians have long recognized that, in the real world, "characteristically deontological" judgments are generally good and are often better *in utilitarian terms* than the "characteristically consequentialist" judgments with which they sometimes compete. (That said, we should expect that in many cases—especially cases involving unfamiliar* problems—characteristically deontological judgments are, from a utilitarian perspective, worse. More on this shortly.)

Darwall's argument is presented as a contest between AC and ARC. He argues that both AC and ARC are consistent with the normative conclusions supported by my empirical analysis. But he claims that ARC is better (because it's not esoteric) and that AC and ARC differ in that AC supports characteristically consequentialist conclusions, while ARC supports characteristically deontological conclusions. I agree that AC and ARC may both be consistent with my empirical analysis (pending one critical matter of interpretation—see below), but I also think that they are equivalent in every way that matters.

I am, once again, not claiming that utilitarianism is the moral truth. I'm recommending utilitarianism (a form of AC) as a metamorality, as a public standard for resolving intertribal moral disagreements. And, I claim, AC and ARC are equivalent as metamoralities. This is because the differences between AC and ARC only matter for individual decision-making. More specifically, these differences matter in exceptional cases in which one believes that doing the most good requires flouting the rules that would (upon general acceptance) do the most good. However, if the practical task at hand is to establish a public normative standard, then the distinction between doing the most good and abiding by the rules that would do the most good disappears, on the assumption that the rules that would do the most good endorse their own adoption.

When serving as metamoralities, AC and ARC both say the same thing: "Let us adopt policies that can be expected to produce the best consequences." Thus, for my purposes, AC and ARC are equivalent, and both can be expected to endorse a mixture—the same mixture—of "characteristically deontological" and "characteristically consequentialist" conclusions.

I defined "characteristically consequentialist" judgments as ones that are naturally justified in terms of impartial cost-benefit reasoning and "characteristically deontological" judgments as ones that are naturally justified by appeals to rights, duties, and so on. When it comes to uncontroversial moral questions, these terms have little meaning. Disapproving of child abuse is both "characteristically consequentialist" and "characteristically deontological," or neither—take your pick. But if we allow that everyday, uncontroversial judgments are both "characteristically consequentialist" and "characteristically deontological," then it's clear that both AC and ARC will endorse many conclusions of both kinds.

These two "characteristically" labels are not very meaningful outside the context of moral dilemmas in which considerations about rights and duties, at least superficially, appear to conflict with an impartial cost-benefit analysis. These can be real-world cases or hypothetical cases. Once again, I believe that both AC and ARC are equivalent in the real world, supporting both "characteristically consequentialist" and "characteristically deontological" conclusions, with more of the former in controversial cases. When it comes to hypothetical dilemmas, such as trolley problems, AC and ARC would seem to come apart, with AC giving characteristically consequentialist answers and ARC giving characteristically deontological answers. However, this is only true if one takes an unnecessarily coarse-grained reading of what counts as the "circumstances" of a hypothetical dilemma.

Darwall defines ARC as follows:

> Acceptance rule consequentialism (ARC): An agent A in circumstance C is morally obligated to perform an action of which it is true that the general acceptance of a rule requiring that action would have better consequences than would the general acceptance of any other rule for circumstances like C.

We all know what AC says about the Footbridge dilemma: If it's really true that pushing the one to save the five will do more good, then one ought to do it. But does ARC say anything different? It depends on how we interpret the "circumstance C" of the Footbridge dilemma. If by "circumstances like C" we mean "cases in which a private citizen acting on his own authority with limited time to think can commit a violent murder that he believes will save several lives," then ARC will (I presume) say that it's wrong to push. But if circumstances like C are "exceedingly rare cases in which one knows with absolute certainty that killing one person will save the lives of several others and that there will be no further negative consequences," then ARC will give the same answer as AC. I see no reason to reject the second interpretation. If we are going to hold AC to the fire of contrived hypotheticals, engineered with unrealistic assumptions to make AC look bad, then why should we not hold ARC to the same standard?

I understand, of course, that some readers will consider this cheating. For many, the whole point of rule consequentialism (of which ARC is a form) is to avoid unpalatable conclusions about Footbridge cases and the like. But even if we insist on defining our "circumstances C" in a more conventional way, such that AC endorses pushing and ARC does not, ARC's advantage is soon lost. What it gains in compatibility with moral intuition, it loses in incompatibility with psychological research casting doubt on the reliability of moral intuition. The Footbridge dilemma is an *unfamiliar** situation in which a generally bad action type (a lethal act of pushing an innocent person) is guaranteed to have good long-term consequences. If ARC treats this unfamiliar* hypothetical case as "similar" to the gazillions of real-world cases in which personal violence leads to bad consequences, then it is, like the automatic settings embodied in our amygdalas, too inflexible.

In sum, deep pragmatism, better known as utilitarianism, may not be a proper moral theory, but it is a metamoral theory, which is the kind of evaluative standard that the modern world actually needs. In the real world utilitarianism provides answers to difficult questions, some of which may be called "characteristically deontological" and some of which may be called "characteristically consequentialist." In hypothetical worlds filled with unfamiliar* problems—cases in which generally bad action types are guaranteed to produce good consequences—utilitarianisms answers are all "characteristically consequentialist," and these answers often strike us as terribly, horribly wrong. But that, surprisingly, is to its credit. Given how unreliable our moral intuitions are proving to be, a moral theory that always gets things "right" is surely on the wrong track.

Acknowledgments

Many thanks to Julia Driver and Stephen Darwall for their thoughtful comments.

Notes

1. In my book (*Moral Tribes: Emotion, Reason, and the Gap between Us and Them*, 2013), I argue that both lay and professional ethicists easily slip into misunderstandings of what it means to be a utilitarian in the real world. I have for this reason chosen to describe my favored philosophy as "deep pragmatism," a term that encourages a more accurate conception of real-world utilitarian thinking, wisely applied in light of the inevitable uncertainty, bias, and parochialism inherent in human decision-making.

2. Cushman's theory is an extension of the dual-process theory that I have advocated, providing a deeper understanding of the competing cognitive processes at work in moral dilemmas, and other contexts as well.

References

Bentham, Jeremy, and John Stuart Mill. 2004. *Utilitarianism and Other Essays.* New York: Penguin.

Crockett, Molly J. 2013. "Models of Morality." *Trends in Cognitive Sciences* 17, no. 8: 363–366.

Cushman, Fiery. 2013. "Action, Outcome, and Value: A Dual-System Framework for Morality." *Personality and Social Psychology Review* 17, no. 3: 273–292.

Dickinson, Anthony, B. Balleine, Andrew Watt, Feli Gonzalez, and Robert A. Boakes. 1995. "Motivational Control after Extended Instrumental Training." *Animal Learning and Behavior* 23, no. 2: 197–206.

Greene, Joshua D. 2013. *Moral Tribes: Emotion, Reason, and the Gap between Us and Them.* New York: Penguin.

Greene, Joshua D., Fiery A. Cushman, Lisa E. Stewart, Kelly Lowenberg, Leigh E. Nystrom, and Jonathan D. Cohen. 2009. "Pushing Moral Buttons: The Interaction between Personal Force and Intention in Moral Judgment." *Cognition* 111, no. 3: 364–371.

Hare, R. M. 1981. *Moral Thinking: Its Levels, Methods and Point.* New York: Oxford University Press.

III

New Methods in Moral Neuroscience

8

Emotional Learning, Psychopathy, and Norm Development

R. J. R. Blair, Soonjo Hwang, Stuart F. White, and Harma Meffert

8.1. Introduction

Considerable progress has been made in understanding the development of morality over the past thirty years. On the basis of this increase in understanding, we will consider ten claims:

Claim 1: Most emotional expressions (e.g., fear, sadness, happiness, and disgust) are reinforcers.

Claim 2: Other individuals' different emotional expressions are processed by at least partially independent emotional learning systems.

Claim 3: Individuals with psychopathy show impairment in processing distress cues.

Claim 4: Individuals with psychopathy show relatively intact processing of anger and disgust expressions.

Claim 5: A developmental consequence of these partially independent emotional learning systems is the development of differential processing of different forms of norms.

Claim 6: Because psychopathy is associated with impairment in the amygdala's role in responding to or learning from fearful, sad, and pained expressions (of other indivduals), individuals with the disorder come to represent care-based transgressions as less aversive than healthy individuals.

Claim 7: Because psychopathy is not associated with impairment in the insula's role in responding to or learning from disgusted expressions and the inferior frontal cortex's role in responding to angry expressions, individuals with the disorder should not show impairment processing disgust-based and conventional transgressions.

Claim 8: The ventromedial prefrontal cortex (VMPFC) allows the representation of reinforcement values: information critical for successful (including norm-based) decision-making.

Claim 9: Moral reasoning requires more than the architecture outlined above.

Claim 10: The development of appropriate processing of justice norms may rely on distress cues sensitivity even if the response to others' unfairness does not.

After a brief description of psychopathy and the model that underpins these claims, this chapter will consider the evidence in support of them.

8.2. Psychopathy

Patients with *psychopathy* show pronounced emotional deficits and are at increased risk for displaying antisocial behavior (Frick 1995; Hare 2003). The emotional deficits involve reduced guilt and empathy (callous and unemotional [CU] traits). Psychopathy is a developmental disorder: it is relatively stable from child- into adulthood (Lynam et al. 2007; L. C. Munoz and Frick 2007). Moreover, the functional impairments seen in adults with psychopathy (e.g., in responding to emotional expressions, aversive conditioning, passive avoidance learning, reversal learning, extinction) are also seen in adolescents with psychopathic tendencies (see below).

There are a variety of assessment scales of psychopathy available. For adolescents, these include the Antisocial Process Screening Device (Frick and Hare 2001) and the Psychopathy Checklist—Youth Version (Forth et al. 2007), while the Psychopathy Checklist-Revised (PCL-R; Hare 2003) is often used for adults. These measures typically identify three dimensions of behavior (Cooke et al. 2006; Frick et al. 2000; Neumann et al. 2006), though the exact number is debated (Cooke et al. 2006). These are (1) an emotional factor that focuses on CU traits; (2) an arrogant and deceitful interpersonal style involving narcissism; and (3) impulsive and irresponsible behavior (Cooke et al. 2006; Frick et al. 2000; Neumann et al. 2006).

Psychopathy is not equivalent to the DSM-IV diagnoses of conduct disorder or antisocial personality disorder (ASPD) or their ICD-10 counterparts. These psychiatric diagnoses concentrate on the presence of antisocial behaviors rather than putative underlying causes such as the emotion dysfunction seen in psychopathy (Blair et al. 2005). Accordingly, they capture a broader array of individuals whose difficulties may relate, for example, to executive dysfunction (Moffitt 1993), increased anxiety, or CU traits (Blair et al. 2005). It should be noted, however, that DSM-5 looks likely to introduce a CU specifier for the diagnosis of CD that will lead to a closer relationship of psychopathy with the DSM categories.

8.2.1. THE INTEGRATED EMOTION SYSTEMS MODEL

The integrated emotion systems (IES) model is a cognitive neuroscience model of psychopathy; that is, the goal is to consider the functional properties of the neural systems involved in psychopathic traits and what the computational implications of their dysfunction might be (R. J. R. Blair 2007). The basic claims of this model are that psychopathic traits in youth are associated with two main forms of impairment. First, there is a specific form of empathic incapacity: reduced responsiveness to the distress of others. Second, there is impairment in aspects of decision-making, including decision-making regarding at least some forms of norm. Neural regions that are most implicated include the amygdala, striatum, and VMPFC. The current chapter considers a series of claims of this model that are relevant to moral development.

Claim 1: Most emotional expressions are reinforcers

Considerable work in both humans and other mammals demonstrates that emotional expressions allow the rapid transmission of valence information to conspecifics. For example, the social referencing literature involves mothers displaying emotional reactions to novel objects in front of their children (Aktar et al. 2013; Klinnert et al. 1987). Infants subsequently approach objects associated with their mother's happiness and avoid objects associated with their mother's fear or disgust. Similarly, observational fear studies in nonhuman primates involve infant monkeys observing their mothers displaying emotional reactions to novel objects. The infant comes to show fear responses to those objects associated with maternal fear (Mineka and Zinbarg 2006).

In humans emotional reactions are also used to modify another individual's social behaviors. Displays of distress—sadness, fear, and pain—typically reduce another individual's aggressive responses and may discourage such aggressive responses in the future—they act as aversive reinforcers (R. J. R. Blair 2003). Displays of disgust are also reinforcers, but these typically provide valence information about foods (Rozin et al. 1993). They allow the rapid transmission of taste aversions, and the observer is less likely to approach the food that the individual is showing a disgusted reaction to.

Displays of anger are typically used to curtail the behavior of others in situations where social rules or expectations have been violated (Averill 1982). Such displays act less as aversive reinforcers than as signals to modulate current behavioral responding, particularly in situations involving hierarchy interactions (R. J. R. Blair 2003). In short, others' angry expressions trigger immediate response change (R. J. R. Blair 2003).

Claim 2: Other individuals' different emotional expressions are processed by at least partially independent emotional learning systems

This second claim remains debated. There are data, for example, suggesting that the amygdala and insula respond to both fearful and disgusted expressions (Fitzgerald et al. 2006). However, such studies have typically been underpowered, and meta-analytic reviews strongly indicate at least partially independent systems that process specific emotional expressions (Murphy et al. 2003). Of course, all are processed via the occipital and temporal cortex (though there may also be a subcortical route to the amygdala for the processing of fearful expressions; Luo et al. 2010; Vuilleumier et al. 2003).

The amygdala is critically involved in aversive (and appetitive) conditioning (Cardinal and Everitt 2004; LeDoux 2007). In line with the suggestion that fearful and sad expressions induce aversive conditioning, both initiate amygdala activity (though sadness to a lesser extent) (Blair et al. 1999; Murphy et al. 2003). Moreover, recent animal work has confirmed that the amygdala is necessary for observational fear learning (Jeon et al. 2010).

The insula is critical for taste aversion learning; lesions of the insula block the acquisition and expression of taste aversion learning (Cubero et al. 1999). In line with the suggestion that disgusted expressions induce taste aversion learning (R. J. R. Blair 2003), these expressions are associated with increased insula activity (see, for a meta-analytic review, Murphy et al. 2003). Moreover, lesions of the amygdala disrupt the recognition of disgust expressions (Calder et al. 2000).

The inferior frontal and anterior insula cortex are critically involved in organizing response change as a function of changes in contingencies or other forms of error information (Budhani et al. 2007; Casey et al. 2001). In line with the suggestion that anger expressions are critical for triggering response change (R. J. R. Blair 2003), neuroimaging work has shown that the angry expressions are associated with increased activity within the inferior frontal and anterior insula cortex (see, for a meta-analytic review, Murphy et al. 2003).

Claim 3: Individuals with psychopathy show impairment in processing distress cues

There is now relatively consistent evidence that children and adults with elevated psychopathic traits show impaired processing of distress cues, that is, the fear, sadness, and pain of others. Following on from the early studies (Blair et al. 2001; Blair et al. 2002; Stevens et al. 2001), a considerable body of work has found impaired recognition of fearful and, to a lesser extent, sad expressions in individuals with psychopathic traits (for meta-analytic reviews of this literature, see Dawel et al., in press; Marsh and Blair 2008). Impaired recognition of fearful and sad vocal tones (Blair et al. 2005; Stevens et al. 2001) and fearful body postures (L. Munoz 2009) has also been reported. In addition, reduced autonomic responses to the fear and sadness of others in youth and adults with psychopathic traits has also been reported (Anastassiou-Hadjicharalambous and Warden 2008; R. J. R. Blair 1999; Blair et al. 1997; de Wied et al. 2012). While recognition of pain expressions has not been investigated, there have been findings of reduced autonomic responsiveness, and atypical EEG responses, to others' pain in individuals with psychopathic traits (Aniskiewicz 1979; Cheng et al. 2012; House and Milligan 1976).

FMRI studies have confirmed this dysfunction in the processing of distress cues at the neural level. Studies with youth with psychopathic traits have consistently reported reduced amygdala responses to fearful expressions (Carre et al., in press; Jones et al. 2009; Marsh et al. 2008; Viding et al. 2012; White, Marsh, et al. 2012). There are also indications that fearful expressions fail to initiate attentional priming, via the amygdala, in associated regions of the temporal, parietal, and posterior cingulate cortex (White, Williams, et al. 2012). In addition, youth with psychopathic traits show reduced amygdala responses to others' pain (Marsh et al. in press). It should be noted, however, that the fMRI literature with adults is not so consistent. The reasons for this remain unclear; one study reported reduced amygdala responses to fearful expressions (Gordon et al. 2004), while another did not (Pardini and Phillips 2010).

Claim 4: Individuals with psychopathy show relatively intact processing of anger and disgust expressions

There is relatively consistent evidence that children and adults with elevated psychopathic traits show intact processing of angry and disgusted expressions. For example, a considerable body of work has examined expression recognition in individuals with psychopathic traits. As confirmed by recent meta-analyses (Dawel et al., in press; Marsh and Blair 2008), there are no indications of impairment in the recognition of either expression. Similarly, fMRI studies have failed to find any indications of reduced responsiveness to angry expressions in at least youth with psychopathic tendencies (disgust expressions have not been tested; Carre et al., in press; Marsh et al. 2008; White, Williams, et al. 2012).

Claim 5: A developmental consequence of these partially independent emotional learning systems is the development of differential processing of different forms of norms

There are at least four distinct forms of norm: care based, conventional, disgust based, and fairness based (Blair et al. 2006). This view was first articulated by the domain theorists who distinguished between what they termed moral norms (which correspond to both care-based and fairness-based norms here) and conventional norms (Nucci et al. 1983; Smetana 1993). A fifth form of norm has also been suggested: in-group / loyalty concerns norms, valuing patriotism, for example (Graham et al. 2011). While there are many individuals who value such norms, it is unclear how they are acquired—though it is plausible that they may be a context-specific form of conventional norm. Given the lack of precision, they will not be considered further. Instead, within this section, three of the four norms will be considered: care based, disgust based, and conventional. Fairness-based norms will be considered in more detail later.

Care-based norms: Care-based norms are norms regarding actions that might harm others (including the theft or damage of others' property). Understanding the development of care-based norms led to the development of the integrated emotion systems model articulated here (R. J. R. Blair 2007). In particular, the model stresses emotional learning mediated by the amygdala. This allows conditioned stimuli (including representations of moral transgressions) to be associated with unconditioned stimuli (including the victim's distress cues). As noted above, the amygdala is crucial for the formation of stimulus-reinforcement associations generally; that is, it allows previously neutral objects to come to be valued as either good or bad according to whether they have been associated with punishment or reward (Everitt et al. 2003; LeDoux 2007). Moreover, the amygdala is critically involved in responding to the distress cue reinforcers (i.e., the observed sadness, fear, and pain of others; see above). Indeed, when it is lesioned, observational learning of fear is disrupted (Jeon et al. 2010). In short, researchers argue that the individual learns that care-based norm violations are "bad" because they are associated with the aversive consequences of the victim's distress that occurred following the norm violation.

The importance of the amygdala in care-based moral judgments can be seen through fMRI studies that have examined neural activity in response to care-based norms. These studies have investigated responses to trolley problems (Greene et al. 2004; Shenhav and Greene 2010), passive responding to scenes of moral transgressions (Harenski and Hamann 2006; Moll et al. 2002), judging descriptions of behaviors as moral or immoral (Borg et al. 2006; Heekeren et al. 2005), and brain activity during performance of a morality implicit association task (Luo et al. 2006). They have relatively consistently shown amygdala responses to care-based transgressions.

Disgust-based norms: For some time, Haidt has emphasized disgust with respect to what he has termed "purity" norms (Haidt 2001; Haidt and Graham 2007). He has suggested that "in many cultures, disgust goes beyond such contaminant-related issues and supports a set of virtues and vices linked to bodily activities in general, and religious activities in particular" (Haidt and Graham 2007, 106). While he does not detail the neurocognitive architecture that might mediate and allow the development of disgust-based ("purity") morality, he has argued for its existence on evolutionary grounds. However, evolutionary arguments are difficult to empirically evaluate.

However, a neurocognitive model of disgust-based norms can be articulated. Disgusted expressions, like fearful, sad, and happy expressions, are reinforcers (R. J. R. Blair 2003). As noted above, they usually provide information about foods (Rozin et al. 1993). However, disgusted expressions can also be used to convey distaste at another individual's actions. By doing so they allow the development of appropriate processing of disgust-based norms where the emotional force behind the proscribed actions is disgust.

As noted above, observing disgusted expressions engages the insula (Phillips et al. 1998; Sprengelmeyer et al. 1998), a region critical for taste aversion learning (Cubero et al. 1999). In line with the architecture proposed here, fMRI work has indicated that disgust-based transgressions are also associated with increased insula activation (Moll et al. 2005), a neurobiological argument for a relatively independent norm system based on the emotion of disgust.

Conventional norms: Conventional norms are norms regarding actions that can cause social disorder (e.g., talking in class). They particularly concern actions that challenge established hierarchies (in the example above, the teacher's status). Elsewhere, we have proposed a neurocognitive model of conventional reasoning; the social response reversal (SRR) system model (e.g., Blair and Cipolotti 2000). According to this model aversive social cues (particularly, angry expressions) or expectations of such cues (i.e., representations of actions that make other individuals angry) guide the individual away from committing conventional transgressions (particularly in the presence of higher-status individuals) and orchestrate a response to witnessed conventional transgressions (particularly when these are committed by lower-status individuals; Blair and Cipolotti 2000).

Principal neural systems implicated in this process include the dorsomedial frontal cortex and inferior frontal / anterior insula cortex. These regions are consistently activated when behavior needs to be altered (Botvinick et al. 2004; Budhani et al. 2007). As noted above, displays of anger are typically used to curtail or change the behavior of others (Averill 1982). The inferior frontal cortex is particularly responsive to angry expressions (Murphy et al. 2003). Importantly, this region shows activity when participants consider conventional transgressions (Berthoz et al. 2002). Moreover, this region is also critically involved in processing hierarchy cues (Marsh et al. 2009).

Claim 6: Because psychopathy is associated with impairment in the amygdala's role in responding to or learning from fearful, sad, and pain expressions, individuals with the disorder come to represent care-based transgressions as less aversive than healthy individuals

There is now considerable work indicating that care-based norm judgments are disrupted in individuals with psychopathy. This was first formally documented by Blair and colleagues, who showed that youth and adults with psychopathy demonstrated significant impairment on what is termed the moral/conventional distinction task (R. J. R. Blair 1995, 1997). Youth and adults with psychopathic traits show a reduced distinction in their judgments between care-based and conventional transgressions. Specifically, following the removal of rules prohibiting the act, they are significantly more likely to judge victim-based and social conventional rules similarly. They are also less likely to make reference to the welfare of others in their justifications of why victim-based transgressions are bad. More recently, work in both subclinical and clinical populations has shown that individuals with psychopathy show reduced endorsement of care-based norms (Aharoni et al. 2011; Glenn et al. 2009). They also show an increased likelihood to allow actions that indirectly harm another (Koenigs et al. 2011) and regard accidents that harm others as more permissible than comparison individuals (Young et al. 2012).

As noted above, the motivational force against care-based transgressions is thought to rely on the amygdala's role in the association of the representation of the transgression with the fear/sadness/pain of the victim. In support of this model, recent work has shown that the recruitment of the amygdala during care-based reasoning is disrupted in both youth and adults with psychopathic traits (Glenn et al. 2008; Harenski et al. 2010; Marsh et al. 2011).

Before continuing, we should note work with a population who can be considered a counterpoint to youth with psychopathic traits; that is, youth with high trait fearfulness. Trait fearfulness can be considered an index of the integrity of the amygdala. Individuals with heightened amygdala responsiveness to threat are likely to be more fearful (R. J. R. Blair 2003). Accordingly, on the basis of the model developed above, trait fearfulness indexes the integrity of the neural system necessary for responding appropriately to distress cues and moral socialization. Heightened trait fearfulness should thus be associated with heightened sensitivity to care-based transgressions. This suggestion is borne out in the literature using a variety of measures (e.g., Asendorpf and Nunner-Winkler 1992; Kochanska et al. 2007).

Claim 7: Because psychopathy is not associated with impairment in the insula's role in responding to or learning from disgusted expressions and the inferior frontal cortex's role in responding to angry expressions, individuals with the disorder should not show impairment processing disgust-based and conventional transgressions

As noted above, individuals with psychopathy fail the moral/conventional distinction task, and this has been attributed to impairment in the processing of care-based transgressions and intact processing of conventional transgressions (R. J. R. Blair 1995). However, more direct evidence that individuals with psychopathy show intact processing of conventional transgressions was provided by a later study (Blair and Cipolotti 2000). This study was a single-case study of a patient with an extensive orbital frontal cortex lesion that included, as comparison populations, individuals with psychopathy. Again impaired performance on the moral/conventional distinction task was seen in the individuals with psychopathy. Performance on another measure, the "social situations task," was also examined. In this task, participants are asked to rate the appropriateness of different actions in particular social circumstances. The transgressions in these vignettes were all conventional and induced anger in observers against the transgressor (Blair and Cipolotti 2000). Replication of this appropriate endorsement of conventional norms has been more recently found using Haidt's Moral Foundations Questionnaire in both subclinical (Glenn et al. 2009) and clinical populations of individuals with psychopathy (Aharoni et al. 2011). In addition, these latter two studies also showed that endorsement of disgust-based norms was intact in individuals with psychopathy (Aharoni et al. 2011; Glenn et al. 2009).

Claim 8: The VMPFC allows the representation of reinforcement values: information critical for successful (including norm-based) decision-making

A basic tenet of the IES model is that emotional learning systems allow norms to acquire emotive force, force that guides attitudes toward these norms. Only one of these emotional learning systems is thought be disrupted in psychopathic traits, but all are thought to feed reinforcement expectancy information to the VMPFC. The VMPFC is thought to represent this information and allow appropriate decision-making. Considerable data support a role for the VMPFC in the representation of reinforcement information (Blair et al. 2006; Knutson and Bossaerts 2007; O'Doherty 2011). Moreover, data support that this region is responsive to norms. Most of the fMRI studies examining the neural response to care-based transgressions report VMPFC activity (Greene et al. 2004; Heekeren et al. 2005; Luo et al. 2006). Importantly, this activity is modulated by the transgression's severity (Luo et al. 2006). Considerable data show that activity within the VMPFC is modulated by the magnitude of the reinforcement expectancy (Blair et al. 2006; Knutson and Bossaerts 2007; O'Doherty 2011).

Claim 9: Moral reasoning requires more than the architecture outlined above

The model developed above provides an account of how emotion-based systems allow the development of judgments of "badness" about different forms of transgression. However, as has been noted (Nichols 2002), this model cannot explain how individuals generate judgments of "immorality." For example, an individual killing five people and a plane crash killing five people are both "bad" events, but only the first is usually considered as immoral. Nichols has proposed that judgments of immorality require the participant accessing semantic knowledge, that an immorality judgment is a form of concept-matching task. This seems plausible but will not be a focus here.

One issue that will be briefly discussed is Theory of Mind. Theory of Mind is defined as the capacity to represent the mental states of others: the beliefs, intentions, and knowledge (Frith and Frith 2006). It has been known for some time that intent information becomes increasingly important for morality judgments across development (Piaget 1932). Thus, children at the age of four years consider the severity of care-based transgressions on the basis of outcome information, the extent to which a victim was harmed. However, children by the age of eight years and adults typically regard intent information to be paramount (Baird and Astington 2004). This is consistent with the idea that emotion-based systems are critical for the early development of moral judgments; they allow the individual to regard actions as bad, but intent information can supersede emotion information in later childhood and adult moral reasoning (cf. Young et al. 2010).

Claim 10: The development of appropriate processing of justice norms may rely on distress cues sensitivity even if the response to others' unfairness does not

Justice norms cover the fairness of decisions regarding the allocation of resources. Allocation of resources regarded as unfair elicit anger in those who believe they have been unjustly treated (Sanfey et al. 2003). Considerable work has examined justice reasoning in the context of cooperation tasks (e.g., the Ultimatum and Trust games). In such games, a proposer suggests an allocation of resources and typically the participant decides whether or not to accept this allocation or punish the proposer for the unfairness of his offer (de Quervain et al. 2004; King-Casas et al. 2008). The greater the difference in the allocation of resources between the individuals, the greater the sense of the unfairness of the offer and the greater the amount that the participant is prepared to pay in order to punish the proposer (e.g., White et al. 2013).

Unfair offers by proposers have been found to elicit activity in participants within both the anterior insula cortex (AIC) and the dorsomedial frontal cortex (DMFC; King-Casas et al. 2008; Rilling et al. 2002; Sanfey et al. 2003; White et al. 2013). There have been suggestions that activity within these regions reflects anger elicited by unfairness to the self (Sanfey et al. 2003). This is consistent with the argument raised above that these regions respond to anger or expectations of anger (including in response to norm violations) and organize changes in behavior (Blair and Cipolotti 2000).

In short, unfair offers make individuals angry and activate regions of the DMFC and AIC/IFG implicated in responding to anger and organizing behavior on the basis of this anger. Of course, this form of response is also implicated in the response to conventional transgressions. Yet impairment in processing justice norms appears to dissociate from impairment in processing conventional norms. This was seen in the moral distinction literature where justice norms are processed like care-based norms and unlike conventional norms (Nucci et al. 1983; Smetana 1993). Moreover, individuals with psychopathic traits have been reported to show reduced endorsement of justice norms but intact endorsement of conventional norms (Aharoni et al. 2011; Glenn et al. 2009).

We suggest that this is due to different computations occurring when one considers an individual who has been unjustly treated as opposed to when processing an unfair allocation of resources. It appears plausible that the representation of an unjustly treated individual is associated with the person's distress. Thus, the unfairness transgression is processed like a care-based transgression (for example, they are considered rule independent; see Nucci et al. 1983; Smetana 1993). In contrast, witnessing an unfair allocation of resources, particularly to the self, results in anger and a motivation to challenge (or punish) the actions of the allocator. Of course, the above speculation is in need of empirical investigation.

8.3. Conclusions

Four classes of norm can be distinguished from a neurocognitive perspective: harm based, disgust based, social conventions, and justice based. Learning the prohibitive power of these norms relies on relatively independent emotional learning systems (see figure 8.1). These are not specified for the learning of social norms but rather are learning systems for the emotional significance of stimuli that have been co-opted to allow the rapid transmission of social values. These emotional learning systems can be selectively impaired, leading to a reduced ability to acquire the prohibitive power of specific forms of norms (e.g., the reduced prohibitive power of care-based and justice-based norms for individuals with psychopathy). The prohibitive power of these norms rests on their ability to generate an aversive reinforcement expectation that can be adequately represented by the ventromedial prefrontal cortex.

The emotion-based systems alone do not allow full moral development. An individual's culturally influenced theories of morality influence what forms of norm he or she

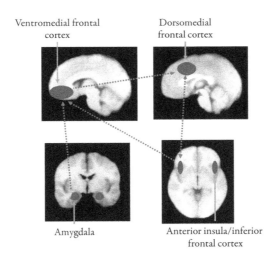

Ventromedial frontal cortex   Dorsomedial frontal cortex

Amygdala   Anterior insula/inferior frontal cortex

FIGURE 8.1 The IES model with respect to moral reasoning. The amygdala is critical for processing distress cues and allowing the development of aversions to transgressions that result in harm to others (i.e., care-based and justice-based transgressions). The insula and inferior frontal cortex are importantly involved in the processing of disgust and anger cues. Processing these cues allows the development of an aversion to disgust-based and conventional norms, respectively. Expectations of the aversiveness of norm violations, fed forward from the amygdala and insula, are represented in the ventromedial frontal cortex, and it is these expectations that bias the healthy individual away from committing violations of these norms. The dorsomedial frontal cortex has access to these expectations, allowing the selection between actions associated with different expectations. Violations of conventional and justice-based norms elicit anger and recruit the dorsomedial frontal cortex and anterior insula/inferior frontal cortex, particularly if these norm violations are against the individual. As such they can be considered provocations that organize responses to the transgressor that may include retribution.

will consider moral. Indeed, the individual will only consider the action immoral if the action matches the individual's concept of what an immoral act is. For most individuals, part of the concept of an immoral act includes its intentional nature. In short, full moral development requires the integration of mental state information provided by theory of mind with outcome information provided by the emotion-learning systems.

Acknowledgment

This work was supported by the Intramural Research Program of the National Institute of Mental Health, National Institutes of Health under grant number 1-ZIA-MH002860-08.

References

Aharoni, E., O. Antonenko, and K. A. Kiehl. 2011. "Disparities in the Moral Intuitions of Criminal Offenders: The Role of Psychopathy." *Journal of Research in Personality* 45, no. 3: 322–327. doi:10.1016/j.jrp.2011.02.005.

Aktar, E., M. Majdandzic, W. de Vente, and S. M. Bogels. 2013. "The Interplay between Expressed Parental Anxiety and Infant Behavioural Inhibition Predicts Infant Avoidance in a Social Referencing Paradigm." *Journal of Child Psychology and Psychiatry* 54, no. 2: 144–156. doi:10.1111/j.1469-7610.2012.02601.x.

Anastassiou-Hadjicharalambous, X., and D. Warden. 2008. "Physiologically-Indexed and Self-Perceived Affective Empathy in Conduct-Disordered Children High and Low on Callous-Unemotional Traits." *Child Psychiatry and Human Develevelopment* 39, no. 4: 503–517. doi:10.1007/s10578-008-0104-y.

Aniskiewicz, A. S. 1979. "Autonomic Components of Vicarious Conditioning and Psychopathy." *Journal of Clinical Psychology* 35: 60–67.

Asendorpf, J. B., and G. Nunner-Winkler. 1992. "Children's Moral Motive Strength and Temperamental Inhibition Reduce Their Immoral Behaviour in Real Moral Conflicts." *Child Development* 63: 1223–1235.

Averill, J. R. 1982. *Anger and Aggression: An Essay on Emotion.* New York: Springer-Verlag.

Baird, J. A., and J. W. Astington. 2004. "The Role of Mental State Understanding in the Development of Moral Cognition and Moral Action." *New Directions in Child and Adolescent Development* 103: 37–49.

Berthoz, S., J. Armony, R. J. R. Blair, and R. Dolan. 2002. "Neural Correlates of Violation of Social Norms and Embarrassment." *Brain* 125, no. 8: 1696–1708.

Blair, K. S., A. A. Marsh, J. Morton, M. Vythilingham, M. Jones, K. Mondillo, . . . R. J. R. Blair. 2006. "Choosing the Lesser of Two Evils, the Better of Two Goods: Specifying the Roles of Ventromedial Prefrontal Cortex and Dorsal Anterior Cingulate Cortex in Object Choice." *Journal of Neuroscience* 26, no. 44: 11379–11386.

Blair, R. J. R. 1995. "A Cognitive Developmental Approach to Morality: Investigating the Psychopath." *Cognition* 57: 1–29.

Blair, R. J. R. 1997. "Moral Reasoning in the Child with Psychopathic Tendencies." *Personality and Individual Differences* 22: 731–739.

Blair, R. J. R. 1999. "Responsiveness to Distress Cues in the Child with Psychopathic Tendencies." *Personality and Individual Differences* 27: 135–145.

Blair, R. J. R. 2003. "Facial Expressions, Their Communicatory Functions and Neuro-cognitive Substrates." *Philosophical Transactions of the Royal Society London B: Biological Sciences* 358, no. 1431: 561–572.

Blair, R. J. R. 2007. "The Amygdala and Ventromedial Prefrontal Cortex in Morality and Psychopathy." *Trends in Cognitive Science* 11, no. 9: 387–392.

Blair, R. J. R., S. Budhani, E. Colledge, and S. Scott. 2005. "Deafness to Fear in Boys with Psychopathic Tendencies." *Journal of Child Psychology and Psychiatry* 46, no. 3: 327–336.

Blair, R. J. R., and L. Cipolotti. 2000. "Impaired Social Response Reversal: A Case of 'Acquired Sociopathy.'" *Brain* 123: 1122–1141.

Blair, R. J. R., E. Colledge, L. Murray, and D. G. Mitchell. 2001. "A Selective Impairment in the Processing of Sad and Fearful Expressions in Children with Psychopathic Tendencies." *Journal of Abnormal Child Psychology* 29, no. 6: 491–498.

Blair, R. J. R., L. Jones, F. Clark, and M. Smith. 1997. "The Psychopathic Individual: A Lack of Responsiveness to Distress Cues?" *Psychophysiology* 34: 192–198.

Blair, R. J. R., A. A. Marsh, E. Finger, K. S. Blair, and Q. Luo. 2006. "Neuro-cognitive Systems Involved in Morality." *Philosophical Explorations* 9, no. 1: 13–27.

Blair, R. J. R., D. G. V. Mitchell, and K. S. Blair. 2005. *The Psychopath: Emotion and the Brain.* Oxford: Blackwell.

Blair, R. J. R., D. G. V. Mitchell, R. A. Richell, S. Kelly, A. Leonard, C. Newman, and S. K. Scott. 2002. "Turning a Deaf Ear to Fear: Impaired Recognition of Vocal Affect in Psychopathic Individuals." *Journal of Abnormal Psychology* 111, no. 4: 682–686.

Blair, R. J. R., J. S. Morris, C. D. Frith, D. I. Perrett, and R. Dolan. 1999. "Dissociable Neural Responses to Facial Expressions of Sadness and Anger." *Brain* 122: 883–893.

Borg, J. S., C. Hynes, J. Van Horn, S. Grafton, and W. Sinnott-Armstrong. 2006. "Consequences, Action, and Intention as Factors in Moral Judgments: An FMRI Investigation." *Journal of Cognitive Neuroscience* 18, no. 5: 803–817.

Botvinick, M. M., J. D. Cohen, and C. S. Carter. 2004. "Conflict Monitoring and Anterior Cingulate Cortex: An Update." *Trends in Cognitive Science* 8, no. 12: 539–546.

Budhani, S., A. A. Marsh, D. S. Pine, and R. J. R. Blair. 2007. "Neural Correlates of Response Reversal: Considering Acquisition." *NeuroImage* 34, no. 4: 1754–1765.

Calder, A. J., J. Keane, F. Manes, N. Antoun, and A. W. Young. 2000. "Impaired Recognition and Experience of Disgust Following Brain Injury." *Nature Neuroscience* 3: 1077–1078.

Cardinal, R. N., and B. J. Everitt. 2004. "Neural and Psychological Mechanisms Underlying Appetitive Learning: Links to Drug Addiction." *Current Opinion in Neurobiology* 14, no. 2: 156–162.

Carre, J. M., L. W. Hyde, C. S. Neumann, E. Viding, and A. R. Hariri. In press. "The Neural Signatures of Distinct Psychopathic Traits." *Social Neuroscience*.

Casey, B. J., S. D. Forman, P. Franzen, A. Berkowitz, T. S. Braver, L. E. Nystrom, . . . D. C. Noll. 2001. "Sensitivity of Prefrontal Cortex to Changes in Target Probability: A Functional MRI Study." *Human Brain Mapping* 13, no. 1: 26–33.

Cheng, Y., A. Y. Hung, and J. Decety. 2012. "Dissociation between Affective Sharing and Emotion Understanding in Juvenile Psychopaths." *Development and Psychopathology* 24, no. 2: 623–636. doi:10.1017/s095457941200020x.

Cooke, D. J., C. Michie, and S. Hart. 2006. "Facets of Clinical Psychopathy: Toward Clearer Measurement." In *The Handbook of Psychopathy*, edited by C. J. Patrick, 91–106. New York: Guilford Press.

Cubero, I., T. E. Thiele, and I. L. Bernstein. 1999. "Insular Cortex Lesions and Taste Aversion Learning: Effects of Conditioning Method and Timing of Lesion." *Brain Research* 839, no. 2: 323–330.

Dawel, A., R. O'Kearney, E. McKone, and R. Palermo. In press. "Not Just Fear and Sadness: Meta-analytic Evidence of Pervasive Emotion Recognition Deficits for Facial and Vocal Expressions in Psychopathy." *Neuroscience and Biobehavioral Reviews*.

de Quervain, D. J., U. Fischbacher, V. Treyer, M. Schellhammer, U. Schnyder, A. Buck, and E. Fehr. 2004. "The Neural Basis of Altruistic Punishment." *Science* 305, no. 5688: 1254–1258. doi:10.1126/science.1100735.

de Wied, M., A. van Boxtel, W. Matthys, and W. Meeus. 2012. "Verbal, Facial and Autonomic Responses to Empathy-Eliciting Film Clips by Disruptive Male Adolescents with High versus Low Callous-Unemotional Traits." *Journal of Abnormal Child Psychology* 40, no. 2: 211–223. doi:10.1007/s10802-011-9557-8.

Everitt, B. J., R. N. Cardinal, J. A. Parkinson, and T. W. Robbins. 2003. "Appetitive Behavior: Impact of Amygdala-Dependent Mechanisms of Emotional Learning." *Annual New York Academy of Sciences* 985: 233–250.

Fitzgerald, D. A., M. Angstadt, L. M. Jelsone, P. J. Nathan, and K. L. Phan. 2006. "Beyond Threat: Amygdala Reactivity across Multiple Expressions of Facial Affect." *NeuroImage* 30, no. 4: 1441–1448.

Forth, A. E., D. S. Kosson, and R. D. Hare. 2007. *The Psychopathy Checklist: Youth Version*. Toronto: Multi-Health Systems.

Frick, P. J. 1995. "Callous-Unemotional Traits and Conduct Problems: A Two-Factor Model of Psychopathy in Children." *Issues in Criminological and Legal Psychology* 24: 47–51.

Frick, P. J., S. D. Bodin, and C. T. Barry. 2000. "Psychopathic Traits and Conduct Problems in Community and Clinic-Referred Samples of Children: Further Development of the Psychopathy Screening Device." *Psychological Assessment* 12, no. 4: 382–393.

Frick, P. J., and R. D. Hare. 2001. *The Antisocial Process Screening Device*. Toronto: Multi-Health Systems.

Frith, C. D., and U. Frith. 2006. "The Neural Basis of Mentalizing." *Neuron* 50, no. 4: 531–534.

Glenn, A. L., R. Iyer, J. Graham, S. Koleva, and J. Haidt. 2009. "Are All Types of Morality Compromised in Psychopathy?" *Journal of Personality Disorders* 23: 384–398.

Glenn, A. L., A. Raine, and R. A. Schug. 2008. "The Neural Correlates of Moral Decision-Making in Psychopathy." *Molecular Psychiatry* 14: 5–6.

Gordon, H. L., A. A. Baird, and A. End. 2004. "Functional Differences among Those High and Low on a Trait Measure of Psychopathy." *Biological Psychiatry* 56, no. 7: 516–521.

Graham, J., B. A. Nosek, J. Haidt, R. Iyer, S. Koleva, and P. H. Ditto. 2011. "Mapping the Moral Domain." *Journal of Personality and Social Psychology* 101, no. 2: 366–385. doi:10.1037/a0021847.

Greene, J. D., L. E. Nystrom, A. D. Engell, J. M. Darley, and J. D. Cohen. 2004. "The Neural Bases of Cognitive Conflict and Control in Moral Judgment." *Neuron* 44, 389–400.

Haidt, J. 2001. "The Emotional Dog and Its Rational Tail: A Social Intuitionist Approach to Moral Judgment." *Psychological Review* 108, no. 4: 814–834.

Haidt, J., and J. Graham. 2007. "When Morality Opposes Justice: Conservatives Have Moral Intuitions That Liberals May Not Recognize." *Social Justice Research* 20, no. 1: 98–116.

Hare, R. D. 2003. *Hare Psychopathy Checklist-Revised (PCL-R)*. 2nd ed. Toronto: Multi-Health Systems.

Harenski, C. L., and S. Hamann. 2006. "Neural Correlates of Regulating Negative Emotions Related to Moral Violations." *NeuroImage* 30, no. 1: 313–324.

Harenski, C. L., K. A. Harenski, M. S. Shane, and K. A. Kiehl. 2010. "Aberrant Neural Processing of Moral Violations in Criminal Psychopaths." *Journal of Abnormal Psychology* 119, no. 4: 863–874. doi:10.1037/a0020979.

Heekeren, H. R., I. Wartenburger, H. Schmidt, K. Prehn, H. P. Schwintowski, and A. Villringer. 2005. "Influence of Bodily Harm on Neural Correlates of Semantic and Moral Decision-Making." *NeuroImage* 24: 887–897.

House, T. H., and W. L. Milligan. 1976. "Autonomic Responses to Modeled Distress in Prison Psychopaths." *Journal of Personality and Social Psychology* 34: 556–560.

Jeon, D., S. Kim, M. Chetana, D. Jo, H. E. Ruley, S. Y. Lin, . . . H. S. Shin. 2010. "Observational Fear Learning Involves Affective Pain System and Cav1.2 Ca2+ Channels in ACC." *Nature Neuroscience* 13, no. 4: 482–488. doi:10.1038/nn.2504.

Jones, A. P., K. R. Laurens, C. M. Herba, G. J. Barker, and E. Viding. 2009. "Amygdala Hypoactivity to Fearful Faces in Boys with Conduct Problems and Callous-Unemotional Traits." *American Journal of Psychiatry* 166: 95–102.

King-Casas, B., C. Sharp, L. Lomax-Bream, T. Lohrenz, P. Fonagy, and P. R. Montague. 2008. "The Rupture and Repair of Cooperation in Borderline Personality Disorder." *Science* 321, no. 5890: 806–810. doi:10.1126/science.1156902.

Klinnert, M. D., R. N. Emde, P. Butterfield, and J. J. Campos. 1987. "Social Referencing: The Infant's Use of Emotional Signals from a Friendly Adult with Mother Present." *Annual Progress in Child Psychiatry and Child Development* 22: 427–432.

Knutson, B., and P. Bossaerts. 2007. "Neural Antecedents of Financial Decisions." *Journal of Neuroscience* 27, no. 31: 8174–8177. doi:10.1523/jneurosci.1564-07.2007.

Kochanska, G., N. Aksan, and M. E. Joy. 2007. "Children's Fearfulness as a Moderator of Parenting in Early Socialization: Two Longitudinal Studies." *Developmental Psychology* 43, no. 1: 222–237.

Koenigs, M., M. Kruepke, J. Zeier, and J. P. Newman. 2011. "Utilitarian Moral Judgment in Psychopathy." *Social, Cognitive, and Affective Neuroscience*. doi:10.1093/scan/nsr048.

LeDoux, J. E. 2007. "The Amygdala." *Current Biology* 17, no. 20: R868–R874.

Luo, Q., T. Holroyd, C. Majestic, X. Cheng, J. C. Schechter, and R. J. R. Blair. 2010. "Emotional Automaticity Is a Matter of Timing." *Journal of Neuroscience* 30, 5825–5829.

Luo, Q., M. Nakic, T. Wheatley, R. Richell, A. Martin, and R. J. Blair. 2006. "The Neural Basis of Implicit Moral Attitude: An IAT Study Using Event-Related fMRI." *NeuroImage* 30, no. 4: 1449–1457.

Lynam, D. R., A. Caspi, T. E. Moffitt, R. Loeber, and M. Stouthamer-Loeber. 2007. "Longitudinal Evidence That Psychopathy Scores in Early Adolescence Predict Adult Psychopathy." *Journal of Abnormal Psychology* 116, no. 1: 155–165.

Marsh, A. A., K. S. Blair, M. M. Jones, N. Soliman, and R. J. R. Blair, 2009. "Dominance and Submission: The Ventrolateral Prefrontal Cortex and Responses to Status Cues." *Journal of Cognitive Neuroscience* 21, no. 4: 713–724.

Marsh, A. A., and R. J. R. Blair. 2008. "Deficits in Facial Affect Recognition among Antisocial Populations: A Meta-analysis." *Neuroscience and Biobehavioral Reviews* 32, no. 3: 454–465.

Marsh, A. A., E. C. Finger, K. A. Fowler, C. J. Adalio, I. T. N. Jurkowitz, J. C. Schechter, . . . R. J. R. Blair. In press. "Empathic Responsiveness in Amygdala and Anterior Cingulate Cortex in Youths with Psychopathic Traits." *Journal of Child Psychology and Psychiatry*.

Marsh, A. A., E. C. Finger, K. A. Fowler, I. T. Jurkowitz, J. C. Schechter, H. H. Yu, . . . , R. J. R. Blair. 2011. "Reduced Amygdala-Orbitofrontal Connectivity during Moral Judgments in Youths with Disruptive Behavior Disorders and Psychopathic Traits." *Psychiatry Research* 194, no. 3: 279–286. doi:10.1016/j.pscychresns.2011.07.008.

Marsh, A. A., E. C. Finger, D. G. V. Mitchell, M. E. Reid, C. Sims, D. S. Kosson, . . . R. J. R. Blair. 2008. "Reduced Amygdala Response to Fearful Expressions in Children and Adolescents with Callous-Unemotional Traits and Disruptive Behavior Disorders." *American Journal of Psychiatry* 165, no. 6: 712–720.

Mineka, S., and R. Zinbarg. 2006. "A Contemporary Learning Theory Perspective on the Etiology of Anxiety Disorders: It's Not What You Thought It Was." *American Psychologist* 61, no. 1: 10–26.

Moffitt, T. E. 1993. "The Neuropsychology of Conduct Disorder." *Development and Psychopathology* 5: 135–152.

Moll, J., R. de Oliveira-Souza, P. J. Eslinger, I. E. Bramati, J. Mourao-Miranda, P. A. Andreiuolo, and L. Pessoa. 2002. "The Neural Correlates of Moral Sensitivity: A Functional Magnetic Resonance Imaging Investigation of Basic and Moral emotions." *Journal of Neuroscience* 22, no. 7: 2730–2736.

Moll, J., R. de Oliveira-Souza, F. T. Moll, F. A. Ignacio, I. E. Bramati, E. M. Caparelli- Daquer, and P. J. Eslinger. 2005. "The Moral Affiliations of Disgust: A Functional MRI Study." *Cognitive and Behavioral Neurology* 18, no. 1: 68–78.

Munoz, L. 2009. "Callous-Unemotional Traits Are Related to Combined Deficits in Recognizing Afraid Faces and Body Poses." *Journal of American Academy of Child and Adolescent Psychaitry* 48, no. 5: 554–562.

Munoz, L. C., and P. J. Frick. 2007. "The Reliability, Stability, and Predictive Utility of the Self-Report Version of the Antisocial Process Screening Device." *Scandinavian Journal of Psychology* 48: 299–312.

Murphy, F. C., I. Nimmo-Smith, and A. D. Lawrence. 2003. "Functional Neuroanatomy of Emotions: A Meta-analysis." *Cognitive, Affective, and Behavioral Neuroscience* 3, no. 3: 207–233.

Neumann, C. S., D. S. Kosson, A. E. Forth, and R. D. Hare. 2006. "Factor Structure of the Hare Psychopathy Checklist: Youth Version (PCL: YV) in Incarcerated Adolescents." *Psychological Assessment* 18: 142–154.

Nichols, S. 2002. "Norms with Feeling: Towards a Psychological Account of Moral Judgment." *Cognition* 84, no. 2: 221–236.

Nucci, L. P., E. Turiel, and G. E. Encarnacion-Gawrych. 1983. "Social Interactions and Social Concepts: Analysis of Morality and Convention in the Virgin Islands." *Journal of Cross Cultural Psychology* 14: 469–487.

O'Doherty, J. P. 2011. "Contributions of the Ventromedial Prefrontal Cortex to Goal-Directed Action Selection." *Annals of the New York Academy of Sciences* 1239, 118–129. doi:10.1111/j.1749-6632.2011.06290.x.

Pardini, D. A., and M. Phillips. 2010. "Neural Responses to Emotional and Neutral Facial Expressions in Chronically Violent Men." *Journal of Psychiatry and Neuroscience* 35, no. 6: 390–398. doi:10.1503/jpn.100037.

Phillips, M. L., A. W. Young, S. K. Scott, A. J. Calder, C. Andrew, V. Giampietro, . . . J. A. Gray. 1998. "Neural Responses to Facial and Vocal Expressions of Fear and Disgust." *Proceedings of the Royal Society London B: Biological Sciences* 265, no. 1408: 1809–1817.

Piaget, J. 1932. *The Moral Development of the Child.* Translated by Marjorie Gabain. London: Routledge and Kegan Paul.

Rilling, J. K., D. Gutman, T. Zeh, G. Pagnoni, G. Berns, and C. Kilts. 2002. "A Neural Basis for Social Cooperation." *Neuron* 35, no. 2: 395–405.

Rozin, P., J. Haidt, and C. R. McCauley. 1993. "Disgust." In *Handbook of Emotions*, edited by M. Lewis and J. M. Haviland, 575–594. New York: Guilford Press.

Sanfey, A. G., J. K. Rilling, J. A. Aronson, L. E. Nystrom, and J. D. Cohen. 2003. "The Neural Basis of Economic Decision-Making in the Ultimatum Game." *Science* 300, no. 5626: 1755–1758. doi:10.1126/science.1082976.

Shenhav, A., and J. D. Greene. 2010. "Moral Judgments Recruit Domain-General Valuation Mechanisms to Integrate Representations of Probability and Magnitude." *Neuron* 67, no. 4: 667–677. doi:10.1016/j.neuron.2010.07.020.

Smetana, J. G. 1993. "Understanding of Social Rules." In *The Child as Psychologist: An Introduction to the Development of Social Cognition*, edited by M. Bennett, 111–141. New York: Harvester Wheatsheaf.

Sprengelmeyer, R., M. Rausch, U. T. Eysel, and H. Przuntek. 1998. "Neural Structures Associated with the Recognition of Facial Basic Emotions." *Proceedings of the Royal Society London B: Biological Sciences* 265: 1927–1931.

Stevens, D., T. Charman, and R. J. R. Blair. 2001. "Recognition of Emotion in Facial Expressions and Vocal Tones in Children with Psychopathic Tendencies." *Journal of Genetic Psychology* 162, no. 2: 201–211.

Viding, E., C. L. Sebastian, M. R. Dadds, P. L. Lockwood, C. A. Cecil, De S. A. Brito, and E. J. McCrory. 2012. "Amygdala Response to Preattentive Masked Fear in Children with Conduct Problems: The Role of Callous-Unemotional Traits." *American Journal of Psychiatry* 169, no. 10: 1109–1116. doi:10.1176/appi.ajp.2012.12020191.

Vuilleumier, P., J. L. Armony, J. Driver, and R. J. Dolan. 2003. "Distinct Spatial Frequency Sensitivities for Processing Faces and Emotional Expressions." *Nature Neuroscience* 6, no. 6: 624–631.

White, S. F., S. J. Brislin, H. Meffert, S. Sinclair, and R. J. R. Blair. 2013. "Callous-Unemotional Traits Modulate the Neural Response Associated with Punishing Another Individual during Social Exchange: A Preliminary Investigation." *Journal of Personality Disorders* 27, no. 1: 99–112.

White, S. F., A. A. Marsh, K. A. Fowler, J. C. Schechter, C. Adalio, K. Pope, . . . R. J. R. Blair. 2012. "Reduced Amygdala Responding in Youth with Disruptive Behavior Disorder and Psychopathic Traits Reflects a Reduced Emotional Response, Not Increased Top-Down Attention to Non-emotional Features." *American Journal of Psychiatry* 169, no. 7: 750–758.

White, S. F., W. C. Williams, S. J. Brislin, S. Sinclair, K. S. Blair, K. A. Fowler, . . . R. J. R. Blair. 2012. "Reduced Activity within the Dorsal Endogenous Orienting of Attention Network to Fearful Expressions in Youth with Disruptive Behavior Disorders and Psychopathic Traits." *Developmental Psychopathology* 24, no. 3: 1105–1116. doi:10.1017/s0954579412000569.

Young, L., J. A. Camprodon, M. Hauser, A. Pascual-Leone, and R. Saxe. 2010. "Disruption of the Right Temporoparietal Junction with Transcranial Magnetic Stimulation Reduces the Role of Beliefs in Moral Judgments." *Proceedings of the National Academy of Sciences* 107, 6753–6758.

Young, L., M. Koenigs, M. Kruepke, and J. P. Newman. 2012. "Psychopathy Increases Perceived Moral Permissibility of Accidents." *Journal of Abnormal Psychology* 121, no. 3: 659–667. doi:10.1037/a0027489.

9

The Neuropsychiatry of Moral Cognition and Social Conduct

Ricardo de Oliveira-Souza, Roland Zahn, and Jorge Moll

9.1. Introduction

This chapter will focus on developmental psychopathy[1] and abnormal antisocial conduct[2] as natural experiments for exploring the neural underpinnings of moral experience and conduct. Information gained from these sources will be contrasted with what is known about normal morality as revealed by behavioral and neuroimaging observations and experiments on normal volunteers. Our main goal is to review and extend previous attempts to infer the neural underpinnings of morality through the analysis of normal and abnormal moral conduct from a broad neurobiological perspective (Mendez 2006; Moll et al. 2003). Although we draw from several sources of information, we will give priority to observations that have been probed by the clinicoanatomic method either in vivo or by postmortem exam. This is so because of the unique cause-and-effect information that strategic lesions provide for the interpretation of mental and behavioral symptoms (Rorden and Karnath 2004). The rationale for this approach rests on the assumption that abnormal moral conduct reflects the malfunction of neural systems that underpin subordinate aspects of moral experience and cognition, such as empathy, impulsiveness, altruism, disgust, aggressiveness, and theory of mind (figure 9.1). Considerable variability is thus created through which nature and nurture may modify the brain and ultimately lead to prosocial or antisocial behaviors (Carré et al. 2012). A major implication of these premises is that antisocial behavior may be produced by dysfunction of one or a few subordinate systems, even if the remaining subsystems remain relatively intact (Godefroy et al. 1998). Psychopathy (a particularly severe form of antisocial personality disorder, as detailed further on), in contrast, probably depends on a narrower and more

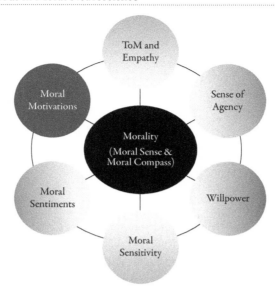

FIGURE 9.1 The puzzle of morality. Subordinate neurobehavioral constructs are often compromised in individuals with acquired sociopathy and developmental psychopathy. None of them, however, is specific to morality (that is, they are not domain-specific); likewise, neither acquired sociopathy nor developmental psychopathy is explained by dysfunction in any one of them.

capricious combination of malfunction of subordinate brain systems, especially those that mediate prosocial sentiments, agency, attachment, and empathy (Gregory et al. 2012; Moll et al. 2011).

No attempt will be made to review the history of psychopathy and acquired sociopathy, a subject on which the interested reader may find excellent accounts in the recent literature (Hervé 2007; Millon et al. 1998). Nevertheless, we wish to emphasize that the concept of antisocial conduct as a nonspecific symptom of diverse neuropsychiatric disorders and its differentiation from psychopathy as a specific developmental disorder of personality is a comparatively recent achievement (de Oliveira-Souza and Moll 2009). The historical record is necessarily inaccurate, and we will probably never be able to translate past into current diagnostic categories reliably. For example, contrary to common opinion, Prichard's concept of "moral insanity" probably originated from cases of mania and acquired cerebral damage rather than from cases of true (i.e., developmental) psychopathy (Berrios 1999). This issue is further complicated by the fact that the word "moral" was not restricted to the ethical connotations with which it was enriched in the twentieth century (Whitlock 1967). The category of moral insanity was the English equivalent of Pinel's concept of *manie sans délire* (insanity without delusion), thus equally heterogeneous in terms of our current diagnostic systems. We must probably grant Benjamin Rush (1746–1813) the earliest formulation of this personality. After stating that in his life he was "consulted in three cases of the total perversion of the moral faculties," Rush goes on to propose, "In all these cases of innate, preternatural moral depravity, there is probably an original defective organization in those parts of the body, which are occupied by the moral faculties of the mind" (Rush 1830, 358). In the beginning of the twentieth century the concept that some individuals suffer from a kind of "moral feeblemindedness" from early life was already well entrenched in the mind of physicians. For example, after describing the case of a thirty-three-year-old engineer who was "stranded" in his asylum, Kraepelin (1856–1926) discussed the psychical mechanisms at play in cases of what he called "morbid personalities" and emphasized the enduring nature of the morbid traits (Kraepelin 1904, 289):

> The patient's moral incapacity from childhood contrasts very sharply with his intellectual talents. But it is well known from every-day life that morality and intellect are to a great extent independent of each other. These cases are therefore generally designated as moral imbecility or *moral feeble-mindedness*. Such men are *born criminals by nature*, and are only distinguished from ordinary criminals by the great extent of their moral incapacity, by their having wills completely unaffected by the restraining experiences of life, and by their being *fundamentally incorrigible*. There is, therefore . . . no other course to be taken, for their own sake, and for the sake of those around them, than to isolate them as being unfit for society, and as far as possible to find them occupation.

The first descriptions of cases of acquired sociopathy resulting from damage to the frontal lobes (Browning 1923; Harlow 1868; Welt 1888) set the stage for the scientific pursuit of the neurological bases of moral conduct (Verplaetse 2009). Originally observed in different contexts (psychopaths in the criminal justice system, acquired sociopaths in medical settings), research on psychopathy and acquired sociopathy has increasingly converged thanks to the technological advances of the past fifty years. The development of psychometrically valid measures of psychopathy/antisocial behaviors and neuroimaging methods, in particular, have played a decisive role.

9.2. The PCL: A Yardstick for Gauging the Amount of Psychopathy across Diagnostic Categories

The operationalization of Cleckley's portrayal of psychopathy into psychometrically valid instruments began in the early 1980s (Hare 1980) and continues up to the present day (Neumann et al. 2012). There is now a large body of evidence supporting the reliability and validity of the Psychopathy Checklist (PCL), originally developed for use in prison inmates, and its derivatives, namely, the PCL-R (Revised), the PCL:SV (Screening Version), the PCL-YV (Youth Version), the Antisocial Process Screening Device, and the P-SCAN (Gacono 2000). These instruments have a high degree of concordance in terms of the unitary construct they measure, that is, psychopathy, and yield four subordinate facets through the factorial analyses of large numbers of individuals regardless of culture, sex, and context (forensic, nonforensic clinical, community). The extension of the PCL to nonforensic settings as well as to children and adolescents (Frick 2009) has opened new horizons for the practical diagnosis and theoretical understanding of psychopathy. For one thing, it is now clear that psychopathy is more prevalent in the general population than usually thought, a finding that somehow endorses our ordinary intuitions (Hare 1993). The validity of the PCL has further been ascertained by anatomical and functional neuroimaging studies. For example, total and individual facets PCL-R scores were negatively related to left amygdala activity, and the Interpersonal Facet was also negatively associated with activity in the right angular gyrus, superomedial prefrontal cortex (SMPFC), and posterior cingulate on an emotional moral decision-making task (Glenn, Raine, and Schug 2009). In a voxel-based morphometric study, we found that psychopathy was associated with reductions of gray matter volume in the frontopolar cortex (FPC), orbitofrontal cortex (OFC), temporopolar cortex (TPC), superior temporal sulcus (STS), and insula; we also found that the severity of psychopathy as reflected by Factor 1 (Interpersonal/Affective) PCL: SV scores was proportional to bilateral reduction in the volume of gray matter in the FPC, posterior OFC, subgenual cortex (SGC), and temporoparietal junction (TPJ) (de Oliveira-Souza et al. 2008a).

Psychopathy is a reliable and valid diagnostic category with high predictive values for interpersonal violence and criminal recidivism (Hare 2006). Although psychopathy and crime have different conceptual roots and are thus not synonymous (Ellis 1890), psychopathy is a strong risk factor for criminality in general, and for violent and predatory crime in particular (Woodworth and Porter 2002). This criminal propensity has also been observed in cases of acquired sociopathy due to cerebral damage (Mendez 2010). Research has also revealed that the amount of psychopathic traits is gauged with psychometrically valid instruments outside forensic or clinical settings (de Oliveira-Souza et al. 2008b; Walters et al. 2007). These traits, or "facets," fall into four subordinate domains, namely, affective, lifestyle, interpersonal, and antisocial (Hare 2003), that do not conflict with the basic tenet that psychopathy is a unitary construct in its own right (Neumann et al. 2007). Besides validating a diagnosis of psychopathy on a cross-sectional analysis, research has also endorsed the long-held view that psychopathy begins in childhood or early adolescence and remains stable throughout the lifespan (Harpur and Hare 1994).

The PCL may also be used to settle a categorical diagnosis of psychopathy. Cutoff scores vary among different authors, but scores higher than 17 on the PCL: SV and 29 on the PCL-R are accepted as diagnostic (de Oliveira-Souza et al. 2008b). The distinction between dimensional versus categorical diagnoses has far-reaching implications for the design of studies, statistical analysis of raw data, and interpretation of neuroimaging findings (Koenigs 2011). The schematic relationship between Conduct Disorder (CD), Antisocial Personality Disorder (ASPD), and psychopathy is shown in figure 9.2. Note that a categorical diagnosis does not preclude the concomitant use of the PCL as

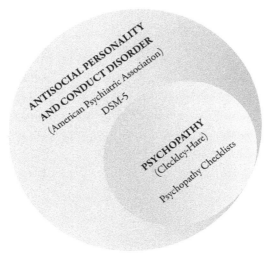

FIGURE 9.2 Relationship between developmental psychopathy and antisocial personality (adults) and conduct (children and adolescents) disorders. Whereas ASPD and CD are diagnosed according to DSM criteria, psychopathy is diagnosed according to PCL criteria.

a measure of the degree of psychopathy in CD or ASPD, and, for that matter, in any other condition of interest. For example, the dimensional structure of the PCL allows us to grade the callousness of psychopaths, thus accounting for the observation that many such individuals may be sympathetic and truly warm to others without obvious gains in mind (de Oliveira-Souza et al. 2008b).

Further evidence on the critical role of a specific emotional impairment in psychopathy comes from studies on the callous-unemotional (CU) traits of children and adolescents (Frick 2009). The CU traits comprise an ensemble of symptoms of impaired interpersonal emotions and attitudes that include a lack of guilt, a lack of concern about the feelings of others, a lack of concern about performance in important activities, and shallow or deficient affect (Frick 2012). The CU traits are found in a subset of children with a variety of disruptive behaviors manifested as early as four years of age; they are stable over the years with a heritability of 0.81, being remarkably impervious to environmental influences. The longitudinal stability of CU traits indicates that they are the youth equivalent of the Affective Facet gauged by the PCL on adult psychopaths (Hare and Neumann 2008).

9.3. Diagnostic Categories in Which Antisocial Behavior Is the Leading or Sole Manifestation (Table 9.1)

Antisocial behaviors comprise the chief manifestation of several neuropsychiatric disorders (Chen et al. 2003), but psychopathy is the most severe of such disorders. The differential diagnosis among these disorders is essential for correct management and

TABLE 9.1

Diagnostic Affiliations of Persistent Abnormal Antisocial Behavior

Condition	Core features	Diagnosis
Acquired sociopathy	A change in personality that may occur at any age, in which a previously socially adjusted and productive individual engages in antisocial acts as a sequel of acquired brain surgery or natural damage, such as head trauma, infarction, tumor, or degenerative disease.	Clinical, essentially qualitative; change in personality traits may be assessed with the Iowa Scales of Personality Change (Barrash et al. 2011)
Antisocial, borderline, histrionic and narcissistic personality disorders	A disturbing and stable pattern of emotional, dramatic, and erratic inner experience and behavior, which are established by early adulthood.	DSM-5
Conduct disorder	A repetitive and persistent pattern of behavior, first observed during childhood or adolescence, in which the basic rights of others or major age-appropriate societal norms or rules are violated. Conduct disorder is often a forerunner of adult antisocial personality disorder and psychopathy.	DSM-5
Psychopathy	A disorder of personality beginning in adolescence or even earlier characterized by a propensity to engage in antisocial acts allied with a particular way of feeling and interacting with others, which is perceived as "callousness" or "lack of empathy." Individuals with a diagnosis of psychopathy often meet criteria for antisocial personality disorder, but the converse is not necessarily true.	PCL and related instruments

DSM-5: *Diagnostic and Statistical Manual of Mental Disorders*, 5th edition.
PCL: Psychopathy Checklist.

prognosis (Dorst et al. 1997; Thorneloe and Crews 1981; Tyrer and Brittlebank 1993). Access to trustworthy and independent collateral sources of information is indispensable, and a final diagnosis can reliably be made after several interviews with different informants.

9.4. The Concept of Moral Sense and the Theoretical Problems Involved in the Study of the Neurology of Morality

The fact that psychopaths, in particular, and antisocial individuals, in general, *seem* to suffer from profound impairments of moral cognition and behavior does not necessarily mean that these disorders *are* a primary disorder of the neural networks that underpin morality. As indicated in figure 9.1, there is so far little evidence supporting the existence of a domain-specific morality circuitry in the brain. From a strict anatomical perspective, the analogy that depicts psychopathy as a kind of "moral daltonism" (Maudsley 1876) is possibly flawed because it implies that, like any sensory system, morality has a peripheral sense organ with a specific pathway that projects onto specific primary and secondary cortical areas, the "cortical 'center' for morality" (Verplaetse 2009, 208). For the sake of brevity, however, in the present chapter we use the expression "moral sense" to refer to the mental capacity or power that intuitively or implicitly imparts a moral quality—the attribution of values of rightness or wrongness—to ideas, actions, and perceptions (Hauser 2006; Jastrow and Marillier 1902; Pfaff 2007).

The neuroanatomical implausibility of the moral center concept has called for fresh neuroscientific inquiries attempting to establish that (1) there are dedicated (domain-specific) networks in the human brain that underpin morality, and that (2) developmental psychopathy and some cases of acquired sociopathy ultimately reflect a primary disorder of these networks (Sobhani and Bechara 2011). Mendez and colleagues have persuasively argued that developmental psychopathy and acquired sociopathy have each distinct merits and limitations regarding their validity as natural experiments on the cerebral organization of morality (Mendez et al. 2005).

Most cerebral regions related to acquired sociopathy and developmental psychopathy pertain to a fronto-temporo-insular network that has a number of distinctive features. For example, one conspicuous feature of the frontoinsular cortex is a large slender neuronal type in layer V described by von Economo in 1926 (see Seeley et al. 2012 for an annotated English translation of von Economo's article). Von Economo neurons (VEN) emerge postnatally and are most abundant in the right cerebral hemisphere of humans, being also numerous in other large-brained mammals with a complex social life, such as the great apes, elephants, and cetaceans. VENs are particularly vulnerable in neuropsychiatric conditions that course with abnormalities of social behavior, such as frontotemporal dementia (FTD), callosal agenesis, and autism (Allman et al. 2011).

9.5. Morality in the Brain

Like the capacity to enjoy beauty and transcendence, morality stands out as one of the components of the mammalian social brain that makes us human (Dunbar 1998). The sense of fairness, beauty, and transcendence are not intrinsic to the physical stimuli that make up our perceptions and ideas, but rather qualitatively distinct states of mind with which we invest perceptions and ideas. The neuroanatomical underpinnings of such unique domains of subjective life have only begun to be scientifically explored (de Oliveira-Souza et al. 2011). A promising avenue of inquiry has investigated morality as a construct with multiple foundations, which may vary in number and structure from three (Rozin et al. 1999) to five (Haidt and Joseph 2007). In a large unselected sample of Internet volunteers, scores on a self-reported measure of psychopathy were inversely related to harm and fairness, but not to the other three foundations of morality, namely, respect to authority, in-group loyalty, and spiritual purity (Glenn, Iyer, et al. 2009). These results are somewhat puzzling (we would expect some impairment in in-group scores) and must be replicated. For the purposes of exposition, in the following paragraphs morality is treated as a unitary phenomenon that is presented as such to conscious awareness, but which can be fractionated into subordinate constructs amenable to experimental inquiry. These constructs have extensively been studied from a neuroscientific perspective. Although there is little doubt that they are ingredients of ordinary moral experience and behavior, none of them in isolation is critical for moral experience.

9.5.1. SENSE OF AGENCY AND AUTHORSHIP, HARMFUL INTENT, PERSONAL RESPONSIBILITY

The moral sense is intimately associated with the subjective experience that the actions one carries out while awake emanate from the self, thus making one immediately responsible for them. This sense of agency, intentionality, or authorship is not unique to the moral sense, as it pervades most of the actions we perform in our ordinary lives when morality is not an issue (Gazzaniga 1985); moreover, the moral sense may be fully at work without primarily involving the sense of personal agency, as when we witness the moral conduct of others. The attribution of intentionality to our own behavior and to the behavior of others, especially to moral behavior, is a critical element of social life. In the criminal justice system, for example, the intent to harm (mens rea), regardless of whether harm is actually inflicted, is critical for court decisions. Dracon's legal code (ca. 624 BCE) was the first to distinguish between murder (killing with intent) and manslaughter (killing without intent), thus incorporating a psychological distinction into law that has since been decisive for making individuals criminally accountable for their acts (Green and Groff 2003). Moral agency is such a complex issue that even today we often feel at a loss when a harmful intent cannot be proven beyond reasonable doubt (Aharoni et al. 2008).

The neurological literature is informative on some of these points. In the frontal type of the "alien hand syndrome," apparently purposeful movements of the right hand are perceived as being autonomous and detached from the patient's stated intentions (Feinberg et al. 1992). The hand is perceived as being part of the self (indicating that there is no abnormality of the body schema)—only its actions are alien to the will (Goldberg 2000). The lesion in such cases usually falls on the left medial frontal lobe with or without involvement of the anterior corpus callosum. A second finding that is particularly germane to the harmful intent discussion is the observation that patients with bilateral VMPFC injury judged attempted harms and even murder as more morally permissible than completed harm; controls, in turn, judged the intent to harm as morally unacceptable as completed harm itself (Young, Bechara, et al. 2010). These results complement previous findings from normal individuals in whom activation of the right TPJ was related to the subjective evaluation of the intent to harm of moral agents (Young and Saxe 2009). Transient inactivation of the same region by transcranial magnetic stimulation (TMS; the "virtual lesion" method) compromised judgments of attempted harm, which was deemed as less forbidden and more morally permissible in comparison to the volunteers own pre-TMS judgments, that is, when right TPJ neural activity was not being disrupted by TMS (Young, Camprodon, et al. 2010). Inactivation of the right TPJ and injury of the VMPFC thus seem to produce overtly similar effects concerning the attribution of harmful intent to others. A related study offered evidence that patients with VMPFC damage are primarily impaired at bringing awareness of harmful intent into their judgment of harmful actions, thus providing clues for a differential role of the VMPFC in this kind of moral judgment (Ciaramelli et al. 2012). In contrast to brain-damaged patients, psychopaths seem to judge accidental harms as more morally permissible than normal controls, indicating that they may be less moved by the suffering of the victims (Young et al. 2012). However, the impairment of judgments of attempted harm does not explain the personality of psychopaths and acquired sociopaths since individuals with high-functioning autism exhibit similar deficits of judgment (Moran et al. 2011).

The preceding studies might compel researchers to reconsider the view that theory of mind (ToM) is unimpaired in psychopaths even when they are assessed with different tools (Blair et al. 1996; Richell et al. 2003). They may also help explain why, under certain circumstances, psychopaths and patients with acquired sociopathy may do well on tasks on which they are expected to tell right from wrong. Clues to a solution to this paradox are provided by seeing how VMPFC patients tackle moral dilemmas with varying degrees of personal involvement. Ciaramelli et al. (2007) have found that, compared to normals, patients with VMPFC damage tend to judge personal moral violations as more acceptable than impersonal violations. Also in contrast to normal controls, VMPFC patients fail to generate galvanic skin responses (GSRs) just before endorsing their moral transgressions in personal dilemmas, indicating that the emotional concomitants of personal moral decisions are impaired (Moretto et al. 2009). The nature of emotional guidance to moral decision-making is still open to discussion, since the GSR is a nonspecific index of emotional arousal of different sorts that may occur even below the fringe of conscious awareness (Bauer 1984). However, the emotional deficit in such cases is not due to a generalized blunting of emotional experience; quite on the contrary, studies on normal adults and patients with localized prefrontal cortex (PFC) or TPC damage have shown that the heightened tendency to provide utilitarian responses reflects, at least in part, an impairment of the moral sentiments of guilt and compassion while leaving other moral sentiments relatively unimpaired (Green et al. 2010; Krajbich et al. 2009). Lesion and functional neuroimaging studies on moral agency concur that nonemotional agency (as elicited by scripts like "You heard your neighbors chatting in the apartment next door; they were talking about business") engage the SGC/septal area and adjoining VMPFC, frontoinsular and temporopolar cortices, and mid-STS (Moll et al. 2007). There is good evidence that this remarkably heterogeneous albeit discrete volume of neural tissue is essential for the most fundamental experience and expression of the self. Bilateral damage to these rostral ventromedial prosencephalic regions, of which the SGC/septal nuclei, ventromedial preoptic area, and anterior hypothalamus seem to be the critical structures (Jefferson 1957), produces the vigilant form of akinetic mutism, a state in which the individual opens and closes his eyes in periodic alternations of wakefulness and sleep, but shows no evidence of mental life whatsoever (Segarra 1972). It is intriguing that the neural systems that underpin moral experience and the fundamental experience of self greatly overlap in the neural space.

9.5.2. MORAL SENTIMENTS

Most authors concur that an impairment of morality lies at the bottom of developmental psychopathy and acquired sociopathy. However, only in the past decade has the role of the moral sentiments in these conditions begun to be investigated (Moll et al. 2003). Two issues that are critical for our present argument are: (1) the neural organization of discrete moral sentiments differs among themselves and from that of the basic emotions, and (2) individuals with psychopathy and acquired sociopathy suffer from impairments of specific moral sentiments (such as guilt and compassion), and these impairments predict at least part of their abnormal personalities. Although there is evidence that both claims are true (Glenn, Iyer, et al. 2009; Roseman et al. 1994), they clearly need to be further investigated.

The emotions that are primarily impaired in psychopaths are precisely those that Adam Smith (1723–1790) called the "social passions" or "benevolent affections" because they are experienced as sympathy and expressed as behaviors that ultimately promote the welfare of others (Smith [1790] 2002). Smith went further and contrasted the social passions with the selfish (grief and joy, "when conceived upon account of our own private good or bad fortune") and the unsocial (hatred and resentment) passions.

The flavor of Smith's taxonomy has been retained in current views of the moral emotions as sentiments that are linked to the interests or welfare either of society as whole or at least of persons other than the judge or agent (Haidt 2003). Typically, moral sentiments—such as guilt, compassion, gratitude—(1) are elicited by ideas and events that benefit or harm others, and (2) incite prosocial action tendencies (Haidt 2003). Contrary to the "basic" emotions,[3] which have been debated since the nineteenth century (Darwin 1872), only recently did the moral sentiments become objects of active investigation, especially by neuroscientists (Gray and Wegner 2011).

One of the few studies that directly probed the neural organization of discrete moral sentiments showed that agency plays a decisive role both in the kind of emotional experience (e.g., anger at oneself vs. anger at another person) and in the related pattern of neural activation (Kédia et al. 2010). Emotional experience in general activated the amygdala and insula, as well as the DMPFC, the TPJ, and the precuneus. When emotional experience was related to someone else (i.e., the agent was a person other than the self), there was increased activity in the DMPFC, the TPJ, and the precuneus. Slightly different regions of the SMPFC and TPJ were engaged by the prosocial sentiments of guilt, compassion, and embarrassment when controlling for nonemotional agency (Moll et al. 2007). Embarrassment was a prosocial sentiment whenever it was elicited by situations in which it opposed some self-centered tendency, like when we feel embarrassed to stay sitting on a bus where a pregnant woman stands by us.

In line with studies that have shown a critical role of the SGC and septal nuclei in altruistic choices (Moll et al. 2006), an investigation on patients with frontotemporal dementia (FTD), who commonly present antisocial behavior (Piguet et al. 2011), showed that the blunting of the prosocial sentiments of guilt, compassion, and embarrassment paralleled the degeneration of the FPC and septal area (Moll et al. 2011). These results are consistent with the verification that patients with long-standing traumatic injury of the OFC and nearby PFC show excessive pride and little shame; when they do express these emotions, they tend to be out of context and inadequate (Beer et al. 2003). For example, one of our FTD patients, a seventy-two-year-old woman with a postgraduate degree in sociology and a lifelong political inclination for socialism, in utter contrast with her usual manners startled her daughter as she approached a street beggar, kissed him warmly, and gave him US$500 in cash. Similar apparently selfless behaviors are sometimes encountered in psychopaths (de Oliveira-Souza et al. 2008b). Part of the social inadequacy of these patients may also be related to a decreased ability to experience indignation, a moral derivation of the basic emotion of disgust, which engages the ventrolateral OFC in normal individuals (Moll et al. 2005). Whether the impairment of moral sentiments exhibited by patients with frontal lobe damage requires associated impairments of basic emotions often seen in such cases (Rolls et al. 1994) remains to be determined.

9.5.3. EMPATHY, THEORY OF MIND (MENTALIZING), AND THEORY OF CONTEXT

Human beings possess a remarkable capacity to behave malleably toward others on a continuum that ranges from extreme antisociality (selfishness) to extreme prosociality (altruism). The selfish/altruistic polarity has been supported by a recent functional magnetic resonance imaging (fMRI) study, which revealed that as we migrate from the

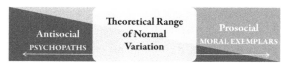

FIGURE 9.3 The prosocial-antisocial continuum of interpersonal inclinations.

selfish toward the prosocial end of the continuum in a "your pain / my gain" paradigm, the distribution of cerebral activations shifts from the dorsal cingulate, OFCm and dorsolateral prefrontal cortex (DLPFC) to the ventral cingulate, right temporal pole, and anterior insula (FeldmanHall et al. 2012). Most people fall within the median region of this prosocial-antisocial continuum—in ordinary life, we sometimes gladly give our seat to an elderly woman, while at other times we may be so tired that we just pretend not to see her (figure 9.3). The closer we get to the prosocial end, the more interpersonal interactions require a host of mental abilities subsumed under the general concepts of empathy, theory of mind ("mentalizing"), and attachment (Eslinger 1998). Already in early life, children are capable of inferring the feelings, intentions, and thoughts of others and to change their behavior accordingly (Gergely et al. 1995). However, no matter how necessary for prosocial conduct, mentalizing is not prosocial in itself, as shown by reports of psychopaths with normal mentalizing abilities (Blair et al. 1996).

The capacity to experience empathy and make a ToM on self and others is a hallmark of morally mature human beings (Narvaez 2008). Although these constructs are related, to some extent they refer to different mental and neural processes. Likewise, although both empathy and ToM are necessary for normal conduct, they are not sufficient for fully grown moral behavior. Empathy is a multidimensional construct that, at the most fundamental level, encompasses the ability to share (i.e., literally, to experience) the feelings of others (Decety and Jackson 2004); the ability to experience the pain or suffering of others, in particular, is tapped by the "personal distress" subscale of the Interpersonal Reactivity Index (IRI), a multidimensional measure of empathy (Davis 1980). During development, this ability is supplemented by growing awareness that the shared emotion derives from someone else (the "empathic concern" subscale of the IRI) and by the ability to suppress one's viewpoint so that the attribution of agency and cognitive perspective to others can take place (the "perspective taking" subscale of the IRI). Note that perspective taking (inferences about what someone is thinking and intending) and empathic concern (inferences on what someone is feeling) do not necessarily require emotional sharing; this is so because perspective taking and empathic concern are recognition processes that primarily depend on perceptual cues such as facial expression and affective prosody. Personal distress, in contrast, does not require a fully developed ToM ability, since in this case the self/nonself boundaries are experientially blurred (Miller et al. 2001). This formulation reconciles empathy with ToM and specifies multiple sites at which subordinate processes may break down. It also concurs with prior observations that although psychopaths show normal moral reasoning abilities when they discuss hypothetical situations (Raine and Yang 2006), they are less likely to feel another's pain (Blair 1999) and, regardless of being capable of telling right from wrong, they "just don't care" (Cima et al. 2010). A similar dissociation between preserved social knowledge and antisocial conduct has been found in cases of acquired sociopathy due to static (Saver and Damasio 1991) or progressive (Mendez 2010) brain damage.

Studies on normal volunteers and patients with localized brain damage indicate that the different dimensions of empathy and ToM are to a certain extent dissociable both at the phenomenological and neural levels. Empathic concern depends on the integrity of the right temporal pole, inferior frontal gyrus, SGC, and VMPFC (Shamay-Tsoory et al. 2005; Leopold et al. 2012), while PT additionally depends on the integrity of the fusiform gyri (Rankin et al. 2006). There are few studies on the personal distress dimension of empathy, which, incidentally, may be relevant to the understanding of the neural basis of the callous-unemotional traits of psychopathy and acquired sociopathy.

Empathy and mentalizing do not occur in a vacuum—rather, they are embedded in a variety of interpersonal and social contexts that transcend the self and often change the meaning of interpersonal inferences themselves (Barrett et al. 2007). Context streamlines the course of ideas and perceptions, thus minimizing the ideational and perceptual ambiguity that inevitably arises when we consider the objects of ideas and perceptions as abstract forms. The accuracy of inferences is greatly enhanced when the meaning of facial expressions, prosody, and body language, for example, emerge from the particular social context within which they take place (de Oliveira-Souza et al. 2013). Based on clinicoanatomic evidence obtained on patients with FTD, Ibáñez and Manes proposed that social context is ultimately integrated by a distributed neural circuitry that encompasses the orbitofrontal, anterior insular, and temporopolar cortices (Ibáñez and Manes 2012). These cortical regions are among the first to undergo degeneration in cases with the most severe impairments in metaphor comprehension, recognition of facial expressions and emotional prosody, and empathy, leading to gross deficits in context appropriate behavior (Lough et al. 2006). Figure 9.4 depicts two pairs of test stimuli on which FTD patients regularly fail, since they find it difficult to offer a plausible contextual description of each picture (e.g., why are the four guys possibly happy/angry with the person in the center?), even if they can still read their individual expressions correctly.

9.5.4. ATTACHMENT

One of the most striking characteristics of psychopaths and acquired sociopaths is their inability to feel attached to other people, to principles, and even to mundane objects. There is regularly some noticeable deficit in attachment that expresses itself as a lack of concern for their children and significant others (a mother goes to a party and leaves her little boy alone at home without food and grooming because, she says, "I wasn't supposed to stay out for more than a few hours"), lack of interpersonal loyalty (a psychopath

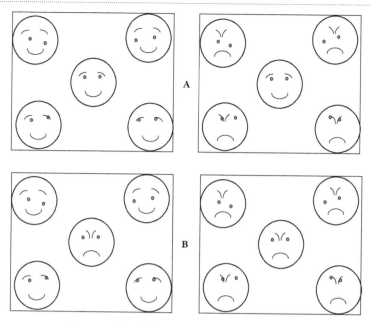

FIGURE 9.4 Contextual modulation of social perception of facial expressions.

spent away his partner's capital, justifying the loss, after the fact and pretending regret, as "a stroke of bad luck"), commitment to values and principles that easily changes in opportunistic ways (Babiak and Hare 2006), lying and unfaithfulness (no commitment to telling the truth or attempting to behave according to what they profess as their minimum codes of conduct). In some cases, there is also a perversion of attachment, which is variously expressed as an exquisite taste for some objects (such as cars, paintings, guns, and stamps), animals, and even persons. In these cases, individuals may be profoundly attached to a specific person to the exclusion of kids, parents, and relatives, as illustrated by the assortative mating of infamous criminal couples like Bonnie and Clyde (Guze et al. 1970).

We have already discussed the role played by attachment in the maintenance of group identity and perpetuation (Moll and Schulkin 2009). We have also argued that attachment attains new dimensions that transcend the universal ones that hold for parents and offspring, romantic couples, friendship, and family ties (Moll and de Oliveira-Souza 2009). In humans, attachment extends to abstract forms, such as concepts and symbols, thus lying at the heart of belief systems and culture (de Oliveira-Souza et al. 2013). The critical substrates of attachment occupy a discrete continuum in the rostral ventromedial basal forebrain encompassing the SGC and septal nuclei, ventromedial preoptic area, and anterior hypothalamus. These structures were activated when normal subjects engaged in altruistic behaviors, such as donating money for charity (Moll et al. 2006). In normal adults the volume of the SGC is proportional to the capacity to establish some forms of attachment (Lewis et al. 2012). Recently, we showed that a relatively discrete region in the rostral ventromedial basal forebrain of normal adults was engaged by scenarios portraying several forms of attachment to kin regardless of the emotional valence of the scenarios (Moll et al. 2012). This region includes the nucleus accumbens, neighboring septal nuclei, and ventromedial preoptic area and hypothalamus, many of which are rich in affiliative neuropeptides such as oxytocin (Loup et al. 1991), as well as basal forebrain associative pathways, especially the medial forebrain bundle and the *ansa peduncularis* (Klingler and Gloor 1960). This region is schematically presented in figure 9.5.

9.5.5. MORAL VALUES, MORAL MOTIVATION, AND SELF-CONTROL ("WILLPOWER")

The moral sense, the sense of agency, the ability to experience guilt and compassion and share the suffering of others, would be of little value in the real social world if we lacked the capacity to oppose our immediate self-centered urges in favor of others (Sellito et al. 2010). The ability to oppose current motivations is classically conceptualized under the rubrics of "will," "willpower," and "self-control" (Bleuler 1912; Kalis et al. 2008). The

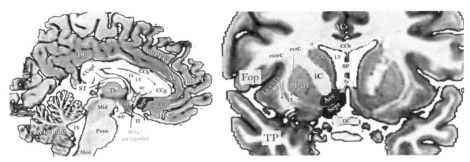

FIGURE 9.5 Parasagittal (left) and coronal (level of the optic chiasma, OC) views of the cerebral hemispheres depicting anatomical structures discussed in the text (schematic renderings modified from MRIcron templates [Rorden and Brett 2000]). Critical structures implied in prosocial and affiliative behaviors surround the intersection of the fornix with the anterior commissure, and comprise a continuum made up by the preoptic area/anterior hypothalamus (POA/ant hypothal), septal nuclei (Sept), and subgenual cortex (SGC) (Moll et al. 2012). This septo-preoptic-anterior hypothalamic continuum is a core component of the default mode network (Bado et al. 2013), damage to which gives rise to the most remarkable forms of akinetic mutism (Segarra 1972). AC: anterior cingulate; ac: anterior commissure; Acc: nucleus accumbens septi; CC: corpus callosum (spl: splenium, b: body, g: genu); Cl: claustrum; CN: caudate nucleus; extC: external capsule; extrC: extreme capsule; Fop: frontal operculum; fx: fornix; H: hypothalamus; iC: internal capsule; mb: mammillary body; LV: lateral ventricle; Med: medulla; mFPC: medial frontopolar cortex; Mid: midbrain; mOFC: medial orbitofrontal cortex; OC: optic chiasma; PC: posterior cingulate; POA/ant hypothalamus: preoptic area/anterior hypothalamus; Put: putamen; SGC: subgenual cortex; smPFC: superomedial prefrontal cortex; Sept: septal nuclei; SP: septum pellucidum; ST: stria terminalis; Th: thalamus; TP: temporal pole; II: optic nerve; IV: fourth ventricle.

will has often been overlooked and even denied by twentieth-century scholars, who attempted to replace it, with arguable success, by constructs such as goal-directed behavior, executive domains, or frontal lobe functions (Tranel et al. 1994); some researchers have further confounded the issue by conflating the concepts of will and motivation (Berrios and Gili 1995). Fortunately, neuroscientists are beginning to consider the will as a legitimate object of inquiry and distinguish it both conceptually and neuroanatomically from motivation (Swanson 2005). Researchers have also shaped mathematical tools to study quantitatively the will and its weaknesses in normal subjects and in patients with neuropsychiatric disorders (Ainslie 2004).

Perhaps in no circumstance does the reality of will become more apparent than in clinical neuropsychiatry. The most obvious instances of an abnormally heightened or reduced will are found in a cluster of symptoms that pertain to the catatonic syndrome and are generally known as "passivity and negativism" phenomena. Lesion studies have shown that structures in the right cerebral hemisphere, especially the ventrolateral prefrontal lobe and anterior cingulate gyrus, are critical for the exertion of willpower (Berman et al. 2012; Matsuda et al. 2004; Saver et al. 1993; Seo 2009). Damage to these regions may transform an individual into a patient extremely compliant with external influences to the point of obeying commands that go against his social composure and even his physical integrity (de Oliveira-Souza et al. 2002). In these cases, patients lack the capacity to refrain from acting on the nearby surroundings and, without prompting, going on using objects at their reach or copying the actions of others, as if magnetized by the environment (Lhermitte 1986). In normal individuals, these regions are part of a network of brain regions engaged by deliberate opposition to some internal (e.g., a physical urge like thirst) or external (e.g., a knock on the door) influence with which the subject would gladly comply (Brass et al. 2001). The opposite pattern, in which the individual vigorously avoids any influence of the environment through the visual, tactile, or gustatory modalities, is observed in cases of bilateral damage to the cortex of the occipito-temporoparietal junction (Mori and Yamadori 1989). The critical structure for the production of such "rejection behavior" seems to be the inferior parietal lobule (Tippin and Dunner 1981; Warren et al. 2004). Departing from observations that damage to the frontal lobes produces a release of exploratory behaviors toward the environment, whereas damage to the parietal lobes produces a rejection of contact with the environment, Denny-Brown advanced a general model of cortical function according to which a delicate balance is established through mutual competition between parietal lobe approach and frontal lobe avoidance behaviors (Denny-Brown 1952). These "cortical tropisms," which are present from the first postnatal weeks, are normally played upon by other cerebral systems that contribute to the overall organization of goal-directed behavior.

A few years ago, we proposed that the workings of the will in everyday life are intermittent, effortful, and conscious (de Oliveira-Souza et al. 2002). The will essentially comes into action when we oppose some ongoing tendency by either enforcing unwanted actions (e.g., rising from bed in the morning to go to work) or by counteracting some desired behavior (e.g., refusing sweets now in order to lose weight in the long term). The concept of will is further supported by a series of independent studies showing that the strength with which subjects oppose current behavioral inclinations ("self-control") in childhood is a strong predictor of health, wealth, and public safety in later epochs of life (Moffitt et al. 2011).

A common denominator of motivation and will is their vectorial nature—both can be graphically represented as opposing arrows departing from the individual and pointing to specific objects, events, and actions in the environment, with measurable magnitudes D (drive) and W (willpower) that are proportional to the length of the arrows (Schott 2000). This vectorial portrayal of morality is aptly conveyed by the classical metaphor of a "moral compass," which implies some kind of awareness, or conscience, of the right action to take especially when we are tempted to deviate from what ought to be done (Lewis 1952).

When it comes to moral behavior, the will is typically engaged by situations in which the individual is compelled to oppose his self-centered inclinations in favor of prosocial courses of action. This process is shaped by the repertoire of moral values that are internalized during moral development as the learning individual interacts with different cultural contexts as he grows up (Narvaez 2008). In adults, the will enforces the translation of moral values into moral actions, especially in circumstances in which such actions oppose the current tendencies of the individual (Bechara 2005; Knoch and Fehr 2007).

The preceding considerations suggest that willpower is a general capacity that varies greatly among individuals, but which intermittently becomes apparent in diverse domains of psychic and social life. The phenomenon of akrasia (incontinence, lack of mastery) refers to a trait of character in which the individual lacks the amount of willpower necessary to resist some current urge or need despite a normal capacity for understanding that complying with such inclinations will be deleterious to himself or to others (Kalis et al. 2008). The importance of akrasia for neuropsychiatry, psychology, and philosophy is obvious; alone or in combination with other psychopathological states, akrasia accounts for a considerable part of human suffering (Bechara 2005). Moreover, even in normal people the translation of moral values into moral behavior is far more tenuous than generally thought. Several years ago, Milgram showed that the moral values held by normal individuals were set aside with relative ease by a calculated restructuring of the social environment (Milgram 1974). Milgram showed that when personal responsibility is transferred to a higher authority, the moral sense shifts to how well the subject is behaving according to the expectations of the authority. In a series of studies, normal volunteers were willing to inflict lethal harm on other human beings without remorse as long as they were supported by another responsible agent. This effect was augmented by a prior devaluation of the victim. fMRI studies on normal adults revealed that SMPFC activity correlates with the choice of punishment intensity (an aversive pressure stimulus to one finger) as well as with the intensity of the stimulus delivered to a competitor in a game of speed of response (Lotze et al. 2007); in the same study, watching the competitor's suffering by the delivered stimulus correlated with activity in the right amygdala, right STS, and medial FPC, the latter also bearing a positive correlation with the amplitude of GSRs. Thus, inflicting pain on someone versus watching its immediate harmful effects seem to engage distinct cerebral mechanisms. This pattern of cerebral response may differ in criminal psychopaths (Veit et al. 2010), but more evidence is needed.

The will operates intermittently against what we have so far called "current ongoing personal inclinations." There is evidence that these inclinations constitute different urges that continuously spring from multiple sources within the body as well as from the environment, which struggle for the control of behavior (Carbanac 1995; Loewenstein 1996). Together they add up to generate what Freud called "instincts" (Freud 1915) and Stellar figured as a "central motive state" (Stellar 1960). Following these authors, the internal milieu of the organism provides an incessant array of stimuli originating from the viscera and from the blood (Craig 2002). These stimuli are converted into specific appetites and aversions at several points in the brainstem (parabrachial and solitary tract nuclei), hypothalamus and nearby basal forebrain regions, thalamus (midline-intralaminar and ventromedial nuclei), and insular and anterior cingulate cortices (Fuller et al. 2011; Phillips et al. 1987; Thompson 1951; van der Werf et al. 2002), where they add up to energize the mind and behavior.[4] The nature of this "psychic energy"—the "élan vital" of classic French psychiatry (Luauté and Saladini 2001)—is still obscure, as are the processes by which the myriad of bodily stimuli are converted into it (figure 9.6). Clinicoanatomic evidence gathered since the lethargic encephalitis epidemic suggests that this transduction process takes place at specific loci in the brainstem, hypothalamus, and basal forebrain (Habib 2000; Ward 2011). Not surprisingly, these structures are included in the collection of neuronal assemblies that send profuse and direct connections to all areas of the isocortex and allocortex of both cerebral hemispheres (Saper 1987). A closer look

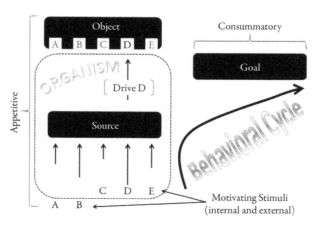

FIGURE 9.6 Essential constituents of motivated behavior as parts of a broader organismic biphasic cycle of appetitive and consummatory phases.

at some clinical syndromes that result from injuries at strategic nodes of these circuits provides clues on how motivation and will differ in critical ways both in phenomenology and in cerebral organization.

The syndrome of abulia captures a common symptom of impairment of the intensive aspect of motivation (drive). Patients with pure abulia are cognitively intact and able to tell exactly what they want or need, but they lack the mental power to transform intention into action. Abulia appears to an observer as a decrease of psychomotor initiative, spontaneity, and agility. This unique symptom reflects impairment of a universal cerebral system that translates the overall intensity of bodily needs and imbalances into mental and behavioral actions (Fisher 1984). Anatomically, it extends bilaterally from the paramedian midbrain and thalamus to the anterior cingulate gyrus (Nauta and Domesick 1981). A ventral leaflet of this system follows a subthalamic course through the hypothalamus and basal forebrain, where it establishes local connections with the medial hypothalamic nuclei, nucleus accumbens and ventral pallidum, septal nuclei, amygdala, and thalamus (dorsomedial and anterior nuclei), thus comprising Cummings's anterior cingulate loop (Cummings 1993). The medial forebrain bundle is a major association pathway of this ventral leaflet that, together with the aforementioned structures, undergoes a remarkable expansion in humans (Coenen et al. 2012; Stephan et al. 1981).

While in abulia the inertia pervades all aspects of mind and behavior, patients suffering from the syndrome of "autoactivation deficit" (AAD) remain still, but awake, their minds being devoid of feelings, intentions, and thoughts most of the time; however, they behave normally when stimulated by their social environment (Laplane 1990). The damage in such cases is bilateral and restricted to the associative and "limbic" sectors of the globus pallidus and the *pars reticulata* of the substantia nigra (Adam et al. 2008; Laplane 2001; Levy and Dubois 2006). The neural structures that are compromised in AAD are probably the same that translate the magnitude of an expected reward into the behavioral activation (effort) necessary to accomplish it in normal individuals—a collection of basal forebrain structures represented by the ventral striatum and pallidum, parts of the extended amygdala, and the basal nucleus of Meynert (Pessiglione et al. 2007). Damage to this region seems to disrupt the link between emotion and motivation, but leaving each one of them intact (Schmidt et al. 2008), thus depriving the motivational system of its most fundamental and powerful instigator—as aptly stated by a leading researcher a few years ago: "Emotional experience, although subjective, is one of the major factors in motivating human behavior" (Heilman 1997, 439). The syndrome of AAD speaks for the existence of discrete neural systems related to different epochs of goal-directed ideation and behavior, from self-initiation to the generation and assessment of alternative courses of action, decision-making, actual changes in the course of action (flexibility), and its conclusion (Schneirla 1959). Each of these links may be the locus of functional derangements in relative isolation from the others, as illustrated by AAD. Further examples of impairments of other discrete links of motivated behavior include ambivalence and indecision (decision-making), perseveration and impersistence (flexibility), and obsessive-compulsive symptoms (completion).

9.5.6. MORAL SENSITIVITY AND MORAL DECISION-MAKING

The cerebral correlates of our constant surveillance of ideas and external events for moral salience has been shown by fMRI experiments in which volunteers were passively exposed to visual scenes of ordinary events and asked to just pay attention to them. In this condition, there was specific activation of the TPJ, medial FPC, and medial OFC (Moll et al. 2002). When volunteers were asked to perform explicit judgments (i.e., make a decision) on stimuli with a moral content, the temporal pole became active (Zahn et al. 2007), while the OFC and TPJ remained active, albeit in different subregions (Moll et al. 2001; Moll et al. 2002). Overall, these findings have been confirmed by other investigators in different experimental settings. Disputes among results are possibly related to the particular design of each study, and the gender (Harenski et al. 2008) and neuropsychiatric (Harrison et al. 2012) composition of their respective samples.

The moral judgment of patients with acquired sociopathy and psychopathy has long puzzled researchers. Amazingly, such patients are often capable of providing plausible logical-verbal judgments on what is right or wrong, and yet their real-world conduct is often utterly immoral.[5] Studies on psychopathic adolescents have shown that they lag behind their normal peers by one Kohlberg moral developmental stage when they reason about real-life or hypothetical moral dilemmas even when social status and IQ are accounted for. Although statistically significant, the difference between normal and psychopathic youth has been small in most studies. Moreover, normal children at moral developmental levels comparable to those of psychopaths—for example, preconventional (Campagna and Harter 1975; Trevethan and Walker 1989)—are, of course, not psychopaths. There is evidence that abnormal moral judgments are more easily detected when psychopaths are asked to reason on moral dilemmas with a strong personal emotional involvement. Even then, the effects are not large, as shown by a thoroughly controlled study in which homicidal psychopaths and normal controls were asked to decide the fate of one or several individuals (Pujol et al. 2012). However, the cerebral correlates of judgments performed by psychopaths were critically distinct from those of normal individuals, especially concerning the intensity of the activation of the superomedial hemispheric wall in the moral dilemma condition, which was significantly reduced in them. Moreover, the intensity of activations in the posterior cingulate and right angular gyrus were inversely related to the severity of psychopathy as gauged by PCL-R scores. In line with studies on psychopathy, some patients with FTD appeared to retain a normal fund of moral knowledge and were able to reason as well as patients with Alzheimer's disease and normal controls about the right and wrong of a situation; they differed from both groups, however, in their unhesitatingly unemotional responses to moral dilemmas with a personal-emotional content (Mendez et al. 2005).

This pattern of dysmorality is comparable to the one reported on patients with focal damage to the VMPFC, who were additionally shown to be abnormally self-indulgent when challenged with moral personal dilemmas (Ciaramelli et al. 2007).

9.6. Final Considerations, Provisional Conclusions, and Prospects

The neural substrates of the mental and behavioral phenomena that engender the moral stance have begun to be identified thanks to the efforts of diverse fields of neuroscientific inquiry. However, despite remarkable advances of knowledge, the ultimate neural correlates of the moral stance still elude us. Although there is plenty of evidence on the neuroanatomical correlates of the subordinate neural systems that compound morality, so far morality could not be reduced to any of them. Therefore, we still do not know how the subjective experience of morality is organized in the brain, or if such experience has (1) a domain-specific neural organization as some authors (with whom we align ourselves) contend (Mendez 2009), or is (2) an emergent property of the concerted workings of domain-general systems like the ones mentioned above (Young and Dungan 2012). The decision between these alternatives will depend on further observations and the design of well-controlled experiments on normal subjects and patients with strategic cerebral lesions. In our opinion, the search for a specific moral domain is heuristically productive, because it incites the formulation of testable hypotheses and because it has already worked in the understanding of other domains of neural organization. This was the case, for example, in the determination of the glutamatergic neurons of the parabrachial nucleus and precoeruleus region as the essential substrates of wakefulness (Fuller et al. 2011).

Although few anatomical studies have directly compared acquired sociopathy with developmental psychopathy (Koenigs et al. 2010), one of the chief differences between them is the higher scores on PCL-R Factor 1 in psychopaths (Mitchell et al. 2006). An immediate challenge for future lesion mapping studies is to refine the lesion correlates of the four major outcomes of injuries that fall within the fronto-temporo-insular region outlined above, namely, acquired sociopathy without psychopathy (Eslinger and Damasio 1985), acquired psychopathy (Angrilli et al. 1999; Dimitrov et al. 1999; Goldar and Outes 1972; Jurado and Junqué 2000; Koenigs and Tranel 2006; Relkin et al. 1996), the often-neglected phenomena of improvement of personality with a concomitant improvement in interpersonal relations (Labbate et al. 1997), and the paradoxical decrease in socio-occupational functioning due to pathologically heightened prosocial sentiments (Ferreira-Garcia et al. 2013). The differential lesion localizations in each one of these groups must then be compared to the regional volumetric decreases of the cerebral substance in developmental psychopaths, which are fairly subtle and circumscribed (Gao et al. 2009; Gregory et al. 2012).

Another important gap in our present knowledge is the scarcity of postmortem studies on the brains of psychopaths. The exciting opportunities afforded by the ever-growing possibilities of studying the human brain in vivo should not distract researchers from the clinicoanatomic, or "lesion," method (Charcot 1874; Cummings 1993; de Oliveira-Souza and Tovar-Moll 2012). In the past three decades, the lesion method has successfully been extended to hitherto inaccessible neuropsychiatric disorders (Fisher 1989). Although the anatomical correlates of acquired sociopathy in FTD and focal brain damage have been the focus of intensive studies, we still know very little about the neuropathology of developmental psychopathy.

An issue of practical importance concerns the translation of a neuroscience of morality into effective treatments for disabling symptoms often found in developmental psychopathy and acquired sociopathy, such as uncontrollable outbursts of rage, and in drug addiction, such as craving (McGregor et al. 2008). From a technical standpoint there seems to be hope for novel pharmacological and surgical strategies. There are no controlled studies on the effects of prosocial drugs, such as oxytocin and ecstasy, on antisocial behaviors. Incidentally, ecstasy, an MDMA-agonistic drug, was originally distinguished from other recreational drugs of abuse for its empathogenic effects and absence of adverse reactions such as psychosis and withdrawal symptoms (Eisner 1994). The recognition that the MDMA system is an important mediator of prosocial behaviors may further the development of new therapeutic drugs that enhance empathy and hasten recovery from chronic drug addiction. A somewhat more remote, yet no less realistic, therapeutic avenue is the extension of functional stereotactic neurosurgery to the treatment of discrete symptoms of antisocial conduct (Schvarcz et al. 1972) and drug addiction (Stelten et al. 2008). The continuing pursuit of more specific neurosurgical targets is bolstered by serendipitous observations that injuries of certain brain regions may produce "salutary" changes in personality (Labbate et al. 1997), as well as in long-standing addictions, such as in cigarette smoking (Naqvi et al. 2007).

Finally, we believe that the neuropsychiatry of morality offers new insights into century-old philosophical disputes concerning the nature of human emotions. Since classical antiquity moral conduct has been represented as a tension between "instincts" (or "passions") and "reason" (Beach 1955). Also for centuries, the idea of a *scala naturae* has been ingrained in Western thought, implying that the fundamental organization of neurobiological and psychological structures and phenomena follows a hierarchy leading from the most elementary to the most complex (Hodos and Campbell 1969). This conception has inspired models of the organization of the human nervous system in which structures usually subsumed under the rubric of an ill-defined "limbic system" (MacLean 1964), which humans supposedly share with mammals and even reptiles, are held in check by "higher order" structures, usually represented by the neocortex (Kukuev 1980). The fallacy of these assumptions, as well as alternative views that are more in line with current facts of human neuroanatomy, were recently discussed (de Oliveira-Souza et al. 2011). The structural reorganization that the human brain underwent in the earliest stages of hominin phylogenesis was marked by a vertical (in contrast to a layered) pattern of differentiation in which subcortical structures traditionally seen as "ancient" or "regressive," with few exceptions (the primary olfactory pathways, in particular), have been subjected to progressive changes that were inextricably linked to the expansion of the isocortex itself (Stephan 1983). In many ways, present-day human neuroanatomy has been "humanized" and provided solid anatomical substrates that are more consistent with human nature—the unique neurobiological features that make us human, from erect bipedalism to morality, transcendence, and aesthetics.

Acknowledgments

The authors are indebted to Mr. José Ricardo Pinheiro and Ms. Monica Garcia (Library of Fundação Oswaldo Cruz, Rio de Janeiro) for untiring helpfulness in the retrieval of bibliographic references. The authors are indebted to Professor Omar da Rosa Santos, MD, PhD, for his insightful comments on earlier versions of the manuscript.

Notes

1. For the purposes of the present chapter, "psychopathy" refers to Cleckley-Hare's psychopathy, a *developmental* unremitting lifelong personality disorder that can reliably be diagnosed by objective criteria (Patrick 2006).

2. Not all antisocial conduct is abnormal, because virtually every human being engages in antisocial acts now and then; however, "normal" antisocial behavior is sharply different from abnormal social behavior in kind, frequency, and adverse impact on others. Unless otherwise stated, antisocial conduct refers to *abnormal* antisocial behavior as defined in the fourth and fifth editions of the Diagnostic and Statistical Manual of Mental Disorders (American Psychiatric Association 2013).

3. There is no consensus on what a basic emotion is or, for that matter, on which emotions should be classified as such. By tradition, all emotions that humans share with other mammals are considered "basic." Most authors would probably concede that the following "big six" should be part of any such classification: fear, surprise, happiness, disgust, rage, and sadness. A more recent claim proposes that basic and moral emotions are distributed along a continuum of elicitors that varies from selfish to altruistic. The closer to the selfish pole, the more basic an emotion is, and vice versa. Sadness, for example, may be either a basic or a moral emotion depending on whether it is elicited by a self-centered (sadness elicited by a personal loss) or other-centered (sadness elicited by sympathy to a friend's personal loss) stimulus or situation. Both views are consistent with the claim that the basic emotions constitute the basic blocks from which more complex emotional experiences are made. For example, compassion, a typical moral sentiment, probably has a core of sadness.

4. Freud and Stellar proposed that what we now call "motivation" consists of four components and two phases, which take place on an approach-avoidance behavioral continuum. The components are the need (which may be physiological or psychological), the goal (the satiation of the need), the physical object or psychological condition through which the goal is achieved, and the intensity of behavior (drive). These components make up the appetitive or ergotropic phase of motivated behavior; as the goal is achieved, satiety sets in, and the second phase

(consummatory or trophotropic) prevails for that particular motivation. Satiety has a positive rewarding value, being subjectively experienced as pleasure or well-being; frustration (failure to accomplish satiety), in contrast, has a negative punishing value being experienced as displeasure or aversion (Berridge 2003).

5. We use the term "immoral" to refer to a person who does morally wrong things but who is capable of telling the difference between right and wrong; we reserve the word "amoral" to refer to a person who does bad things because he is not capable of knowing the difference between right and wrong.

References

Adam, J., M. Baulac, J. J. Hauw, D. Laplane, and C. Duyckaerts. 2008. "Behavioral Symptoms after Pallido-Nigral Lesions: A Clinico-Pathological Case." *Neurocase* 14: 125–130.

Aharoni, E., C. Funk, W. Sinnott-Armstrong, and M. Gazzaniga. 2008. "Can Neurological Evidence Help Courts Assess Criminal Responsibility? Lessons from Law and Neuroscience." *Annals of the New York Academy of Sciences* 1124: 145–160.

Allman, J. M., N. A. Tetreault, A. Hakeem, and S. Park. 2011. "The von Economo Neurons in Apes and humans." *American Journal of Human Biology* 23: 5–21.

American Psychiatric Association. *Diagnostic and Statistical Manual of Mental Disorders.* 5th ed. (*DSM-5*). Washington DC: American Psychiatric Association, 2013.

Angrilli A., D. Palomba, A. Cantagallo, A. Maietti, and L. Stegagno. 1999. "Emotional Impairment after Right Orbitofrontal Lesion in a Patient without Cognitive Deficits." *NeuroReport* 10: 1741–1746.

Babiak, P., and R. D. Hare. 2006. *Snakes in Suits: When Psychopaths go to Work.* New York: HarperCollins.

Bado, P., A. Engel, R. de Oliveira-Souza, I. E. Bramati, F. F. Paiva, R. Basílio, J. R. Sato, F. Tovar-Mol, and J. Moll. 2012. "Functional Dissociation of Ventral and Dorsal Default Mode Network Components during Resting State and Emotional Autobiographical Recall." *Journal of Neuroscience* 32: 12499–12505.

Barrash, J., E. Asp, K. Markon, K. Manzel, S. W. Anderson, and D. Tranel. 2011. "Dimensions of Personality Disturbance after Focal Brain Damage: Investigation with the Iowa Scales of Personality Change." *Journal of Clinical and Experimental Neuropsychology* 33: 833–852.

Barrett, L. F., K. A. Lindquist, and M. Gendron. 2007. "Language as Context for the Perception of Emotion." *Trends in Cognitive Sciences* 11: 327–332.

Bauer, R. M. 1984. "Autonomic Recognition of Names and Faces in Prosopagnosia: A Neuropsychological Application of the Guilty Knowledge Test." *Neuropsychologia* 22: 457–469.

Beach, F. A. 1955. "The Descent of Instinct." *Psychological Review* 62: 401–410.

Bechara, A. 2005. "Decision Making, Impulse Control and Loss of Willpower to Resist Drugs: A Neurocognitive Perspective." *Nature Neuroscience* 8: 1458–1461.

Beer, J. S., E. A. Heerey, D. Keltner, D. Scabini, and R. T. Knight. 2003. "The Regulatory Function of Self-Conscious Emotion: Insights from Patients with Orbitofrontal Damage." *Journal of Personality and Social Psychology* 85: 594–604.

Berman, B. D., S. G. Horovitz, B. Morel, and M. Hallett. 2012. "Neural Correlates of Blink Suppression and the Buildup of a Natural Bodily Urge." *NeuroImage* 59: 1441–1450.

Berridge, K. C. 2003. "Pleasures of the Brain." *Brain and Cognition* 52: 106–128.

Berrios, G. E. 1999. "J. C. Prichard and the Concept of 'Moral Insanity.'" *History of Psychiatry* 10: 111–116.

Blair, R. J. R. 1999. "Responsiveness to Distress Cues in the Child with Psychopathic Tendencies." *Personality and Individual Differences* 27: 135–145.

Blair, R. J. R., C. Sellars, I. Strickland, F. Clark, A. Williams, M. Smith, and L. Jones. 1996. "Theory of Mind in the Psychopath." *Journal of Forensic Psychiatry* 7: 15–25.

Bleuler, E. 1912. *The Theory of Schizophrenic Negativism*. New York: Nervous and Mental Disease Publishing Company.

Brass, M., S. Zysset, and D. Y. von Cramon. 2001. "The Inhibition of Imitative Response Tendencies." *NeuroImage* 14: 1416–1423.

Browning, W. 1921. "The Moral Center in the Brain (Cortical Region for Control of Morals): Its Location and Significance." *Medical Record* 99: 1043–1048, 1089–1094.

Campagna, A. F., and S. Harter. 1975. "Moral Judgment in Sociopathic and Normal Children." *Journal of Personality and Social Psychology* 31: 199–205.

Carbanac, M. 1995. "Palatability *vs*. Money: Experimental Study of a Conflict of Motivations." *Appetite* 25: 43–49.

Carré, J. M., L. W. Hyde, C. S. Neumann, E. Viding, and A. R. Hariri. 2013. "The Neural Signatures of Distinct Psychopathic Traits." *Social Neuroscience* 8: 122–135.

Charcot, J. M. 1874. *Leçons Cliniques sur les Maladies des Vieillards et les Maladies Chroniques*. Paris: Adrien Delahaye.

Chen, P. S., S. J. Chen, Y. K. Yang, T. L. Yeh, C. C. Chen, and H. Y. Lo. 2003. "Asperger's Disorder: A Case Report of Repeated Stealing and the Collecting Behaviour of an Adolescent Patient." *Acta Psychiatrica Scandinavica* 107: 73–76.

Ciaramelli, E., D. Braghittoni, and G. di Pellegrino. 2012. "It Is the Outcome That Counts! Damage to the Ventromedial Prefrontal Cortex Disrupts the Integration of Outcome and Belief Information for Moral Judgment." *Journal of the International Neuropsychological Society* 18: 962–971.

Ciaramelli, E., M. Miccioli, E. Làdavas, and G. di Pellegrino. 2007. "Selective Deficit in Personal Moral Judgment Following Damage to Ventromedial Prefrontal Cortex." *Social, Cognitive, and Affective Neuroscience* 2: 84–92.

Cima, M., F. Tonnaer, and M. D. Hauser. 2010. "Psychopaths Know Right from Wrong but Don't Care." *Social, Cognitive, and Affective Neuroscience* 5: 59–67.

Cleckley, H. 1976. *The Mask of Sanity*. 5th ed. St. Louis, MO: Mosby.

Coenen, V. A. 2012. "Human Medial Forebrain Bundle (MFB) and Anterior Thalamic Radiation (ATR): Imaging of Two Major Subcortical Pathways and the Dynamic Balance of Opposite Affects in Understanding Depression." *Journal of Neuropsychiatry* 24: 223–236.

Craig, A. D. 2002. "How Do You Feel? Interoception: The Sense of the Physiological Condition of the Body." *Nature Reviews Neuroscience* 3: 655–666.

Cummings, J. L. 1993. "Frontal-Subcortical Circuits and Human Behavior." *Archives of Neurology* 50: 873–880.

Darwin, C. 1872. *The Expression of the Emotions in Man and Animals*. London: J. Murray.

Davis, M. H. 1980. "A Multidimensional Approach to Individual Differences in Empathy." *JSAS Catalog of Selected Documents in Psychology* 10: 85.

Decety, J., and P. L. Jackson. 2004. "The Functional Architecture of Human Empathy." *Behavioral and Cognitive Neuroscience Reviews* 3: 71–100.

Denny-Brown, D. 1952. "The Biological Tropisms of the Cerebral Cortex." *Arquivos de Neuro-Psiquiatria* 10: 399–404.

de Oliveira-Souza, R., R. D. Hare, I. E. Bramati, G. J. Garrido, F. A. Ignácio, F. Tovar-Moll, and J. Moll. 2008. "Psychopathy as a Disorder of the Moral Brain: Fronto-Temporo-Limbic Grey Matter Reductions Demonstrated by Voxel-Based Morphometry." *NeuroImage* 40: 1202–1213.

de Oliveira-Souza, R., and J. Moll. 2009. "The Neural Bases of Normal and Deviant Moral Cognition and Behavior." *Topics in Magnetic Resonance Imaging* 20: 261–270.

de Oliveira-Souza, R., J. Moll, and P. J. Eslinger. 2004. "Neuropsychological Assessment." In *Principles and Practice of Behavioral Neurology and Neuropsychology*, edited by M. Rizzo and P. J. Eslinger, 47–64. New York: Oxford University Press.

de Oliveira-Souza, R., J. Moll, and J. Grafman. 2011. "Emotion and Social Cognition: Lessons from Contemporary Human Neuroanatomy." *Emotion Review* 3: 310–312.

de Oliveira-Souza, R., J. Moll, F. A. Ignácio, and P. J. Eslinger. 2002. "Catatonia: A Window into the Cerebral Underpinnings of Will." *Behavioral and Brain Sciences* 25: 582–584.

de Oliveira-Souza, R., J. Moll, F. A. Ignácio, and R. D. Hare. 2008. "Psychopathy in a Civil Psychiatric Outpatient Sample." *Criminal Justice and Behavior* 35: 427–437.

de Oliveira-Souza, R., and F. Tovar-Moll. 2012. "The Unbearable Lightness of the Extrapyramidal Concept." *Journal of the History of the Neurosciences* 21: 280–292.

de Oliveira-Souza, R., R. Zahn, and J. Moll. 2013. "The Neural Bases of Moral Belief Systems." In *The Neural Basis of Human Belief Systems*, edited by F. Krueger and J. Grafman, 111–135. New York: Psychology Press.

Dimitrov, M., M. Phipps, T. P. Zahn, and J. Grafman. 1999. "A Thoroughly Modern Gage." *Neurocase* 5: 345–354.

Dorst, R., K. Jabotinsky-Rnbin, and M. Fliman. 1997. "Psychopathic Schizophrenia: A Neglected Diagnostic Entity with Legal Implications." *Medicine and Law* 16: 487–498.

Dunbar, R. I. M. 1998. "The Social Brain Hypothesis." *Evolutionary Anthropology* 6: 178–190.

Eisner, B. 1994. *Ecstasy: The MDMA Story*. Berkeley, CA: Ronin Publishing.

Ellis, H. 1890. *The Criminal*. New York: Scribner and Welford.

Eslinger, P. J. 1998. "Neurological and Neuropsychological Bases of Empathy." *European Neurology* 39: 193–199.

Feinberg, T. E., R. J. Schindler, N. G. Flanagan, and L. D. Haber. 1992. "Two Alien Hand Syndromes." *Neurology* 42: 19–24.

FeldmanHall, O., T. Dalgleish, R. Thompson, D. Evans, S. Schweizer, and D. Mobbs. 2012. "Differential Neural Circuitry and Self-Interest in Real vs. Hypothetical Moral Decisions." *Social, Cognitive, and Affective Neuroscience* 7: 743–751.

Ferreira-Garcia, R., L. F. Fontenelle, J. Moll, and R. de Oliveira-Souza. 2014. "Pathological Generosity: An Atypical Impulse Control Disorder after a Left Subcortical Stroke." *Neurocase* 20: 496–500.

Fisher, C. M. 1989. "'Catatonia' Due to Disulfiram Toxicity." *Archives of Neurology* 46: 798–804.

Fisher, C. M. 1984. "Abulia Minor vs. Agitated Behavior." *Clinical Neurosurgery* 31: 9–31.

Fisher, C. M. 1993. "Concerning Mind." *Canadian Journal of Neurological Sciences* 20: 247–253.

Freud, S. 1915. "Triebe und Triebschicksale." *Internationale Zeitschrift für Psychoanalyse* 3: 84–100.

Frick, P. J. 2009. "Extending the Construct of Psychopathy to Youth: Implications for Understanding, Diagnosing, and Treating Antisocial Children and Adolescents." *Canadian Journal of Psychiatry* 54: 803–812.

Frick, P. J. 2012. "Developmental Pathways to Conduct Disorder: Implications for Future Directions in Research, Assessment, and Treatment." *Journal of Clinical Child and Adolescent Psychology* 41: 378–389.

Fuller, P., D. Sherman, N. P. Pedersen, C. B. Saper, and J. Lu. 2011. "Reassessment of the Structural Basis of the Ascending Arousal System." *Journal of Comparative Neurology* 519: 933–956.

Gacono, C. B. 2000. *The Clinical and Forensic Assessment of Psychopathy: A Practitioner's Guide*. Mahwah, NJ: Lawrence Erlbaum.

Gao, Y., A. L. Glenn, R. A. Schug, Y. Yang, and A. Raine. 2009. "The Neurobiology of Psychopathy: A Neurodevelopmental Perspective." *Canadian Journal of Psychiatry* 54: 813–823.

Gazzaniga, M. S. 1985. "The Social Brain." *Psychology Today* 19: 29–38.

Gergely, G., Z. Nadasdy, G. Csibra, and S. Biro. 1995. "Taking the Intentional Stance at 12 Months of Age." *Cognition* 56: 165–193.

Glenn, A. L., R. Iyer, J. Graham, S. Koleva, and J. Haidt. 2009. "Are All Types of Morality Compromised in Psychopathy?" *Journal of Personality Disorders* 23: 384–398.

Glenn, A. L., A. Raine, and R. A. Schug. 2009. "The Neural Correlates of Moral Decision-Making in Psychopathy." *Molecular Psychiatry* 14: 5–6.

Godefroy, O., A. Duhamel, X. Leclerc, T. S. Michel, H. Hénon, and D. Leys. 1998. "Brain-Behaviour Relationships: Some Models and Related Statistical Procedures for the Study of Brain-Damaged Patients." *Brain* 121: 1545–1556.

Goldar, J. C., and D. L. Outes. 1972. "Fisiopatología de la Desinhibición Instintiva." *Acta Psiquiátrica y Psicológica de América Latina* 18: 177–185.

Goldberg, G. 2000. "When Aliens Invade: Multiple Mechanisms for Dissociation between Will and Action." *Journal of Neurology, Neurosurgery and Psychiatry* 68: 7.

Gray, K., and D. M. Wegner. 2011. "Dimensions of Moral Emotions." *Emotion Review* 3: 258–260.

Green, C. D., and P. R. Groff. 2003. *Early Psychological Thought: Ancient Accounts of Mind and Soul*. Westport, CT: Praeger.

Green S., M. A. Ralph, J. Moll, E. A. Stamatakis, J. Grafman, and R. Zahn. 2010. "Selective Functional Integration between Anterior Temporal and Distinct Fronto-Mesolimbic Regions during Guilt and Indignation." *NeuroImage* 52: 1720–1726.

Gregory, S., D. ffytche, A. Simmons, V. Kumari, M. Howard, S. Hodgins, and N. Blackwood. 2012. "The Antisocial Brain: Psychopathy Matters. A Structural MRI Investigation of Antisocial Male Violent Offenders." *Archives of General Psychiatry* 69: 962–972.

Guze, S. B., D. W. Goodwin, and J. B. Crane. 1970. "A Psychiatric Study of the Wives of Convicted Felons: An Example of Assortative Mating." *American Journal of Psychiatry* 126: 1773–1776.

Habib, M. 2000. "Disorders of Motivation." In *Behavior and Mood Disorders in Focal Brain Lesions*, edited by J. Bogousslavsky and J. L. Cummings, 261–284. New York: Cambridge University Press.

Haidt, J. 2003. "The Moral Emotions." In *Handbook of Affective Sciences*, edited by R. J. Davidson, K. R. Scherer, and H. H. Goldsmith, 852–870. Oxford: Oxford University Press.

Haidt, J., and C. Joseph. 2007. "The Moral Mind: How 5 Sets of Innate Intuitions Guide the Development of Many Culture-Specific Virtues, and Perhaps Even Modules." In *The Innate Mind*, vol. 3, edited by P. Carruthers, S. Laurence, and S. Stich, 852–870. New York: Oxford University Press.

Hare, R. D. 1980. "A Research Scale for the Assessment of Psychopathy in Criminal Populations." *Personality and Individual Differences* 1: 111–119.

Hare, R. D. 1993. *Without Conscience: The Disturbing World of the Psychopaths among Us.* New York: Guilford Press.

Hare, R. D. 2006. "Psychopathy: A Clinical and Forensic Overview." *Psychiatric Clinics of North America* 29: 709–724.

Hare, R. D. 2003. *The Hare Psychopathy Checklist—Revised.* 2nd ed. Toronto: Multi-Health Systems.

Hare, R. D, and C. S. Neumann. 2008. "Psychopathy as a Clinical and Empirical Construct." *Annual Review of Clinical Psychology* 4: 217–246.

Harenski, C. L., O. Antonenko, M. S. Shane, and K. A. Kiehl. 2008. "Gender Differences in Neural Mechanisms Underlying Moral Sensitivity." *Social, Cognitive, and Affective Neuroscience* 3: 313–321.

Harlow, J. M. 1868. "Recovery from the Passage of an Iron Bar through the Head." *Massachusetts Medical Society Publications* 2: 327–346.

Harpur, T. J, and R. D. Hare. 1994. "Assessment of Psychopathy as a Function of Age." *Journal of Abnormal Psychology* 103: 604–609.

Harrison, B. J., J. Pujol, C. Soriano-Mas, Hernández-R. Ribas, M. López-Solà, H. Ortiz, P. Alonso, et al. 2012. "Neural Correlates of Moral Sensitivity in Obsessive-Compulsive Disorder." *Archives of General Psychiatry* 69: 741–749.

Hauser, M. D. 2006. *Moral Minds. The Nature of Right and Wrong.* New York: HarperCollins.

Heilman, K. H. 1997. "The Neurobiology of Emotional Experience." In *The Neuropsychiatry of Limbic and Subcortical Disorders*, edited by S. Salloway, P. Malloy, and J. L. Cummings, 133–142. Washington, DC: American Psychiatric Press.

Hervé, H. 2007. "Psychopathy across the Ages: A History of the Hare Psychopath." In *The Psychopath: Theory, Research, and Practice*, edited by H. Hervé and J. C. Yuille, 21–55. London: Lawrence Erlbaum.

Hodos, W., and C. B. G. Campbell. 1969. "*Scala Naturæ*: Why There Is No Theory in Comparative Psychology." *Psychological Review* 76: 337–350.

Ibáñez, A., and F. Manes. 2012. "Contextual Social Cognition and the Behavioral Variant of Frontotemporal Dementia." *Neurology* 78: 1354–1362.

Jastrow, J., and L. Marillier. 1902. "Will." In *Dictionary of Philosophy and Psychology*, vol. 2, edited by J. M. Baldwin, 815–817. New York: Macmillan.

Jefferson, G. 1957. "The Reticular Formation and Clinical Neurology." In *Reticular Formation of the Brain. Henry Ford Hospital, Detroit, International Symposium*, edited by H. H. Jasper, L. Proctor, R. Knighton, and R. T. Costello, 729–738. London: Churchill.

Jurado, M. A., and C. Junqué. 2000. "Conducta Delictiva tras Lesiones Prefrontales Orbitales: Estudio de Dos Casos." *Actas Españolas de Psiquiatría* 28: 337–341.

Kalis, A., A. Mojzisch, T. S. Schweizer, and S. Kaiser. 2008. "Weakness of Will, Akrasia, and the Neuropsychiatry of Decision Making: An Interdisciplinary Perspective." *Cognitive, Affective, and Behavioral Neuroscience* 8: 402–417.

Kédia, G., S. Berthoz, M. Wessa, D. Hilton, and J.-L. Martinot. 2008. "An Agent Harms a Victim: A Functional Magnetic Resonance Imaging Study on Specific Moral Emotions." *Journal of Cognitive Neuroscience* 20: 1788–1798.

Klingler, J., and P. Gloor. 1960. "The Connections of the Amygdala and of the Anterior Temporal Cortex in the Human Brain." *Journal of Comparative Neurology* 115: 333–369.

Knoch, D., and E. Fehr. 2007. "Resisting the Power of Temptations: The Right Prefrontal Cortex and Self-Control." *Annals of the New York Academy of Sciences* 1104: 123–134.

Koenigs, M., A. Baskin-Sommers, J. Zeier, and J. P. Newman. 2011. "Investigating the Neural Correlates of Psychopathy: A Critical Review." *Molecular Psychiatry* 16: 792–799.

Koenigs, M., M. Kruepke, and J. P. Newman. 2010. "Economic Decision-Making in Psychopathy: A Comparison with Ventromedial Prefrontal Lesion Patients." *Neuropsychologia* 48: 2198–2204.

Koenigs, M., and D. Tranel. 2006. "Pseudopsychopathy: A Perspective from Cognitive Neuroscience." In *The Orbitofrontal Cortex*, edited by D. H. Zald and S. L. Rauch, 597–619. New York: Oxford University Press.

Kraepelin, E. 1904. *Lectures on Clinical Psychiatry*. Revised and edited by Thomas Johnstone. New York: William Woody.

Krajbich, I., R. Adolphs, D. Tranel, N. L. Denburg, and C. F. Camerer. 2009. "Economic Games Quantify Diminished Sense of Guilt in Patients with Damage to the Prefrontal Cortex." *Journal of Neuroscience* 29: 2188–2192.

Kukuev, L. A. 1980. "The Concept of Nervous System Levels." *Neuroscience and Behavioral Physiology* 10: 1–5.

Labbate, L. A, D. Warden, and G. B. Murray. 1997. "Salutary Change after Frontal Brain Trauma." *Annals of Clinical Psychiatry* 9: 27–30.

Laplane, D. 1990. "La Perte d'Auto-activation Psychique." *Revue Neurologique* (Paris) 146: 397–404.

Laplane, D., and B. Dubois. 2001. "Auto-activation Deficit: A Basal Ganglia Related Syndrome." *Movement Disorders* 16: 810–814.

Leopold, A., F. Krueger, O. dal Monte, M. Pardini, S. J. Pulaski, J. Solomon, and J. Grafman. 2012. "Damage to the Left Ventromedial Prefrontal Cortex Impacts Affective Theory of Mind." *Social, Cognitive, and Affective Neuroscience* 7: 871–880.

Levy, R., and B. Dubois. 2006. "Apathy and the Functional Anatomy of the Prefrontal Cortex-Basal Ganglia Circuits." *Cerebral Cortex* 16: 916–928.

Lewis, C. S. 1952. *Mere Christianity*. New York: HarperCollins.

Lewis, G. J., R. Kanai, T. C. Bates, and G. Rees. 2012. "Moral Values Are Associated with Individual Differences in Regional Brain Volume." *Journal of Cognitive Neuroscience* 24: 1657–1663.

Loewenstein, G. 1996. "Out of Control: Visceral Influences on Behavior." *Organizational Behavior and Human Decision Processes* 65: 272–292.

Lotze, M., R. Veit, S. Anders, and N. Birbaumer. 2007. "Evidence for a Different Role of the Ventral and Dorsal Medial Prefrontal Cortex for Social Reactive Aggression: An Interactive fMRI Study." *NeuroImage* 34: 470–478.

Lough, S., C. M. Kipps, C. Treise, P. Watson, R. J. R. Blair, and J. R. Hodges. 2006. "Social Reasoning, Emotion and Empathy in Frontotemporal Dementia." *Neuropsychologia* 44: 950–958.

Loup, F., E. Tribollet, M. Dubois-Dauphin, and I. I. Dreifuss. 1991. "Localization of High-Affinity Binding Sites for Oxytocin and Vasopressin in the Human Brain." An Autoradiographic Study." *Brain Research* 555: 220–232.

Luauté, J. P., and O. Saladini. 2001. "Le Concept Français d'Athymhormie de 1922 à Nos Jours." *Revue Canadienne de Psychiatrie* 46: 639–646.

MacLean, P. D. 1964. "Man and His Animal Brains." *Modern Medicine* 32: 95–106.

Maudsley, H. 1876. *Responsibility in Mental Disease*. 3rd ed. London: Henry S. King.

McGregor, I. S., P. D. Callaghan, and G. E. Hunt. 2008. "From Ultrasocial to Antisocial: A Role for Oxytocin in the Acute Reinforcing Effects and Long-Term Adverse Consequences of Drug Use?" *British Journal of Pharmacology* 154: 358–368.

Mendez, M. F. 2006. "What Frontotemporal Dementia Reveals about the Neurobiological Basis of Morality." *Medical Hypotheses* 67: 411–418.

Mendez, M. F. 2009. "The Neurobiology of Moral Behavior: Review and Neuropsychiatric Implications." *CNS Spectrums* 14: 608–620.

Mendez, M. F. 2010. "The Unique Predisposition to Criminal Violations in Frontotemporal Dementia." *Journal of the American Academy of Psychiatry and the Law* 38: 318–323.

Mendez, M. F, A. K. Chen, J. S. Shapira, and B. L. Miller. 2005. "Acquired Sociopathy and Frontotemporal Dementia." *Dementia and Geriatric Cognitive Disorders* 20: 99–104.

Miller, B. L., W. W. Seeley, P. Mychack, H. J. Rosen, I. Mena, and K. Boone. 2001. "Neuroanatomy of the Self: Evidence from Patients with Frontotemporal Dementia." *Neurology* 57: 817–821.

Milgram, S. 1974. *Obedience to Authority: An Experimental View*. New York: Harper Perennial.

Millon, T., E. Simonsen, and M. Birket-Smith. 1998. "Historical Conceptions of Psychopathy in the United States and Europe." In *Psychopathy: Antisocial, Criminal, and Violent Behavior*, edited by T. Millon, E. Simonsen, M. Birket-Smith, and R. D. Davis, 3–31. New York: Guilford Press.

Mitchell, D. G. V., S. B. Avny, and R. J. R. Blair. 2006. "Divergent Patterns of Aggressive and Neurocognitive Characteristics in Acquired versus Developmental Psychopathy." *Neurocase* 12: 164–178.

Moffitt, T. E., L. Arseneault, D. Belsky, N. Dicksonc, R. J. Hancox, H. L. Harrington, R. Houtsa, et al. 2011. "A Gradient of Childhood Self-Control Predicts Health, Wealth, and Public Safety." *Proceedings of the National Academy of Sciences USA* 108: 2693–2698.

Moll, J., P. Bado, R. de Oliveira-Souza, I. E. Bramati, D. O. Lima, F. F. Paiva, J. R. Sato, F. Tovar-Moll, and R. Zahn. 2012. "A Neural Signature of Affiliative Emotion in the Human Septohypothalamic Area." *Journal of Neuroscience* 32: 12499–12505.

Moll, J., and R. de Oliveira-Souza. 2009. "'Extended Attachment' and the Human Brain: Internalized Cultural Values and Evolutionary Implications." In *The Moral Brain: Essays on the Evolutionary and Neuroscientific Aspects of Morality*, edited by J. Verplaetse, J. De Schrijver, S. Vanneste, and J. Braeckman, 69–85. New York: Springer.

Moll, J., R. de Oliveira-Souza, I. E. Bramati, and J. Grafman. 2002. "Functional Networks in Emotional Moral and Nonmoral Social Judgments." *NeuroImage* 16: 696–703.

Moll J., R. de Oliveira-Souza, and P. J. Eslinger. 2003. "Morals and the Human Brain: A Working Model." *NeuroReport* 14: 299–305.

Moll, J., R. de Oliveira-Souza, G. J. Garrido, I. E. Bramati, E. M. A. Caparelli-Dáquer, M. L. M. F. Paiva, R. Zahn, and J. Grafman. 2007. "The Self as a Moral Agent: Linking the Neural Bases of Social Agency and Moral Sensitivity." *Social Neuroscience* 2: 336–352.

Moll, J., R. de Oliveira-Souza, F. Tovar-Moll, F. A. Ignácio, I. E. Bramat, E. M. A. Caparelli-Dáquer, and P. J. Eslinger. 2005. "The Moral Affiliations of Disgust: A Functional MRI Study." *Cognitive and Behavioral Neurology* 18: 68–78.

Moll, J., P. J. Eslinger, and R. de Oliveira-Souza. 2001. "Frontopolar and Anterior Temporal Cortex Activation in a Moral Judgment Task." *Arquivos de Neuro-Psiquiatria* 59: 657–664.

Moll, J., F. Krueger, R. Zahn, M. Pardini, R. de Oliveira-Souza, and J. Grafman. 2006. "Human Fronto-Mesolimbic Networks Guide Decisions about Charitable Donation." *Proceedings of the National Academy of Sciences USA* 103: 15623–15628.

Moll, J., and J. Schulkin. 2009. "Social Attachment and Aversion in Human Moral Cognition." *Neuroscience and Biobehavioral Reviews* 33: 456–465.

Moll, J., R. Zahn, R. de Oliveira-Souza, I. E. Bramati, F. Krueger, B. Tura, A. L. Cavanagh, and J. Grafman. 2011. "Impairment of Prosocial Sentiments Is Associated with Frontopolar and Septal Damage in Frontotemporal Dementia." *NeuroImage* 54: 1735–1742.

Moran, J. M., L. L. Young, R. Saxe, S. M. Lee, D. O'Young, and P. L. Mavros. 2011. "Impaired Theory of Mind for Moral Judgment in High-Functioning Autism." *Proceedings of the National Academy of Sciences USA* 108: 2688–2692.

Moretto G., E. Mattioli, F. Làdavas, and G. di Pellegrino. 2009. "A Psychophysiological Investigation of Moral Judgment after Ventromedial Prefrontal Damage." *Journal of Cognitive Neuroscience* 22: 1888–1899.

Mori, E., and A. Yamadori. 1989. "Rejection Behaviour: A Human Homologue of the Abnormal Behaviour of Denny-Brown and Chambers' Monkey with Bilateral Parietal Ablation." *Journal of Neurology, Neurosurgery and Psychiatry* 52: 1260–1266.

Naqvi, N. H., D. Rudrauf, H. Damasio, and A. Bechara. 2007. "Damage to the Insula Disrupts Addiction to Cigarette Smoking." *Science* 315: 531–534.

Nauta, W. J. H., and V. B. Domesick. 1981. "Ramifications of the Limbic System." In *Psychiatry and the Biology of the Human Brain: A Symposium Dedicated to Seymour S. Kety*, edited by S. Matthysse, 165–188. New York: Elsevier.

Narvaez, D. 2008. "Human Flourishing and Moral Development: Cognitive Science and Neurobiological Perspectives on Virtue Development." In *Handbook of Moral and Character Education*, edited by L. Nucci and D. Narvaez, 310–327. Mahwah, NJ: Erlbaum.

Neumann, C. S., R. D. Hare, and J. P. Newman. 2007. "The Super-ordinate Nature of the Psychopathy Checklist—Revised." *Journal of Personality Disorders* 21: 102–117.

Neumann, C. S., D. S. Schmitt, R. Carter, I. Embley, and R. D. Hare. 2012. "Psychopathic Traits in Females and Males across the Globe." *Behavioral Sciences and the Law* 30: 557–573.

Patrick, C. J. 2006. "Back to the Future: Cleckley as a Guide to the Next Generation of Psychopathy Research." In *Handbook of Psychopathy*, edited by C. J. Patrick, 605–617. New York: Guilford Press.

Pessiglione, M., L. Schmidt, B. Draganski, R. Kalisch, H. Lau, R. J. Dolan, and C. D. Frith. 2007. "How the Brain Translates Money into Force: A Neuroimaging Study of Subliminal Motivation." *Science* 316: 904–906.

Pfaff, D. W. 2007. *The Neuroscience of Fair Play: Why We (Usually) Follow the Golden Rule.* New York: Dana Press.

Phillips, S., V. Sangalang, and G. Sterns. 1987. "Basal Forebrain Infarction: A Clinicopathologic Correlation." *Archives of Neurology* 44: 1134–1138.

Piguet, O., M. Hornberger, E. Mioshi, and J. R. Hodges. 2011. "Behavioural-Variant Frontotemporal Dementia: Diagnosis, Clinical Staging, and Management." *Lancet Neurology* 10: 162–172.

Pujol, J., I. Batalla, O. Contreras-Rodríguez, B. J. Harrison, V. Pera, R. Hernández-Ribas, E. Real, et al. 2012. "Breakdown in the Brain Network Subserving Moral Judgment in Criminal Psychopathy." *Social, Cognitive, and Affective Neuroscience* 7: 917–923.

Raine, A., and Y. Yang. 2006. "Neural Foundations to Moral Reasoning and Antisocial Behavior." *Social, Cognitive, and Affective Neuroscience* 1: 203–213.

Rankin, K. P., M. L. Gorno-Tempini, S. C. Allison, C. M. Stanley, S. Glenn, M. W. Weiner, and B. L. Miller. 2006. "Structural Anatomy of Empathy in Neurodegenerative Disease." *Brain* 129: 2945–2956.

Relkin, N., F. Plum, S. Mattis, D. Eidelberg, and D. Tranel. 1996. "Impulsive Homicide Associated with an Arachnoid Cyst and Unilateral Frontotemporal Cerebral Dysfunction." *Seminars in Clinical Neuropsychiatry* 1: 172–183.

Richell, R. A., D. G. V. Mitchell, C. Newman, A. Leonard, S. Baron-Cohen, and R J. R. Blair. 2003. "Theory of Mind and Psychopathy: Can Psychopathic Individuals Read the 'Language of the Eyes'?" *Neuropsychologia* 41: 523–526.

Rolls, E. T., J. Hornak, D. Wade, and J. McGrath. 1994. "Emotion-Related Learning in Patients with Social and Emotional Changes Associated with Frontal Lobe Damage." *Journal of Neurology, Neurosurgery and Psychiatry* 57: 1518–1524.

Rorden, C., and M. Brett. 2000. "Stereotaxic Display of Brain Lesions." *Behavioral Neurology* 12: 191–200.

Rorden, C., and O. H. Karnath. 2004. "Using Human Brain Lesions to Infer Function: A Relic from a Past Era in the fMRI Age?" *Nature Reviews Neuroscience* 5: 813–819.

Roseman, I. J., C. Wiest, and T. S. Swartz. 1994. "Phenomenology, Behaviors, and Goals Differentiate Discrete Emotions." *Journal of Personality and Social Psychology* 67: 206–221.

Rozin, P., L. Lowery, S. Imada, and J. Haidt. 1999. "The CAD Triad Hypothesis: A Mapping between Three Moral Emotions (Contempt, Anger, Disgust) and Three Moral Codes (Community, Autonomy, Divinity)." *Journal of Personality and Social Psychology* 76: 574–586.

Rush, B. 1830. *Medical Inquiries and Observations upon the Diseases of the Mind.* 4th ed. Philadelphia: Kimber and Richardson.

Saper, C. B. 1987. "Diffuse Cortical Projection Systems: Anatomical Organization and Role in Cortical Function." In *Handbook of Physiology*, vol. 5: *Higher Functions of the Brain*, edited by F. Plum, 169–210. Bethesda, MD: American Physiological Society.

Saver, J. L., and A. R. Damasio. 1994. "Preserved Access and Processing of Social Knowledge in a Patient with Acquired Sociopathy Due to Ventromedial Frontal Damage." *Neuropsychologia* 29: 1241–1249.

Saver, J. L., P. Greenstein, M. Ronthal, and M. M. Mesulam. 1993. "Asymmetric Catalepsy after Right Hemisphere Stroke." *Movement Disorders* 8: 69–73.

Schmidt, L., B. F. d'Arc, G. Lafargue, A. Galanaud, V. Czernecki, M. Grabli, M. Schupbach, et al. 2008. "Disconnecting Force from Money: Effects of Basal Ganglia Damage on Incentive Motivation." *Brain* 131: 1303–1310.

Schneirla, T. C. 1959. "An Evolutionary and Developmental Theory of Biphasic Processes Underlying Approach and Withdrawal." In *Nebraska Symposium on Motivation*, edited by M. R. Jones, 1–42. Lincoln: University of Nebraska Press.

Schott, G. D. 2000. "Illustrating Cerebral Function: The Iconography of Arrows." *Philosophical Transactions of the Royal Society London B* 355: 1789–1799.

Schvarcz, J. R., R. Driollet, E. Rios, and O. Betti. 1972. "Stereotactic Hypothalamotomy for Behaviour Disorders." *Journal of Neurology, Neurosurgery and Psychiatry* 35: 356–359.

Seeley W. W., F. T. Merkle, S. E. Gaus, A. D. Craig, J. M. Allman, and P. R. Hof. 2012. "Distinctive Neurons of the Anterior Cingulate and Frontoinsular Cortex: A Historical Perspective." *Cerebral Cortex* 22: 245–250.

Segarra, J. M. 1970. "Cerebral Vascular Disease and behavior. I. The Syndrome of the Mesencephalic Artery (Basilar Artery Bifurcation)." *Archives of Neurology* 22: 408–418.

Seo, S. W., K. Jung, H. You, B. H. Lee, G. M. Kim, C.-S. Chung, K. H. Lee, and D. L. Na. 2009. "Motor-Intentional Disorders in Right Hemisphere Stroke." *Cognitive and Behavioral Neurology* 22: 242–248.

Shamay-Tsoory, S. G., R. Tomer, B. D. Berger, D. Goldsher, and J. Aharon-Peretz. 2005. "Impaired 'Affective Theory of Mind' Is Associated with Right Ventromedial Prefrontal Damage." *Cognitive and Behavioral Neurology* 18: 55–67.

Smith, A. [1790] 2002. *The Theory of Moral Sentiments*. 6th ed. Edited by Knud Haasonssen. Cambridge: Cambridge University Press.

Sobhani, M., and A. Bechara. 2011. "A Somatic Marker Perspective of Immoral and Corrupt Behavior." *Social Neuroscience* 6: 640–652.

Stellar, E. 1960. "Drive and Motivation." In *Handbook of Physiology*, vol. 3, edited by John Field, 1501–1527. Baltimore: American Physiological Society, distributed by Williams and Wilkins.

Stelten, B. M., L. H. Noblesse, L. Ackermans, Y. Temel, and V. Visser-Vandewalle. 2008. "The Neurosurgical Treatment of Addiction." *Neurosurgical Focus* 25(1): E5.

Stephan, H. 1983. "Evolutionary Trends in Limbic System Structures." *Neuroscience and Biobehavioral Reviews* 7: 367–374.

Swanson, L. W. 2005. "Anatomy of the Soul as Reflected in the Cerebral Hemispheres: Neural Circuits Underlying Voluntary Control of Basic Motivated Behaviors." *Journal of Comparative Neurology* 493: 122–131.

Thompson, G. N. 1951. "Cerebral Area Essential to Consciousness." *Bulletin of the Los Angeles Neurological Society* 16: 311–334.

Tippin, J., and F. J. Dunner. 1981. "Biparietal Infarctions in a Patient with Catatonia." *American Journal of Psychiatry* 138: 1386–1387.

Thorneloe, W. F., and E. L. Crews. 1981. "Manic Depressive Illness Concomitant with Antisocial Personality Disorder: Six Case Reports and Review of the Literature." *Journal of Clinical Psychiatry* 42: 5–9.

Tranel, D. 1994. "'Acquired Sociopathy': The Development of Sociopathic Behavior Following Focal Brain Damage." In *Progress in Experimental Personality and Psychopathology Research*, vol. 17, edited by D. C. Fowles, P. Sutker, and S. H. Goodman, 285–311. New York: Springer.

Tranel, D., S. W. Anderson, and A. L. Benton. 1994. "Development of the Concept of 'Executive Behavior' and Its Relationship to the Frontal Lobes." In *Handbook of Neuropsychology*, vol. 9, edited by F. Boller and J. Grafman, 125–148. Amsterdam: Elsevier.

Trevethan, S. D., and L. J. Walker. 1989. "Hypothetical versus Real-Life Moral Reasoning among Psychopathic and Delinquent Youth." *Developmental Psychopathology* 1: 91–103.

Tyrer, S. P., and A. D. Brittlebank. 1993. "Misdiagnosis of Bipolar Affective Disorder as Personality Disorder." *Canadian Journal of Psychiatry* 38: 587–589.

van der Werf, Y. D., M. P. Witter, and H. J. Groenewegen. 2002. "The Intralaminar and Midline Nuclei of the Thalamus: Anatomical and Functional Evidence for Participation in Processes of Arousal and Awareness." *Brain Research Reviews* 39: 107–140.

Veit, R., Lotze, M., S. Sewing, H. Missenhardt, T. Gaber, and N. Birbaumer. 2010. "Aberrant Social and Cerebral Responding in a Competitive Reaction Time Paradigm in Criminal Psychopaths." *NeuroImage* 49: 3365–3372.

Verplaetse, J. 2009. *Localizing the Moral Sense: Neuroscience and the Search for the Cerebral Seat of Morality, 1800–1930*. New York: Springer.

von Economo, C. 1926. "Eine neue Art Spezialzellen des Lobus cinguli und Lobus insulæ." *Zeitschrift für die gesamte Neurologie und Psychiatrie* 100: 706–712.

Walters, G. D., N. S. Gray, R. L. Jackson, K. W. Sewell, R. Rogers, J. Taylor, and R. J. Snowden. 2007. "A Taxometric Analysis of the Psychopathy Checklist: Screening Version (PCL: SV): Further Evidence of Dimensionality." *Psychological Assessment* 19: 330–339.

Ward, C. D. 2011. "On Doing Nothing: Descriptions of Sleep, Fatigue, and Motivation in Encephalitis Lethargica." *Movement Disorders* 26: 599–604.

Warren, J. D., M. T. M. Hu, M. Galloway, R. J. Greenwood, and M. N. Rossor. 2004. "Observations on the Human Rejection Behaviour Syndrome: Denny-Brown Revisited." *Movement Disorders* 19: 860–862.

Welt, L. 1888. "Ueber Charakterveränderungen des Menschen infolge von Läsionen des Stirnhirns." *Deutsches Archiv für Klinische Medizin (München)* 42: 339–390.

Whitlock, F. A. 1967. "Prichard and the Concept of Moral Insanity." *Australian and New Zealand Journal of Psychiatry* 1: 72–79.

Woodworth, M., and S. Porter. 2002. "In Cold Blood: Characteristics of Criminal Homicides as a Function of Psychopathy." *Journal of Abnormal Psychology* 111: 436–445.

Young, L., A. Bechara, D. Tranel, H. Damasio, M. Hauser, and A. Damasio. 2010. "Damage to Ventromedial Prefrontal Cortex Impairs Judgment of Harmful Intent." *Neuron* 65: 845–851.

Young, L., J. A. Camprodon, M. Hauser, A. Pascual-Leone, and R. Saxe. 2010. "Disruption of the Right Temporoparietal Junction with Transcranial Magnetic Stimulation Reduces the Role of Beliefs in Moral Judgments." *Proceedings of the National Academy of Sciences USA* 107: 6753–6758.

Young, L., and J. Dungan. 2012. "Where in the Brain Is Morality? Everywhere and Maybe Nowhere." *Social Neuroscience* 7: 1–10.

Young, L., M. Koenigs, M. Kruepke, and J. P. Newman. 2012. "Psychopathy Increases Perceived Moral Permissibility of Accidents." *Journal of Abnormal Psychology* 121: 659–667.

Young, L., and R. Saxe. 2009. "Innocent Intentions: A Correlation between Forgiveness for Accidental Harm and Neural Activity." *Neuropsychologia* 47: 2065–2072.

Zahn, R., J. Moll, G. Garrido, F. Krueger, E. D. Huey, and J. Grafman. 2007. "Social Concepts Are Represented in the Superior Anterior Temporal Cortex." *Proceedings of the National Academy of Sciences USA* 104: 6430–6435.

Morphing Morals

NEUROCHEMICAL MODULATION OF MORAL JUDGMENT

AND BEHAVIOR

Molly J. Crockett

HOW DOES BRAIN chemistry affect morality? Simple observations and introspection reveal that people sometimes feel motivated to help others, but not always. Moral sentiments are diverse and dynamic: they differ between individuals, and within individuals over time. This observation suggests that moral sentiments could be shaped by *neuromodulators*, brain chemicals that modify neuronal dynamics, excitability, and synaptic function. Here I will review recent studies examining how the neuromodulator serotonin influences moral judgment and behavior.

In our work, we focused on serotonin for several reasons (Crockett et al. 2008). If one were to engineer a neurotransmitter system for the purpose of governing something as complex as moral behavior, one would want a system that is evolutionarily old yet easily modifiable, widely distributed in the brain, with many receptor subtypes to allow for maximum flexibility in control of behavior. The serotonin system fulfills all of these requirements (Insel and Winslow 1998), and has been implicated in regulating a wide range of social behaviors across species. In both primates and humans, serotonin function tends to covary positively with "prosocial" behaviors, such as grooming, cooperation, and affiliation, and tends to covary negatively with "antisocial" behaviors such as aggression and social isolation (Higley and Linnoila 1997; Higley et al. 1996; Higley et al. 1996; Knutson et al. 1998; Krakowski 2003; Linnoila et al. 1983; Moskowitz et al. 2001; Raleigh et al. 1991). Such prosocial and antisocial behaviors are likely precursors to human morality (Brosnan and Waal 2012; Proctor et al. 2013; Stevens et al. 2005).

In one study, we examined how serotonin influences moral judgments in the domain of harm and care. Humans have a basic aversion to harming others that infuses moral judgment and moral behavior. Such harm aversion is thought to underlie deontological moral judgments, for example, judging it to be morally unacceptable to kill one person in order to save five others. One particularly elegant demonstration of how harm aversion is related to deontological moral judgment comes from a study by Cushman and colleagues. In the lab, subjects were asked to perform and observe various "fake" harmful acts, such as shooting a fake gun and smashing a doll's head against a table. Subjects' physiological reactivity to both performing and observing the harmful acts was correlated with subsequent deontological moral judgments (Cushman et al. 2012).

How does serotonin affect deontological moral judgments? We conducted a study in which participants judged the moral permissibility of harmful actions in hypothetical scenarios on three separate occasions (Crockett et al. 2010). On one occasion, they received the drug citalopram, a selective serotonin reuptake inhibitor. Citalopram enhances serotonin function by blocking its reuptake after it has been released into the synapse, thus prolonging serotonin's actions on postsynaptic receptors. On another occasion, they received a different drug, atomoxetine, a noradrenaline reuptake inhibitor. Finally, on a third occasion, they received a placebo pill.

We compared the effects of citalopram, atomoxetine, and placebo on judgments in three types of scenarios: neutral scenarios that contained no moral content, "personal" moral scenarios in which harmful actions were emotionally salient, and "impersonal" moral scenarios in which harmful actions were not emotionally salient. There were no differences across treatments on judgments in the neutral scenarios or the impersonal scenarios. However, in the personal scenarios, we found that citalopram seemed to increase harm aversion—participants were more deontological, that is, less likely to endorse harming one to save many others.

We also examined how the drug effects interacted with individual differences in empathy. We might expect that individuals who have a stronger baseline level of harm aversion could be more susceptible to the effects of serotonin manipulations. Our data supported this prediction. We split participants into low- and high-empathy groups, defined by scores in the Interpersonal Reactivity Index (Davis 1983). We found no effect of citalopram on judgments in the low-empathy group, but a strong effect in the high-empathy group. In our sample, the most harm-averse individuals were those who scored high on empathy and also received citalopram.

In another set of studies, we examined how serotonin shapes morality in the domain of fairness and reciprocity. Humans care deeply about fairness, to the extent that they are willing to incur personal costs in order to punish unfair behavior and enforce fair outcomes. Such "costly punishment" plays an important role in encouraging and sustaining cooperation (Fehr and Fischbacher 2003).

In our studies, we measured costly punishment behavior using the Ultimatum game (Güth et al. 1982). This game has two players, a proposer and a responder. They have to agree on how to split a sum of money, or neither of them gets any money. The proposer makes an offer to the responder. The responder can accept the offer, in which case both players are paid accordingly. Or he can reject the offer, in which case neither player is paid. A receiver motivated solely by self-interest will accept any offer, because something is better than nothing. But many studies have shown that most receivers would rather have nothing than let the proposer get away with taking the lion's share.

We were interested in how costly punishment in the ultimatum game would be sensitive to manipulations of the serotonin system. In our first study (Crockett et al. 2008), we used a technique called acute tryptophan depletion, which temporarily lowers the amount of serotonin that is available to the brain, allowing us to observe behavior when the brain is in a low-serotonin state. We compare the effects of acute tryptophan depletion to a placebo treatment in a double-blind study.

Participants played the role of responder in a series of one-shot ultimatum games, interacting with a different proposer on each round. We deliberately used one-shot games to rule out strategic motivations for rejecting unfair offers. In a repeated game, rejecting an unfair offer can induce the proposer to offer higher amounts in subsequent rounds. We were interested in rejection behavior that is motivated solely by the desire to punish unfair behavior, which can be measured cleanly in one-shot games.

We found that impairing serotonin function with acute tryptophan depletion increased the rejection of unfair offers, without affecting the (low) rejection of fair offers. In a second study, we examined the effects of enhancing serotonin function with citalopram on costly punishment in the ultimatum game (Crockett et al. 2010). We compared the effects of citalopram with those of atomoxetine and placebo. As with the moral judgment study, we found that citalopram influenced decision-making, but atomoxetine had no effect. Specifically, citalopram reduced the rejection of unfair offers, producing the opposite effect to acute tryptophan depletion. Again, the effects of citalopram were strongest in participants high in empathy.

Note that the effects of serotonin manipulations on moral judgment and behavior cannot be explained by changes in mood. In all studies, we were careful to measure mood at baseline and postmanipulation. We did not observe any reliable effects of serotonin manipulations on subjects' mood, and subjects were blind to the treatment they received. Despite this, we found significant effects of serotonin manipulations on moral judgment and behavior.

In light of these behavioral findings, we became interested in better understanding the motivational processes that give rise to these effects. Although costly punishment is usually framed in terms of fairness and reciprocity, it is worth considering that punishing a norm violation requires harming the norm violator—whether economically (as in ultimatum games), emotionally (as in scolding or gossiping), or even physically (as in corporal punishment). Decisions *not* to punish (which were enhanced by citalopram) could therefore be driven by some form of harm aversion.

There is indeed converging evidence that similar sorts of motivational processes could influence both moral judgments in hypothetical scenarios, and costly punishment decisions. In our studies, citalopram made people less likely to reject unfair offers and less likely to endorse harmful actions in personal moral scenarios. Meanwhile, patients with damage to the ventromedial prefrontal cortex show the opposite pattern—they reject *more* unfair offers (Koenigs and Tranel 2007) and are *more* likely to endorse harmful actions in personal moral scenarios (Koenigs et al. 2007). Finally, psychopaths and healthy people with psychopathic traits show a behavioral pattern similar to that of the ventromedial patients—they also reject more unfair offers (Koenigs et al. 2010) and are more likely to endorse personal harms (Bartels and Pizarro 2011; Koenigs et al. 2011). Together these studies support the notion that costly punishment and moral judgment are similarly governed by a medial fronto-striatal circuit concerned with "moral sentiments" like harm aversion.

In our most recent study, we investigated how depleting serotonin shapes the neural circuitry of costly punishment behavior (Crockett et al. 2013). One advantage of examining brain activations is that they can provide clues about the motivational processes that drive behavior. Specifically, we tested whether serotonin influences punishment behavior through affecting a more "altruistic" motive to enforce fairness norms, versus a more "antisocial" motive for revenge. These competing explanations generate different predictions about the effects of serotonin manipulations on brain activity.

Previous work has identified brain regions associated with motives for revenge. In one classic neuroimaging study, participants first played a series of trust games with two confederates. One confederate played fairly, and the other played unfairly. Next, participants watched as the fair and unfair confederates received electric shocks.

When participants passively observed the unfair players receive shocks, they showed activation in the ventral striatum, and this activation was correlated with self-reported desire for revenge (Singer et al. 2006). Other studies have reported ventral striatum activation when sports fans observed fans of their rival team suffer (Cikara et al. 2011; Hein et al. 2010). These findings suggest that watching a rival suffer has motivational value. There is also evidence that actively delivering punishment has motivational value. When people punish unfair behavior, they show increased activity in the dorsal striatum (de Quervain et al. 2004; Strobel et al. 2011).

Together these findings suggest that if depleting serotonin increases costly punishment behavior by enhancing the motivational value of punishment, we should see that serotonin depletion increases activity in the striatum when people punish. This is precisely what we observed. Serotonin depletion increased activity in the dorsal striatum during punishment, and individual differences in the neural effects of depletion were correlated with individual differences in the behavioral effects of depletion.

An alternative (though not mutually exclusive) possibility is that serotonin depletion increases punishment by enhancing altruistic motives to enforce fairness norms. Previous studies have shown that fair outcomes activate value-processing regions, including the ventral striatum and medial prefrontal cortex (Tabibnia et al. 2008; Tricomi et al. 2010). Thus, if serotonin depletion amplifies preferences for fairness, we should expect that serotonin depletion would increase fairness-related responses in these regions. Instead, we observed the opposite effect: serotonin depletion blunted ventral striatal responses to fair outcomes, suggesting that depletion made fairness goals less salient.

We observed a similar, albeit weaker, effect in the medial prefrontal cortex. The cluster showing the interaction was located in anterior MPFC (Brodmann area 10), a region that has been implicated in the representation of abstract and social rewards (Haber and Knutson 2009; Rademacher et al. 2010), mentalizing (Amodio and Frith 2006), and moral cognition (Moll et al. 2011). It may therefore be involved in assessing the long-term benefits arising from mutual cooperation (Rilling and Sanfey 2011). Supporting this view, patients with damage to the MPFC show impaired prosocial emotions (Moll et al. 2011) and are less likely to reciprocate trust (Krajbich et al. 2009). Thus, serotonin may normally increase cooperation (and inhibit retaliation, which can damage social relationships) by enhancing the subjective value of the distant rewards associated with repeated cooperation. This would be consistent with our previous finding that serotonin depletion increased impulsive choice in tandem with its effects on costly punishment (Crockett et al. 2010) and could also explain the observation that serotonin depletion reduces cooperation in the repeated prisoner's dilemma (Wood et al. 2006), while enhancing serotonin function has the opposite effect (Tse and Bond 2002). An obvious next step would be to test whether enhancing serotonin function promotes positive reciprocity by boosting ventral striatal and MPFC responses to mutual cooperation.

The pattern of results we observed suggests that serotonin depletion decreased the subjective value of social exchange while simultaneously enhancing the subjective value of retaliation via punishment. More broadly, our observations are compatible with the hypothesis that serotonin regulates social preferences, where enhancing (versus impairing) serotonin function leads individuals to value the outcomes of others more positively (versus negatively; Siegel and Crockett 2013). This hypothesis unifies a range of empirical data describing positive associations between serotonin function and prosocial behavior on the one hand, and negative associations between serotonin function and antisocial behavior on the other hand. To test this hypothesis, future work will combine more precise computational models of social preferences with pharmacological manipulations and neuroimaging.

Studies demonstrating effects of neurochemical manipulations on morality may have potential normative implications. We have shown that moral judgments and decisions are sensitive to fluctuations in brain chemistry; others have discovered similar effects of stress (Starcke et al. 2012; Youssef et al. 2012) and even time of day (Danziger et al. 2011). Together these studies have shown that moral judgments respond to factors that are clearly nonnormative. However, certain kinds of moral judgments appear to be more sensitive to nonnormative factors than others. In particular, moral judgments about physical harms (e.g., Greene's "personal" scenarios in which harms are emotionally salient) seem to be more susceptible to the influence of neuromodulators (Crockett et al. 2010; Terbeck et al. 2013) and acute stress (Starcke et al. 2012; Youssef et al. 2012). This raises the question of whether we should generally be more skeptical of judgments in such "personal" cases, compared with judgments in "impersonal" cases involving more indirect harms, which appear to be less susceptible to nonnormative influences.

In addition, some individuals may be more vulnerable to influence by nonnormative factors than others; for instance, we have shown that the effects of manipulating serotonin on moral judgments interact with individual differences in empathy (Crockett et al. 2010). This is hardly surprising, given that genotypic variability affects how an individual's nervous system reacts to perturbations in neurotransmitter levels (Rogers 2011). But this individual variability raises important ethical issues, particularly in the realm of applied ethics: if certain individuals are less influenced by nonnormative factors than others, by way of their genetic makeup or some other stable underlying trait, should the judgments of these individuals be privileged above those who are more influenced by such factors? Take, for example, a recent study showing that judges are more likely to grant parole if the parole hearing takes place immediately after a snack break (Danziger et al. 2011). Suppose we discover a biomarker that reliably detects an individual's susceptibility to the influence of snack breaks on judgments. Should such evidence be used to bar certain individuals from making judicial decisions? Obviously we are a long way off from such a test, but the fact that different people can be more or less sensitive to nonnormative factors begs the question of whether we should be more skeptical of the former's judgments compared to those of the latter.

The evidence reviewed here shows that moral judgments are not fixed, but malleable and contingent on neuromodulator levels, stress, and so on. Many of us would rather believe that such judgments are not so dependent on the vagaries of neurochemistry. This raises the question whether there exists any "neutral" physiological state from which one can generate reliable ethical principles (Crockett and Rini 2015). Although the idea of finding such a state is certainly attractive, in practice it is far from straightforward. Neuromodulator levels are constantly in flux and extremely difficult to measure in humans; for this reason there is not even a scientific consensus on what constitutes a "healthy" level of serotonin, dopamine, and so on, if such a state even exists. Moreover, determining which state is the "neutral" one, for the purpose of establishing a neutral ethical baseline, is itself a sort of value judgment that would be subject to influence by the same neurochemical factors—an inescapable problem. In the coming decade it will be important to systematically investigate these questions and debate their significance for morality.

References

Amodio, D. M., and C. D. Frith. 2006. "Meeting of Minds: The Medial Frontal Cortex and Social Cognition." *Nature Reviews Neuroscience* 7, no. 4: 268–277. doi:10.1038/nrn1884.

Bartels, D. M., and D. A. Pizarro. 2011. "The Mismeasure of Morals: Antisocial Personality Traits Predict Utilitarian Responses to Moral Dilemmas." *Cognition* 121, no. 1: 154–161. doi:10.1016/j.cognition.2011.05.010.

Brosnan, S. F., and F. B. M. de Waal. 2012. "Fairness in Animals: Where to from Here?" *Social Justice Research* 25, no. 3: 336–351. doi:10.1007/s11211-012-0165-8.

Cikara, M., M. M. Botvinick, and S. T. Fiske. 2011. "Us versus Them: Social Identity Shapes Neural Responses to Intergroup Competition and Harm." *Psychological Science* 22, no. 3: 306–313. doi:10.1177/0956797610397667.

Crockett, M. J., A. Apergis-Schoute, B. Herrmann, M. D. Lieberman, U. Muller, T. W. Robbins, and L. Clark. 2013. "Serotonin Modulates Striatal Responses to Fairness and Retaliation in Humans." *Journal of Neuroscience* 33, no. 8: 3505–3513. doi:10.1523/JNEUROSCI.2761-12.2013.

Crockett, M. J., L. Clark, M. D. Hauser, and T. W. Robbins. 2010. "From the Cover: Serotonin Selectively Influences Moral Judgment and Behavior through Effects on Harm Aversion." *Proceedings of the National Academy of Sciences* 107, no. 40: 17433–17438. doi:10.1073/pnas.1009396107.

Crockett, M. J., L. Clark, M. D. Lieberman, G. Tabibnia, and T. W. Robbins. 2010. "Impulsive Choice and Altruistic Punishment Are Correlated and Increase in Tandem with Serotonin Depletion." *Emotion* 10, no. 6: 855–862. doi:10.1037/a0019861.

Crockett, M. J., L. Clark, G. Tabibnia, M. D. Lieberman, and T. W. Robbins. 2008. "Serotonin Modulates Behavioral Reactions to Unfairness." *Science* 320, no. 5884: 1739–1739. doi:10.1126/science.1155577.

Crockett, M. J., and R. A. Rini. 2015. "Neuromodulators and the (In)stability of Moral Cognition." In *The Moral Brain*, edited by J. Decety and T. Wheatley, 221–235. Cambridge, MA: MIT Press,

Cushman, F., K. Gray, A. Gaffey, and W. B. Mendes. 2012. "Simulating Murder: The Aversion to Harmful Action." *Emotion* 12, no. 1: 2.

Danziger, S., J. Levav, and L. Avnaim-Pesso. 2011. "Extraneous Factors in Judicial Decisions." *Proceedings of the National Academy of Sciences* 108, no. 17: 6889–6892.

Davis, M. H. 1983. "Measuring Individual Differences in Empathy: Evidence for a Multidimensional Approach." *Journal of Personality and Social Psychology* 44, no. 1: 113–126. doi:10.1037/0022-3514.44.1.113.

De Quervain, D. J.-F., U. Fischbacher, V. Treyer, M. Schellhammer, U. Schnyder, A. Buck, and E. Fehr. 2004. "The Neural Basis of Altruistic Punishment." *Science* 305, no. 5688: 1254–1258. doi:10.1126/science.1100735.

Fehr, E., and U. Fischbacher. 2003. "The Nature of Human Altruism." *Nature* 425, no. 6960: 785–791. doi:10.1038/nature02043.

Güth, W., R. Schmittberger, and B. Schwarze. 1982. "An Experimental Analysis of Ultimatum Bargaining." *Journal of Economic Behavior and Organization* 3, no. 4: 367–388. doi:10.1016/0167-2681(82)90011-7.

Haber, S. N., and B. Knutson. 2009. "The Reward Circuit: Linking Primate Anatomy and Human Imaging." *Neuropsychopharmacology* 35, no. 1: 4–26. doi:10.1038/npp.2009.129.

Hein, G., G. Silani, K. Preuschoff, C. D. Batson, and T. Singer. 2010. "Neural Responses to Ingroup and Outgroup Members' Suffering Predict Individual Differences in Costly Helping." *Neuron* 68, no. 1: 149–160. doi:10.1016/j.neuron.2010.09.003.

Higley, J. D., S. T. King Jr., M. F. Hasert, M. Champoux, S. J. Suomi, and M. Linnoila. 1996. "Stability of Interindividual Differences in Serotonin Function and Its Relationship to Severe Aggression and Competent Social Behavior in Rhesus Macaque Females." *Neuropsychopharmacology* 14, no. 1: 67–76. doi:10.1016/S0893-133X(96)80060-1.

Higley, J. D., and M. Linnoila. 1997. "Low Central Nervous System Serotonergic Activity Is Traitlike and Correlates with Impulsive Behavior." *Annals of the New York Academy of Sciences* 836, no. 1: 39–56. doi:10.1111/j.1749-6632.1997.tb52354.x

Higley, J. D., P. T. Mehlman, R. E. Poland, D. M. Taub, J. Vickers, S. J. Suomi, and M. Linnoila. 1996. "CSF Testosterone and 5-HIAA Correlate with Different Types of Aggressive Behaviors." *Biological Psychiatry* 40, no. 11: 1067–1082. doi:10.1016/S0006-3223(95)00675-3.

Insel, T. R., and J. T. Winslow. 1998. "Serotonin and Neuropeptides in Affiliative Behaviors." *Biological Psychiatry* 44, no. 3: 207–219. doi:10.1016/S0006-3223(98)00094-8.

Knutson, B., O. M. Wolkowitz, S. W. Cole, T. Chan, E. A. Moore, R. C. Johnson, . . . V. I. Reus. 1998. "Selective Alteration of Personality and Social Behavior by Serotonergic Intervention." *American Journal of Psychiatry* 155, no. 3: 373–379.

Koenigs, M., M. Kruepke, and J. P. Newman. 2010. "Economic Decision-Making in Psychopathy: A Comparison with Ventromedial Prefrontal Lesion Patients." *Neuropsychologia* 48, no. 7: 2198–2204. doi:10.1016/j.neuropsychologia.2010.04.012.

Koenigs, M., M. Kruepke, J. Zeier, and J. P. Newman. 2011. "Utilitarian Moral Judgment in Psychopathy." *Social Cognitive and Affective Neuroscience* 7, no. 6: 708–714. doi:10.1093/scan/nsr048.

Koenigs, M., and D. Tranel. 2007. "Irrational Economic Decision-Making after Ventromedial Prefrontal Damage: Evidence from the Ultimatum Game." *Journal of Neuroscience* 27, no. 4: 951–956. doi:10.1523/JNEUROSCI.4606-06.2007.

Koenigs, M., L. Young, R. Adolphs, D. Tranel, F. Cushman, M. Hauser, and A. Damasio. 2007. "Damage to the Prefrontal Cortex Increases Utilitarian Moral Judgements." *Nature* 446, no. 7138: 908–911. doi:10.1038/nature05631.

Krajbich, I., R. Adolphs, D. Tranel, N. L. Denburg, and C. F. Camerer. 2009. "Economic Games Quantify Diminished Sense of Guilt in Patients with Damage to the Prefrontal Cortex." *Journal of Neuroscience* 29, no. 7: 2188–2192. doi:10.1523/JNEUROSCI.5086-08.2009.

Krakowski, M. 2003. "Violence and Serotonin: Influence of Impulse Control, Affect Regulation, and Social Functioning." *Journal of Neuropsychiatry and Clinical Neurosciences* 15, no. 3: 294–305. doi:10.1176/appi.neuropsych.15.3.294.

Linnoila, M., M. Virkkunen, M. Scheinin, A. Nuutila, R. Rimon, and F. K. Goodwin. 1983. "Low Cerebrospinal Fluid 5-hydroxyindoleacetic Acid Concentration Differentiates Impulsive from Nonimpulsive Violent Behavior." *Life Sciences* 33, no. 26: 2609–2614. doi:10.1016/0024-3205(83)90344-2.

Moll, J., R. Zahn, R. de Oliveira-Souza, I. E. Bramati, F. Krueger, B. Tura, . . . J. Grafman. 2011. "Impairment of Prosocial Sentiments Is Associated with Frontopolar and Septal Damage in Frontotemporal Dementia." *NeuroImage* 54, no. 2: 1735–1742. doi:10.1016/j.neuroimage.2010.08.026.

Moskowitz, D. S., G. Pinard, D. C. Zuroff, L. Annable, and S. N. Young. 2001. "The Effect of Tryptophan on Social Interaction in Everyday Life: A Placebo-Controlled Study." *Neuropsychopharmacology* 25, no. 2: 277–289.

Proctor, D., R. A. Williamson, F. B. M. de Waal, and S. F. Brosnan. 2013. "Chimpanzees Play the Ultimatum Game." *Proceedings of the National Academy of Sciences* 110(6: 2070–2075. doi:10.1073/pnas.1220806110.

Rademacher, L., S. Krach, G. Kohls, A. Irmak, G. Gründer, and K. N. Spreckelmeyer. 2010. "Dissociation of Neural Networks for Anticipation and Consumption of Monetary and Social Rewards." *NeuroImage* 49, no. 4: 3276–3285. doi:10.1016/j.neuroimage.2009.10.089.

Raleigh, M. J., McM. T. Guire, G. L. Brammer, D. B. Pollack, and A. Yuwiler. 1991. "Serotonergic Mechanisms Promote Dominance Acquisition in Adult Male Vervet Monkeys." *Brain Research* 559, no. 2: 181–190. doi:10.1016/0006-8993(91)90001-C.

Rilling, J. K., and A. G. Sanfey. 2011. "The Neuroscience of Social Decision-Making." *Annual Review of Psychology* 62, no. 1: 23–48. doi:10.1146/annurev.psych.121208.131647.

Rogers, R. D. 2011. "The Roles of Dopamine and Serotonin in Decision Making: Evidence from Pharmacological Experiments in Humans." *Neuropsychopharmacology* 36, no. 1: 114–132. doi:10.1038/npp.2010.165.

Siegel, J. Z., and M. J. Crockett. 2013. "How Serotonin Shapes Moral Judgment and Behavior." *Annals of the New York Academy of Sciences* 1299, no. 1: 42–51.

Singer, T., B. Seymour, O'J. P. Doherty, K. E. Stephan, R. J. Dolan, and C. D. Frith. 2006. "Empathic Neural Responses Are Modulated by the Perceived Fairness of Others." *Nature* 439, no. 7075: 466–469. doi:10.1038/nature04271.

Starcke, K., A.-C. Ludwig, and M. Brand. 2012. "Anticipatory Stress Interferes with Utilitarian Moral Judgment." *Judgment and Decision Making* 7, no. 1: 61–68.

Stevens, J. R., F. A. Cushman, and M. D. Hauser. 2005. "Evolving the Psychological Mechanisms for Cooperation." *Annual Review of Ecology, Evolution, and Systematics* 36: 499–518.

Strobel, A., J. Zimmermann, A. Schmitz, M. Reuter, S. Lis, S. Windmann, and P. Kirsch. 2011. "Beyond Revenge: Neural and Genetic Bases of Altruistic Punishment." *NeuroImage* 54, no. 1: 671–680. doi:10.1016/j.neuroimage.2010.07.051.

Tabibnia, G., A. B. Satpute, and M. D. Lieberman. 2008. "The Sunny Side of Fairness: Preference for Fairness Activates Reward Circuitry (and Disregarding Unfairness Activates Self-Control Circuitry)." *Psychological Science* 19, no. 4: 339–347. doi:10.1111/j.1467-9280.2008.02091.x.

Terbeck, S., G. Kahane, McS. Tavish, J. Savulescu, N. Levy, M. Hewstone, and P. J. Cowen. 2013. "Beta Adrenergic Blockade Reduces Utilitarian Judgement." *Biological Psychology* 92, no. 2: 323–328. doi:10.1016/j.biopsycho.2012.09.005.

Tricomi, E., A. Rangel, C. F. Camerer, and J. P. O'Doherty. 2010. "Neural Evidence for Inequality-Averse Social Preferences." *Nature* 463, no. 7284: 1089–1091. doi:10.1038/nature08785.

Tse, W., and A. Bond. 2002. "Serotonergic Intervention Affects Both Social Dominance and Affiliative Behaviour." *Psychopharmacology* 161, no. 3: 324–330. doi:10.1007/s00213-002-1049-7.

Wood, R. M., J. K. Rilling, A. G. Sanfey, Z. Bhagwagar, and R. D. Rogers. 2006. "Effects of Tryptophan Depletion on the Performance of an Iterated Prisoner's Dilemma Game in Healthy Adults." *Neuropsychopharmacology* 31, no. 5: 1075–1084.

Youssef, F. F., K. Dookeeram, V. Basdeo, E. Francis, M. Doman, D. Mamed, . . . G. Legall. 2012. "Stress Alters Personal Moral Decision Making." *Psychoneuroendocrinology* 37, no. 4: 491–498. doi:10.1016/j.psyneuen.2011.07.017.

Hendrix and Pearson pulled Romona into a dilapidated house. They took her down to a basement where they tortured her, beat her up, and raped her for four days. They took off her clothes and put her in chains. They sodomized her. They tried to saw off her hands and feet. They beat her face with a hammer when she screamed. They cut the webbing between her fingers. They burned her face with a lit cigarette. Then they kept her under a tarp. When a friend stopped by, they brought him to basement where Ramona was being kept. As they were smoking pot on the couch, Hendrix said out loud: "Say hi, bitch." The friend asked: "Who y'all talking to?" Hendrix and Pearson pulled up a tarp on the floor to show their proud work. They made Ramona recount everything they had done to her to their friend. Then they dropped the tarp back to the floor. Romona was eventually bludgeoned to death with a hammer and a barbell. Hendrix and Pearson were later reported to say their interaction with Ramona was "fun."

—A compilation from Gardiner 2008; Katz 2006; Ginsberg 2006.

Every murder raises terrible questions that no trial, no law, no punishment can answer. What forces make it possible for one human being to take the life of another? . . . Scholars ranging from theologians and psychologists to evolutionary biologists have offered theories about murder—theories of evil, theories of disease, theories of disposition—but the analytical burden placed on any general discussion of murder, freighted, as it is, with atrocity, is nearly unbearable. Nothing suffices, or can.

—Lepore 2009

11

Of Mice and Men

THE INFLUENCE OF RODENT MODELS OF EMPATHY ON HUMAN MODELS OF HARM PREVENTION

Jana Schaich Borg

THE ACTS HENDRIX and Pearson committed in the story above were morally very wrong. For many, it seems impossible to even imagine doing such horrible things to another being. This raises fundamental questions. One question discussed in this volume is why we *judge* or *believe* it to be morally wrong to cause harm to others. An equally essential question, however, is why some people (hopefully most people) *act* morally while other people, like Hendrix and Pearson, *act* so immorally. In other words, what leads to moral or immoral action, as opposed to its related cousins, moral judgment and moral belief?

Moral judgment and moral action must be differentiated; what people think or report is morally wrong or obligatory does not always correspond with what people do (Blasi 1980, 1983), or even what they say they will do (Schaich Borg 2006). The past decade of neuroscience research on morality has taught us a lot about the neural systems involved in making moral judgments. The next decade of neuroscience research needs to focus on delineating the brain systems involved in morally relevant action. In particular, it should focus on a particularly devastating type of morally relevant action: unjustified physical violence.

A major reason we do not yet know how to prevent unjustified violence is that biomedical studies of human antisocial behavior are rife with ethical and practical challenges (Ward and Willis 2010). To start, one of the most efficient ways to identify study participants who are likely to commit violence in the future is to identify people who have committed violence in the past; thus, prisoners are an informative population to study. However, federal rules severely limit the amount of biomedical research that can be carried out in prison populations, especially if such research does not benefit the research participants themselves (to protect prisoners from coercion) (Osganian 2008). Research that ultimately benefits incarcerated research participants is often restricted as well, because some (including granting agencies) feel that individuals who have already committed immoral actions should be punished without an opportunity for treatment (Taylor 2011; Beck 2010; Eastman 1999). Such ethical concerns motivate some researchers to study antisocial behavior outside of the prison, but antisocial research outside the prison is plagued by its own difficulties. People who consistently commit violent or immoral action do not usually seek treatment or research participation voluntarily, and when they do, clinical service providers may be obligated to turn them away to avoid the inherent physical risks of working with such a dangerous population (Howells and Day 2007). Finally, there is concern that studying the biological basis of violent behavior will undermine notions of responsibility, culpability, and free will, and that identifying or treating potential offenders can lead to discrimination or stigmatization (Beck 2010; Pickersgill 2011; Pustilnik 2009). Perhaps these challenges explain why so few attempts have been made to develop or test biomedical treatments for violent or immoral behavior (Gibbon et al. 2010; Khalifa 2010), and why no biomedical treatments currently exist (Salekin et al. 2010).

Ethical concerns surrounding the study of human immoral and antisocial action are very important, but they must be balanced with our obligations to protect the rights of our fellow members of society, including the right to live a life without unjustified physical or emotional harm. We now know that the most persistent 5 percent to 8 percent of offenders are responsible for between 50 percent and 70 percent of documented violent crimes (Farrington et al. 1986; Moffitt 1993; Vaughn et al. 2011). We also now know that a considerable amount of variance in immoral and antisocial behavior can be accounted for by one's genetics (Ferguson 2010; Gunter et al. 2010). This raises the strong possibility that there is something genetically and biologically different about the most persistent violent offenders that, when fully understood, may shed some light on how to change their violent, immoral behavior. Given the disproportionate amount of damage this small population of destructive individuals causes, a change in these individuals' behavior could have a dramatic impact on how much violence is committed worldwide. If it is feasible to develop treatments for the biological causes of violent behavior in an ethically appropriate way, we should try to do so.

One critical advance from the past decade that has made the development of treatments for unjustified violent behavior a realistic possibility is the development of rodent models of empathy (which will be renamed "negative intersubjectivity" in later parts of this chapter). As discussed in sections 11.1 and 11.2 of this chapter, empathy is a phenomenon that contributes to violence aversion, and we now know some of the brain regions that likely contribute to human empathy. However, these advances, by themselves, have not been sufficient to make significant progress toward developing methods for treating biological causes of violent behavior. Fortunately, rodent models of empathy have become available at the same time as field-changing technologies that allow us to dissect rodent neural circuits with unprecedented accuracy and efficiency. Section 11.3 will describe these rodent models and explain how they provide powerful and realistic opportunities for neuroscience to help prevent unjustified violence in more mechanistic ways than were previously thought possible. Sections 11.1–11.3 will collectively provide evidence that the most efficient way to understand moral action and prevent immoral action is to pursue rodent research and human research in parallel.

11.1. "Negative Intersubjectivity"?

"Negative intersubjectivity" will be defined as *feeling negative affect when another feels negative affect*. In the story recounted earlier, Hendrix and Pearson certainly did not have negative intersubjectivity because they did not feel negative when they saw Ramona's wounds or heard her screaming in pain. Instead, they were entertained by, and eventually bored by, her distress. Ramona would be alive and unharmed if Hendrix and Pearson had felt aversion to Ramona's distress cues. This illustrates a fundamental principle: if we could learn how to induce negative intersubjectivity, or aversion to actions that cause pain and distress in others, we could prevent the type of violent behavior performed by Hendrix and Pearson.

11.1.1. NEGATIVE INTERSUBJECTIVITY'S RELATIONSHIP TO "EMPATHY"

"Empathy" is one of the first words that comes to mind to describe the phenomenon of feeling negative in response to another person's distress, and any discussion of negative intersubjectivity would be remiss to ignore the term. However, despite this natural association, the term "empathy" is not very useful because (despite much effort) there remains little or no consensus about what it means in either a scientific or colloquial context. As some researchers in the field wrote, "Psychologists are known for using terms loosely, but in our use of empathy we have outdone ourselves" (Batson et al. 1987, 19). Providing support for the spirit of that exclamation, all of the following subprocesses have been incorporated into some published definitions of empathy:

(1) **Motor mimicry:** adopting the posture, position, or facial expression of an observed other. *Example*: grabbing your own elbow when you see a friend fall and grab his elbow.

(2) **Personal distress:** a self-oriented reactive emotion in response to the perception or recognition of another's negative emotion or situation. Personal distress does not need to be congruent with the emotion or situation of the observed other, but it does need to describe a negative personal state in the observer. *Example*: feeling anxious about your own job upon hearing that your friend was laid off.

(3) **Emotional contagion:** feeling the same emotion as the emotion perceived or recognized in another. Most theorists specify that emotional contagion does not require observers to be able to distinguish between themselves and the person they are observing. *Example*: a newborn infant's reactive cry to the distress cry of another infant.

(4) **Affective intersubjectivity:** feeling emotions that are "more congruent with another's situation than with one's own situation" (Hoffman 2000, 30). This affective reaction does not necessarily require an accompanying state of understanding. Unlike emotional contagion, affective intersubjectivity does not require that the subject and target feel the exact same emotions, although it does tend to require that the subject and target feel emotions of the same valence. *Example*: feeling sad when you hear that your friend's parent died.

(5) **Theory of mind:** the ability to understand another's perspective (Wellman 2010). This can be broken down into (*a*) "perceptual perspective-taking," the ability to understand and report what another is likely to perceive, (*b*) "emotional perspective-taking," the ability to understand and report what another is likely to feel (sometimes this is also referred to as "empathic accuracy"), and (*c*) "cognitive perspective-taking," the ability to understand and report what another is likely to think. *Examples*: Knowing that someone sitting with his back to the wall is not likely to see a sign posted on the wall above his head

(perceptual perspective-taking); knowing that somebody will be angry if he is not reimbursed the money he lent (emotional perspective-taking); knowing that somebody thinks the meeting is scheduled for Monday because he was not told that it had been rescheduled for Tuesday (cognitive perspective-taking).

(6) **Sympathy:** caring for another's well-being as it relates to his emotion or situation (Darwall 1998). This term usually implies that an observer is motivated to alleviate another's suffering, or has judged that another's suffering should be alleviated (Wispé 1986; Eisenberg and Strayer 1987). *Example*: Wanting to give money to a homeless person on the street because you believe he's hungry.

(7) **Moral judgment or motivation:** principles of right or wrong that motivate and structure behaviors within social environments. It is under debate whether these principles exist because humans have innate emotions toward their perceptions of how other people feel or because humans have unemotional and impartial cognitive processes that allow them to deduce relevant social and behavioral rules (Haid 2004, 2001; Greene et al. 2001). *Example*: Most people believe that it is wrong to physically beat children and consequently may be motivated to prevent other people from physically beating children.

(8) **Altruism:** the intention of increasing another's welfare, even at the expense of harm to oneself. Colloquial conceptions of empathy often incorporate altruistic intentions, but empathy and altruism are usually differentiated in the academic literature (Batson et al. 2011, 417). *Example*: Giving your food to a homeless person, even though you are very hungry yourself, because you want to end the homeless person's hunger.

Using different combinations of these processes, empathy has been defined with various descriptions including:

> When we have (a) an affective state, (b) which is isomorphic to another person's affective state, (c) which was elicited by observing or imagining another person's affective state, and (d) when we know that the other person's affective state is the source of our own affective state (de Vignemont and Singer 2006, 435). [This definition includes some aspects of emotional contagion, may include either personal distress or theory of mind, and has an extra knowledge component that requires the observer to know the other person's state is the source of one's own state.]

> The capacity to a) be affected by and share the emotional state of another, b) assess the reasons for the other's state, and c) identify with the other, adopting his or her perspective. This definition extends beyond what exists in many animals, but I employ the term "empathy" even if only the first criterion is met as I believe all of these elements are evolutionarily connected (de Waal 2008, 281). [This definition can include any of the subprocesses listed above.]

Empathy is defined as an affective state that stems from the apprehension of another's emotional state or condition, and that is congruent with it. Thus, empathy can include emotional matching and the vicarious experiencing of a range of emotions consistent with those of others (Eisenberg and Miller 1987, 91). [This definition specifies that empathy cannot only be theory of mind because it requires affect, and suggests that empathy is usually differentiated from sympathy.]

"The intellectual or imaginative apprehension of another's condition or state of mind [which] is central for understanding a broad range of social phenomena including, in particular, moral development. Within this latter context, an empathic disposition can be regarded as the capacity to adopt a broad moral perspective, that is, to take "the moral point of view" (Hogan 1969, 307). [This definition says empathy requires theory of mind and moral judgment.]

Empathy is the ability to experience and understand what others feel without confusion between oneself and others (Decety and Lamm 2006, 1146). [This definition specifies that empathy is not emotional contagion and likely not personal distress, since personal distress is often elicited via confusion between oneself and others.]

11.1.2. "NEGATIVE INTERSUBJECTIVITY" IS RELATED TO, BUT NOT IDENTICAL TO, DEFINITIONS OF "EMPATHY"

The phenomenon critical for this chapter is *feeling negative affect when another feels negative affect*. In order to discuss this phenomenon without bringing conflicting definitions of "empathy" to bear, the term "negative intersubjectivity" will be used instead of "empathy" to refer to this phenomenon of interest. The word "intersubjectivity" in this phrase refers to subjective experiences initiated by interactions with others, and the word "negative" specifies that those subjective experiences must have a negative valence. It is therefore similar to "affective intersubjectivity" (described earlier), but does not include subjective experiences with a positive valence. It departs from many colloquial definitions of empathy because it does not require the recognition of moral content or altruistic intentions. Negative intersubjectivity, said simply, is disliking (for any reason, selfish or not) when another individual feels bad. This term represents the phenomenon relevant to antisocial and prosocial action better than other terms currently available.

To further clarify how this phenomenon relates to other academic definitions of empathy, negative intersubjectivity as it is being operationalized here *does* require negative affect in both an observer and a receiver. Since negative intersubjectivity requires affect, neither (1) motor mimicry nor (5) theory of mind is sufficient on its own to meet the criteria of negative intersubjectivity, and (7) moral judgment would only be sufficient if it involved negative affect. Beyond that, however, negative intersubjectivity may or may not involve mimicry systems, personal distress, identical emotions between the observer and receiver, or cognitive apprehension of what is happening in either a receiver or oneself. Most importantly, again, negative intersubjectivity *does not require* motivation to help the individual in distress or feelings or judgments about what is right or wrong.

Although the term "empathy" will be avoided whenever possible, many studies relevant to the goals of this chapter utilize published measures of "empathy" or "callousness." These measures ask participants to rate items such as "I often have tender, concerned feelings for people less fortunate than me" (taken from the Interpersonal Reactivity Index) (Davis 1980), and are clearly related to negative intersubjectivity. As a consequence, the only times the word "empathy" will be used in this chapter will be when describing results of these studies that explicitly report empathy measurements. The following points must be kept in mind when considering these studies. First, as already discussed, empathy self-report tools incorporate processes (1)–(7) described above to different degrees, so it is difficult to quantify how much self-reported "empathy" scores uniquely represent negative intersubjectivity as opposed to other phenomena like theory of mind (Lovett and Sheffield 2007). Second, it is unclear how well such self-report questions map onto negative intersubjectivity, given that empathy self-reports can be poorly correlated with nonverbal measures of responses to others' distress, such as autonomic outputs or facial expressions (Eisenberg and Fabes 1990). Third, it is uncertain how honest people are when responding to these questionnaires. Nonetheless, studies using empathy self-report scales provide important evidence corroborating that negative intersubjectivity consistently correlates with human moral behavior, and therefore deserve attention in section 11.2, which summarizes what is known about this critical link.

11.2. Human Negative Intersubjectivity and Moral Behavior

11.2.1. NEGATIVE INTERSUBJECTIVITY PREDICTS ANTISOCIAL AND PROSOCIAL BEHAVIOR

One of the most consistent lines of evidence linking negative intersubjectivity to behavior comes from studies referencing the "affective" components of trait empathy self-reports. Affective components attempt to capture one's "emotional" responses to others' experiences, and therefore come close to indexing negative intersubjectivity as I have defined it. Indeed, scores on the affective components of self-reported empathy correlate with antisocial behavior, or behavior that imposes harm on others (Jolliffe and Murray 2012; Björkqvist et al. 2000; Jolliffe and Farrington 2004; LeSure-Lester 2000). Similar evidence comes from research with "callous" personality traits in children and adolescents. Callousness is when an individual does not feel guilt, appears more concerned about the effects of his actions on himself than on others (even when his actions result in substantial harm to others), and generally disregards others' feelings (American Psychiatric Association's Proposed Draft Revisions to DSM Disorders and Criteria). Callous traits often cluster with "unemotional" traits (found in individuals who have low levels of affect overall), so the two traits are usually combined and called "callous-unemotional" (CU) traits. Consistent with the correlations found with self-reports of trait empathy, CU traits are good predictors of the persistence and intensity of violence within juvenile and adolescent delinquents, and some evidence suggests that CU traits also predict offenders' resistance to treatment (Frick and White 2008; Hawes and Dadds 2005). In addition, persistent violent offenders are disproportionately likely to have high CU traits when they are adolescents compared to other offenders (Vaughn and DeLisi 2008). CU traits in adults can be indexed by items in the "affective factor" of the Psychopathy Checklist (Revised, PCL-R), a semistructured interview used to diagnose psychopathy. When present simultaneously with high impulsivity (another trait of psychopathy), scores on the affective factor of the PCL-R correlate with increased violence in adult psychopaths (Hare 1991, 2003). Conversely, the personality traits that lead to low scores on the affective items of the PCL-R may be protective against the influence of impulsive traits on violent behavior (Walsh and Kosson 2008). Finally, scores on the newly developed Inventory of Callous Unemotional Traits, a self-report assessment designed for both adolescents and young adults (Essau et al. 2006; Kimonis et al. 2008), correlate with number of arrests and charges for violent crime (Kahn et al. 2012). In fact, a study in young adults reported that callousness, on its own and separated from unemotional traits, correlated with repeated and violent offending even after controlling for prior criminal behavior and other well-established risk factors (Kahn et al. 2012). Thus, there is a well-documented correlation between negative intersubjectivity deficits and persistent antisocial behavior, suggesting that if we could determine how to appropriately modulate negative intersubjectivity, we might be able to decrease antisocial behavior.

Whereas antisocial behavior harms others, prosocial behavior is defined as voluntary behavior that benefits others, either intentionally or unintentionally (Eisenberg 1986). Consistent with the studies above suggesting that increased negative intersubjectivity correlates with reduced antisocial behavior, it is well documented that increased negative intersubjectivity (or reduced callousness) also correlates with increased helping and prosocial behavior (Batson et al. 2011, 417; Eisenberg and Miller 1987; Hoffman 2008; Eisenberg 2008; Trommsdorff et al. 2007; Batson and Shaw 1991; Batson and Oleson 1991; Barraza and Zak 2009). For example, self-reports of empathy when viewing videos of emotional scenes correlate positively with helping (preparing gifts to send people in the emotional movies) in children (Miller et al. 1996), and positively with more generous monetary offers in an ultimatum game in adults (Barraza and Zak 2009). Further, educational training programs aimed to enhance children's empathy and empathy-related skills have been reported to increase cooperation, helping, and generosity (Feshbach 1979; Feshbach and Feshbach 1982). Of note, many reports suggest there may be a nonlinear relationship such that although moderate levels of negative intersubjectivity correlate with increased helping as summarized above, extremely high levels of negative intersubjectivity may actually inhibit prosocial behavior to redirect efforts toward minimizing one's own distress (rather than others' distress) (Batson et al. 2011, 417; Eisenberg 2008; Feshbach and Feshbach 1982). Taking this into account, if we succeed in developing methods to regulate negative intersubjectivity appropriately, the literature suggests we may be able to increase prosocial behavior.

11.2.2. NEURAL BASIS OF HUMAN NEGATIVE INTERSUBJECTIVITY

Understanding the mechanisms that cause negative intersubjectivity helps provide insight into how to manipulate negative intersubjectivity. Toward this end, much effort has been dedicated to elucidating the neural basis of human negative intersubjectivity. This now fairly large body of work has been discussed in many excellent reviews (Shirtcliff et al. 2009; Walter 2012; Bernhardt and Singer 2012; Decety 2011), so rather than duplicate these reviews, the three primary themes of human negative intersubjectivity neuroscience research will be summarized below.

Overlapping, but not identical, brain regions are involved in receiving pain oneself and observing pain in another. Two recent meta-analyses of "empathy" functional magnetic resonance imaging (fMRI) studies converged on identifying the anterior cingulate (ACC) and the anterior insula (AI) as brain regions consistently activated both when receiving pain and when observing others in pain (Fan et al. 2011; Lamm et al. 2007). Further, Lamm et al. calculated that approximately 60 percent of studies measuring self-reported acute empathy in response to task stimuli, and many studies measuring general trait empathy using self-report questionnaires, show that self-reported empathy positively correlates with AI and ACC activity evoked when participants observe others in pain. Of note, similar correlations have been reported when observing people in negative affective states other than physical pain, such as during social exclusion (Meyer et al. 2013) or while smelling a disgusting odor (Jabbi et al. 2008; Wicker et al 2003). These observations have led to the "observing is feeling" hypothesis: observing pain in others activates the same neural circuitry as when you are in pain yourself, and activation of this neural circuitry mediates empathy.

The established relationships between AI and ACC activity and negative intersubjectivity are qualified by two considerations. First, despite the consistent overlap in the AI and ACC, there are also many differences in the neural representation of observing and receiving pain. Even within the insula, there is a topographical gradient localizing the sensory components of physical pain experience to the more posterior regions, and the affective components of physical pain experience to the more anterior regions (Fan et al. 2011; Lamm et al. 2007; Corradi-Dell'Acqua 2011). Vicarious pain only elicits activity in the more anterior regions. Second, the role of the AI in negative intersubjectivity might be more consistent than the role of the ACC. Whereas the AI seems to be preferentially active in response to all vicarious pain conditions, the ACC is only preferentially active when responding to others in pain under certain high-attention conditions, suggesting it might be more involved in the conscious voluntary control of behaviors relevant to negative intersubjectivity than negative intersubjectivity itself (Gu et al. 2010; Azevedo et al. 2013; Gu et al. 2012). Perhaps through this putative attentional role, the ACC is also hypothesized to help coordinate the recruitment of other task-relevant brain networks as well, like those involved in understanding another person's actions or mental states (Bruneau et al. 2012). In sum, there is compelling evidence that the AI and ACC are involved in negative intersubjectivity in some way, but without methods for manipulating activity in brain regions located deep within the human brain, it is not known whether AI or ACC activity is either necessary or sufficient for executing moral actions.

Mirror neurons might have a role in responses to others' pain. Drawn from a completely different set of observations and principles, another popular hypothesis posits that "mirroring mechanisms" mediate negative intersubjectivity (Gallese et al. 2011; Spunt and Lieberman 2012). Mirror neurons are neurons in the parietal and premotor cortices of macaque monkeys that fire both when a monkey performs a particular action and when a monkey observes a human or another monkey intentionally perform the same action (Rizzolatti and Craighero 2004). Encouraged by the fMRI studies reviewed above that show affective brain areas are active both when humans observe and when they receive pain, proponents of mirror-neuron explanations of negative intersubjectivity have postulated that there may be "affective mirror neurons" in brain areas identified in those fMRI studies—including the ACC or AI—that mediate physical pain to oneself and aversion to pain in others (Iacoboni 2009). According to this view, witnessing somebody else in pain activates the same neurons in the ACC or AI that fire when you yourself are in physical pain, reinforcing the notion introduced earlier that at least to some extent, "empathetic" pain is a type of physical pain.

Two primary potential roles for mirror neurons in negative intersubjectivity have been discussed. First, we may automatically *physically* imitate the actions or facial expressions of others in distress using motor mirror neurons. Then, second, doing so may make it easier for us to automatically *affectively* imitate the feelings of others in distress using affective mirror neurons. In partial support, some studies report that the magnitude of motor "mirroring," defined by observable motor imitation or activity in one's own motor system when observing another person perform an action, correlates with self-reports of state empathy (Sonnby-Borgström 2002; Sonnby-Borgstrom et al. 2008; Gazzola et al. 2006; Kaplan and Iacoboni 2006; Dimberg et al. 2011; Chartrand and Bargh 1999). A recent fMRI study provided some additional compelling evidence using multivariate pattern analysis (MVPA) showing that the anterior insula, and perhaps the middle insula and cingulate cortex, had identical patterns of hemodynamic activity both when receiving pain and when observing pain (Corradi-Dell'Acqua et al. 2011). Of course, fMRI studies cannot provide single-cell resolution and are only correlational. Thus, though the "mirror-neuron hypothesis of negative intersubjectivity" remains a very popular (and very controversial) hypothesis in academic and popular literature (Gallese et al. 2011; Baird et al. 2011; Hickok 2009), it has never been tested directly.

Oxytocin's potential role in negative intersubjectivity is unclear, and likely indirect. Oxytocin is popularly called the "love" or "empathy" hormone (see lovehormone.org). More accurately, it is a neuropeptide secreted from the paraventricular nucleus, accessory magnocellular nuclei, and the supraoptic nucleus of the hypothalamus during many social behaviors (such as birthing or sex). In rodents, oxytocin receptor expression patterns correlate strongly with sociality and pair-bonding.[92] In humans, one study demonstrated that oxytocin levels in the blood correlated positively with self-reported positive feelings of "empathy" and negative feelings of distress when people watched videos of a father describing his son's terminal brain cancer (Barraza and Zak 2009). Oxytocin nasal inhalations have also been shown to increase generosity in a one-shot game asking participants to split a sum of money with a stranger (Zak et al. 2007) and change brain activity in response to infant cries (Riem et al. 2011). In addition, some oxytocin gene variants correlate with self-reports of trait empathy (Rodrigues et al. 2009; Wu et al. 2012). Reports like these have led to speculations that oxytocin could potentially be used to enhance prosocial behavior (Walter 2012; Yamasue et al. 2012; McKaughan 2012).

Enthusiasm for using oxytocin as a "love hormone" to increase negative intersubjectivity and prosocial behavior has been tempered by conflicting evidence about whether such applications would work, and more evidence that even if oxytocin did affect negative intersubjectivity or prosocial behavior, it would likely do so in an indirect fashion. First, some studies fail to detect any effects of oxytocin on human negative intersubjectivity or responses to others' pain (Singer et al. 2008; Bartz et al. 2011), and others have observed oxytocin effects that are in the opposite direction of ideal social behavior (Zhong et al. 2012; Radke and 2012; Sheng et al. 2013; De Dreu 2012). Second, other studies report qualified interactions such that oxytocin only affected subgroups of people with either a specific gender, set of development conditions, or baseline social abilities (Wu et al. 2012; Bartz et al. 2011; Riem et al. 2013; Hurlemann et al. 2010; Bartz et al. 2010; Huffmeijer et al. 2012).

Part of the explanation for these complex results is likely based in oxytocin anatomy, which has been characterized mostly through rodent research rather than human research. Regardless of the task, most studies find that the observed oxytocin effects are mediated by decreased activity in the amygdala, a limbic brain region involved in many aspects of emotion (Singer et al. 2008; Hurlemann et al. 2010; Striepens et al. 2012; Hirosawa et al. 2012; Tost et al. 2010). Indeed, oxytocin receptors are densely expressed in the amygdala (Veinante and Freund-Mercier 1998; Loup et al. 1991). Importantly, at least in rats, they are much less densely expressed in the insula, and perhaps not expressed at all in the ACC (Tribollet et al. 1992). This hints that oxytocin's role in social behavior may not be directly through negative intersubjectivity circuits, but rather through amygdala-dependent social circuits that are modulated or preferentially enlisted in specific contexts, including (but not limited to) circuits related to general anxiety and/or fear (Churchland and Winkielman 2012). Thus, despite great interest in the role of oxytocin in negative intersubjectivity and prosocial behavior, its potential therapeutic applications remain controversial.

To conclude, efforts to map out the neural bases of intersubjectivity have led to many interesting and compelling biological models of how negative intersubjectivity might manifest. Unfortunately, two of the reigning hypotheses about the neural basis of negative intersubjectivity have yet to be proven or refuted: (1) the putative overlap between neural circuits involved in observing and receiving distress (are some of the same cells involved? If so, which ones, and why?), and (2) the related "mirror-neuron hypothesis of negative intersubjectivity" (do cells exist that respond to both being in distress and affectively imitating another's distress, and do these cells have any relation to the motor system?). Slightly more progress has been made testing the oxytocin hypothesis of negative intersubjectivity, but efforts have yielded conflicting results. Up to this point, our ability to more definitively test these hypotheses of the neural basis of negative intersubjectivity has been obstructed by the technological constraints of human research. The last section of this chapter will discuss how rodent research can rectify this problem.

11.3. Evidence of Negative Intersubjectivity in Rodents

11.3.1. HUMANS VERSUS RODENTS AS EXPERIMENTAL SUBJECTS

The fact that morality research has almost exclusively used humans as experimental subjects is understandable given the popular view that humans are the only species to have morality (although some argue that nonhuman primates, dolphins, and elephants have rudimentary moral systems) (de Waal 2009, 2008). Furthermore, a lot of morality research aims to study emotions or beliefs, and it is challenging to develop methods that allow us to infer the internal state or beliefs of animals with whom we cannot communicate. The downside of restricting morality research to humans, of course, is that it will only be able to advance as far as techniques available in humans and human research ethics permit. Neuroscience tools available in humans index a wide variety of biological functions and can cover many brain or body regions at once, but they also all have poor temporal and spatial resolution for the types of processes we believe are responsible for cognition and behavior (Homberg 2013; de Waal 2012).

To illustrate, consider the limitations of using fMRI to address the observing-is-feeling or the mirror-neuron hypothesis of negative intersubjectivity. The following details of brain anatomy might at first seem detached from complex phenomena like morality, but they are extremely important for understanding why we have not yet been able to test popular theories of the neural basis of negative intersubjectivity. Brain tissue is populated by heterogeneous populations of cells. Brain cells can be excitatory or inhibitory (or be different types of neurons within these classifications), can have diverse anatomical projections that allow them to participate in different anatomical circuits, can use different neurotransmitters or peptides, and most of the time aren't even neurons! (Allen and Barres 2009). Critical for the methods of human research, the BOLD (blood oxygen level dependent) signal measured by fMRI is due to hemodynamics that respond to activity of any of these cells, regardless of whether they are stimulating or inhibiting functioning in a brain area, and regardless of whether or not they are neurons (Schulz et al. 2012). Therefore, the BOLD signal is too imprecise a measurement to provide us information about many types of neural circuits. Furthermore, the BOLD signal can sometime be too insensitive a measurement. Very small populations of cells within a given brain area may have incredibly important roles in an animal's behavior (Witten et al. 2010), but not be detectable with fMRI because the hemodynamic response of the brain area is dominated by the metabolic needs of surrounding cells. In sum, if the neural processes underlying moral behavior are not mediated by relatively large, homogeneous populations of cells firing in a relatively homogeneous way, we will not be able to detect or study those mechanisms using human fMRI studies, and such studies may actually mislead us. Neither the observing-is-feeling nor the mirror-neuron hypothesis of negative intersubjectivity makes any claims about whether relevant cells are in large homogeneous populations.

If not humans, in what species should we study negative intersubjectivity? At first, nonhuman primates might seem like the ideal model organism. Monkeys and apes have a close evolutionarily relationship to humans and under certain conditions can be used to examine many detailed mechanisms of cognition. Primate work has its own set of methodological challenges, however. First, the financial cost and regulation governing the use of research monkeys dictates that only two or three animals can be used per experiment. If monkeys have the same diversity in social behavior as humans, it would be unwise to infer general mechanisms of social decision-making from such a small number of animals. Second, although it is controversial to cause distress in any experimental species, it is particularly controversial to cause distress or pain in monkeys (Suran and Wolinsky 2009), making it difficult to study how monkeys respond to other monkeys in distress or pain. Third, even if both of these challenges are surmounted, monkeys are a difficult species to use to study the molecular or anatomical mechanisms underlying behavior because it is costly and ethically contentious to genetically alter primates or collect their brains. To be most effective, moral neuroscience needs to be able to study negative intersubjectivity and social behavior in a model species that can be used in large numbers, that allows us to record from and manipulate the activity of single neurons, and that is compatible with techniques for robust and controlled circuit dissection and manipulation. The most efficient way to meet these criteria, despite nonhuman primates' evolutionary proximity to humans, is to study negative intersubjectivity in the dominant mammalian species used in basic neuroscience research: rodents.

In stark contrast to human research, rodent research permits exquisite control over environmental and genetic factors affecting its participants and affords data with extremely high spatial and temporal resolution. In rodents we can (with enough time) not only determine precisely what neurons fire in response to a certain stimulus or action, but also the genetic identity of those neurons, what those neurons look like, where those neurons project to or receive projections from, and how those neurons share information with other neurons. This is the type of information needed to address the observing-is-feeling and mirror-neuron hypotheses of negative intersubjectivity. This is also the type of information that permitted (preliminary) explanations of the confusing data collected while testing the oxytocin hypothesis of negative intersubjectivity.

Another strong advantage of using rodents as model organisms is that they offer a relatively unique opportunity to study the causal relationship between neural properties and associated phenotypes. Popular science writing has exposed most people to the idea that we can lesion or temporarily inactivate specific brain regions in rodents, and either knock out or knock in specific genes. What might be less known is that we can actually knock out or knock in specific genes in specific brain regions at specific times during a behavior or development (Luo et al. 2008). Furthermore, thanks to a new technology called optogenetics, we can now activate or inhibit genetically targeted populations of cells with precise temporal precision (Fenno et al. 2011). We can also use advances in brain-computer interfaces to train algorithms that can determine how and when to make specific neurons fire to create precise behaviors, like grasping an object or even kicking a soccer ball (Thorsten and Christian 2011; Nicolelis 2012). It would be terribly exciting and perhaps revolutionary to apply all of these techniques to the study of moral behavior and moral decision-making. Of course, the primary challenge in using rodents to study morality is this: do rodents do or think anything that is morally relevant?

11.3.2. REQUIREMENTS OF A RODENT MODEL OF NEGATIVE INTERSUBJECTIVITY

Evidence supporting a strong relationship between negative intersubjectivity and moral behavior has been presented, and the limitations of studying moral behavior exclusively in humans has been discussed. The groundwork has been laid to argue that a primary goal of moral neuroscience over the next decade should be to develop, establish, and use a standardized rodent model of negative intersubjectivity to (a) identify the biological systems and neural processes that lead to humans *disliking* pain and distress in other humans, and (b) understand how these systems and processes lead to *avoidance* of causing pain and distress in other humans, or stated in reverse, how dysfunction in these systems and processes lead to persistent callous or violent behavior. The next step towards making this argument is to delineate what such a model would look like.

To address (a), a rodent behavioral model of negative intersubjectivity needs to convincingly demonstrate that rodents *dislike* witnessing other rodents in distress. To interpret the literature discussed in the following section, it is important to know that rodents (and some would argue humans) have three natural defense mechanisms against something they don't like: flight (avoidance), freezing, or fight (aggressive attack). In theory, any one of these defense mechanisms could be used to index negative affect. However, to simultaneously address (b), a rodent behavioral model of negative intersubjectivity must demonstrate that rodents are motivated to actively *avoid* distress in other rodents. Given the purposes of the modeling negative intersubjectivity, clearly a model that induces attack in an animal observing another animal's distress would not be appropriate. When considering the other two defense mechanisms, it is useful to consider their ethological functions. Avoidance is the defense mechanism typically used when threats are defined, present, and avoidable. Freezing, on the other hand, is the defense mechanism typically used when threats are undefined, not yet present, and unavoidable (Eilam 2005). If we want to understand how negative intersubjectivity contributes to behavior when a person has an option to prevent violence from happening, avoidance would be the most appropriate natural defense mechanism. This becomes even more clear when one considers that avoidance and freezing are behaviorally mutually exclusive (because you can't be fleeing if you are freezing) and are known to be mediated by different neural circuits (Eilam 2005; Fanselow 1994). For these reasons, a rodent model of intersubjective avoidance would be a better model for human negative intersubjectivity than a rodent model of intersubjective freezing (the importance of this distinction will be become clear later). Putting these concepts together, an ideal rodent model of intersubjective avoidance would do the following:

a. Convincingly show that rodents do not like witnessing distress in other rodents
b. Incorporate an active avoidance or choice behavior, rather than a freezing behavior
c. Have an analogue test that could be run in humans for validation and comparison

It is important to recognize that such a model of negative intersubjectivity would not meet many definitions of empathy, because it does not make any assumptions about intentions, especially altruistic intentions. The next section reviews where the field is in developing such a model.

11.3.3. PROGRESS IN DEVELOPING RODENT MODELS OF NEGATIVE INTERSUBJECTIVITY

Although interest in rodent negative intersubjectivity has increased over the past decade, evidence that rodents might be useful for studying intersubjectivity has been around for a long time. It is commonly known in animal husbandry that exposing rodents to stress cues from other rodents can increase baseline stress, even if no harm is incurred to the observing animals themselves. This vicarious stress is so well accepted that the American Veterinary Medical Association recommends rodent euthanasia be performed away from locations where other animals are housed to prevent potential stress in the noneuthanized animals (AVMA Guidelines on Euthanasia, 2007) (Špinka 2012). Furthermore, in support of these practical guidelines, experimental observations have documented that observing, smelling, and hearing other mice get shocked for an extended period of time can increase morphine self-administration (Kuzmin et al. 1996), cocaine self-administration (Ramsey and Van Ree 1993), saccharine preference (Pijlman et al. 2003), locomotor activity (Pijlman et al. 2003; Gutiérrez-García et al. 2006), and immobility in a forced-swim test (Gutiérrez-García and Contreras 2009; Gutiérrez-García et al. 2007), and disrupt sleep (Cui et al. 2008). These studies make it clear that rodents perceive at least some cues from other animals in distress that can affect their overall behavior. That said, these documented observations only prove that rodents perceive distress cues in other rodents; they don't yet prove that rodents have negative emotions that motivate them to avoid other rodents in distress.

Fortunately, more explicit behavioral reports of rodents perceiving other rodents' distress have been documented as well. Male mice will modulate writhing pain behaviors when they see other mice exhibiting the same writhing pain behaviors, a response modulated by the physical proximity between the mice being tested (Langford et al. 2006, 2011). In addition, rats show increased locomotor activity and startle amplitude when they are returned to a home cage with a rat who was recently shocked in a separate room (Knapska 2006), and their ability to learn to associate a shock with a conditioned stimulus will be improved by observing a conspecific receive shock (Chen et al. 2009; Guzman et al. 2009; Kiyokawa et al. 2009; Bruchey et al. 2010; but see Bredy and Barad 2009) or get worse if they are paired with a conspecific who did *not* receive shock in association with that same stimulus (Guzman et al. 2009; Kiyokawa et al. 2009). Outside of an explicit learning context, rats and mice who have experienced foot shock themselves will freeze upon witnessing a cagemate experience foot shock (Atsak et al. 2011) or upon witnessing a cagemate vocalize in response to a stimulus previously paired with foot shock (Kim et al. 2010). Perhaps most relevant, even if an observing mouse has never experienced foot shock itself, it may freeze upon witnessing a noncagemate experience foot shock, as long as the noncagemate is shocked with very intense strength and frequency (Jeon et al. 2010). These data demonstrate that distress cues from other rodents will affect freezing responses in observing rodents, which in turn suggests that the experience of perceiving other rodents' distress cues can have a negative valence. This is encouraging for developing a rodent model of negative intersubjectivity, but for the reasons stated earlier, freezing is not the ideal behavior for studying the role of negative intersubjectivity in violence. We must look elsewhere in the literature to find examples of behaviors relevant to avoiding distress in others.

Interestingly, most of the studies suggesting that rodents will perform active behaviors to avoid another rodents' distress were published half a century ago and were implemented in rats rather than mice. The most famous of these was published by Russell Church in 1959. The explicit goal of this study was to determine whether the "sympathetic" response that "animals and people" often have to the emotional states of others could be explained by others' emotional states acting as conditioned stimuli, or neutral stimuli that are learned through experience to be associated with other valenced (in this case negatively valenced) stimuli to oneself. To address this, Church taught a group of hungry observer rats to press a lever to obtain food. Then Church conditioned the rats. In the first conditioning sessions, a light would come on for one minute followed by another minute of a rat in an adjacent box getting shocked. This taught the observers to associate the light with the other rat getting shocked. In the next set of conditioning sessions, the rat in the adjacent box would get shocked for thirty seconds followed by a one-second shock to the observer rat. This taught the observers to associate the other rat getting shocked with shock to themselves. Then Church tested how much the observer rats would press a lever to obtain food in the presence of the rat in the adjacent box getting shocked, even if the observers were no longer shocked themselves. He found that, indeed, shock to another rat initially served as an effective conditioned stimulus: observers that were conditioned to associate shock to another rat in the adjacent chamber with shock to themselves reduced their lever-pressing for food during testing days. However, this decrease in lever pressing habituated each day over the course of ten days. Church also found that a control group who never received shocks to themselves during training did not decrease their lever pressing at all during testing (and, if anything, increased their lever pressing). Based on this data the authors concluded, "The difference between the experimental and unshocked control group was considered support for a conditioned-response interpretation of some cases of 'sympathy'" (Church 1959, 134). In other words, Church hypothesized that humans may dislike observing distress in others because we learn through experience that distress in others is usually associated with some type of distress in ourselves. Of note, even if this hypothesis is true, humans (or rats) would still have negative intersubjectivity as it is defined in this chapter.

The Church (1959) study is famous because it is one of the first studies designed to assess whether rats change their behavior in response to other rats' distress. However, the results were not particularly encouraging as a model of negative intersubjectivity because observers' response to other rats' distress habituated quite rapidly and was therefore not very robust. In addition, the primary observation was related to a lack of lever pressing rather than an increase in lever pressing. This makes it difficult to interpret whether the observing rats were just freezing when the other rats were getting shocked or whether they were intentionally withholding lever presses because doing so would prevent further distress.

The first study to address whether rodents are motivated to perform a directed action to avoid distress in another rat was published by Rice and Gainer in 1962. In a rather strange experimental paradigm, they began by training observer rats to press a lever to avoid (or escape) a shock to themselves. A five-second signal light preceded the escapable shock. At the same time as the observer rats were performing this avoidance task, they could see a styrofoam block suspended from a hoist being raised up and down adjacent to the training chamber. Whenever an observer rat pressed the lever to avoid or escape a shock, the block was lowered to the floor, where it remained for fifteen seconds before being raised again. The signal light that preceded the shock to the observer was presented when the block was at its zenith. After learning this avoidance task, all observer rats underwent extinction training until bar pressing in response to the signal light disappeared. This suggested that the rats no longer associated the signal light with a future experience of shock to themselves. After extinction was verified, testing commenced. During testing, the procedure changed in two ways. First, unlike training, the observer rats never got shocked themselves. Second, the styrofoam block was replaced with a live rat who "typically squealed and wriggled satisfactorily while suspended, and if it did not, it was prodded with a sharp pencil until it exhibited signs of discomfort" (Rice and Gainer 1962, 123). Although the observer rats would not be shocked during testing, as in the conditioning phase, whenever an observer rat pressed the lever in their chamber, the hoist would be lowered until the hoisted rat had all four feet on the ground for fifteen seconds. Under these conditions, Rice and Gainer compared the bar pressing of observer rats who did and did not receive previous avoidance training. They also examined the bar pressing of observer rats who did and did not receive previous avoidance training when the suspended rat was replaced with a styrofoam block. They made the following observations: *both* groups of observers who witnessed a rat being suspended from the hoist, regardless of previous avoidance training, pressed the lever significantly more times than their matched controls. Over the course of ten minutes, the experimental groups with a hoisted rat pressed the lever an average of fifteen and eighteen times (for the trained and untrained rats, respectively), whereas the control groups with a hoisted styrofoam block pressed an average of one and five times. This clearly demonstrated that rats will perform active actions when they observe another rat in distress. Since the study suggested that rats might be willing to press a lever to bring a suspended rat to safety, the authors controversially concluded, "It is suggested that this behavior might operationally be termed altruistic" (Rice and Gainer 1962, 124).

Half a century later, a relevant paradigm was reported by Inbal Ben-Ami Bartal, Jean Decety, and Peggy Mason (2011). The purpose of this paradigm was to test whether rats had enough prosocial motivation to release a trapped cagemate from captivity. To test this, they placed two rats in an open arena. The observer was free to run around, while its cagemate was trapped in a plastic restrainer. If the observer pressed the door to the restrainer with enough force, it could open the restrainer and release its cagemate. During training, the observer and receiver were placed in the arena for ninety minutes and the latency to door opening was recorded. If the observer did not open the door of the restraining chamber by a certain time, it was opened by the experimenter and the rats were allowed to interact before being returned to their shared home cage. Control experiments were run in which (a) an observer was placed in the arena with an empty restrainer, but no other rat, present, (b) an observer was placed in the arena with an empty restrainer present, and a cagemate in a separate adjacent compartment, (c) the observer could open the restrainer, but the cagemate was released into a separate compartment, (d) the observer was placed in the arena with one restrainer holding its cagemate and another restrainer holding chocolate chips, and (e) the observer was placed in the arena with one restrainer holding chocolate chips and another empty restrainer. The following observations were made: observers took an average of seven days to learn how to open the door to the restrainer to "free" the restrained rat before the time limit, and by the end of this learning curve the observers opened the door between five and ten minutes after the beginning of the session. The average opening rate was similar for the experimental group as for the group when the observer could open the restrainer but the cagemate was released into a separate compartment (suggesting the observer wasn't just opening the restrainer to have social interaction), but much higher than either group with empty restrainers. Finally, when given a choice between opening a restrainer with a rat or a restrainer with chocolate chips, observers opened both restrainers equally quickly, but when given a choice between opening a restrainer with chocolate chips or an empty re-strainer, it opened the restrainer with the chocolate chips faster (although it also opened the empty restrainer). The authors concluded, "The most parsimonious interpretation of the observed helping behavior is that rats free their cagemate in order to end distress, either their own or that of the trapped rat, that is associated with the circumstances of the trapped cagemate" (Bartal et al. 2011, 1430).

Although both studies by Rice and Gainer (1962) and Bartal et al. (2011) show clearly that rats' active behaviors are affected by other rats in distress, they also share a characteristic that confounds their interpretation: general arousal (Lucke and Baton 1980; Lavery and Foley 1963). In order for these behaviors to be useful models of negative intersubjectivity, the behaviors need to convincingly show that the observers feel negative affect when other rats are in distress, and no plausible explanations for the observed behavior should exist that do not require the subjective state of the observer to have a negative valence. To the contrary, both behaviors reported by Rice and Gainer (1962) and Bartal et al. (2011) could potentially be explained by increased general arousal without corresponding negative valence. Generalized arousal is the large-scale readiness of many potential behavioral responses to respond to environmental conditions (Pfaff et al. 2008). (Arousal, itself, is unvalenced, but it can interact with either positive or negative valence circuits to affect subjective states or behavior; Kensinge 2004). Arousal manifests in rodents as increased locomotor behavior when no other stimulus is present to initiate motivated action (Pfaff et al. 2008). Thus, if a suspended rat or a restrained rat increased arousal without "dislike" in an observing rat, an observing rat should increase its locomotion and interact with its environment in a nonspecific way. Bartal et al. measured locomotor activity in their study and reported that observers were more active before learning to open the restrainer, consistent with this prediction.

The best way to determine whether the reported responses were specifically linked to distress in another animal in either the Rice and Gainer study or the Bartal et al. study would have been to give observers the opportunity to perform a task-irrelevant action in the testing environment. For example, an inactive lever could have been provided in the Rice and Gainer study, or a separate empty restrainer could have been provided in the Bartal et al. study; researchers could then have tested whether responding toward the lever associated with lowering the suspended rat or the restrainer with the rat, as opposed to the unpaired level or the empty restrainer, was selectively increased. Neither study reported such a control. Even without these controls, there is reason to be skeptical of a negative intersubjectivity interpretation of the Bartal et al. study because both when (d) the observer was placed in the arena with one restrainer holding its cagemate and another restrainer holding chocolate chips and (e) the observer was placed in the arena with one restrainer holding chocolate chips and another empty restrainer, the observer opened both restrainers. This suggests that, indeed, the observer was more likely to respond to many cues, not just the restrainer with a rat in it. Further, inspection of the videos published with the Bartal et al. study suggests that neither the observer nor the restrained rat avoided the restrainer once the restrained rat was released. In fact, as soon as the restrained rat was released, both rats competed to enter the restrainer again, perhaps using the restrainer as a toy. This suggests that being in the restrainer was not likely very aversive (or aversive at all), which in turn suggests that the observer may never have had an opportunity to perceive distress cues from the other rat. In sum, the Rice and Gainer and Bartal et al. studies provide convincing evidence that witnessing another rat be suspended or be restrained is a salient stimulus for rats, which may be relevant to negative intersubjectivity in some way. However, they are still not ideal behaviors for modeling how negative intersubjectivity inhibits violence. If a violent human commits violence against a victim, we don't want the violent human to get generally aroused and start causing more damage to everything in his environment, including the victim. Rather, we want the violent human to perceive the victim's distress cues and feel so negative about those distress cues that he stops the violence he is currently performing and goes out of his way to avoid causing victims' distress cues in the future. Neither the Rice and Gainer nor the Bartal et al. study provides convincing evidence that rats can have these avoidance responses to other rats' distress.

Five other published studies do provide convincing evidence that rodents will avoid other rodents in distress, but unlike Rice and Gainer and Bartal et al. studies, none of them are well known or cited. The first of these studies put rats in a T-maze and trained them to go to either end of the T to receive a sucrose award. When receiving sucrose at one end of the T was paired with another rat getting shocked, the observers selectively avoided that end of the T and sought sucrose at the other end (Evans and Braud 1969). A similar behavior was reported in mice who avoided odors of a distressed mouse (distressed by hypertonic saline injection or by foot shock) in a shuttle box or tube where the odors were only pumped into one side of the box or tube (Rottman and Snowdon 1972; Zalaquett and Thiessen 1991). Perhaps the most convincing demonstration of rodent negative intersubjectivity, though, was reported by Simonov and colleagues using rats (Preobrazhenskaya and Simonov 1970; Wetzel and Simonov 1978). They designed a three-chamber apparatus such that an observer could be put in two chambers, one having a roof and the other having no roof. The observer could move freely between both of these chambers, and they were arranged in an "L" around a third receiver chamber. The observers could see, but not interact with, a receiver placed in the inner chamber from either the covered or the uncovered area. Observers and receivers were placed in this apparatus for five minutes daily, and the amount of time the observers spent in the covered versus uncovered chambers was recorded. During baseline, most observers preferred the covered chamber (although the researchers did not test baseline preference in all animals). During testing, whenever an observer went into the covered chamber, the rat in the inside chamber would get shocked until the observer entered the uncovered chamber. In twelve rats, Preobrazhenskaya and Simonov showed that some observers dramatically avoided the covered chamber under these conditions. Further, when the observers avoided the covered area during testing, they did so consistently over many days (sometimes over twenty days in a row). The authors also made the following interesting observations: (*a*) four of the twelve animals started to prefer the uncovered area after only two or three days of testing, (*b*) five of the twelve animals started to prefer the uncovered area only after they had been used as the shocked rat for three or five days, (*c*) three of the twelve rats never preferred the uncovered chamber, even after having been used as the shocked rat, and (*d*) the four rats that avoided the covered chamber without having experienced shock themselves tended to be less anxious as measured by an open field test, while the three rats that never avoided the covered chamber were very anxious. Further, at the end of the conditioning experiments, Preobrazhenskaya and Simonov tested observers in an "aggression" test. In this test, pairs of rats were placed in a compartment with a wire floor and observed as electrical charge was gradually introduced into the floor. The voltage at which the rats responded by attacking their neighbor was recorded. The four rats that avoided the covered chamber without having experienced shock themselves in the three-chamber experiment tended to respond to the shocked floor by cooperating with the other rat to short-circuit the nociceptive stimulation with their hind limbs. The three rats that never avoided the covered chamber showed aggressive responses at low voltages.

These studies provide five independent reports that mice and rats will change their physical location to avoid distress cues from other mice or rats. These behaviors aren't easily explained by general arousal, because the animals' change in location is specific to where the distress cues originate. Furthermore, the study by Preobrazhenskaya and Simonov suggests that rats will change their location in a dramatic and persistent way that may not habituate even after weeks of training. Even more impressively, how much rats change their physical location to avoid distress cues from other mice or rats may negatively correlate with how likely they are to engage in aggression as a defensive reaction, suggesting that even in rats, avoidance of other's pain may correlate with decreased general aggression.

In sum, these studies support the hypothesis that it is possible to meet the criteria for an ideal rodent model of intersubjective avoidance. Amazingly, rodents avoid others' pain, a behavior human violent offenders do not perform and psychopaths may not have the affective neural machinery to perform (Aniskiewicz 1979; House and Milligan 1976; Blair et al. 1997). To clarify, these studies do *not* indicate *why* observer rodents feel negative in response to other rodents' distress (are they scared? do they feel sympathy?), nor whether observer rodents have conscious intentions toward other rodents' distress (do they want to help, or do they simply want to get away?). However, as discussed in sections 11.1 and 11.2 of this chapter, neither a specific origin nor a specific intention is necessary for negative intersubjectivity to mediate violence aversion. What is most important is simply that observers avoid others' distress cues, as opposed to ignoring them or freezing upon perceiving them. Indeed, the studies described above convincingly show that rodents can and will avoid other rodents' distress. The studies published thus far have not designed their behavioral paradigms to be able to quantify how much each rodent does not like witnessing distress in other rodents, but the paradigms could easily be adapted to do so by simply varying the intensity of negative stimulus rats are required to endure to avoid another rat in distress (intensity of light in the Preobrazhenskaya and Simonov studies) or varying the amount of positive stimulus rats are required to give up in order to avoid another rat in distress (amount of sucrose reward in the Evans and Braud study). Once the exact paradigm is established, it would be relatively easy to implement parallel studies in humans for validation and comparison. A few labs are actively working on developing these kinds of behavioral models for rodents, so the question is no longer *if* a robust rodent model of negative intersubjectivity can be established, but rather *when* such models will be standardized.

11.3.4. THE FUTURE OF RODENT MODELS OF NEGATIVE INTERSUBJECTIVITY

When rodent intersubjective avoidance models become serviceable, multiple kinds of information will become instantly attainable that may facilitate treatments for antisocial behavior. As a few examples, the observing-is-feeling and mirror-neuron hypotheses of negative intersubjectivity can finally be proved or disproved by recording from single cells or populations of cells while rodents are avoiding other animals' distress. The hypothesis that oxytocin is involved in intersubjective avoidance can finally be tested rigorously using causal manipulations of specific populations or types of oxytocin cells. The pharmacological basis of negative intersubjectivity can be characterized to help identify potential pharmaceutical treatments for antisocial behavior in humans. High- or low-intersubjectivity rat lines can be bred to provide insight into what types of traits or biological markers tend to correlate with high or low intersubjective avoidance, and to help identify candidate genes responsible for prosocial or antisocial behavior in humans. More nuanced questions can also be addressed, such as whether the anatomical connections to putative mirror neurons help clarify why pain to oneself still feels subjectively different than observing pain in another, even if both pain experiences activate some of the same neurons. And, of course, new models of negative intersubjectivity can be developed and refined. The past decade of neuroscience has yielded more information than we imagined possible, and, similarly, the next decade of neuroscience has the potential to use rodent models to understand violence aversion in creative and insightful ways that far surpass what is described here. Very little—if any—of this progress will be achieved if antisocial behavior is only studied in humans.

This chapter has focused on how rodent research can inform our understanding of violence aversion. Will rodent research tell us anything about other types of moral action? As I final thought, I'd like to propose that *we should find out* (and I suspect the answer will be yes). There are two main mechanisms by which rodent negative inter-subjectivity research is likely to influence human morality research: (1) by providing an increasingly sophisticated knowledge base to operationalize biologically based definitions and questions about moral judgment and moral action in general, and (2) by motivating very specific, testable hypotheses about what causes and influences judgments and behaviors that we believe have moral relevance. In particular, rodent research will be helpful both for delineating the different computations that contribute to moral judgments and for understanding subconscious forces that influence our moral behaviors. Such empirical observations may then, in turn, influence theoretical accounts of morality by providing opportunities to better define terms like "emotion" and "reason," and by providing more clarity to what "causes" us to commit to a moral judgment or perform a moral action. Of course, it is likely that some aspects of human morality cannot be studied in other species. However, it will be just as useful to determine what aspects of human behavior are unique to humans as it will be to determine what aspects of human behavior are shared with other species. In fact, such comparisons may be instrumental for understanding what makes humans feel something is "moral" in the first place.

To be clear, not all aspects of morality can be understood with empirical research, and rodent research cannot answer all empirical questions about morality. We should not perform all future morally relevant research in rodents. Rather, just like most other fields of biomedical research, rodent research and human research should be pursued in parallel with a commitment to compare and combine relevant findings. Rodent models should be used to generate hypotheses about moral action or judgment, and human studies should be used to test these hypotheses in verifiably moral situations (or vice versa). The results of these tests will then be used to refine and revise hypotheses in rodents (or humans), and the cycle will begin again. This approach has helped us make great advances in our understanding and treatment of phenomena as complex as addiction (Gardner 2010), and it may do the same for morality research. Most importantly, if the moral decision-making field commits to taking a multispecies, mechanism-grounded strategy to understanding moral action, we may dramatically improve human lives by reducing violence and increasing prosocial behavior. This, I believe, is the next frontier of morality research.

Our evolved reverence for the sanctity of life makes random violence and cruelty one of the most devastating of our strange behaviors, and one that seems like it will never be explainable. Caleb Mallery, a victim of violence in 1780, is reported to have cried out to his murderer in between blows, "Tell me what you do it for!" (Lepore 2009). While the past decade has done much to advance our understanding of moral judgment, the next frontier is to find an answer to Caleb's question. We must learn how to explain immoral action.

References

Allen, N. J., and B. A. Barres. 2009. "Neuroscience: Glia—More Than Just Brain Glue." *Nature* 457, no. 7230: 675–677.

Aniskiewicz, A. S. 1979. "Autonomic Components of Vicarious Conditioning and Psychopathy." *Journal of Clinical Psychology* 35, no. 1: 60–67.

Atsak, P., et al. 2011. "Experience Modulates Vicarious Freezing in Rats: A Model for Empathy." *PLoS One* 6, no. 7: e21855.

Azevedo, R. T., et al. 2013. "Their Pain Is Not Our Pain: Brain and Autonomic Correlates of Empathic Resonance with the Pain of Same and Different Race Individuals." *Human Brain Mapping* 34, no. 12: 3168–3181.

Baird, A. D., I. E. Scheffer, and S. J. Wilson. 2011. "Mirror Neuron System Involvement in Empathy: A Critical Look at the Evidence." *Social Neuroscience* 6, no. 4: 327–335.

Barraza, J. A., and P. J. Zak. 2009. "Empathy toward Strangers Triggers Oxytocin Release and Subsequent Generosity." *Annals of the New York Academy of Sciences* 1167, no. 1: 182–189.

Bartal, I. B. A., J. Decety, and P. Mason. 2011. "Empathy and Pro-social Behavior in Rats." *Science* 334, no. 6061: 1427–1430.

Bartz, J. A., et al. 2010. "Oxytocin Selectively Improves Empathic Accuracy." *Psychological Science* 21, no. 10: 1426–1428.

Bartz, J. A., et al. 2011. "Social Effects of Oxytocin in Humans: Context and Person Matter." *Trends in Cognitive Sciences* 15, no. 7: 301–309.

Batson, C. D., N. Ahmad, and D. A. Lishner. 2011. "Empathy and Altruism." In *The Oxford Handbook of Positive Psychology*, edited by Shane J. Lopez and C. R. Snyder, 417–426. New York: Oxford University Press.

Batson, C. D., J. Fultz, and P. A. Schoenrade. 1987. "Distress and Empathy: Two Qualitatively Distinct Vicarious Emotions with Different Motivational Consequences." *Journal of Personality* 55, no. 1: 19–39.

Batson, C. D., and K. C. Oleson. 1991. "Current Status of the Empathy-Altruism Hypothesis." In *Prosocial behavior: Review of Personality and Social Psychology*, edited by M. S. Clark, 62–85. Newbury Park, CA: Sage.

Batson, C. D., and L. L. Shaw. 1991. "Evidence for Altruism: Toward a Pluralism of Prosocial Motives." *Psychological Inquiry* 2, no. 2: 107–122.

Beck, J. C. 2010. "Dangerous Severe Personality Disorder: The Controversy Continues." *Behavioral Sciences and the Law* 28, no. 2: 277–288.

Bernhardt, B. C., and T. Singer. 2012. "The Neural Basis of Empathy." *Annual Review of Neuroscience* 35: 1–23.

Björkqvist, K., K. Österman, and A. Kaukiainen. 2000. "Social Intelligence – Empathy = Aggression?" *Aggression and Violent Behavior* 5, no. 2: 191–200.

Blair, J., et al. 1997. "The Psychopathic Individual: A Lack of Responsiveness to Distress Cues?" *Psychophysiology* 34, no. 2: 192–198.

Blasi, A. 1980. "Bridging Moral Cognition and Moral Action: A Critical Review of the Literature." *Psychological Bulletin* 88, no. 1: 1–45.

Blasi, A. 1983. "Moral Cognition and Moral Action: A Theoretical Perspective." *Developmental Review* 3, no. 2: 178–210.

Bredy, T. W., and M. Barad. 2009. "Social Modulation of Associative Fear Learning by Pheromone Communication." *Learning and Memory* 16, no. 1: 12–18.

Bruchey, A. K., C. E. Jones, and M. H. Monfils. 2010. "Fear Conditioning by Proxy: Social Transmission of Fear during Memory Retrieval." *Behavioural Brain Research* 214, no. 1: 80–84.

Bruneau, E. G., A. Pluta, and R. Saxe. 2012. "Distinct Roles of the 'Shared Pain' and 'Theory of Mind' networks in Processing Others' Emotional Suffering." *Neuropsychologia* 50, no. 2: 219–231.

Chartrand, T. L., and J. A. Bargh. 1999. "The Chameleon Effect: The Perception-Behavior Link and Social Interaction." *Journal of Personality and Social Psychology* 76, no. 6: 893–910.

Chen, Q., J. B. Panksepp, and G. P. Lahvis. 2009. "Empathy Is Moderated by Genetic Background in Mice." *PLoS One* 4, no. 2: e4387.

Church, R. M. 1959. "Emotional Reactions of Rats to the Pain of Others." *Journal of Comparative and Physiological Psychology* 52, no. 2: 132–134.

Churchland, P. S., and P. Winkielman. 2012. "Modulating Social Behavior with Oxytocin: How Does It Work? What Does It Mean?" *Hormones and Behavior* 61, no. 3: 392–399.

Corradi-Dell'Acqua, C., C. Hofstetter, and P. Vuilleumier. 2011. "Felt and Seen Pain Evoke the Same Local Patterns of Cortical Activity in Insular and Cingulate Cortex." *Journal of Neuroscience* 31, no. 49: 17996–18006.

Cui, R., et al. 2008. "The Effects of Atropine on Changes in the Sleep Patterns Induced by Psychological Stress in Rats." *European Journal of Pharmacology* 579, no. 31–3: 153–159.

Darwall, S. 1998. "Empathy, Sympathy, Care." *Philosophical Studies* 89, no. 32: 261–282.

Davis, M. 1980. "A Multidimensional Approach to Individual Differences in Empathy." In *JSAS Catalog of Selected Documents in Psychology*. Washington, DC: American Psychological Association.

De Dreu, C. K. 2012. "Oxytocin Modulates Cooperation within and Competition between Groups: An Integrative Review and Research Agenda." *Hormones and Behavior* 61, no. 3: 419–428.

de Vignemont, F., and T. Singer. 2006. "The Empathic Brain: How, When and Why?" *Trends in Cognitive Sciences* 10, no. 10: 435–441.

de Waal, F. B. 2008. "Putting the Altruism Back into Altruism: The Evolution of Empathy." *Annual Review of Psychology* 59, no. 1: 279–300.

de Waal, F. B. 2009. *The Age of Empathy*. New York: Harmony.

de Waal, F. B. 2012. "Research Chimpanzees May Get a Break." *PLoS Biology* 10, no. 3: e1001291.

Decety, J. 2011. "Dissecting the Neural Mechanisms Mediating Empathy." *Emotion Review* 3, no. 1: 92–108.

Decety, J., and C. Lamm. 2006. "Human Empathy through the Lens of Social Neuroscience." *Scientific World Journal* 6: 1146–1163.

Dimberg, U., P. Andréasson, and M. Thunberg. 2011. "Emotional Empathy and Facial Reactions to Facial Expressions." *Journal of Psychophysiology* 25, no. 1: 26–31.

Eastman, N. 1999. "Who Should Take Responsibility for Antisocial Personality Disorder? Fallon Suggests Emphasising Custody, but Psychiatrists' Future Role Remains Unclear." *BMJ: British Medical Journal* 318, no. 7178: 206–207.

Eilam, D. 2005. "Die Hard: A Blend of Freezing and Fleeing as a Dynamic Defense: Implications for the Control of Defensive Behavior." *Neuroscience and Biobehavioral Reviews* 29, no. 8: 1181–1191.

Eisenberg, N. 1986. *Altruistic Emotion, Cognition, and Behavior.* Hillsdale, NJ: Erlbaum.

Eisenberg, N. 2008. "Empathy-Related Responding and Prosocial Behaviour." In *Empathy and Fairness*, edited by Greg Bock and Jamie Goode, 71–88. Chichester: John Wiley & Sons.

Eisenberg, N., N. D. Eggum, and L. Di Giunta. 2010. "Empathy-Related Responding: Associations with Prosocial Behavior, Aggression, and Intergroup Relations." *Social Issues and Policy Review* 4, no. 1: 143–180.

Eisenberg, N., and R. Fabes. 1990. "Empathy: Conceptualization, Measurement, and Relation to Prosocial Behavior." *Motivation and Emotion* 14, no. 2: 131–149.

Eisenberg, N., and P. A. Miller. 1987. "The Relation of Empathy to Prosocial and Related Behaviors." *Psychological Bulletin* 101, no. 1: 91–119.

Eisenberg, N., and J. Strayer. 1987. "Critical Issues in the Study of Empathy." In *Empathy and Its Development*, edited by N. Eisenberg and J. Strayer, 3–13. New York: Cambridge University Press.

Essau, C. A., S. Sasagawa, and P. J. Frick. 2006. "Callous-Unemotional Traits in a Community Sample of Adolescents." *Assessment* 13, no. 4: 454–469.

Evans, V. E., and W. G. Braud. 1969. "Avoidance of a Distressed Conspecific." *Psychonomic Science* 15, no. 3: 166.

Fan, Y., et al. 2011. "Is There a Core Neural Network in Empathy? An fMRI Based Quantitative Meta-analysis." *Neuroscience and Biobehavioral Reviews* 35, no. 3: 903–911.

Fanselow, M. 1994. "Neural Organization of the Defensive Behavior System Responsible for Fear." *Psychonomic Bulletin and Review* 1, no. 4: 429–438.

Farrington, D., Ohlin, L., and Wilson, J. Q. 1986. *Understanding and Controlling Crime.* New York: Springer-Verlag.

Fenno, L., O. Yizhar, and K. Deisseroth. 2011. "The Development and Application of Optogenetics." *Annual Review of Neuroscience* 34, no. 1: 389–412.

Ferguson, C. J. 2010. "Genetic Contributions to Antisocial Personality and Behavior: A Meta-analytic Review from an Evolutionary Perspective." *Journal of Social Psychology* 150, no. 2: 160–180.

Feshbach, N. D. 1979. "Empathy Training: A Field Study in Affective Education." In *Aggression and Behavior Change: Biological and Social Processes*, edited by Seymour Feshbach and Adam Fraczek, 234–249. New York: Praeger.

Feshbach, N. D., and S. Feshbach. 1982. "Empathy Training and the Regulation of Aggression: Potentialities and Limitations." *Academic Psychology Bulletin* 4: 399–413.

Frick, P. J., and S. F. White. 2008. "Research Review: The Importance of Callous-Unemotional Traits for Developmental Models of Aggressive and Antisocial Behavior." *Journal of Child Psychology and Psychiatry* 49, no. 4: 359–375.

Gallese, V., et al. 2011. "Mirror Neuron Forum." *Perspectives on Psychological Science* 6, no. 4: 369–407.

Gardiner, S. 2008. "NYPD Inaction over a Missing Black Woman Found Dead Sparks a Historic Racial-Bias Lawsuit." *Village Voice*, May 6.

Gardner, E. L. 2010. "What We Have Learned about Addiction from Animal Models of Drug Self-Administration." *American Journal on Addictions* 9, no. 4: 285–313.

Gazzola, V., L. Aziz-Zadeh, and C. Keysers. 2006. "Empathy and the Somatotopic Auditory Mirror System in Humans." *Current Biology* 16, no. 18: 1824–1829.

Gibbon, S., et al. 2010. "Psychological Interventions for Antisocial Personality Disorder." *Cochrane Database of Systematic Reviews*, doi:10.1002/14651858.CD007668.pub2.

Ginsberg, A. 2006. "Killer's 'Fun' Day in Court." *New York Post*, November 21.

Greene, J. D., et al. 2001. "An fMRI Investigation of Emotional Engagement in Moral Judgment." *Science* 293, no. 5537: 2105–2108.

Gu, X., et al. 2010. "Functional Dissociation of the Frontoinsular and Anterior Cingulate Cortices in Empathy for Pain." *Journal of Neuroscience* 30, no. 10: 3739–3744.

Gu, X., et al. 2012. "Anterior Insular Cortex Is Necessary for Empathetic Pain Perception." *Brain* 135, no. 9: 2726–2735.

Gunter, T. D., M. G. Vaughn, and R. A. Philibert. 2010. "Behavioral Genetics in Antisocial Spectrum Disorders and Psychopathy: A Review of the Recent Literature." *Behavioral Sciences and the Law* 28, no. 2: 148–173.

Gutiérrez-García, A. G., and C. M. Contreras. 2009. "Stressors Can Affect Immobility Time and Response to Imipramine in the Rat Forced Swim Test." *Pharmacology Biochemistry and Behavior* 91, no. 4: 542–548.

Gutiérrez-García, A. G., et al. 2006. "A Single Session of Emotional Stress Produces Anxiety in Wistar Rats." *Behavioural Brain Research* 167, no. 1: 30–35.

Gutiérrez-García, A. G., et al. 2007. "Urine from Stressed Rats Increases Immobility in Receptor Rats Forced to Swim: Role of 2-Heptanone." *Physiology and Behavior* 91, no. 1: 166–172.

Guzman, Y. F., et al. 2009. "Social Modeling of Conditioned Fear in Mice by Non-fearful Conspecifics." *Behavioural Brain Research* 201, no. 1: 173–178.

Haidt, J. 2001. "The Emotional Dog and Its Rational Tail: A Social Intuitionist Approach to Moral Judgment." *Psychological Review* 108, no. 4: 814–834.

Haidt, J. 2004. "The Emotional Dog Gets Mistaken for a Possum." *Review of General Psychology* 8, no. 4: 283–290.

Hare, R. D. 1991. *The Hare Psychopathy Checklist—Revised (PCL-R)*. Toronto, ON: Multi-Health Systems.

Hare, R. D. 2003. *Manual for the Revised Hare Psychopathy Checklist*. 2nd ed. Toronto, ON: Multi-Health Systems.

Hawes, D. J., and M. R. Dadds. 2005. "The Treatment of Conduct Problems in Children with Callous-Unemotional Traits." *Journal of Consulting and Clinical Psychology* 73, no. 4: 737–741.

Hickok, G. 2009. "Eight Problems for the Mirror Neuron Theory of Action Understanding in Monkeys and Humans." *Journal of Cognitive Neuroscience* 21, no. 7: 1229–1243.

Hirosawa, T., et al. 2012. "Oxytocin Attenuates Feelings of Hostility Depending on Emotional Context and Individuals' Characteristics." *Scientific Reports* 2, doi: 10.1038/srep00384.

Hoffman, M. L. 2000. *Empathy and Moral Development: Implications for Caring and Justice.* Cambridge: Cambridge University Press.

Hoffman, M. L. 2008. "Empathy and Prosocial Behavior." *Handbook of Emotions*, edited by Michael Lewis, Jeannette M. Haviland-Jones, and Lisa Feldman Barrett, 440–455. 3rd ed. New York: Guilford Press.

Hogan, R. 1969. "Development of an Empathy Scale." *Journal of Consulting and Clinical Psychology* 33, no. 3: 307–316.

Homberg, J. R. 2013. "Measuring Behaviour in Rodents: Towards Translational Neuropsychiatric Research." *Behavioural Brain Research* 236, no. 1: 295–306.

House, T. H., and W. L. Milligan. 1976. "Autonomic Responses to Modeled Distress in Prison Psychopaths." *Journal of Personality and Social Psychology* 34, no. 4: 556–560.

Howells, K., and A. Day. 2007. "Readiness for Treatment in High Risk Offenders with Personality Disorders." *Psychology, Crime and Law* 13, no. 1: 47–56.

Huffmeijer, R., et al. 2012. "Asymmetric Frontal Brain Activity and Parental Rejection Predict Altruistic Behavior: Moderation of Oxytocin Effects." *Cognitive, Affective, and Behavioral Neuroscience* 12, no. 2: 382–392.

Hurlemann, R., et al. 2010. "Oxytocin Enhances Amygdala-Dependent, Socially Reinforced Learning and Emotional Empathy in Humans." *Journal of Neuroscience* 30, no. 14: 4999–5007.

Iacoboni, M. 2009. "Imitation, Empathy, and Mirror Neurons." *Annual Review of Psychology* 60: 653–670.

Insel, T. R. 2010. "The Challenge of Translation in Social Neuroscience: A Review of Oxytocin, Vasopressin, and Affiliative Behavior." *Neuron* 65, no. 6: 768–779.

Jabbi, M., J. Bastiaansen, and C. Keysers. 2008. "A Common Anterior Insula Representation of Disgust Observation, Experience and Imagination Shows Divergent Functional Connectivity Pathways." *PLoS One* 3, no. 8: e2939.

Jeon, D., et al. 2010. "Observational Fear Learning Involves Affective Pain System and Cav1.2 Ca2+ Channels in Acc." *Nature Neuroscience* 13, no. 4: 482–488.

Jolliffe, D., and D. P. Farrington. 2004. "Empathy and Offending: A Systematic Review and Meta-analysis." *Aggression and Violent Behavior* 9, no. 5: 441–476.

Jolliffe, D., and J. Murray. 2012. "Lack of Empathy and Offending." In *The Future of Criminology*, edited by R. Loeber and B. C. Welsh, 62–69. New York: Oxford University Press.

Kahn, R. E., A. L. Byrd, and D. A. Pardini. 2012. "Callous-Unemotional Traits Robustly Predict Future Criminal Offending in Young Men." *Law and Human Behavior*, advance online publication.

Kaplan, J. T., and M. Iacoboni. 2006. "Getting a Grip on Other Minds: Mirror Neurons, Intention Understanding, and Cognitive Empathy." *Social Neuroscience* 1, nos. 3–4: 175–183.

Katz, N. L. 2006. "Attorney Knifed as Suspects Bring Bloody Mayhem to Brooklyn Murder Trial." *New York Daily News*, January 20.

Kensinger, E. A. 2004. "Remembering Emotional Experiences: The Contribution of Valence and Arousal." *Reviews in the Neurosciences* 15, no. 4: 241–252.

Khalifa, N., et al. 2010. "Pharmacological Interventions for Antisocial Personality Disorder." *Cochrane Database of Systematic Reviews*, doi:10.1002/14651858.CD007667.pub2.

Kim, E. J., et al. 2010. "Social Transmission of Fear in Rats: The Role of 22-kHz Ultrasonic Distress Vocalization." *PLoS One* 5, no. 12: e15077.

Kimonis, E. R., et al. 2008. "Assessing Callous-Unemotional Traits in Adolescent Offenders: Validation of the Inventory of Callous-Unemotional Traits." *International Journal of Law and Psychiatry* 31, no. 3: 241–252.

Kiyokawa, Y., et al. 2009. "Main Olfactory System Mediates Social Buffering of Conditioned Fear Responses in Male Rats." *European Journal of Neuroscience* 29, no. 4: 777–785.

Knapska, E., et al. 2006. "Between-Subject Transfer of Emotional Information Evokes Specific Pattern of Amygdala Activation." *Proceedings of the National Academy of Sciences* 103, no. 10: 3858–3862.

Kuzmin, A., et al. 1996. "Enhancement of Morphine Self-Administration in Drug Naive, Inbred Strains of Mice by Acute Emotional Stress." *European Neuropsychopharmacology* 6, no. 1: 63–68.

Lamm, C., C. D. Batson, and J. Decety. 2007. "The Neural Substrate of Human Empathy: Effects of Perspective-Taking and Cognitive Appraisal." *Journal of Cognitive Neuroscience* 19, no. 1: 42–58.

Langford, D. J., et al. 2006. "Social Modulation of Pain as Evidence for Empathy in Mice." *Science* 312, no. 5782: 1967–1970.

Langford, D. J., et al. 2011. "Varying Perceived Social Threat Modulates Pain Behavior in Male Mice." *Journal of Pain* 12, no. 1: 125–132.

Lavery, J. J., and P. J. Foley. 1963. "Altruism or Arousal in the Rat?" *Science* 140, no. 3563: 172–173.

Lepore, J. 2009. "Rap Sheet: Why Is American History So Murderous?" *New Yorker*, November 9.

LeSure-Lester, G. E. 2000. "Relation between Empathy and Aggression and Behavior Compliance among Abused Group Home Youth." *Child Psychiatry and Human Development* 31, no. 2: 153–161.

Loup, F., et al. 1991. "Localization of High-Affinity Binding Sites for Oxytocin and Vasopressin in the Human Brain: An Autoradiographic Study." *Brain Research* 555, no. 2: 220–232.

Lovett, B. J., and R. A. Sheffield. 2007. "Affective Empathy Deficits in Aggressive Children and Adolescents: A Critical Review." *Clinical Psychology Review* 27, no. 1: 1–13.

Lucke, J. F., and C. D. Baton. 1980. "Response Suppression to a Distressed Conspecific: Are Laboratory Rats Altruistic?" *Journal of Experimental Social Psychology* 16, no. 3: 214–227.

Luo, L., E. M. Callaway, and K. Svoboda. 2008. "Genetic Dissection of Neural Circuits." *Neuron* 57, no. 5: 634–660.

McKaughan, D. 2012. "Voles, Vasopressin, and Infidelity: A Molecular Basis for Monogamy, a Platform for Ethics, and More?" *Biology and Philosophy* 27, no. 4: 521–543.

Meyer, M. L., et al. 2013. "Empathy for the Social Suffering of Friends and Strangers Recruits Distinct Patterns of Brain Activation." *Social Cognitive and Affective Neuroscience* 8, no. 4: 446–454.

Miller, P. A., et al. 1996. "Relations of Moral Reasoning and Vicarious Emotion to Young Children's Prosocial Behavior toward Peers and Adults." *Developmental Psychology* 32, no. 2: 210.

Moffitt, T. E. 1993. "Adolescence-Limited and Life-Course-Persistent Antisocial Behavior: A Developmental Taxonomy." *Psychological Review* 100, no. 4: 674–701.

Nicolelis, M. A. 2012. "Mind in Motion." *Scientific American* 307, no. 3: 58–63.

Osganian, A. L. 2008. "Limitations on Biomedical and Behavioral Research Involving Prisoners: An Argument Supporting the Institute of Medicine's Recommendations to Revise Regulations." *New England Journal on Criminal and Civil Confinement* 34: 429.

Pfaff, D., et al. 2008. "Concepts and Mechanisms of Generalized Central Nervous System Arousal." *Annals of the New York Academy of Sciences* 1129, no. 1: 11–25.

Pickersgill, M. 2011. "'Promising' Therapies: Neuroscience, Clinical Practice, and the Treatment of Psychopathy." *Sociology of Health and Illness* 33, no. 3: 448–464.

Pijlman, F. T. A., G. Wolterink, and J. M. Van Ree. 2003. "Physical and Emotional Stress Have Differential Effects on Preference for Saccharine and Open Field Behaviour in Rats." *Behavioural Brain Research* 139, nos. 1–2: 131–138.

Preobrazhenskaya, L. A., and P. V. Simonov. 1970. "Conditioned Avoidance Responses to Nociceptive Stimulation of Another Individual." *Neuroscience and Behavioral Physiology* 4, no. 4: 15–20.

Pustilnik, A. C. 2009. "Violence on the Brain: A Critique of Neuroscience in Criminal Law." *Wake Forest Law Review* 44: 183–238.

Radke, S., and E. R. De Bruijn. 2012. "The Other Side of the Coin: Oxytocin Decreases the Adherence to Fairness Norms." *Frontiers in Human Neuroscience* 6: Article 193.

Ramsey, N. F., and J. M. Van Ree. 1993. "Emotional but Not Physical Stress Enhances Intravenous Cocaine Self-Administration in Drug-Naive Rats." *Brain Research* 608, no. 2: 216–222.

Rice, G., and P. Gainer. 1962. "'Altruism' in the Albino Rat." *Journal of Comparative and Physiological Psychology* 55: 123–125.

Riem, M. M. E., et al. 2011. "Oxytocin Modulates Amygdala, Insula, and Inferior Frontal Gyrus Responses to Infant Crying: A Randomized Controlled Trial." *Biological Psychiatry* 70, no. 3: 291–297.

Riem, M. M. E., et al. 2013. "Does Intranasal Oxytocin Promote Prosocial Behavior to an Excluded Fellow Player? A Randomized-Controlled Trial with Cyberball." *Psychoneuroendocrinology* 38, no. 8: 1418–1425.

Rizzolatti, G., and L. Craighero. 2004. "The Mirror-Neuron System." *Annual Review of Neuroscience* 27, no. 1: 169–192.

Rodrigues, S. M., et al. 2009. "Oxytocin Receptor Genetic Variation Relates to Empathy and Stress Reactivity in Humans." *Proceedings of the National Academy of Sciences* 106, no. 50: 21437–21441.

Rottman, S. J., and C. T. Snowdon. 1972. "Demonstration and Analysis of an Alarm Pheromone in Mice." *Journal of Comparative and Physiological Psychology* 81, no. 3: 483–490.

Salekin, R. T., C. Worley, and R. D. Grimes. 2010. "Treatment of Psychopathy: A Review and Brief Introduction to the Mental Model Approach for Psychopathy." *Behavioral Sciences and the Law* 28, no. 2: 235–266.

Schaich Borg, J., et al. 2006. "Consequences, Action, and Intention as Factors in Moral Judgments: An fMRI Investigation." *Journal of Cognitive Neuroscience* 18, no. 25: 803–817.

Schulz, K., et al. 2012. "Simultaneous BOLD fMRI and Fiber-Optic Calcium Recording in Rat Neocortex." *Nature Methods* 9, no. 6: 597–602.

Sheng, F., et al. 2013. "Oxytocin Modulates the Racial Bias in Neural Responses to Others' Suffering." *Biological Psychology* 92, no. 2: 380–386.

Shirtcliff, E. A., et al. 2009. "Neurobiology of Empathy and Callousness: Implications for the Development of Antisocial Behavior." *Behavioral Sciences and the Law* 27, no. 2: 137–171.

Singer, T., et al. 2008. "Effects of Oxytocin and Prosocial Behavior On Brain Responses to Direct and Vicariously Experienced Pain." *Emotion* 8, no. 6: 781–91.

Sonnby-Borgström, M. 2002. "Automatic Mimicry Reactions as Related to Differences in Emotional Empathy." *Scandinavian Journal of Psychology* 43, no. 5: 433–443.

Sonnby-Borgstrom, M., P. Jönsson, and O. Svensson. 2008. "Gender Differences in Facial Imitation and Verbally Reported Emotional Contagion from Spontaneous to Emotionally Regulated Processing Levels." *Scandinavian Journal of Psychology* 49, no. 2: 111–122.

Špinka, M. 2012. "Social Dimension of Emotions and Its Implication for Animal Welfare." *Applied Animal Behaviour Science* 138, nos. 3–4: 170–181.

Spunt, R. P., and M. D. Lieberman. 2012. "An Integrative Model of the Neural Systems Supporting the Comprehension of Observed Emotional Behavior." *NeuroImage* 59, no. 3: 3050–3059.

Striepens, N., et al. 2012. "Oxytocin Facilitates Protective Responses to Aversive Social Stimuli in Males." *Proceedings of the National Academy of Sciences* 109, no. 44: 18144–18149.

Suran, M., and H. Wolinsky. 2009. *The End of Monkey Research? New Legislation and Public Pressure Could Jeopardize Research with Primates in Both Europe and the USA.*" EMBO reports, 10, no. 10: 1080.

Taylor, C. 2011. "Nothing Left to Lose? Freedom and Compulsion in the Treatment of Dangerous Offenders." *Psychodynamic Practice* 17, no. 3: 291–306.

Thorsten, O. Z., and K. Christian. 2011. "Towards Passive Brain-Computer Interfaces: Applying Brain-Computer Interface Technology to Human-Machine Systems in General." *Journal of Neural Engineering* 8, no. 2: 025005.

Tost, H., et al. 2010. "A Common Allele in the Oxytocin Receptor Gene (Oxtr) Impacts Prosocial Temperament and Human Hypothalamic-Limbic Structure and Function." *Proceedings of the National Academy of Sciences* 107, no. 31: 13936–13941.

Tribollet, E., et al. 1992. "Oxytocin Receptors in the Central Nervous System." *Annals of the New York Academy of Sciences* 652, no. 1: 29–38.

Trommsdorff, G., W. Friedlmeier, and B. Mayer. 2007. "Sympathy, Distress, and Prosocial Behavior of Preschool Children in Four Cultures." *International Journal of Behavioral Development* 31, no. 3: 284–293.

Vaughn, M. G., and M. DeLisi. 2008. "Were Wolfgang's Chronic Offenders Psychopaths? On the Convergent Validity between Psychopathy and Career Criminality." *Journal of Criminal Justice* 36, no. 1: 33–42.

Vaughn, M. G., et al. 2011. "The Severe 5%: A Latent Class Analysis of the Externalizing Behavior Spectrum in the United States." *Journal of Criminal Justice* 39, no. 1: 75–80.

Veinante, P., and M. J. Freund-Mercier. 1998. "Distribution of Oxytocin and Vasopressin Binding Sites in the Rat Extended Amygdala: A Histoautoradiographic Study." *Journal of Comparative Neurology* 383, no. 3: 305–325.

Walsh, Z., and D. S. Kosson. 2008. "Psychopathy and Violence: The Importance of Factor Level Interactions." *Psychological Assessment* 20, no. 2: 114–120.

Walter, H. 2012. "Social Cognitive Neuroscience of Empathy: Concepts, Circuits, and Genes." *Emotion Review* 4, no. 1: 9–17.

Ward, T., and G. Willis. 2010. "Ethical Issues in Forensic and Correctional Research." *Aggression and Violent Behavior* 15, no. 6: 399–409.

Wellman, H. M. 2010. "Developing a Theory of Mind." In *The Wiley-Blackwell Handbook of Childhood Cognitive Development*, edited by Usha Goswami, 258–284. 2nd ed. Malden, MA: Wiley-Blackwell.

Wetzel, W., and P. V. Simonov. 1978. "Avoidance Reaction to Painful Stimulation of Another Rat: Effect of Methylglucamine Orotate." *Pharmacology Biochemistry and Behavior* 9, no. 4: 401–404.

Wicker, B., et al. 2003. "Both of Us Disgusted in My Insula: The Common Neural Basis of Seeing and Feeling Disgust." *Neuron* 40, no. 3: 655–664.

Wispé, L. 1986. "The Distinction between Sympathy and Empathy: To Call Forth a Concept, a Word Is Needed." *Journal of Personality and Social Psychology* 50, no. 2: 314–321.

Witten, I. B., et al. 2010. "Cholinergic Interneurons Control Local Circuit Activity and Cocaine Conditioning." *Science Signalling* 330, no. 6011: 1677.

Wu, N., Z. Li, and Y. Su. 2012. "The Association between Oxytocin Receptor Gene Polymorphism (Oxtr) and Trait Empathy." *Journal of Affective Disorders* 138, no. 3: 468–472.

Yamasue, H., et al. 2012. "Integrative Approaches Utilizing Oxytocin to Enhance Prosocial Behavior: From Animal and Human Social Behavior to Autistic Social Dysfunction." *Journal of Neuroscience* 32, no. 41: 14109–14117.

Zak, P. J., A. A. Stanton, and S. Ahmadi. 2007. "Oxytocin Increases Generosity in Humans." *PLoS One* 2, no. 11: e1128.

Zalaquett, C., and D. Thiessen. 1991. "The Effects of Odors from Stressed Mice on Conspecific Behavior." *Physiology and Behavior* 50, no. 1: 221–227.

Zhong, S., et al. 2012. "U-Shaped Relation between Plasma Oxytocin Levels and Behavior in the Trust Game." *PLoS One* 7, no. 12: e51095.

IV

Philosophical Lessons

12

Is, Ought, and the Brain

Guy Kahane

12.1. Introduction: Between Two Extremes

This chapter is about the relation between normative ethics and the psychology and neuroscience of morality. In one direction, the relation is fairly straightforward. Ethics tries to answer normative questions about what is morally right and wrong. The psychology and neuroscience of morality try to answer empirical questions about the psychological and neural processes that take place *when* we try to answer questions of the first kind. This is why concepts, examples, and thought experiments that are central to normative inquiry within ethics also turn out to be of interest to empirical inquiry: if moral philosophers distinguish between utilitarian and deontological approaches to morality, or between doing and allowing, or intending and foreseeing, then cognitive scientists can in turn study what, at the psychological level, underlies such distinctions.

Things get far more controversial, however, when we consider the relation in the other direction—when we ask whether there are ways of getting from

empirical evidence about the psychological and neural processes that underlie moral judgment, emotion and behavior,

to

normative conclusions about what's right and wrong—about what we morally ought to do.

Views on this issue tend to cluster around two extremes. On one side, many scientists and some philosophers find it simply obvious that evidence from the psychology and neuroscience of morality has radical normative implications.[1] At the farthest extreme, we even find the view that traditional ethical inquiry, pursued in the armchair, is an antiquated and confused practice, and that ethics should be entirely assimilated into science. Something like this view was famously proposed by E. O. Wilson, who once wrote,

> The hypothalamus and limbic system ... flood our consciousness with all the emotions—hate, love, guilt, fear, and others—that are consulted by ethical philosophers who wish to intuit the standards of good and evil. What, we are then compelled to ask, made the hypothalamus and the limbic system? They evolved by natural selection. That simple biological statement must be pursued to *explain ethics*.[2]

Contemporary authors rarely put things so bluntly, but recent literature offers numerous attempts to challenge the philosopher's armchair, and to infer dramatic normative conclusions from various empirical findings—some authors, for example, argue that evidence from recent cognitive science lends powerful new support to utilitarianism—though others think that such evidence supports exactly the opposite conclusion.[3]

On the other side, we find the opposing view, held by many moral philosophers, that such inferences invariably involve confusion or error. What we learn about the psychology and neuroscience of morality may be a fascinating, but it has no normative significance. It is simply irrelevant to the inherently a priori business of trying to figure out what we ought to do. If an argument seems to lead us from scientific findings about moral psychology to some interesting normative conclusion, this is usually because the argument already implicitly presupposes the ethical view it was claimed to support.[4] (Some philosophers actually seem to view the intrusion of empirical methods into ethics as a kind of repugnant purity violation . . .)

Faced with this opposition, it is natural to reply that the answer must lie somewhere in the middle, that it must be possible for the cognitive science of ethics to somehow inform substantive ethical reflection without at the same time undermining ethics as a distinctive, nonempirical source of guidance.

But to say that the answer must lie somewhere in the middle is to say little. We need to trace concrete ways of validly getting from psychological premises to normative conclusions. In this chapter, I will present several valid arguments of this form—and this is by no means meant to be an exhaustive list.[5]

There *are* ways of getting from empirical evidence to normative conclusions, and more than one. But as we shall see, each of the arguments we will consider also requires some nontrivial (and often controversial) further premises to go through. For example, some of these premises involve demanding metaethical commitments—in fact we shall see that different metaethical starting points can lead to very different normative implications.[6] Moreover, we shall see that some of these arguments require empirical evidence of a sort that we do not currently possess. One of the lessons of this chapter will actually be that if we want to draw normative implications from cognitive science, we may need to pursue new directions of empirical inquiry.

Although in what follows I will make use of various examples drawn from current research, my main aim isn't to criticize (or support) any particular empirical claim, or even any specific normative argument. My aim is rather to clarify the structure of such arguments, to identify the kind of premises that *would* be needed if we are to arrive at any interesting normative conclusions. I have to admit, however, that I myself doubt that current scientific research actually supports any very significant normative conclusions.

This chapter has a further lesson: the flashiest forms of neuroscience actually turn out to have, at best, little normative significance. It turns out that more traditional, pedestrian psychological methods, of the kind that receives less attention, are of far greater interest to ethics.[7]

12.2. Hume's Law and the Naturalistic Fallacy

When people debate the normative significance of cognitive science, they almost invariably assume that the primary obstacles here are David Hume's famous dictum that we can't infer an "ought" from an "is," and G. E. Moore's (misleadingly named) naturalistic fallacy. Moral philosophers who want protection from science often find comfort in Hume and Moore. Scientists who want to draw dramatic ethical conclusions feel that they must first launch an assault on Hume and Moore, often with endearingly clumsy results (see, e.g., Harris 2011; Churchland 2012).

This isn't a helpful starting point. It obscures what is really at issue—and not only because Hume and Moore are often misunderstood, even at a basic level.

Let's start with some common misconceptions. I do not have space to present the views of Hume and Moore in any detail, nor is that necessary for our purposes. Stated very briefly and schematically, Hume argued that we can't validly infer an "ought" from an "is"—a normative statement from purely descriptive ones (Hume [1739] 1975; see also Hudson 1972; Schurz 1997). Moore argued that goodness is a simple, unanalyzable property—that goodness cannot be identified with any natural (or for that matter supernatural) set of facts (Moore [1903] 1983; see also Frankena 1939; Baldwin 1992). And some think that Moore's argument can extend beyond goodness to other normative notions, such as moral wrongness.

It is easy to misunderstand what follows from these two metaethical claims. Consider, for example, Ralph Waldo Emerson's proto-Nietzschean principle that "the only right is what is after my constitution, the only wrong what is against it" ([1841] 1994) or the common view that we ought to do what is natural. It is often assumed that these views are conclusively refuted by Hume's law, or the naturalistic fallacy.

But that's simply false. These views about the moral significance of the natural are *substantive* claims about what's right and wrong. They needn't violate Hume's law, since they needn't be based on any kind of inference—they could be claimed to be self-evident truths. Nor must these views assert anything about the meaning or nature of right or wrong; they just ascribe moral rightness or wrongness to certain ways of acting. So they also needn't commit the naturalistic fallacy.

Of course once you accept the normative principle that we ought to do what is natural for humans, you can infer various ethical conclusions from empirical facts about what's natural. But neither Hume nor Moore has any problem with *that*: such inferences will always assume this general normative principle; they don't derive an ought from a bare is.

The real problem with this kind of normative appeal to nature has nothing to do with Hume or Moore. The real problem is that these are utterly implausible ethical views— views that don't survive ethical reflection, and, when they are taken literally, have absurd implications. War and pestilence and cruelty and deceit are all natural, but this hardly means that they are desirable or right.[8]

Now the view that we should follow nature does at least seem attractive to some people. It can have a strong intuitive appeal. But, *considered on their own*, unadorned facts about our brain don't even have a prima facie normative significance. There isn't even the appearance of plausibility to the claim that we ought to act in certain ways simply because, say, our amygdala is firing; no claim of this form is even remotely a candidate for being a self-evident truth. So the idea that we could just derive ethical conclusions from neural premises alone is hopeless *regardless* of our views about Hume's law or the naturalistic fallacy. We will anyway need some extra premises.

So we don't need Hume or Moore to see that there is a glaring gap in arguments of the form:

Empirical. Some bit of evidence about the psychology or neuroscience of ethics.

.

.

Therefore
Normative. We ought to X.[9]

But, contrary to a common assumption, that we need to add further premises is not a problem. The real question is whether we can identify premises that will take us from empirical claims to interesting moral conclusions without presupposing the result, or begging the question.

So what premises do we need to add? This depends on our answer to another question. In most domains, our psychology is a guide only to how we *think* about things, not to how things actually *are*. We don't think of our psychology as a useful guide to the weather, or the age of the universe, or mathematics (I'm not aware of any large volumes on the mathematical implications of the neuroscience of maths). Why, then, should our psychology (and neurobiology) be any kind of guide to what we ought to do?

This is the question we need to start with. We need to establish some appropriate relation between our psychology and the domain we want to use our psychology find out about—in our case, some appropriate relation between facts about our psychology and what we ought to do. If Moore is right, then this relation isn't simply that of identity,[10] and if Hume is right, it isn't simply one of entailment. But there are plenty of other ways in which empirical facts and normative claims might be related.

12.3. The Argument from Antirealism

Now such a relation would admittedly hold in the most direct way if what we ought to do really was ultimately reducible to facts about our psychology, or was at least grounded in such facts. The first type of argument I will examine assumes such a naturalist antirealist view of morality. The kind of antirealism that is most relevant here is subjectivist or response-dependent views that ground moral facts in subjective attitudes such as our desires and emotions.[11] These antirealist views do need to reject Moore's argument, or at least find some way around it, but the metaethical details about how exactly they might do so are actually not very important for our purposes.[12]

Once we adopt such an antirealist view, we can in principle infer normative conclusions from psychological facts.[13] In their simplest form, such inferences could go something like this:[14]

P1. Metaethical. *Simple subjectivism*: We ought to V iff we approve of Ving.
P2. Empirical. We approve Xing.

Therefore

C. Normative. We ought to X.

We do need to add an extra, metaethical premise, but as I said, this doesn't make such arguments less interesting. And notice that this is a positive argument: if sound, it can directly tell us what we ought to do, not just debunk some of our existing moral beliefs.[15]

If we are antirealists of this kind, then we can draw normative conclusions from facts about our psychology.[16] What is unclear, however, is whether cognitive science (let alone the cognitive science of ethics) has an interesting role to play in such inferences.

Now it's true that subjectivists (and their more sophisticated antirealist relatives) tie what we ought to do to *psychological* facts—to what, for example, we most deeply desire. But desires are best understood as dispositional states, manifested in complex patterns of behavior across a range of situations, both actual and counterfactual. It's unlikely that understanding the deep structure of our moral psychology, let alone its neurobiology, is a useful way to find out what people desire. If you want to find out what people really want, you should begin by looking at what they do and say.[17]

There is an even greater problem. Current cognitive science studies our *actual* moral psychology. But only the crudest and least plausible forms of antirealism ground what we ought to do in what we *actually* happen to desire or disapprove. Many antirealists ground what we ought to do in what we would desire or disapprove of in some ideal state, when, for example, we have full information, are fully rational and impartial, and so forth (see, e.g., Firth 1952; Johnston 1989). And it is only from these *ideal psychological facts* that we can infer, on these views, what we ought to do.

Now it's still a kind of empirical question what we would desire in these ideal conditions, a question that psychology can in principle try to answer. But it's very different from the questions psychologists actually try to answer, and it's actually far from obvious how to even go about answering it.

Setting this worry aside, let me just briefly touch on the question of what specific normative implications are likely to follow from the argument from antirealism. At least to the extent that such metaethical views tie what we ought to do to the core desires and sentiments we *actually* have, then the implications are likely to spell trouble for many utilitarian views. It would mean, for example, that if most people have a strong aversion to pushing the fat man in Footbridge and disapprove of this act, then we can simply conclude, from this psychological fact, that it's wrong to push the fat man. We could similarly justify a range of other nonutilitarian views: our special attachment to ourselves and to those dear or near to us, or our preference for humans over other animals, and so forth.[18]

We could also, in a similar way, try to derive normative conclusions that are both antiutilitarian and antiliberal from Haidt's moral foundations theory (see, e.g., Haidt 2007). If, for example, most or all of us are strongly disposed to care about purity or loyalty, then, on a metaethical view on which such subjective concerns ground what we ought to do, there is at least some moral reason to avoid acting in ways that violate purity or compromise loyalty, regardless of the consequences.[19] This much is straightforward. But again things are less clear if our antirealism is of the more idealized sort, tying what we ought to do to, for example, what our ideal self would want us to do.[20]

I won't say more about the argument from antirealism because I find its metaethical premise highly implausible, at best. So I want to turn next to a different way in which what we ought to do might be constrained by facts about us, a way that doesn't presuppose any controversial metaethical view.

12.4. The Argument from "Ought Implies Can"

I have in mind here the principle that ought implies can. Something like this principle is widely accepted within ethics, often even taken to be a conceptual truth.[21]

Kant was one of the first to make this principle explicit, but Kant took it *literally*: he argued that from that fact that we *ought* to do certain things, even that we ought to do *anything at all*, we can infer facts about what we *can* do, and thus draw radical conclusions about our psychology, and even about the world.[22] This is a way of inferring, not ought from is, but *is* from *ought*.

In contemporary ethics, the inference usually goes in the opposite direction. From the fact that we *can't* do something, we can infer that it's *not* true that we ought to do it—if you're unable to cure cancer right now, it can't be true that you have a moral obligation to cure cancer right now (see, e.g., Howard-Snyder 2006).

This form of argument also allows us to infer normative conclusions from empirical claims:

P1. Conceptual. Ought implies can.[23]

P2. Empirical. We can't *X*.

Therefore

C. Normative. It's not true we ought to *X*.

This is a more limited form of argument, since its conclusions are purely negative. This form of argument can't tell us what our obligations are, only what obligations we don't have.

So while this principle can demarcate the space of possible human moralities, it still leaves open a vast space of possible things we *might* ought to do. So it's only really useful if we also have some other, positive way of finding out what we should do.

Still, some philosophers think that this principle can do a lot of work. James Griffin, for example, thinks that "moral norms must be tailored to fit the human moral torso. . . . There are no moral norms outside the boundary set by our capacities" (1992, 131). And Owen Flanagan defends the following principle:

> *The Principle of Minimal Psychological Realism.* Make sure when constructing a moral theory or projecting a moral ideal that the character, decision processing, and behavior prescribed are possible, or are perceived to be possible, for creatures like us. (Flanagan 1993, 32)

And both Griffin and Flanagan think that once we pay attention to the psychological limits on what humans can be or do, then it turns out that act utilitarianism is one of the ethical views that aren't compatible with our psychology. That would be a pretty significant result.[24]

Now, this claim wouldn't make sense if we took the principle that "ought implies can" to only apply to what we can *physically do*—to what causal effects we can bring about in the world. That we are not omnipotent is of course not a threat to utilitarianism, which tells us to promote the good to the best of our ability. After all, we obviously can do something (in fact many things) to make the world at least a little better, impartially speaking. And at least some of us have the physical ability to push the fat man in Footbridge. In any event, if we wanted to find out what causal impact we can make on the world, our moral psychology won't be the best place to start. It would be wiser to focus instead on, say, the effectiveness of various charities.

So the idea must be that we need to apply "ought implies can," not only to what we can *physically do*, but also to what, for example, we can *believe* or be *motivated* by.[25] And the question now is what cognitive science can tell us about that.

This depends on what we mean by "can." If we understand it rather loosely, then it seems that there is no propositional content that we understand that it's simply impossible for us to believe, or be motivated by. This would include both the utilitarian principle, as well as many far crazier ethical views. On the other hand, if we understand "can" too strongly, then, if psychological determinism is true, it follows that we can never believe (or do) anything other than we actually do, and thus that we can never do wrong. So it's rather unclear how exactly we're supposed to understand the relevant psychological limits.

Whatever our solution to this problem, it seems that looking at our neurobiology isn't the best way to find out whether people are able to follow some ethical theory. For example, even if we were all born with an intricate set of deontological intuitions, as Mikhail, Hauser, and others hold (Hauser 2006; Mikhail 2007), or a set of "moral foundations" disposing us to care about purity and loyalty, as Haidt thinks (2012), this would hardly show that we can't learn to ignore these intuitions, however persistent.

In fact many people actually do succeed in ignoring these intuitions, including, of course, utilitarians. This is an obvious problem for such an argument against utilitarianism: at least some people out there claim to believe in utilitarianism, and to be motivated by this belief. If such belief and motivation are actual, then of course it is also possible. Now some people think that there is no one alive, not even Peter Singer, who literally lives the life of someone who follows act utilitarianism without qualification.[26] But even that would hardly show (as this argument requires) that this is simply *impossible* "for creatures like us." After all, we generally tend to underestimate what it's possible for humans to do.

Studying people's actual moral psychology, and how they *actually* make moral decisions, tells us rather little about the limits to how humans *could* make such decisions. If you want to find out whether people *can* follow some ethical theory, a more sensible approach is *to try to get them to follow it.*[27]

So again we face the problem that current cognitive science studies the way we actually are, where it's rather facts about what we *could be* that might set a limit to ethical theory. Facts about what we could be are also empirical facts, but again it's unclear how psychology should go about establishing such facts about our limits—and it is doubtful that the current cognitive science of ethics is of much help here.

To complicate things further, one thing we *have* learned over the past decade is that our moral psychology is not fixed or immutable. It can be altered in significant ways by taking a single pill.[28] And this means that it is now even harder to draw firm limits to our psychology, and to what it could become.[29]

Before we move on, let me just quickly distinguish that the kind of argument I have been considering in this section from rather different arguments with which it may be easily confused. One such argument claims that certain deep-seated features of human nature make some political systems or even moral norms unrealistic or otherwise dangerous, since trying to impose them on actual human beings would lead to disastrous consequences. A similar but weaker form of argument claims that, given our psychology, certain moral views are extremely difficult for us to accept or follow.[30] But these aren't versions of the argument from "ought implies can"—that something is difficult or will have some negative consequences hardly means that it's simply beyond our reach, and that it's extremely hard to us to follow a certain moral view, or that trying to impose it would have bad consequences, tells us nothing about the *truth* of that view. Nobody said that the true morality must be easy, or has to have only good consequences. Even if, for example, humans are born strongly disposed to care about purity and find it extremely difficult to avoid doing so, and even if because of that a moral system that gives no weight to considerations of purity would have some rather unpleasant consequences, this in no way shows the ethics of purity to have any kind of validity.

12.5. Alethic versus Epistemic Arguments

So far, we have examined two "alethic" (i.e., truth-focused) arguments that try to take us from psychological premises to conclusions about what we ought (or ought not) to do. I now want to consider two forms of argument that I think are more promising. These arguments have the advantage that they *don't* require us to infer ought from is, and thus don't require us to assume any kind deep metaphysical relation between the two.

Instead, these arguments take us from psychological premises to conclusions about what we ought to *believe* that we ought to do. These are essentially *epistemic* arguments about moral justification, not about moral truth (or, if you prefer, correctness). And it's not at all mysterious how facts about our psychology can be relevant to the *justification* of our moral beliefs—even if these beliefs are about truths that are utterly mind-independent.

To illustrate these two types of arguments, I will use the example of the influential attempt by Joshua Greene to use his work in moral psychology to undermine deontological ethics.[31] But this is just an example: I am not concerned here with whether Greene's empirical claims are correct—though I have expressed doubts about them elsewhere (Kahane and Shackel 2008, 2011; Kahane et al. 2012, 2015; Kahane 2012, 2014b)—or even with the specifics of the normative arguments that Greene defends. What I want to do is to clarify how such arguments might best work.

Greene's argument draws on a growing body of research where participants confront dilemmas such as the famous Footbridge case, where one must decide whether to sacrifice the life of a large man by pushing him onto the track of a runaway trolley in order to save the lives of five others. We know that most people respond in a deontological way to such dilemmas—they think it's wrong to push the fat man to save five (see Cushman et al. 2006).

At least in its earlier version, Greene's normative argument against these deontological intuitions appealed to three distinct empirical claims. Greene claimed that these intuitions are responding to the fact that the harm one is asked to commit in footbridge is "up close and personal" (you need to physically push the fat man from the footbridge); that these intuitions are based in an immediate *emotional* response; and that such responses are probably *innate*, selected by evolution.[32]

These empirical claims actually offer answers to two distinct questions and are relevant to two (or more) distinct types of arguments that are often conflated. The first type of argument relates to the causal origins of our intuitions. The second one relates to what factors our intuitions are responsive to. I will start with the first type of argument.

12.6. The Argument from Unreliability
12.6.1. THE BASIC ARGUMENT

When we consider dilemmas such as the Footbridge case, it can feel as if we can just directly *see* that it would be wrong to push the fat man. From the inside, there is little more that we can say to justify such judgments, or to explain where they come from. But as our understanding of the psychology and neuroscience of morality advances, we can move beyond thinking of such judgments as mysteriously springing from some obscure faculty of intuition. We can begin to place them in the causal order, as responses that have their source in specific internal processes and mechanisms—whether in affective areas of the brain, or a series of intricate unconscious computations, and so forth. To think of our moral judgments as having such an elaborate causal history can be disturbing. What I want to consider now is whether this growing understanding of the causal sources of our moral judgments has any real normative significance.

Many believe that such causal stories must matter in some way. Anthony Appiah, for example, suggests that the fact that our emotions guide our intuition about Footbridge "is the right sort of thing we might want to consider in deciding whether that intuition is right" (Appiah 2008, 111).

At first sight, this can sound like the genetic fallacy—it is normally a fallacy to infer, from the *causal history* of some belief of ours, the *truth* or *falsity* of the proposition that we believe. For surely, what (and how) we think is one thing, how things actually are another. But it's not at all a fallacy to think that facts about the causal origins of our beliefs can affect their *justification*—this is actually a central focus of contemporary epistemology.

So consider this epistemic argument:

P1. Empirical. Our deontological beliefs are caused by emotion.

P2. Epistemic. Beliefs that have their source in emotion are unreliable.

Therefore

C. Epistemic. Our deontological beliefs lack justification.

This argument takes us from an empirical premise about the causal origins of our beliefs, coupled with an epistemic premise about the unreliability of that causal source, to the conclusion that we should be suspicious of beliefs that originate from that causal source.

Notice that such an argument cannot directly show that our deontological beliefs are false. It *isn't* an inference from "is" to "ought." The conclusion of this argument isn't *that* we ought (or ought not to) do something, but that our prior *beliefs about* what we ought to do are unjustified. But such a result would be significant enough.

A second thing to notice is that such arguments require an epistemic premise, which is either explicitly or implicitly a normative claim.[33] But this isn't in itself a problem, since that normative premise is epistemic, not moral. It would only be problematic if it appealed to controversial epistemological assumptions that are rejected by the moral view we wish to assess.

Now this is only a sketch of an argument, but I think that it is basically valid. This doesn't mean that it is sound. One could raise some doubts about its empirical premise: it is by no means obvious that deontological intuitions are exclusively caused by emotion (see Huebner et al. 2009; Terbeck et al. 2013), but, more importantly, many have pointed out that its epistemic premise is dubious. Who ever said that emotion is such a bad thing? Why think that it's an unreliable guide to what we ought to do? These are controversial claims that need to be defended, and that many reject.[34] And we must also be careful to distinguish the extremely strong claim that emotion in *all* its forms is unreliable, from the commonsensical point that *extreme emotional agitation* is often a biasing influence (and even this claim has many exceptions); it's rather unlikely, to say the least, that subjects in experiments going through boring hypothetical dilemmas are anywhere near such a state of emotional agitation.

12.6.2. WHAT NORMATIVE STANDARD?

So this particular argument is unpersuasive, or at best incomplete.[35] But again I'm more interested here in how such "debunking" arguments *might* work. And you might think that there is a deeper problem with this kind of argument. The worry is that in order to assess the reliability of emotion or any other process that shapes our moral beliefs, we need some normative standard. We need to be able to determine whether the moral outputs of a given process are on or off track.[36] But to do so, don't we already need to know whether these outputs are correct or not?

But if so then it seems that such arguments require us to already make many substantive moral assumptions. The problem is that in the moral domain, even foundational claims are often subject to intense controversy. It is uninteresting to point out that from a *utilitarian* point of view, the processes that generate nonutilitarian beliefs count as unreliable. This is trivial. But this won't persuade any deontologist to change her mind. So it now appears that such arguments are really circular, and that the empirical evidence they appeal to is redundant.

This is a genuine worry, but it is important not to exaggerate it. While we do need some external standard to assess the reliability of the processes that generate our moral intuitions and judgments, there are several strategies that would allow us to do so without simply presupposing the controversial substantive moral claims we wish to defend. However, while these strategies may in principle address the worry, putting them to work in practice is not going to be easy.[37]

12.6.3. EXTRAPOLATION FROM OTHER DOMAINS

One way to address the normative standard problem is to try to extrapolate from evidence about the reliability of a given process in a domain where we *do* possess an agreed normative standard, to its reliability in the moral domain. For example, if we know that intuitions are often biased in the context of, say, thinking about probability, we may try to argue that it is therefore likely that intuitions are also biased in the moral context. Similar arguments could be made about the reliability of emotion, effortful deliberative processing, and the like.

It seems to me that such inferences can sometimes be warranted, but I am rather doubtful that they can do much work—I think that they can at best support only very weak claims. After all, a process might be unreliable in one domain, but highly reliable in another, especially if the subject matter of that domain is very different (probability and moral wrongness are *very* different things). That a microscope isn't a useful instrument for studying the stars hardly shows that it's not highly reliable for studying microbes.

There are also related issues about how to individuate the relevant processes. It seems silly to talk in general terms about the reliability of emotion or intuition or deliberative processing. Surely it matters *which* emotion, or *what* it is exactly we do when we deliberate.[38] Perhaps disgust is unreliable, but empathy is; perhaps seeking reflective equilibrium is reliable, but applying the explicit rules you were taught as a child isn't, and so forth.

So more work needs to be done to tinker with this kind of argument for unreliability, but I am rather pessimistic that this strategy is likely to do much work when applied to significant moral questions. It seems to me that it has some persuasive force only in rather uncommon contexts: when we have absolutely no other way of assessing the reliability of the process; when we can at least sketch an account of why reliability in one domain might carry over to the other;[39] and when the normative conclusion we draw from the argument doesn't challenge our prior convictions. Even if intuitions about probability are really highly unreliable, this gives us no reason at all to doubt our moral intuition that torturing infants for sadistic pleasure is wrong.[40]

12.6.4. UNCONTROVERSIAL MORAL TRUISMS

A second strategy for addressing the problem does assume some substantive moral claims. But this needn't be a problem if these are just *uncontroversial truisms*. For example, if we knew what processes underlie our beliefs in, say, the wrongness of torturing infants for sadistic pleasure—or, for that matter, what makes some people think that this *isn't* wrong—then, in principle, we might be able to use this to assess the reliability of the processes that generate more controversial moral beliefs: the uncontroversial truisms can serve as an agreed normative standard. Since we all agree that torturing infants for sadistic pleasure is deeply wrong, then we can also agree that the processes that lead to this and similarly truistic judgments are to some degree reliable, whereas clearly something is defective in processes that lead to clearly false verdicts.[41]

In a way, the focus of so much current research on difficult and highly controversial moral dilemmas gets things exactly backward. We should start with simpler cases and work our way up. But even current research suggests ways in which this second strategy could potentially be applied. Think, for example, of the recent finding that greater rates of utilitarian judgment in "personal" moral dilemmas are associated with higher levels of psychopathy (see Bartels and Pizarro 2011; Koenigs et al. 2012; as well as Wiech et al. 2013; Kahane et al. 2015). Now it would be a fallacy to conclude that, because psychopaths are nasty characters, this association with utilitarian judgments casts doubt on such judgments. Nasty characters may get all sorts of things right. But to the extent that psychopaths are not so very good in making moral judgments in uncontroversial contexts (something that is far from obvious), then this *would* give us some reason to doubt their judgments in trolley cases.

This is so far a claim only about the unreliability of the moral judgments of psychopaths—not a very exciting result. But we might be able to go further. If, for example, psychopaths make unreliable judgments about easy cases because they lack certain emotional responses, then we could try to extrapolate from this that these emotional responses play an important part in making our moral judgments reliable in harder cases—and this claim could apply even to the thinking of nonpsychopaths.[42]

12.6.5. OFF-TRACK PROCESSES

Let me say a bit more about a third strategy. In some cases, we don't actually need to assume *any* substantive claim to conclude that certain ways of forming beliefs are utterly unreliable. If someone forms her moral views by throwing dice, then you don't need to make any substantive assumptions to conclude that her beliefs are epistemically defective. For why think that there is any relation whatsoever between what the dice say, and what we actually ought to do?

Other influences on our moral intuitions and beliefs may be claimed to be arbitrary in the same way. If your moral judgments change depending on whether or not there is an unpleasant smell in the room, or whether you have eaten lunch, or whether cases are presented in one order or another, then they seem to be affected by influences that are epistemically irrelevant—*influences that seem to bear no plausible relation to the moral truth* (however that is to be understood).[43]

It is important not to confuse the claim that some moral intuitions are shaped by *epistemically* irrelevant *influences* (i.e., by processes that are "off track" with respect to the moral truth) and the rather different claim that these intuitions are *responsive* to *morally* irrelevant *factors*—the conclusion of a different kind of argument I will discuss in the next section. These two distinct claims (and arguments) are often conflated.[44]

Put schematically, the argument from epistemically irrelevant influences goes like this: if we can identify certain causal processes that are random or arbitrary, or that clearly *don't* track the moral truth, then we *can* use empirical evidence to defeat the justification of the intuitions and beliefs that these processes produce:[45]

P1. Empirical. Our belief that p is caused by X.
P2. Epistemic. X doesn't track the moral truth.
Therefore
C. Epistemic. Our belief that p lacks justification.

Notice that compared to the previous strategies we had considered, this one is rather blunt. It is not a way of *measuring* the degree to which some epistemic process is reliable; it is a way of identifying some process as completely *un*reliable.

One weakness of this type of argument is that it is rather hard to show that some moral belief has its source *only* in a process we have shown to be unreliable, or to show that a given process has *no* relation to the truth whatsoever. But if the process is only one of the things that shaped our belief, and if this process might bear some relation, however weak, to the moral truth, then the conclusion of the argument would need to be significantly qualified.

12.6.6. PROXIMAL VERSUS DISTAL SOURCES OF MORAL BELIEF

I now again want to ask what role the cognitive science of ethics might play in this kind of argument. Clearly, recent work in moral psychology has identified numerous ways in which our moral judgments seem to be swayed by influences that are clearly epistemically arbitrary. But so far as I can see, few of these influences really explain our core moral beliefs. This work does show that the processes that generate our moral intuitions and beliefs are often enough *susceptible* to irrelevant influences, which is worrying enough, but this doesn't yet show that these processes themselves are *completely* off track. And this is what we would need to show for debunking argument of the kind outlined above to have interesting applications.[46]

For example, much of Haidt's work aims to show that by modulating emotion, we can affect moral judgment in surprising ways. Many of these manipulations do involve epistemically irrelevant factors. In itself, this just shows that in these contexts, our intuitions might not be fully reliable. But we are also supposed to draw a more general lesson from these experiments: that emotion drives moral judgment (Haidt 2001). The problem is that even if this general conclusion followed, it doesn't in itself have any epistemic implications. It just takes us back to where we started—to questions about the reliability of emotion.

Now much of contemporary cognitive science of ethics is focused in this way on the immediate proximal causes of our core moral beliefs. But unless we can successfully pursue the first two strategies I outlined earlier, I doubt that we can learn all that much about the reliability of our moral beliefs by studying these proximal causes. Let me explain why.

We want to assess the reliability of the processes that shape our moral intuitions. Even if, say, emotion is the immediate cause of some intuitions, this in itself doesn't tell us whether these intuitions have a reliable source. The question about reliability is just pushed back. For to answer it, we now need to know *why* we are disposed to respond with this particular pattern of emotion. We need to know where *this* disposition comes from—does it have its source in a reliable source or in one that is off track? Its source might be natural selection, as Greene and others speculate, but it might also be due to our past experience, or to something we were taught, and so forth. The epistemic status of our intuitions will often depend on whether these *distal* causes are reliable influences, not on whether their immediate cause is emotional or not.[47]

12.6.7. EVOLUTIONARY DEBUNKING ARGUMENTS

One distal cause of our moral beliefs is culture. I won't say much about this form of debunking argument. The idea that the cultural genealogy of our moral beliefs could be used to debunk them is of course familiar from Nietzsche and Marx (see Leiter 2004). But such debunking arguments focus on history and sociology. It's doubtful that the cognitive science of morality has a huge role to play here. Cognitive science, however, does have something to say about the possible evolutionary sources of our moral beliefs.

Evolutionary debunking arguments take this form: they start from an empirical premise about the supposed evolutionary origins of some moral belief. Coupled with the (nonobvious) epistemic claim that evolution doesn't track the moral truth, they allow us to conclude that this belief is unjustified.[48] As an example, consider the following argument:[49]

P1. Empirical. Deontological intuitions were selected by evolution.
P2. Epistemic. Natural selection doesn't track the moral truth.
Therefore
C. Normative. Deontological beliefs based on these intuitions are lack justification.

Notice that this argument says *nothing* about neural activity, emotion, dual processing, or any other proximal cause. If it works, it would work *just as* well even if our intuitions were due to an intricate universal moral grammar, without even a touch of emotion. All the work is done by claims about the evolutionary sources of certain intuitions or beliefs. So most of the work at the heart of the cognitive science of morality is pretty much irrelevant to this argument.[50] In fact, even most of the evolutionary detail is irrelevant, since all that matters for this argument is whether some intuition is the product of evolution. It matters little how and why that intuition was selected.

Earlier in this chapter I briefly discussed and dismissed the common idea that the natural has normative authority—that we ought to follow our nature. The argument from "ought implies can" is in a sense an attempt to inject a degree of plausibility to something like this view. But if the evolutionary debunking argument just outlined works, we get an ironic result. The natural, far from being a *guide* to what we ought to do, turns out to be exactly the opposite: if some belief is due to our nature, this is precisely a reason to be *suspicious*.

Now evolutionary debunking arguments are pretty controversial. Both their empirical and their epistemic premises can be questioned. There are, to begin with, unresolved empirical questions about the extent to which our moral beliefs really have an evolutionary basis—it is likely that our evolutionary history has some role in shaping moral views, but learning, reflection, and social input presumably also play their part. Then there are difficult questions as to whether evolution really isn't truth-tracking in the relevant sense, and as to what it would even mean to track (or fail to track) the moral truth (which, at the fundamental level, may involve necessary truths)—is it enough, as some think, if in explaining the process that shaped a given belief, we needn't at any point refer to the moral truth?

I don't have space here to enter into these difficult questions. Instead, let me just highlight three general points.

First, this kind of debunking argument goes through in a straightforward way only if we assume a robustly realist, mind-independent understanding of morality. After all, if moral truth is in some way grounded in our own desires and emotions, then there is anyway no independent moral truth that evolutionary processes might fail to track. And this means that the force of these debunking arguments will often ultimately depend on our metaethical commitments.[51] The above argument against deontology may have force if we think about morality in strongly realist terms, but we can simply dismiss it if our metaethical views are broadly subjectivist—and as we saw earlier, on such antirealist views it might actually be fairly easy to support strong *deontological* conclusions. In this way, whether empirical evidence supports utilitarianism or its opponents can depend on our prior metaethical commitments. Yet debunking arguments of the kind we considered in this chapter are often presented as if they are valid on their own, and their metaethical commitments not made explicit.

Second, if such arguments work, they are likely to support, not utilitarianism or any other ethical theory, but rational egoism. If evolutionary debunking arguments against particular ethical theories have force, then, given the evolutionary basis of our basic moral capacities and dispositions, parallel arguments against morality *as a whole* are likely to have even *greater* force.[52]

But it's unlikely that the evolutionary debunking argument would stop even there. If it works, it is likely to undermine the justification of *all* of our normative beliefs, *including* our beliefs about self-interest, leaving us with general skepticism about what we ought to do.[53] If this is so, then attempts to use such debunking arguments to defend specific ethical views may ultimately be self-defeating.[54]

12.7. The Argument from What Our Intuitions Track

12.7.1. MORALLY IRRELEVANT FACTORS

The last argument I want to examine is, to my mind, the most promising. This argument focuses, not on the *causal origins* of our intuitions, but on what they are *responsive* to.

Consider, as an illustration, another strand of Greene's normative argument against deontological ethics. In his earlier work, Greene claimed that there is psychological evidence that our deontological intuitions about trolley cases are responding to whether some harm is up close and personal (call this PERSONAL HARM): it seems to us that it's wrong to push the fat man in the Footbridge case simply because this involves pushing rather than, say, switching a trolley by pulling a lever. Let us suppose for the moment that this claim is correct. Now PERSONAL HARM doesn't seem to mark a morally relevant difference. And if so, this should lead us to dismiss this intuition.[55]

Put schematically, the argument goes like this:

P1. Empirical. Deontological intuitions in trolley cases respond to whether some harm is up close and personal.
P2. Moral. Whether or not harm is up close or personal isn't a morally relevant difference.
Therefore

C. Normative. Our deontological beliefs in trolley cases lack justification.[56]

This again seems like a valid argument. Now it's doubtful that deontological intuitions in trolley cases are really responding just to the presence of PERSONAL HARM—something that Greene himself no longer exactly holds. I'll get back to this in a moment. But I want to first look at the structure of the argument.

The first thing to notice is that this argument again makes no reference *at all* to what internal processes generate our intuitions—it would work just as well if it was emotion or some "cold" universal moral grammar. And what happens at the neural level is even less relevant. For the purposes of this argument, all that matters is whether our intuitions track PERSONAL HARM or some other factor (or factors). In a sense, this is a purely behavioral question. What goes "inside"—whether our intuitions track PERSONAL HARM by recruiting emotional processes, or through an innate module, or via amygdala activation—is simply irrelevant. In a way, all that matters is what differences in input explain our pattern of intuitive output: whether the presence or absence of certain factors in the moral situation that people are considering (for example, by changing the text of some hypothetical moral dilemma) leads to corresponding changes in their pattern of intuitions.[57]

Notice that since this argument says nothing about the processes that generate our intuitions, it also doesn't rely on any claim about the unreliability of these processes. It simply claims that some particular set of intuitions is spurious (though this trivially implies that *these* intuitions do not track the moral truth). But of course there is a connection between the reliability of processes, and what these processes track. For example, if what generates some intuitions really *is* utterly unreliable, then we should also expect these intuitions to be tracking factors that are morally irrelevant. Conversely, if some process repeatedly generates intuitions that respond to such irrelevant factors, then this gives us grounds for thinking that this process is unreliable. But notice that a process can be broadly reliable yet still occasionally misfire. The mere fact that, say, emotional processes sometimes respond to irrelevant factors hardly shows that emotion is generally unreliable.

The second point to notice is that the claim that PERSONAL HARM is a morally irrelevant property is not an empirical claim. It's *itself* a substantive normative claim.[58] And not only is it made from the armchair, it is actually based on intuition: it's hard to see how one is supposed to *infer* that PERSONAL HARM is morally irrelevant.[59] This, by the way, is perfectly fine—appealing to intuition is a problem only to those who are on some general crusade against moral intuitions. What is important is that the normative claim about moral irrelevance is one on which we can all agree—that it doesn't simply beg the question, for example, against deontological views. (Utilitarians think that *all* factors that don't invoke consequences are morally irrelevant, but an argument that would invoke this assumption would have no persuasive force for nonutilitarians.)

However, this covert reliance on the armchair *isn't* the most interesting thing about this argument. The most interesting things about it is that, once the argument is made explicit, its structure turns out to *exactly mirror the structure of standard ethical theorizing*. After all, when we reflect in the armchair, we also start with some pattern of intuitions and try to figure out what property they track. We then ask whether that property is morally relevant. If it is, then we take that to support the corresponding moral principle (or general moral claim). If that property is morally irrelevant, then we discard the intuitions and the principle.

The most interesting thing about the argument outlined above isn't that we need the armchair to decide whether or not some factor is morally relevant. The most interesting thing is actually the *previous* stage, the one that actually *does* take place in the lab—the claim about what our intuitions track. Notice that we could, in principle, have reached the same conclusion from the armchair, simply by reflecting on our intuitions about cases. But here this conclusion is based on *psychological* evidence.

In other words, this argument from morally irrelevant factors actually *assumes* that there is a stage of ethical reflection that is in one sense tied to an *empirical question*—to what our intuitions track.[60] This form of argument also assumes that scientific methods are often *better* than armchair methods at answering this empirical question. And, on reflection, that is not surprising. The armchair process of coming up with hypotheses about what our intuitions are tracking, and then testing these hypotheses against yet further examples and thought experiments, is sometimes effective, but it also has obvious limits—as demonstrated by the fact that even after over forty years of armchair reflection, philosophers still do not agree about what underlies our intuitions about trolley cases. But we should be able to do better if we stop relying exclusively on introspection and instead make use of powerful statistical methods to distinguish, for example, between genuine tracking and merely accidental correlations, and if we begin to take into account constraints of psychological plausibility.

These are controversial claims that I have defended elsewhere.[61] But if they are correct, they would have significant implications for the way we do ethics. It doesn't follow that we need to burn any armchair. But the philosopher's armchair will be pushed further to the corner.

12.7.2. A POSITIVE ARGUMENT FROM EMPIRICAL EVIDENCE TO MORAL PRINCIPLES

So I'm essentially suggesting that evidence from psychology can contribute in a pretty direct way to a key stage in ethical theorizing. What is important to see, however, is that this contribution needn't be negative or critical, as many assume. This is often overlooked because people tend to focus on cases where our intuitions seem to track properties that are morally irrelevant. But as we saw, deciding whether some factor is morally relevant is a further step that already takes place in the philosopher's armchair. The science itself leaves it entirely open whether the properties that underlie our intuitions are morally relevant or not.

It might be useful to illustrate this point using an example that, again, comes from Greene.

In more recent work, Greene and his colleagues report that deontological intuitions in trolley cases track, not PERSONAL HARM, but whether the act was *intended*, and something they call PERSONAL FORCE—when the act involve impacting something else using the force of one's own muscles, unmediated by intervening causal mechanisms (Greene et al. 2009).

Now PERSONAL FORCE will still sound to many like a morally irrelevant property, and Greene et al. seem to think that their empirical results still support a skeptical conclusion about these deontological intuitions (Greene et al. 2009). But no such skeptical conclusion follows. After all, many *do* find intention to be morally relevant—or at least it's not clearly morally irrelevant.[62] So this experiment actually offers psychological evidence in support of a familiar deontological distinction. Actually, this empirical evidence might lead us to revise our intuitions in a more *deontological* direction, once we get rid of the biasing influence of PERSONAL FORCE.

It's easy to miss this because of Greene's utilitarian agenda. For our purposes, the important point is that this is a nice illustration of how a psychological experiment can offer *positive* evidence in *favor* of a general moral principle.

We can set this form of positive argument more explicitly as follows:[63]

P1. Empirical. There is psychological evidence that some pattern of intuitions is responsive to factor X.
P2. Moral. Factor X is morally relevant, or at least doesn't seem morally *ir*relevant.
Therefore
C. Epistemic. We have prima facie reason to accept the parallel moral principle concerning X.

This approach can be applied not just to the trolley problem, but also to any other controversy in normative ethics where it is unclear what factors our intuitions are responsive to.

Notice that this isn't really an argument from "is" to "ought"; if you want, it's an argument from psychological evidence about our *beliefs* about many "particular" oughts to reasons to also endorse a "general" ought or moral principle.

A great deal current work in so-called experimental ethics has a negative aim and is driven by a naturalist, even skeptical agenda. It often aims to undermine our intuitions and cast doubt on their reliability. By contrast, the argument I have just outlined is positive in aim and is compatible even with the strongest forms of moral realism. Moreover, it actually begins by assuming that our moral intuitions *are* broadly reliable.[64]

However, although this form of argument outlines a way of using cognitive science to draw normative conclusions, flashy neuroimaging and other exciting neuroscience techniques will at best play only a limited role here. If you want to find out what our intuitions track, you should start by finding out how people's intuitions vary as we vary particular cases. In other words, you should focus on experiments that use old-fashioned and boring pen-and-paper methods—the kind of experiments that even William James and Wilhelm Wundt could have done.[65]

12.8. Conclusion

Let me summarize the main lessons of this chapter. I argued, first, that there are multiple ways to validly draw potentially interesting normative conclusions from empirical premises. And the most interesting arguments of this form are actually epistemic—arguments that don't directly infer an "ought" from an "is."

Second, I've argued that findings about the internal structure of our moral psychology, or about its underlying neurobiology, will have only a limited role to play in such arguments—these arguments draw most heavily on low-tech and unexciting experimental methods.

There is a more general lesson. It's a mistake to think that we should just let the cognitive science of ethics pursue its independent theoretical aims, and then ask what normative implications might follow. Scientists aim to uncover the subpersonal causal mechanisms that underlie our moral capacities. Such research is undoubtedly of great theoretical interest. But it might nevertheless be only of limited ethical significance. The kind of psychological evidence that is of greatest ethical interest is often actually relatively superficial from a scientific point of view—for example, evidence about the external factors to which our intuitions are responsive—or even relates to questions that cognitive scientists don't actually ask, such as questions about our psychological limits, or our ideal psychology. Thus, if we want to use cognitive science to draw ethical conclusions, we might need to do empirical research differently—or even to do different research.[66]

Notes

1. There are of course uninteresting ways of getting from such empirical evidence to normative conclusions. Empirical evidence is often relevant to the *application* of certain moral principles. For example, if moral responsibility requires possession of certain cognitive capacities, and evidence about the frontal lobes can provide evidence relevant to this question, then this empirical evidence may help us decide whether some population can be held morally responsible. But here we are just using empirical evidence to apply some prior moral principle—in exactly the same unexciting way that empirical evidence about the health risks of some drug can bear on various ethical questions. In this chapter I will be concerned with whether the

psychology and neuroscience of morality can provide support for moral conclusions at a more fundamental level.

2. Wilson 1975, 3. Notice the ambiguity in the phrase "explain ethics"—to causally explain why ethical sentiments and dispositions evolved, or even how people come to believe that certain acts are wrong or why they follow certain moral norms, is not yet to explain (or explain away) *why* certain acts really are morally wrong.

3. For prominent examples of attempts to infer normative conclusions from recent empirical research, see Singer 2005; Greene 2008; Sinnott-Armstrong 2008; Harris 2011; Churchland 2012; Haidt 2012.

4. Berker 2009 is sometime interpreted as defending such a claim, though I believe Berker's view is rather more nuanced.

5. Given the focus of this volume, I will say relatively little about more familiar forms of empirical argument in which neuroscience obviously plays little or no role, such as arguments appealing to cultural diversity in moral intuitions.

6. Notice, however, that although I will underscore the role of metaethical assumptions in some inferences from empirical evidence to substantive ethical conclusions, I will not be considering here whether empirical evidence could be used to support interesting conclusions in metaethics—though such inferences should be simpler to make for the simple reason that some core metaethical claims are explicitly meant to be psychological or semantic in character.

7. Although I am more optimistic than Berker (2009) about the normative interest of the cognitive science of morality, one theme of this chapter is broadly in line with Berker's main conclusion: I will argue that of the work currently done in the cognitive science of morality, the research done in neuroscience proper is probably of least normative significance.

8. There are of course various ways of developing such views to avoid obvious counterexamples, for example by refining what is meant by "natural." For our purposes all that matters is that the plausibility of such views is a matter for substantive debate, and needn't depend on the metaethical issues raised by Hume and Moore.

9. To simplify things, I will follow others in writing as if the conclusions of such arguments need to be statements about what we *ought* to do. But it's more plausible that such arguments will only provide some *reasons* for acting in certain ways (or, as we shall see below, some reasons for *believing* that we have certain reasons)—reasons that need to be considered alongside other reasons before we can conclude what we ought to do, all things considered.

10. It is not important for our purposes here whether Moore intended to deny identity at the level of properties or only at the level of meaning.

11. For a survey of antirealist views, see Joyce 2015.

12. There are different ways to get around Moore's argument. The meaning of moral notions may not be as transparent as Moore assumes. Or the tie between what we ought to do and our subjective attitudes might be synthetic, at the level of reference rather than meaning. Or even if moral claims are not claims *about* our subjective attitudes, they may still *express* such attitudes, as noncognitivists claim.

13. In what follows, I focus on broadly subjectivist accounts of morality. This isn't an especially popular view among contemporary metaethicists. More popular are broadly subjectivist (or "desire based") accounts of practical reason. On this kind of view, what we have normative reason to do, and thus what we overall ought to do, is grounded in our desires—even if what

is morally right and wrong (and thus what we morally *ought* to do) isn't. But this kind of view would still allow us to infer normative conclusions from psychological facts.

14. Jesse Prinz (2007) develops a specific instance of this form of argument. But Prinz's argument presupposes a particular variant of antirealism that he also defends on empirical grounds, whereas my aim here is to set out this form of argument in its most general form.

15. As I set out the argument above, the relevant psychological facts are facts about our emotions and desires. This may give the impression that this kind of argument requires a broadly sentimentalist view of moral psychology. But this isn't so. First, even if what we ought to do is grounded in noncognitive attitudes, it doesn't necessarily follow from this that our *judgments* about what we ought to do are causally based in noncognitive attitudes. Second, there are forms of moral antirealism that ground what we ought to do in psychological states that aren't sentiments or desires—for example, what we ought to do might be grounded instead in what we would *judge* in certain ideal conditions (see e.g. Wright 1995).

16. Some further remarks about this form of argument: (1) Once we accept such an identity between psychological states and what we ought to do, then we can deductively infer, in this way, an ought from an is, circumventing Hume's law. But it is not even clear that Hume himself would object—after all, on a common reading, he was himself a kind of subjectivist. In any event, this form of argument doesn't require identity. Weaker relations would suffice, so long as they involve a *necessary correlation* between psychological states and normative claims. In fact, even a probabilistic relation would allow us to make such inference to normative conclusions, though these conclusions would need to be appropriately qualified. (2) This form of inference works in the most straightforward way for subjectivist or (reductive) response-dependent views. But it can also go through on other metaethical views. Consider, for example, noncognitivism. Noncognitivists typically deny that normative claims are made literally true or false by our subjective attitudes; they take normative claims to *express* such attitudes. But even on noncognitivist views, there should be a necessary correlation between subjective attitudes and what we ought to do, allowing for inferences broadly of the kind outlined here. (3) Strictly speaking, any reductive naturalist view would allow inferences from empirical claims to normative conclusions. This includes some realist views, such as reductive forms of moral naturalism. Relativist views also ground what we ought to do in natural facts, but these are facts of the kind studied by sociology rather than psychology.

17. Facts about what we want—even about what we *really* want, deep down—are facts about our psychology, but they are also at the *person* level, the level of folk psychology. They are distinct from subpersonal claims about internal processes or neural activity. So they are already at least one remove from the kinds of evidence with which much cognitive science is concerned. To complicate things further, on at least some views, such person-level facts are irreducible to lower-level states or processes, meaning that there may be no smooth inference to facts about what we believe or want from subpersonal-level evidence. It's often simply assumed that if we can infer ought from is, then it must be possible to infer ought from scientific claims. But this won't follow if there are kinds of "is" that aren't reducible to any set of scientific claims.

18. This is a major background theme in the antiutilitarianism of Bernard Williams (see e.g. Williams 2008). To be sure, some important utilitarians were themselves antirealist. But such antirealists typically defend their view by making strong (and implausible) assumptions about various "objective" conceptual constraints on moral discourse. For a famous example, see Hare 1981.

19. Haidt himself is rather unclear about his metaethical commitments. In some early writings, he flirted with the idea, suggested by Wiggins (1987), that morality is anthropocentric—essentially a response-dependence theory (see Haidt and Bjorklund 2007; Wiggins, however, is actually a nonreductive response-dependence theorist). But in later work, Haidt seems to hold that we should give some weight to "nonliberal" foundations only because of the consequence of doing so, as measured by the "liberal" values of harm and justice (Haidt 2012). This is closer to the form of argument I will consider in the next section.

20. One familiar worry is that substantive assumptions get smuggled into the specification of the idealization process. It is actually hard to imagine that the attitudes of our idealized selves would tend in a utilitarian direction without such "assistance."

21. For doubts about this principle, see Sinnott-Armstrong 1984; Stern 2004. I actually share some of these doubts. Those who reject this principle typically still accept that if someone can't act in some way, the person cannot be *blamed* for not acting in this way. This weaker principle would still allow us to infer normative conclusions from empirical claims, but these would be far more modest and tell us nothing about foundational morality.

22. For discussion of Kant's view, see Stern 2004.

23. I'll assume, with most others, that, if this principle is true, it is a conceptual truth.

24. As Flanagan is careful to acknowledge, this form of argument might spell trouble for act utilitarianism understood as a decision procedure (a way of making moral decisions), but it's harder to see how it could challenge act utilitarianism qua criterion of rightness (an account of what makes some act right or wrong). Griffin, however, rejects this distinction. He thinks that "ought implies can" can undermine act utilitarianism even when it's understood to be a criterion of rightness. Casebeer and Churchland (2003) and Churchland (2012) sometimes *seem* to be appealing to "ought implies can" to dismiss utilitarianism in a similar way.

25. One possible form of this extension inward of something like the "ought implies can" principle is the view known as (reasons) internalism, famously defended by Bernard Williams, on which it is a necessary condition for our having a normative reason to do something that it is possible for us to be motivated to act in this way, through some extension of our existing motivational set (see Williams 1981).

26. See, e.g., the interview with Frances Kamm in Voorhoeve 2009.

27. Here I'm setting aside the point that few contemporary utilitarians think we should directly follow such a decision procedure. But it's worth pointing out that when utilitarians tell us that it would be psychologically impossible or counterproductive to try to directly follow such a utilitarian decision procedure, they are also relying on no more than (all too convenient) armchair speculation about empirical matters.

28. See, e.g., Crockett et al. 2009; Terbeck et al. 2012. For discussion of the possible use of biotechnology to change moral dispositions, see Douglas 2009.

29. Perhaps considerations relating to neural plasticity can lend support to doubts about deriving interesting normative conclusions from the ought-implies-can principle. If so, then evidence from neurobiology does have some indirect normative interest.

30. The normative and political lessons that Haidt draws from his work in moral psychology seem to be of this form.

31. See Greene 2008. For a closely related argument, see Singer 2005.

32. For a detailed presentation of the argument and the empirical evidence it appeals to, see Greene 2008. Berker 2009 offers detailed criticism of this argument.

33. Claims about unreliability are not clearly themselves normative, but to support the inference to a conclusion about justification, some normative assumption about the relation between reliability and justification must be assumed. On some epistemic views, the unreliability of the process generating some belief of ours entails that it is not justified. On other views, this result would follow only if we *knew* that our belief has an unreliable source. But we can ignore this distinction here.

34. See e.g. Berker 2009. Of course some Kantians might independently think of emotion as a distorting influence on belief. *These* Kantians may be forced to accept the conclusion of this argument, given their background epistemology. But nonutilitarian views needn't have such epistemic commitments.

35. In more recent work, Greene seems to have abandoned this particular argument, though appeals to unreliability still figure heavily in his criticism of deontological ethics.

36. In what follows, I'll assume that in order to undermine the epistemic credentials of some belief-forming process, we need to show that it is unreliable. But on some moral epistemologies, it may be just a conceptual truth that some processes are biasing—perhaps it's constitutive of justified moral belief that it must be free of emotional influence. Since such claims are at best controversial, I'll ignore them in what follows.

37. There is one further strategy I will not discuss here because it is rather familiar and because it obviously has nothing to do with neuroscience. If a certain process tends to produce conflicting verdicts (whether intrapersonally or interpersonally), then that is sufficient for us to conclude that this process is unreliable. Without some external standard, we cannot tell which of these verdicts is the correct one. But we don't need an external standard to know that they can't *both* be correct.

38. This is really just an instance of the "generality problem" for process reliabilism. See Conee and Feldman 1998.

39. For example, Derek Parfit (2011) essentially argues that we can extrapolate from reason's general reliability in assessing the intrinsic plausibility of a priori claims about mathematics, logic, and epistemic justification, to its reliability in assessing claims about moral and other practical reasons, since the latter are just a subcategory of the a priori. De Lazari-Radek and Singer (2012) also endorse this strategy.

40. Berker 2009, 328–329, appears to argue that such extrapolations are never valid. I think that this is too strong. His argument for this seems to be that if a process that we take to be highly reliable in another domain (say effortful deliberation) produced a clearly preposterous judgment in the moral domain (say that it's fine to torture babies for fun), then evidence about the reliability of that process in other domains would have no epistemic force whatsoever. This seems right. But to move from *this* extreme (and essentially skeptical) case to the conclusion that such inferences about reliability are *never* correct is itself a pretty dramatic extrapolation that seems to me implausible.

41. When I talk about uncontroversial moral truisms, I mean moral claims that are accepted by both sides to some disputes. There is a sense in which deontological claims about trolley problems are uncontroversial—as I noted, these deontological claims are endorsed by a large majority. But they are *not* uncontroversial truisms in the context of the debate between utilitarians and their opponents. Conversely, there may be psychopaths out there who will not blink an eye at the prospect of torturing infants. But this hardly makes the claim that it's wrong to torture infants controversial—we are not engaged in a moral debate with these psychopaths.

42. This strategy, however, will not take us very far if (as I think is likely) the psychological processes involved in responding to easy moral questions are different from the processes engaged in the context of difficult moral dilemmas. And this strategy also inherits the problems of the first strategy, even if on a smaller scale: it is not so obvious that we can just extrapolate from reliability in simple cases to reliability in difficult ones.

43. Sinnott-Armstrong proposes that we assess the moral reliability of processes by determining the degree to which they are susceptible to such epistemically irrelevant influences (see Sinnott-Armstrong 2011). It's important to see, however, that such a project is purely negative. If some process is highly susceptible to such influences, it is to that extent unreliable. But the mere fact that a process is generally invulnerable to such influences doesn't yet show it bears any *positive* relation to the truth. And it can sometimes be more rational to be guided by a process that is highly influenced by biasing factors but known to have at least *some* relation to the truth, than to be guided by a process that isn't biased in this way, but which may not bear such a relation.

44. *Morally* irrelevant factors are factors present *within* the scenario we are making a moral judgment about—a scenario that may of course relate to distant or merely hypothetical events. By contrast, *epistemically* irrelevant influences are influences that operate *on* (or in) the agent herself, while leaving the scenario that is being morally assessed unaffected. If the mere presence of an unpleasant smell in the room makes people judge that some hypothetical transgression should be punished more severely, this is an epistemically irrelevant influence. But if people judge a transgression more severely when the person committing the hypothetical transgression is *described* as smelly, that would (in most cases!) be a morally irrelevant factor.

According to the principle of supervenience, if we morally assess a given situation in a certain way, we are logically committed to assessing an identical situation in the same way. Epistemically irrelevant influences like the presence of an unpleasant smell thus clearly violate supervenience. However, the mere fact of inconsistency between our moral judgments in different contexts leaves it open which of these contexts is epistemically worse—it leaves it open, for example, that our judgments are *more* reliable in the presence of an unpleasant smell.

45. Notice that this form of argument claims that some of our beliefs are *actually* formed in ways that seem to bear no relation to the moral truth. It does not merely point out the mere skeptical *possibility* that this is the case (a possibility that needn't threaten the justification of these beliefs), nor does it challenge the defender of these beliefs to give a *positive* account of how these beliefs track the truth (a challenge that can be rejected as overly demanding).

46. But see Sinnott-Armstrong 2008 for an attempt to draw stronger conclusions from this kind of evidence.

47. Of course once we have a grip on the reliability of these distal influences, we can in principle also assess the reliability of these proximal causes. If evolutionary influence is an off-track influence, *and* our emotions have been selected by evolution, then to cast doubt about some moral belief, it will be enough to show that it is based in emotion. But again, the real work is done by the claim about the distal influence. If evolution is an off-track influence, then the same conclusion would follow even if the evolutionary influence worked through some utterly unemotional "moral organ."

48. For further detail and nuance, see Kahane 2011.

49. See Singer 2005; Greene 2003, 2008. I should note that this is *one* natural way to interpret the evolutionary arguments sketched by Singer and Greene. I think that Singer and Greene actually fail to distinguish between this debunking argument and a rather different

kind of argument, which we can call the evolutionary argument from moral heuristics. The latter argument makes a weaker claim: it claims that although our deontological intuitions may be reliable in the context in which they were originally selected, there is no reason to expect them to be reliable in the very different contexts thrown up by the modern world. This weaker argument actually *denies* the epistemic premise of the evolutionary debunking argument, since it assumes that evolution *is* truth-tracking in the environment in which it operates. So this form of argument is inconsistent with the evolutionary debunking argument I will be discussing. As I point out in Kahane 2011, 20 n. 23, this second form of argument, once it is made explicit, actually seems to support extreme deontological views, rather than utilitarianism.

50. Evidence from cognitive science is at best indirectly relevant to this argument, by providing support to the claim that some intuition has its source in evolution. So far as I can see, very little of the work in current cognitive science of morality really strongly bears on this kind of question—Internet surveys purporting to show that certain intuitions are universal at most provide thin evidence that these intuitions are innate.

51. In Kahane 2011, I somewhat overstated this point. As Joyce (forthcoming) points out, there are conceivable antirealist views on which it might still be possible that evolutionary pressures have pushed our moral beliefs in directions that bear no relation to what we really ought to do. To complicate things further, evolutionary debunking arguments may also have force against sophisticated expressivist views that try to mimic realism; and they may have no force against some forms of moral naturalism, since these *can* give an account of how evolutionary pressures are truth-tracking. For our purposes here, what matters is that whether (and how) such arguments work depends on our metaethical commitments.

52. But see de Lazari-Radek and Singer 2013 for an attempt to block this extension of the argument. I criticize this attempt in Kahane, 2014a.

53. For full-blown development of such skeptical arguments, see Street 2006; Joyce 2007. For criticism, see Enoch 2010; Wielenberg 2010; Skarsaune 2011; Parfit 2011; Shafer-Landau 2012; and many others.

54. If evolutionary debunking arguments end up supporting such general moral skepticism, they cannot support any interesting substantive normative conclusions. But they may still do so indirectly. Street thinks that, because such moral skepticism is implausible, this debunking argument should lead us to endorse a form of antirealism—and, moreover, a form of antirealism that is likely to end up supporting the *antiutilitarian* form of the argument from antirealism that I outlined earlier (Street doesn't herself make this further step).

55. Greene 2001, 2008. It's important to distinguish such arguments from morally irrelevant factors from what we might called the argument from rationalization (also employed by Greene), which claims that the intricate theories developed by moral philosophers are just ex post rationalizations of their intuitions. The first type of argument makes a claim about intuitions and the beliefs directly based on them; the second aims to debunk general principles and theories. A common mistake in this literature is to assume that if some theory gives special weight to intuitions and tries to find ways of preserving them, then this theory is based in ex post rationalization. But to say this is just to misuse the term "rationalization," which should be applied only to biased forms of motivated cognition. To give weight to one's intuitions in one's theorizing (so long as they have not been *shown* to be biased) can be perfectly rational—it can be perfectly rational *even* if, as a matter of act, these intuitions

later turn out to be spurious. Conversely, our ethical theorizing may completely fail to match the factors that our intuitions actually track. This would be a problem for the theories constructed on the basis of these intuitions, but it would not, in itself, in any way show that the intuitions themselves are defective.

56. Notice that even if the intuitive support for a moral belief turns out to be spurious, that belief may still be true, and perhaps even justifiable on nonintuitive grounds.

57. Though to the extent that a competence/performance distinction can be drawn here in a useful way, then some aspects of our internal psychology might still be relevant. And internal states might still serve an indirect, diagnostic role. For example, if a certain emotional response covaries both with certain moral judgments and with the presence of a certain factor, this could provide some evidence that these judgments are responsive to that factor. I'm grateful here to Matthew Liao.

58. Berker 2009 makes this point.

59. Intuitions about the moral relevance of factors seem quite different in character than intuitions about the wrongness of acts in particular cases, such as those elicited by the trolley cases. It's a pity that no psychological work has yet been done on this second category of intuitions.

60. Few would deny that ethical reflection about intuitions attempts to uncover the factors to which our intuitions respond. But some will deny that this is an empirical matter. For a reply to this objection, see Kahane 2013, 429–422.

61. Kahane 2013 (see esp. 433–436). For a similar claim and an example of how this approach can be applied to a specific problem, see Sripada and Konrath 2011. Sripada and Konrath suggest that statistical methods of causal modeling offer an especially promising way of identifying what "critical" features our intuitions track.

62. Though of course further ethical reflection, and perhaps other kinds of empirical evidence, may still ultimately lead us to dismiss the impression that intention is morally relevant.

63. For more detailed discussion, see Kahane 2013.

64. Of course to the extent that *some* set of intuitions has been shown to be unreliable, then it won't serve as an appropriate basis for such an inference. But in such a case, we should anyway expect to find that the factors these intuitions track are morally irrelevant. Notice further that this argument doesn't require that we take our intuitions to have noninferential justification. It just requires that we take there to be some cases where some pattern of intuitions provides evidential support for more general moral claims. As I argued in Kahane 2013, this assumption is actually widely accepted in normative ethics, often (at least implicitly) even by those who claim to reject such appeals to intuitions.

65. See Kahane 2013 for further discussion of this point.

66. This chapter is based on a talk given at "The Moral Brain" conference at the NYU Centre for Bioethics in 2012. I am grateful to the audience for useful feedback. I would also like to thank S. Matthew Liao and an anonymous referee for extremely helpful comments.

References

Appiah, K. A. 2008. *Experiments in Ethics*. Princeton, NJ: Princeton University Press.
Baldwin, T. 1990. *G.E. Moore*. Routledge: New York.

Bartels, D. M., and D. A. Pizarro. 2011. "The Mismeasure of Morals: Antisocial Personality Traits Predict Utilitarian Responses to Moral Dilemmas." *Cognition* 121, no. 1: 154–161.

Berker, S. 2009. "The Normative Insignificance of Neuroscience." *Philosophy and Public Affairs* 37, no. 293–329.

Casebeer, W. D., and P. S. Churchland. 2003. "The Neural Mechanisms of Moral Cognition." *Biology and Philosophy* 18: 169–194.

Churchland, P. 2012. *Braintrust*. Princeton, NJ: Princeton University Press.

Conee, E., and R. Feldman. 1998. "The Generality Problem for Reliabilism." *Philosophical Studies* 89: 1–29.

Crockett, M. J., L. Clark, M. D. Hauser, and T. W. Robbins. 2010. "Serotonin Selectively Influences Moral Judgment and Behavior through Effects on Harm Aversion." *Proceedings of the National Academy of Sciences* 107: 17433–1748.

de Lazari-Radek, K., and P. Singer. 2012. "The Objectivity of Ethics and the Unity of Practical Reason." *Ethics* 123: 9–31.

Emerson, R. W. [1841] 1994. "Self-Reliance." In *Self-Reliance and Other Essays*. New York: Dover Thrift.

Enoch, D. 2010. "The Epistemological Challenge to Metanormative Realism: How Best to Understand It, and How to Cope with It." *Philosophical Studies* 148: 413–438.

Firth, R. 1952. "Ethical Absolutism and the Ideal Observer." *Philosophy and Phenomenological Research* 12, no. 3: 317–345.

Flanagan, O. 1993. *Varieties of Moral Personality*. Cambridge, MA: Harvard University Press.

Frankena, W. 1939. "The Naturalistic Fallacy." *Mind* 48: 464–477.

Greene, J. D. 2003. "Neural 'Is' to Moral 'Ought': What Are the Moral Implications of Neuroscientific Moral Psychology?" *Nature Reviews Neuroscience* 4: 846–850.

Greene, J. D. 2008. "The Secret Joke of Kant's Soul." In *Moral Psychology: The Neuroscience of Morality*, edited by W. Sinnott-Armstrong, 35–79. Cambridge, MA: MIT Press.

Greene, J. D., R. B. Sommerville, L. E. Nystrom, J. M. Darley, and J. D. Cohen. 2001. "An fMRI Investigation of Emotional Engagement in Moral Judgment." *Science* 293: 2105–2107.

Griffin, J. 1992. "The Human Good and the Ambitions of Consequentialism." *Social Philosophy and Policy* 9, no. 2: 118–132.

Haidt, J. 2001. "The Emotional Dog and Its Rational Tail: A Social Intuitionist Approach to Moral Judgment." *Psychological Review* 108: 814–834.

Haidt, J. 2007. "The New Synthesis in Moral Psychology." *Science* 316: 998–1002.

Haidt, J. 2012. *The Righteous Mind*. New York: Pantheon.

Haidt, J., and F. Bjorklund. 2008. "Social Intuitionists Answer Six Questions about Moral Psychology." In *Moral Psychology*, vol. 2: *The Cognitive Science of Morality: Intuition and Diversity*, edited by W. Sinnott-Armstrong, 181–218. Cambridge, MA: MIT Press.

Hare, R. M. 1981. *Moral Thinking*. Oxford: Oxford University Press.

Harris, S. 2011. *The Moral Landscape*. New York: Bantam.

Hauser, M. 2006. "The Liver and the Moral Organ." *Social Cognitive and Affective Neuroscience* 1: 214–220.

Howard-Snyder, F. 2006. "'Cannot' Implies 'Not Ought.'" *Philosophical Studies* 130, no. 2: 233–246.

Hudson, W. D. 1969. *The Is/Ought Question: A Collection of Papers on the Central Problem in Moral Philosophy*. London: Macmillan.

Huebner, B., S. Dwyer, and M. Hauser. 2009. "The Role of Emotion in Moral Psychology." *Trends in Cognitive Sciences* 13, no. 1: 1–6.

Hume, D. [1739] 1975. *A Treatise of Human Nature*. Edited by L. A. Selby-Bigge. 2nd ed. revised by P. H. Nidditch. Oxford: Clarendon Press.

Johnston, M. 1989. "Dispositional Theories of Value." *Proceedings of the Aristotelian Society* suppl. vol. 62: 139–174.

Joyce, R. 2007. *The Evolution of Morality*. Cambridge, MA: MIT Press.

Joyce, R. 2015. "Moral Anti-realism." In *Stanford Encyclopedia of Philosophy*, edited by Edward N. Zalta. Fall 2015 ed.

Joyce, R. Forthcoming. "Evolution, Truth-Tracking, and Moral Skepticism." In *Problems of Goodness: New Essays on Metaethics*, edited by B. Reichardt.

Kahane, G. 2011. "Evolutionary Debunking Arguments." *Noûs* 45, no. 1: 103–125.

Kahane, G. 2012. "On the Wrong Track: Process and Content in Moral Psychology." *Mind and Language* 25, no. 5: 519–545.

Kahane, G. 2013. "The Armchair and the Trolley." *Philosophical Studies* 162, no. 2: 421–445.

Kahane, G. 2014a. "Evolution and Impartiality." *Ethics* 124, no. 2: 327–341.

Kahane, G. 2014b. "Intuitive and Counterintuitive Morality." In *The Science of Ethics: Moral Psychology and Human Agency*, edited by D. Jacobson and J. D'Arms, 9–39. Oxford: Oxford University Press.

Kahane, G., J. Everett, B. Earp, M. Farias, and J. Savulescu. 2015. "'Utilitarian' Judgment in Sacrificial Dilemmas Does Not Reflect Impartial Concern for the Greater Good." *Cognition* 134: 193–209.

Kahane, G., and N. Shackel. 2008. "Do Abnormal Responses Show Utilitarian Bias?" *Nature* 452: 7185.

Kahane, G., and N. Shackel. 2010. "Methodological Issues in the Neuroscience of Moral Judgment." *Mind and Language* 25, no. 5: 561–582.

Kahane, G., K. Wiech, N. Shackel, M. Farias, J. Savulescu, and I. Tracey. 2012. "The Neural Basis of Intuitive and Counterintuitive Moral Judgement." *Social, Cognitive, and Affective Neuroscience* 7, no. 4: 393–402.

Koenigs, M., M. Kruepke, J. Zeier, and J. P. Newman. 2012. "Utilitarian Moral Judgment in Psychopathy." *Social, Cognitive, and Affective Neuroscience* 7, no. 6: 708–714.

Leiter, B. 2004. "The Hermeneutics of Suspicion: Recovering Marx, Nietzsche and Freud." In *The Future for Philosophy*, edited by B. Leiter, 74–105. Oxford: Clarendon Press.

Mikhail, J. 2007. "Universal Moral Grammar: Theory, Evidence and the Future." *Trends in Cognitive Science* 11, no. 4: 143–152.

Moore, G. E. 1903/1983. *Principia Ethica*. Cambridge: Cambridge University Press.

Parfit, D. 2011. *On What Matters*. Vol. 2. Oxford: Oxford University Press.

Prinz, J. 2007. "Can Moral Obligations Be Empirically Discovered?" *Midwest Studies in Philosophy* 31, no. 1: 271–291.

Schurz, G. 1997. *The Is-Ought Problem: An Investigation in Philosophical Logic*. Dordrecht: Kluwer.

Shafer-Landau, R. 2012. "Evolutionary Debunking, Moral Realism and Moral Knowledge." *Journal of Ethics and Social Philosophy* 7: 1–37.

Singer, P. 2005. "Ethics and Intuitions." *Journal of Ethics* 9: 331–352.

Sinnott-Armstrong, W. 1984. "Ought Conversationally Implies Can." *Philosophical Review* 93, no. 2: 249–259.

Sinnott-Armstrong, W. 2008. "Framing Moral Intuitions." In *Moral Psychology*, vol. 2: *The Cognitive Science of Morality: Intuition and diversity*, edited by W. Sinnott-Armstrong, 47–76. Cambridge, MA: MIT Press.

Sinnott-Armstrong, W. 2011. "Emotion and Unreliability in Moral Psychology." *Emotion Review* 3, no. 3: 288–289.

Sripada, C., and S. Konrath. 2011. "Telling More Than We Can Know about Intentional Action." *Mind and Language* 26, no. 3: 353–380.

Stern, R. 2004. "Does Ought Imply Can? And Did Kant Think It Does?" *Utilitas* 16, no. 1: 42–61.

Street, S. 2006. "A Darwinian Dilemma for Realist Theories of Value." *Philosophical Studies* 127: 109–166.

Terbeck, S., G. Kahane, S. McTavish, N. Levi, J. Savulescu, P. Cowen, and M. Hewstone. 2013. "Beta-Adrenergic Blockade Reduces Utilitarian Judgment." *Biological Psychology* 92, no. 2: 323–328.

Voorhoeve, A. 2009. *Conversations On Ethics*. New York: Oxford University Press.

Wiech, K., G. Kahane, N. Shackel, M. Farias, J. Savulescu, and I. Tracey. 2013. "Cold or Calculating? Reduced Activity in the Subgenual Cingulate Reflects Decreased Aversion to Harming in Counterintuitive Utilitarian Judgment." *Cognition* 126: 364–372.

Wielenberg, E. 2010. "On the Evolutionary Debunking of Morality." *Ethics* 120: 441–464.

Wiggins, D. 1987. "A Sensible Subjectivism?" In *Needs, Values, Truth: Essays in the Philosophy of Value*, 185–214. New York: Oxford University Press.

Williams, B. 1981. "Internal and External Reasons." In *Moral Luck*, 101–113. Cambridge: Cambridge University Press.

Williams, B. 2008. "The Human Prejudice." In *Philosophy as a Humanistic Discipline*, edited by A. W. Moore, 77–97. Princeton, NJ: Princeton University Press.

Wilson, E. O. 1975. *Sociobiology: The New Synthesis*. Cambridge, MA: Harvard University Press.

Wright, C. 1995. "Truth in Ethics." *Ratio* 8, no. 3: 209–226.

13

Are Intuitions Heuristics?

S. Matthew Liao

13.1. Introduction

Many philosophers appeal to intuitions as evidence for the truth of philosophical claims. However, what, if anything, gives intuitions their evidentiary status? In recent years, a number of psychologists, philosophers, and neuroscientists have tended to equate intuitions with heuristics, that is, some kind of mental rules of thumb. A number of those who equate intuitions with heuristics have then questioned the evidentiary status of intuitions by pointing to the tendency of heuristics to be inaccurate. For instance, consider the famous research program on heuristics and biases (Kahneman et al. 1982; Kahneman and Frederick 2005). As Kahneman and Frederick describe this program,

> The heuristics and biases approach began with a study of the statistical intuitions of experts, who were found to be excessively confident in the replicability of results from small samples. . . . The persistence of such systematic errors in the intuitions of experts implied that their intuitive judgments may be governed by fundamentally different processes than the slower, more deliberate computations they had been trained to execute. (2005, 267)

In other words, the heuristics and biases program appears to treat intuitions as synonymous with heuristics; it then aims to show how heuristics can lead even the experts astray.

Likewise, a number of philosophers and neuroscientists have argued that moral intuitions are moral heuristics and therefore moral intuitions as moral heuristics tend to be inaccurate (Baron 1994; Sinnott-Armstrong et al. 2010; Sunstein 2005). For instance, agreeing with Kahneman and Tversky that intuitions are heuristics that often go astray,

Cass Sunstein proclaims that "moral heuristics exist and indeed are omnipresent. We should not treat the underlying moral intuitions as fixed points for analysis, rather than as unreliable and potentially erroneous" (2005, 531). Or consider Joshua Greene's work on the neuroscience of moral judgments (Greene et al. 2001; Greene 2008 and this volume). Using functional magnetic resonance imaging (fMRI), Greene finds that when people make "characteristically deontological judgments," the emotional, "intuitive" regions of the brain are activated.[1] In contrast, when people make "characteristically consequentialist judgments," the cognitive, reasoning regions of the brain are activated.[2] Greene then makes the normative claim that "characteristically deontological judgments" tend to be distorting and that we should give them up and rely instead on "characteristically consequentialist judgments," which are, in his view, more accurate. As Greene explains (this volume), underpinning his normative claim is a particular dual-processing model of moral judgment, according to which moral intuitions tend to be inaccurate, whereas moral reasoning tends to be accurate. Greene offers the following analogy based on DSLR cameras. DSLR cameras have an automatic mode and a manual mode. The automatic mode employs heuristics that are efficient but not very flexible. The manual mode is flexible but not efficient. Greene argues that the automatic mode is better suited for familiar problems, whereas the manual mode is better suited for unfamiliar problems. According to Greene, moral intuitions that produce characteristically deontological judgments are like the automatic mode. They are heuristics that may have operated well for familiar problems in our evolutionary past. But these heuristics are not well suited to handle the kind of unfamiliar problems that we face today. In contrast, moral reasoning that produces characteristically consequentialist judgments is like the manual mode. It is flexible and can be adapted to solve the kind of problems that we face today.

In response to such a challenge to the evidentiary status of intuitions, some people accept that intuitions are heuristics but try to show that heuristics can be fairly accurate in certain circumstances. For instance, Gerd Gigerenzer takes this approach (Gigerenzer and Todd 1999; Gigerenzer 2008) and says that "what intuitionist theories could gain from the science of heuristics is to explicate intuition in terms of fast and frugal heuristics" (Gigerenzer 2008, 9). In this chapter, I take a different tack and question whether intuitions are in fact heuristics. One could of course semantically attach the label "intuition" to any cognitive process. But the question I have in mind is not a semantic one. Instead, it is the following: there is a distinct cognitive process that is of interest to (some) philosophers, namely, the intuitive process. This intuitive process is different from another distinct cognitive process that is of interest to (some) philosophers, namely, the reasoning process. Is this intuitive process best understood as a kind of heuristic? I shall argue that the answer is no. Note that showing that intuitions are not heuristics does not mean that intuitions therefore have evidential value. The task of giving a full account of intuitions and their evidential value is distinct from the task of showing that intuitions are not heuristics. In other words, the argument that intuitions are heuristics is intended, at least as employed by Kahneman, Tversky, Sunstein, and

Greene, to be a kind of an epistemic defeater that undercuts the evidentiary status of intuitions. Removing this defeater leaves unsettled the evidential value of intuitions. Nevertheless, given the widespread endorsement of this argument that intuitions are heuristics, it is important to show that these two types of cognitive processes, intuitions and heuristics, are not equivalent.

To start, I shall present the views of those who think that intuitions are heuristics and how they understand one in terms of the other. In particular, I shall identify three ways of understanding intuitions as heuristics: (a) intuitions are heuristics that involve attribute substitution; (b) intuitions are heuristics that involve unconscious attribute substitution; and (c) intuitions are heuristics that are fast and frugal and that make a more complex problem simpler. Obviously (b) is a subset of (a), but the relation of (a) and (b) to (c) is, as we shall see, less clear.

Next, I offer a working definition of intuitions and reasoning and I argue that intuitions are not heuristics in the three ways discussed above. I then offer a general argument why intuitions are never heuristics. As we shall see, my definition of intuitions is a minimal one. Accordingly, my argument against the idea that intuitions are heuristics does not depend on any particularly controversial account of intuitions. Finally, I shall explore the implications of my arguments for ongoing research in psychology, philosophy, and neuroscience.

Before proceeding, a brief word on language use. I shall use the term "reasoning" and "the reasoning process" interchangeably. Also, I shall take the term "intuition" to be an umbrella term that encompasses both "the intuitive process," which is a certain kind of cognitive process; and "intuitive judgment," which is a judgment that is produced from the use of the intuitive process. I shall use the terms "the intuitive process" and "intuitive judgment" when it is appropriate to do so.

13.2. Intuitions as Heuristics

Why might someone think that intuitions are heuristics? To answer this question, it is helpful to begin with a brief overview of the research program on heuristics and biases. Consider Kahneman and Tversky's classic newspaper study in which they asked people the following questions (Tversky and Kahneman 1984).

> Question 1: In two pages of a newspaper, how many words will have "ing" as the last three letters?

> Question 2: In the same two pages of a newspaper, how many words will have "n" as the second to last letter?

Kahneman and Tversky found that most people give a higher value to the first question than to the second question. However, as Kahneman and Tversky rightly pointed out, this seems to be a mistake since every word that has "ing" as the last three letters will also have "n" as the second to last letter. Kahneman and Tversky hypothesize that people make this mistake because they are giving answers on the basis of how easily they can come up with examples, that is, they are using *the availability heuristic*. Since it is easier to think of words that have "ing" as the last three letters than it is to think of words that have "n" as the second to last letter, so the argument goes, people assign a higher value to the former than to the latter. In other words, when people use the availability heuristic, they base their beliefs about an attribute that is difficult to assess (the number of words of a given type in a newspaper) on an attribute that is easier to assess (how easy it is to think up examples of such words). A real-life use of the availability heuristic might be the following: Someone who is asked, "Do you go to the movie theater often?" might answer this question as if she had been asked, "Do instances of going to the movie theater come readily to mind?"

Consider also Tversky and Kahneman's Linda case (Tversky and Kahneman 1982).

Linda is 31 years old, single, outspoken, and very bright. She majored in philosophy. As a student, she was deeply concerned with issues of discrimination and social justice and also participated in antinuclear demonstrations. Which is more probable?

(1) Linda is a bank teller.
(2) Linda is a bank teller and is active in the feminist movement.

Tversky and Kahneman found that most people chose (2) (Tversky and Kahneman 1982). However, as Tversky and Kahneman point out, the probability of two events occurring together (in "conjunction") is always less than or equal to the probability of either one occurring alone. Tversky and Kahneman hypothesize that people make this mistake because they are trying to determine the probability of an event that is difficult to assess by comparing it to a more well-known, existing paradigm and judging that the probability will be similar, that is, they are using *the representativeness heuristic*. Given the description of Linda, Linda seems to resemble more "bank teller and active in the feminist movement" than just "bank teller." Consequently, so the argument goes, people tend to assign a higher probability to (2). As Stephen Jay Gould comments, "I know [the right answer], yet a little homunculus in my head continues to jump up and down, shouting at me—'but she can't just be a bank teller; read the description'" (1991, 469). A real-life use of the representativeness heuristic might be the following: an academic who has just given a talk in a department and who now considers the question "How friendly is the department?" might answer the following question instead: "How friendly were the faculty who asked the questions at the talk?"

From these studies, Kahneman and Frederick propose the following generalization: Whenever an object (the target attribute) is more difficult to detect directly than a related object that is easier to detect (the heuristic attribute), people tend to substitute the target attribute with the heuristic attribute (Kahneman and Frederick 2005). In other words, Kahneman and Frederick believe that intuitions are heuristics that involve a kind of attribute substitution. For instance, in the newspaper study and the Linda case, people are substituting availability and representativeness for frequency and probability, since availability and representativeness are easier to detect than frequency and probability. As Kahneman and Frederick put it, "When confronted with a difficult question, people may answer an easier one instead and are often unaware of the substitution" (2005, 268). Kahneman and Frederick claim further that "the substitution of one [the target attribute] for the other [the heuristic attribute] inevitably introduces systematic biases" (270). According to Kahneman and Frederick, this explains why subjects responding to the newspaper study and the Linda case tend to make mistakes. Kahneman and Frederick point out that reasoning can sometimes correct these mistakes by bringing additional considerations to bear (272–273).

The idea that intuitions are heuristics that involve attribute substitution is shared by a number of those who believe that moral intuitions are (moral) heuristics. Indeed, Sunstein basically accepts this idea as his starting point, and his main thesis is that because moral intuitions are also heuristics of this kind, moral intuitions often lead us astray (2005, 532). For instance, Sunstein proposes that "Do not knowingly cause a human death" is a moral heuristic.[3] He then argues that a problem with using this heuristic is that it is sometimes acceptable to cause death knowingly, "at least if the deaths are relatively few and an unintended byproduct of generally desirable activity" (2005, 536.). To support this claim, Sunstein offers the following example: When governments build new highways, they know that people will die on those highways. But, so argues Sunstein, while governments should take extra steps to reduce the risks, it does not follow that they should disapprove, from the moral point of view, of any action taken when deaths are foreseeable. Similarly, Sunstein also thinks that "Do not tamper with nature" is a moral heuristic. Sunstein then argues that this heuristic tends to lead people to overestimate the carcinogenic risk from pesticides and underestimate the risks of natural carcinogens (2005, 539). Sunstein recognizes that the claim that moral intuitions are heuristics is complicated by the fact that while nonmoral cases of the kinds considered by Kahneman and Tversky have definite correct answers, it seems more controversial to assert that there are correct answers in the moral cases. In response to this complication, Sunstein suggests that we accept "weak consequentialism," according to which "the social consequences of the legal system are relevant, other things being equal, to what law ought to be doing" (2005, 534). Sunstein claims that weak consequentialism is something that most people, except perhaps for ardent deontologists, would accept.

Sinnott-Armstrong, Young, and Cushman (SYC) also hold that moral intuitions are heuristics that involve attribute substitution. However, SYC place greater emphasis on the idea that heuristics are *unconscious* attribute substitutions. As SYC say, "Most characteristic uses of heuristics are unconscious" (Sinnott-Armstrong et al. 2010, 250). In contrast, in Kahneman and Frederick's paper, for example, the term "unconscious" is not used.

To make the case that heuristics are unconscious attribute substitutions, SYC first argue that moral intuitions are moral heuristics that involve attribute substitutions. According to SYC, the target attribute, that is, moral wrongness, is relatively inaccessible (2010, 255–256). As an example, SYC point out that on a consequentialist view, according to which whether an act is morally wrong depends only on whether some alternative has better consequences overall, it would be quite difficult to determine which act would maximize pleasure and pain, much less the good. SYC then consider various candidates of moral heuristics, and SYC propose that the affect heuristic, according to which "If thinking about the act (whatever the act may be) makes you feel bad in a certain way, then judge that it is morally wrong," may be the best candidate, because, among other things, affect is relatively accessible and seems to correlate strongly with a person's judging that an act is wrong (2010, 260).

To show that moral heuristics are *unconscious* attribute substitutions, SYC point to studies that found that people's moral judgments tend to fit with the doctrine of double effect (DDE), but very few subjects mention the DDE when asked to justify their judgments (Mikhail 2002). To elaborate, consider the following two cases:

> **Standard Trolley:** A runaway trolley is headed toward five innocent people who are on the track and who will be killed unless something is done. Abigail can push a button, which will redirect the trolley onto a second track, saving the five. However, on this second track is an innocent bystander, who will be killed if the trolley is turned onto this track.

> **Fat Man:** A runaway trolley is headed toward five innocent people who are on the track and who will be killed unless something is done. Brandon can push an innocent bystander off a bridge to fall in front of the trolley, thereby killing the bystander. The bystander is very large and the runaway trolley would be stopped by hitting the innocent bystander, thereby saving the five.

Intuitively, it seems permissible to redirect the trolley in Standard Trolley but impermissible to push the fat man. The DDE, which distinguishes between acting with the intention of doing harm and acting in a way that merely foresees harm, appears to be capable of explaining these judgments. [4] In particular, on the DDE, since Abigail merely foresees the death of the bystander, but does not intend him to be hit as a means to saving the five other innocent people, redirecting the trolley appears to be permissible. In contrast, on the DDE, since it appears that Brandon intends the bystander to be hit by the trolley as a means of stopping the trolley from hitting the five other innocent people, it would be impermissible for Brandon to push the fat man. The studies to which SYC are referring found that while people's moral judgments about these two cases tend to fit with the DDE, people do not mention the DDE when asked to justify their judgments. SYC interpret these findings as suggesting that these subjects are unconsciously substituting moral wrongness with acting with the intention of doing harm.

As another piece of evidence that moral heuristics are unconscious attribute substitutions, SYC cite studies that show that people have a tendency to reject certain principles on reflection. For instance, consider again Standard Trolley and Fat Man. Another way to explain one's judgments about these cases is through the Contact Principle, according to which people are more likely to judge harmful acts as morally wrong when an agent physically comes into contact with the victim and less likely to judge acts as morally wrong when an agent does not touch the victim (Cushman et al. 2006). Since the agent pushes, and therefore physically comes into contact with, the victim in Fat Man, but does not physically come into contact with the victim in Standard Trolley, the agent's action in Fat Man is judged to be more impermissible than the agent's action in Standard Trolley. However, it has been found that when subjects are asked whether physical contact is morally relevant, they tend to deny that this is a morally relevant principle. According to SYC, the fact that people deny that physical contact is morally relevant when asked suggests that they could not have used this principle consciously.[5]

As we have seen, Gigerenzer also believes that intuitions are heuristics. However, his understanding of what this amounts to is somewhat different than Kahneman and Tversky's. According to Gigerenzer, a heuristic is a cognitive process that is fast and frugal, where "fast" means making a decision in little time, and "frugal" means ignoring parts of the information (Gigerenzer 2008, 4). For Gigerenzer, heuristics involve a kind of simplification whereby one turns a more complex problem into a simpler one (2008, 4). Gigerenzer agrees with Kahneman and Tversky that people tend to make mistakes when they try to use heuristics in situations involving logic or probability. However, Gigerenzer argues that heuristics can be quite accurate in real-world situations. Consider the following question:

Which US city has more inhabitants: San Diego or San Antonio?

Posing this question to students at the University of Chicago and the University of Munich, Gigerenzer found that 62 percent of the American students and 100 percent of the German students answered correctly (Gigerenzer and Todd 1999, 42). How were the German students so accurate? Gigerenzer learned that all of the German students had heard of San Diego, but many of them had not heard of San Antonio. Gigerenzer hypothesizes that the German students were able to be so accurate because they used *the recognition heuristic*, according to which if one of two objects is recognized and the other is not, then assign a higher value to the recognized object. In the case of the German students, since they recognized San Diego but did not recognize San Antonio, according to Gigerenzer, they assigned a higher value to San Diego when asked to consider which city has more inhabitants.

Gigerenzer claims further that the recognition heuristic can be employed only when one of the two objects is not recognized, that is, only when a subject is under partial ignorance. According to Gigerenzer, since the American students recognized both cities, they were not able to employ the recognition heuristic, and hence they made more mistakes than the German students (Gigerenzer and Todd 1999, 43). Since the German students were able to be more accurate than the American students by using the recognition heuristic, Gigerenzer believes that in real-world situations, those who are able to use intuitions as heuristic can actually be more accurate than those who are not able to do so.

In summary, those who think that intuitions are heuristics have tended to understand this idea in one of three ways: (*a*) intuitions are heuristics that involve attribute substitution; (*b*) intuitions are heuristics that involve unconscious attribute substitution; and (*c*) intuitions are heuristics that are fast and frugal and that make a more complex problem simpler.

13.3. Why Intuitions Are Not (Unconscious) Attribute Substitutions

To assess the claim that intuitions are heuristics, it will be helpful to say something about the nature of intuitions and reasoning.

Let's start with reasoning. Roughly, reasoning seems to be the process of forming certain conclusion-judgments on the basis of certain premise-judgments. For instance, consider deductive reasoning:

P1. All men are mortal.
P2. Socrates is a man.
C3. So Socrates is mortal.

The conclusion-judgment "Socrates is mortal" is formed on the basis of the premise judgments, P1 and P2.

In contrast, an intuition appears to be the process of forming certain conclusion-judgments *not* on the basis of certain premise-judgments. One may form the conclusion-judgment in part because one understands the concepts or the circumstances involved. But one does not form the conclusion-judgment on the basis of premise-judgments. For instance, consider the following: is it permissible to torture innocent people? Intuitively, it seems impermissible. This conclusion-judgment—that it is impermissible to torture innocent people—appears to be formed not on the basis of certain premise-judgments. Indeed, someone asked to justify this conclusion-judgment might say, "It's just obvious—torturing innocent people is wrong."

Notice that this definition of intuitions is a minimal one in that it specifies only one necessary feature that intuitions should have, namely, that they should be noninferential. Accordingly, this definition is compatible with more robust accounts of intuitions such as conceptual accounts, rationalist accounts, virtue-based accounts, and naturalistic accounts of intuitions, since, as far as I am aware, these other accounts all hold that intuitions should be noninferential.[6] Hence, this definition of intuitions should be fairly uncontroversial.

I shall now argue against the idea that intuitions are heuristics. To start, intuitions are not heuristics that involve attribute substitutions because attribute substitutions involve reasoning, and reasoning, we have supposed, is distinct from intuitions. To see this, consider the availability heuristic and the newspaper study. Suppose I am asked, "In two pages of a newspaper, how many words will have "ing" as the last three letters?" Suppose I then think to myself, because I can think of many words that end in "ing," I should give a higher value to this possibility. This is a piece of reasoning. The reasoning is something like

P1.　When there are many incidences of x, x occurs with a frequency of a higher value.
P2.　There are many incidences of words that end in "ing."
C2.　Therefore, words that end in "ing" occurs with a frequency of a higher value.

In this case, my evidence for P2 comes from the incidences of words that end in "ing" that I can recall. The problem with this reasoning is of course that the fact that I can recall many instances of words that end in "ing" is not necessarily good evidence for P2, which states that there are many instances of words that end in "ing." Still, suppose that I reason this way. I will have formed my conclusion-judgment, that is, my answer regarding how likely words will have "ing" as the last three letters, on the basis of premise-judgments, P1 and P2.

Or, suppose I am asked, "In the same two pages of a newspaper, how many words will have "n" as the second to last letter?" Suppose I then think to myself, because I can think of only a few words that have "n" as the second to last letter, I should give a lower value to this possibility. Again this is a piece of reasoning. The reasoning is something like

Q1.　When there are few incidences of x, x occurs with a frequency of a lower value.
Q2.　There are few incidences of words that have "n" as the second to last letter.
C3.　Therefore, words that have "n" as the second to last letter occur with a frequency of a lower value.

Here my evidence for Q2 comes from the incidences of words that have "n" as the second to last letter that I can recall. The problem with this reasoning is of course that the fact that I can recall few instances of words that have "n" as the second to last letter is not necessarily good evidence for Q2. Still, suppose that I reason this way. I will have formed my conclusion-judgment, that is, my answer regarding how likely words will have "n" as the second to last letter, on the basis of premise-judgments, Q1 and Q2.

Or, consider the representativeness heuristics and the case of Linda. Again, one is employing reasoning in this case. The reasoning is something like the following:

R1. When the description of a case suggests that someone is more/less similar to our concept of a paradigm case of X, there is a higher/lower probability that the person is X.

R2. The description of Linda suggests that she is more similar to "bank teller and active in the feminist movement" than to just "bank teller."

C3. Therefore, there is a higher probability that Linda is a "bank teller and active in the feminist movement."

One forms the conclusion-judgment that Linda more likely to be a "bank teller and active in the feminist movement" on the basis of premise-judgments, R1 and R2. Indeed, Gould's remark, "I know [the right answer], yet a little homunculus in my head continues to jump up and down, shouting at me—'but she can't just be a bank teller; *read the description*,"* suggests that he is reasoning in this way.

The problem with this piece of reasoning is of course that R1 seems problematic; one should not necessarily determine how probable it is that someone is X just on how similar the person is to our concept of a paradigm case of X. However, although this piece of reasoning is problematic, it is still reasoning. As such, it is not an intuition.

Similar things can be said about moral attribute substitutions. For example, consider the affect heuristic, according to which if thinking about an act (whatever the act may be) makes you feel bad in a certain way, then judge that it is morally wrong. When one uses the affect heuristic, one is reasoning. Suppose I am not sure whether an act is wrong or not. So I think to myself:

S1. If an act produces negative feelings, then the act is wrong.

S2. This act produces negative feelings.

C3. Therefore, this act is wrong.

Again, this seems like a case of reasoning. I have formed the conclusion-judgment that the act is wrong on the basis of the premise-judgments, S1 and S2.

To be clear, the argument here is not that affect could not accompany intuitions. If one is a motivational internalist about moral judgments, one may well hold that affects necessarily accompany judgments, whether the judgments are intuitive judgments or judgments based on reasoning (Smith 1993). The claim here concerns only the use of affect heuristics, and the argument here is that when one uses the affect heuristics, one is still engaged in reasoning.

If intuitions are not heuristics that involve attribute substitutions, it should follow that intuitions are not heuristics that involve *unconscious* attribute substitutions.

However, some people might think that if a cognitive process is unconscious, then it must be an intuitive process, and that reasoning is always conscious. If so, this might lead them to think that perhaps intuitions are heuristics that involve *unconscious* attribute substitutions after all. To put this thought to rest, I shall argue that (1) reasoning can be unconscious and that (2) one can be conscious of the intuitive process, which means that intuitions are not necessarily unconscious.

To give an example of (1), suppose that a detective has been trying to solve a murder case. Suppose that it was the detective's day off from working on the case and she was in her car listening to music and on her way to do some grocery shopping. All of a sudden the detective had a eureka moment and she said, "The butler did it." When asked why she thought this, she explained, "I just realized that the murderer has to be a member of household staff and has to be a left hander, and the only member of household staff who is left handed is the butler." In this case, it seems that the detective had reached the conclusion that "the butler did it" in an unconscious way. Indeed, she was not aware that she was even thinking about who the murderer was. However, her thought process appears to be a typical example of (deductive) reasoning. In this case, the detective formed the conclusion-judgment that the butler did it on the basis of certain premise-judgments, namely, the murderer has to be a member of household staff and has to be a left hander, and the only member of the household staff who is left handed is the butler. If so, this shows that reasoning can be unconscious.

What about the evidence SYC have cited for unconscious attribute substitutions, such as the fact that people's moral judgments tend to fit with the doctrine of double effect (DDE) and the fact that people have a tendency to reject certain moral heuristics on reflection? Even if we grant that these are indeed evidence for unconscious attribute substitutions, if I am right that attribute substitutions are a form of reasoning, then this evidence could just be evidence for unconscious reasoning. However, there are reasons to doubt that these examples are evidence for unconscious attribute substitutions, because there are reasons to doubt that these are evidence for attribute substitutions at all.

For instance, consider the findings that show that people's moral judgments tend to fit with the DDE even though very few subjects mention the DDE when asked to justify their judgments. There are at least two reasons why this is not a good piece of evidence for attribute substitutions. First, earlier in their paper, SYC actually rejected the idea of acting with the intention of harming as a plausible candidate for heuristic attribute on the ground that "the attribute of intention as a means is not so easy to access," whereas heuristics attributes are supposed to be easy to access (Sinnott-Armstrong et al. 2010, 260). Since, by SYC's own light, acting with the intention of harming is not a plausible candidate for heuristic attribute, these findings are not good evidence for attribute substitutions. Therefore, these findings are not good evidence for unconscious attribute substitutions. Second, there are reasons to doubt that people are substituting moral wrongness with acting with the intention of harming. For one thing, there are people who would reject the DDE but who nevertheless have the same kind of judgments regarding certain cases as someone who accepts the DDE would. Consider again Standard Trolley and Fat Man. Earlier we noted that the DDE appears to explain these judgments. However, the DDE is not the only way to explain these intuitive judgments. For instance, Kamm has rejected the DDE and has argued that these judgments can be explained in terms of causal structures of an act (Kamm 2007). In particular, redirecting the trolley in Standard Trolley is permissible, so argues Kamm, because the bad of killing the innocent bystander in Standard Trolley is downstream from the good of saving the five. In contrast, according to Kamm, pushing the innocent bystander in Fat Man is impermissible because the bad of killing the innocent bystander in Fat Man is upstream from the good of saving the five. For our purpose, since there are people who would reject the DDE and who still have the same judgments about these cases as someone who holds the DDE would, this suggests that it is not necessary to substitute moral wrongness with acting with the intention of harming in order to arrive at these judgments.

Here it is worth pointing out that there is a better and more straightforward explanation of why very few subjects mention the DDE when asked to justify their judgments about these cases, namely, these judgments are intuitive judgments. As such, their judgments are not based on any premise judgments at all, including the DDE. In other words, whereas SYC take the fact that very few subjects mention the DDE when asked to justify their judgments about these cases as evidence that these subjects are appealing to the DDE unconsciously, it seems more plausible to think that these subjects do not mention the DDE because they are not appealing to it. Indeed, these findings provide good empirical evidence that people have intuitive judgments and that the DDE and Kamm's causal structure theory are post hoc principles to which people may or may not appeal in order justify their initial, intuitive judgments.

Similar things can be said about SYC's point that people have a tendency to reject certain moral heuristics such as the Contact Principle upon reflection. First, earlier in their paper, SYC also explicitly rejected the Contact Principle as a plausible candidate for heuristic attribute (Sinnott-Armstrong et al. 2010, 260). Since, by SYC's own light, the Contact Principle is not a plausible candidate for heuristic attribute, findings about the Contact Principle are not good evidence for attribute substitutions. Therefore, they are not good evidence for unconscious attribute substitutions. Second, there are reasons to doubt that people are substituting moral wrongness with the Contact Principle. To see this, consider

> **Push:** A runaway trolley is headed toward five innocent people who are on the track and who will be killed unless something is done. Claire can push a button, which will activate a moveable platform that will move an innocent bystander in front of the trolley. The runaway trolley would be stopped by hitting the innocent bystander, thereby saving the five but killing the innocent bystander.

Push is very similar to Fat Man, but no up-close-and-personal contact with the innocent bystander is necessary to save the five. It nevertheless seems impermissible to push the button in this case. Given the similarity of Push and Fat Man, presumably whatever explains the impermissibility of one would explain the impermissibility of the other. Since the Contact Principle does not seem relevant for explaining the impermissibility of Push, this suggests that the Contact Principle is not necessary to explain the impermissibility of Fat Man. If so, this suggests that it is not necessary to substitute moral wrongness with the Contact Principle in order to arrive at the judgments that Fat Man is a case of impermissible action.

As before, there is, I think, a better and more straightforward explanation of why people have a tendency to reject the Contact Principle upon reflection, namely, their judgments about Fat Man and Push are intuitive judgments. As such, their judgments are not based on any premise judgments, including the Contact Principle. Indeed, these findings provide further empirical evidence that people have intuitive judgments. These findings also suggest that the Contact Principle is a post hoc principle to which people may or may not appeal in order justify their initial, intuitive judgments; and that the Contact Principle is something people may reject upon reflection while maintaining their initial intuitive judgments. If all of this is right, we have reasons to believe that the evidence SYC have provided is not good evidence for attribute substitutions at all; and therefore, it is not good evidence for *unconscious* attribute substitutions.

Next, let me show that one can also be conscious of the intuitive process. To give an example, consider the following case:

Loop: A trolley is headed toward five people and can be redirected onto another track where one innocent bystander sits. However, the track loops back toward the five. Hence, if it were not the case that the trolley would hit the one and grind to a halt, the trolley would go around and kill the five.

It seems that one can consciously be thinking about whether it is permissible to redirect the trolley or not and that one can arrive at an intuitive judgment about the permissibility of redirecting the trolley, that is, one can form a conclusion-judgment about this case not on the basis of any premise judgments. Importantly, it seems that one can be aware that one is intuiting. As far as I can tell, this phenomenon seems ubiquitous; that is, in many cases, we know, through introspection, that we are intuiting. Potentially, those who are in the business of using their intuitions such as philosophers are better than others at knowing whether they are intuiting or not. Also, there are a number of ways one can figure out whether one is intuiting or not. For example, we can eliminate incidences in which we are reasoning or employing cognitive processes other than intuiting (e.g., recall). We may also be able to use some kind of "dumbfounding" test, where we have convictions that we are incapable of justifying but which we nevertheless continue to hold.[7]

It might be thought that the intuitive process must be an unconscious one because being conscious requires that one is aware of the premise-judgments from which a conclusion-judgment is derived. Since, by the account of intuition given above, the intuitive process is a process of forming a conclusion-judgment without basing the conclusion-judgment on certain premise-judgments, this means that in the case of intuitions, it is never possible for one to be aware of the premise-judgments from which a conclusion-judgment is derived. However, it seems that this would reach the conclusion that the intuitive process must be an unconscious one by defining "conscious" in a way that rules out the account of intuition given above. Since the account of intuition given above seems plausible, defining conscious this way seems question-begging. If so, this suggests that one can be conscious of the intuitive process.

If all of this is right, there are reasons to believe that intuitions are not heuristics that involve unconscious attribute substitutions.

13.4. Why Intuitions Are Not Fast-and-Frugal Heuristics

Let us now consider the idea, à la Gigerenzer, that intuitions are fast-and-frugal heuristics that make a more complex problem simpler. A couple of remarks are in order. First, just because a cognitive process is fast does not mean that it is an intuition. A cognitive process can be fast because it is a recall of a piece of recent memory. Indeed, I can recall very quickly that I had soup for lunch, but this would not be an intuition. Also, a cognitive process can be fast because it is a piece of simple reasoning. For instance, when asked, what is 10 + 10? I can easily give the answer, 20. But this would also not be an intuition; this appears just to a piece of simple reasoning. Here it is worth pointing out that Gigerenzer is not the only person to regard fast cognitive processes as intuitions. Kahneman, Tversky, Greene, and many others all assume this as well. In fact, this is a key way by which the heuristic and biases program purports to show how intuitions tend to lead us astray. For instance, consider Kahneman and Frederick's bat and ball study in which they gave subjects the following problem to solve (see, e.g., Kahneman and Frederick 2005):

> A bat and a ball cost $1.10 in total. The bat costs $1 more than the ball. How much does the ball cost?

Kahneman and Frederick found that almost all subjects reported an initial tendency to answer "10 cents," because "the sum $1.10 separates naturally into $1 and 10 cents, and 10 cents is about the right magnitude" (Kahneman and Frederick 2005, 273). Moreover, Kahneman and Frederick found that many people did in fact yield to this immediate impulse. Indeed, even among undergraduates at elite institutions, about half get this problem wrong when it is included in a short IQ test (Kahneman and Frederick 2005, 273). On the basis of these findings, Kahneman and Frederick draw the conclusion that "the surprisingly high rate of errors in this easy problem illustrates how lightly system 2 monitors the output of system 1: People are often content to trust a plausible judgment that quickly comes to mind" (Kahneman and Frederick 2005, 273–274). In other words, Kahneman and Frederick are suggesting that people who answered that the ball costs 10 cents were using their intuitions, that is, system 1, and that their use of quick intuitions is why they got the problem wrong.

But this is not the lesson we should draw from Kahneman and Frederick's study. Instead, the lesson we should draw is that people got this problem wrong because they had not reasoned through the problem *fully*. Consider one way by which one can solve this problem.

1. Let x = the cost of a bat and y = the cost of a ball.
2. "A bat and a ball cost $1.10 in total" can be represented as $x + y = 1.10$. Call this Equation 1.
3. "The bat costs $1 more than the ball" can be represented as $x - y = 1.00$. Call this Equation 2.

To figure out what x and y are, one can add Equations 1 and 2 together. One would get $2x = 2.10$, which means that $x = 1.05$ and $y = .05$. So the answer to the question "How much does the ball cost" is 5 cents.

When people are given the problem, what they notice is that if the bat is 1 dollar and the ball is 10 cents, this would satisfy Equation 1, that is, $1 + .10 = 1.10$. When they see that Equation 1 is satisfied, many tend to stop further deliberation. Their thought process is something like the following: "I have found a set of values for x and y that satisfies Equation 1. Therefore, I can stop further deliberation." If so, however, this does not show that their judgment is the result of an intuition. Instead, it shows that they have not reasoned through the problem fully. Had these people tested these values of x and y on Equation 2, they would have seen that $x = 1$ and $y = .10$ would not satisfy Equation 2. Hence, just because a judgment is reached quickly does not mean that this judgment is the result of an intuition. This judgment may be the result of not reasoning through a problem fully.

Second, it is not the case that if a judgment is the result of an intuition, then the judgment must have been formed quickly. For instance, consider

Brain Transplant: Suppose that there are two human beings, Abbey and Brenda. Both have their cerebrums removed. The cerebrum that had been in Brenda is then destroyed, while the cerebrum that had been in Abbey is transplanted into the skull that had encased Brenda's cerebrum. Let us call the being that receives the cerebrum transplant "Brenbey" while the name "Cerebrumless" will refer to the now mindless body that had earlier contained Abbey's cerebrum. And let us suppose that Brenbey has Abbey's psychology and is now able to (quasi-)know and (quasi-)remember things that Abbey had known and remembered.

Suppose that one is asked whether Abbey is Cerebrumless or Brenbey (or neither). It might take some time for one to understand this case, after which it might take still more time for one to form a judgment regarding whether Abbey is Cerebrumless or Brenbey (or neither). This would not mean that one's judgment was therefore not an intuitive judgment. Of course, if one sat down and worked out a theory of personal identity from first principles and then explicitly applied the theory to the case, then one's judgment would not be the result of an intuition. But the point here is that there is no reason why one couldn't take time to form a conclusion-judgment where the conclusion-judgment is not based on certain premise-judgments. If so, the fact that a judgment is an intuitive judgment need not mean that it must therefore have been formed quickly.

Third, intuitions are not heuristics that make a more complex problem simpler because simplifications are also reasoning. To see this, consider the recognition heuristic and the question Gigerenzer posed to German and American students: "Which US city has more inhabitants: San Diego or San Antonio?" Suppose that I think to myself,

T1.   An object that is recognized has a higher value than an object that is not recognized.
T2.   San Diego is recognized; San Antonio is not recognized.
C3.   Therefore, San Diego has a higher value.

Here I am forming a conclusion-judgment on the basis of premise-judgments, T1 and T2. By the account of reasoning given above, this is a piece of reasoning. In fact, Gigerenzer agrees. As he says, "I suggest that the intuitions can be explicated by heuristics *relying on reasons*. . . . The opposition is not between intuition and reasoning, in my view, but between the (unconscious) reasons underlying intuition and the conscious, after-the-fact reasons" (2008, 15). Gigerenzer may be right that for the purpose of deciding how accurate heuristics are, the relevant distinction may be between unconscious and conscious reasoning. But for our purpose, Gigerenzer is in effect acknowledging that the recognition heuristic could be a form of reasoning. If so, this further supports the idea that recognition heuristic is not an intuition.

We are now in the position to make the general claim that intuitions are never heuristics. It seems that all heuristics employ the following kind of reasoning:

U1:   The heuristic attribute represents/covaries with the target attribute.
U2:   The heuristic attribute has a higher/lower value.
C3:   Therefore the target attribute has a higher/lower value.

If all heuristics employ this kind of reasoning, then they are reasoning rather than intuitions. If so, intuitions are never heuristics.

13.5. Implications

If the claim that intuitions are heuristics is false, this has a number of implications for ongoing research in psychology, philosophy, and neuroscience.

One implication is that *moral* intuitions are not heuristics. This means that even if Sunstein were correct that people who use moral heuristics tend, for example, to overgeneralize, this would be a problem for the use of moral heuristics but not for the use of moral intuitions.

Another implication is that Greene's normative claim that deontological intuitions tend to be inaccurate because they are heuristics, much like the automatic mode on a DSLR camera, is unsupported. Earlier we saw that deontological intuitions are not heuristics; very few subjects mention the DDE when asked to justify their judgments about trolley cases, and people tend to reject the Contact Principle upon reflection, both of which suggest that people are not substituting moral wrongness with the DDE or the Contact Principle and that instead they are intuiting in these cases. Suppose that this is the case. Since deontological intuitions are not heuristics, they are not like the automatic mode on a DSLR camera. If so, and if Greene still wants to maintain that consequentialist judgments are more accurate than deontological judgments, he will need to give some other argument to undercut the evidentiary status of deontological intuitions, and he cannot rely on the argument that intuitions are heuristics that tend to lead us astray. Again, the point here is not that deontological intuitions have evidential value. Instead, the point is that Greene still needs to give us reasons to think that they do not have evidential value.

Finally, if heuristics are a form of reasoning, then Kahneman and Tversky's program of showing how heuristics can be biased in fact shows how some forms of reasoning can be inaccurate. It also means that we should rethink the kind of simple dichotomy between accurate reasoning and inaccurate intuition that we often see psychology, philosophy, and neuroscience and that underlies much of the literature on dual-processing models of judgments.

Acknowledgments

I would like to thank Collin O'Neil, Katherine Keene, Dan Khokhar, Gina Rini, Irena Cronin, Elisabetta Sirgiovanni, and audiences at the 2015 Pacific APA in Vancouver, the CUNY Graduate Student Philosophy Conference, and the Moral Brain Conference at New York University for their helpful comments on earlier versions of this paper.

Notes

1. According to Greene, this includes the medial prefrontal cortex, the posterior cingulate, the posterior superior temporal sulcus, the orbitofrontal/ventromedial prefrontal cortex, and the amygdale. Greene 2008, 44.

2. According to Greene, this includes the dorsolateral surfaces of the prefrontal cortex and parietal lobes. Greene 2008, 44.

3. Although Sunstein endorses the idea that heuristics involve attribute substitutions, as far as I can tell, he does not explicitly discuss how the moral heuristics he considers involve attribute substitutions.

4. According to one interpretation of the DDE, there is a moral constraint on acting with the intention of doing harm, even when the harm will be used as a means to a greater good. However, it can be permissible to act with the intention of employing neutral or good means to promote a greater good, even though one foresees the same harmful side-effects, if (*a*) the good is proportionate to the harm, and (*b*) there is no better way to achieve this good. See, e.g., Kamm 2007.

5. SYC offer a third reason why moral heuristics are unconscious attribute substitutions, namely, moral heuristics are correctable by conscious reflection. As they say, "When asked whether an act is morally wrong, people who initially use the affect heuristic can later correct their initial impressions if they take time to reflect on additional features, such as the consequences of actions" (Sinnott-Armstrong et al. 2010, 266). The implicit assumption here seems to be that if a judgment is correctable by conscious reflection, then the judgment must initially be formed unconsciously. This assumption seems false. Suppose I came up with an argument and, after reflecting on it, I decided that it was false. The fact that the argument was correctable by conscious reflection does not mean that I therefore came up with the argument unconsciously.

6. For a conceptual account of intuition, see, e.g., Goldman 2007. For a rationalist account, see, e.g., Bealer 2000. For a virtue-based account, see, e.g., Sosa 2007. For a naturalistic account, see, e.g., Kornblith 1998. As far as I can tell, the minimalistic account I have offered is compatible with these accounts.

7. For the phenomenon of moral dumbfounding, see Haidt 2001.

References

Baron, J. 1994. "Nonconsequentialist Decisions." *Behavioral and Brain Sciences* 17: 1–10.

Bealer, George. 2000. "A Theory of the A Priori." *Pacific Philosophical Quarterly* 81, no. 1: 1–30.

Cushman, Fiery, Liane Young, and Marc Hauser. 2006. "The Role of Conscious Reasoning and Intuition in Moral Judgment." *Psychological Science* 17, no. 12: 1082–1089.

Gigerenzer, Gerd. 2008. "Moral Intuition = Fast and Frugal Heuristics?" In *Moral Psychology*, vol. 2: *The Cognitive Science of Morality: Intuition and Diversity*, edited by W. Sinnott-Armstrong, 1–26. Cambridge MA: MIT Press.

Gigerenzer, Gerd, and Peter M. Todd. 1999. *Simple Heuristics That Make Us Smart*. Oxford: Oxford University Press.

Goldman, Alvin. 2007. "Philosophical Intuitions: Their Target, Their Source, and Their Epistemic Status." *Grazer Philosophische Studien* 74: 1–25.

Gould, S. J. 1991. *Bully for Brontosaurus: Reflections in Natural History*. New York: W. W. Norton.

Greene, Joshua D. 2008. "The Secret Joke of Kant's Soul." In *Moral Psychology: The Neuroscience of Morality*, edited by Walter Sinnott-Armstrong, 35–79. Cambridge, MA: MIT Press.

Greene, Joshua D., R. Brian Sommerville, Leigh E. Nystrom, John M. Darley, and Jonathan D. Cohen. 2001. "An fMRI Investigation of Emotional Engagement in Moral Judgment." *Science* 293, no. 5537: 2105–2108.

Haidt, J. 2001. "The Emotional Dog and Its Rational Tail: A Social Intuitionist Approach to Moral Judgment." *Psychological Review* 108: 814–834.

Kahneman, D., and S. Frederick. 2005. "A Model of Heuristic Judgment." In *The Cambridge Handbook of Thinking and Reasoning*, edited by K. J. Holyoak and R. G. Morrison, 267–93. New York: Cambridge University Press.

Kahneman, D., P. Slovic, and A. Tversky. 1982. *Judgement under Uncertainty: Heuristics and Biases*. Cambridge: Cambridge University Press.

Kamm, Frances M. 2007. *Intricate Ethics: Rights, Responsibilities, and Permissible Harm*. New York: Oxford University Press.

Kornblith, Hilary. 1998. "The Role of Intuition in Philosophical Inquiry: An Account with No Unnatural Ingredients." In *Rethinking Intuition: The Psychology of Intuition and Its Role in Philosophical Inquiry*, edited by Michael DePaul and William Ramsey, 129–142. Lanham, MD: Rowman and Littlefield.

Mikhail, J. 2002. "Aspects of a Theory of Moral Cognition: Investigating Intuitive Knowledge of the Prohibition of Intentional Battery and the Principle of Double Effect." http://ssrn.com/abstracts=762385.

Railton, Peter. 2014. "The Affective Dog and Its Rational Tale: Intuition and Attunement." *Ethics* 124, no. 4: 813–859.

Sinnott-Armstrong, Walter, Liane Young, and Fiery Cushman. 2010. "Moral Intuitions." In *The Moral Psychology Handbook*, edited by J. Doris, 246–272. Oxford: Oxford University Press.

Smith, Michael. 1993. *The Moral Problem*. Oxford: Blackwell.

Sosa, Ernest. 2007. *A Virtue Epistemology: Apt Belief and Reflective Knowledge*. Vol. 1. New York: Oxford University Press.

Sunstein, Cass. 2005. "Moral Heuristics." *Behavioral and Brain Sciences* 25: 531–573.

Tversky, Amos, and Daniel Kahneman. 1982. "Judgments of and by Representativeness." In *Judgement under Uncertainty: Heuristics and Biases*, edited by Daniel Kahneman, Paul Slovic, and Amos Tversky, 84–98. Cambridge: Cambridge University Press.

Tversky, Amos, and Daniel Kahneman. 1984. "Extensional versus Intuitive Reasoning: The Conjunction Fallacy in Probability Judgment." *Psychological Review* 90: 293–315.

Woodward, James, and John Allman. 2007. "Moral Intuition: Its Neural Substrates and Normative Significance." *Journal of Physiology-Paris* 101, nos. 4–6: 179–202.

14

The Disunity of Morality

Walter Sinnott-Armstrong

ONE OF THE most important lessons from the first decade of research in moral neuro-science is that morality is not unified in the brain or anywhere else. This lesson should shape the next decade of research into moral neuroscience. However, many neuroscien-tists, psychologists, philosophers, and others still assume that all moral judgments share some common and distinctive neural basis.

Some neuroscientists say so explicitly. For example, in a review Moll et al. (2005, 799) write, "Recent functional imaging and clinical evidence indicates that a remarkably consistent network of brain regions is involved in moral cognition." Notice the lack of qualification. Moll and colleagues do not say that this network is involved in *some* moral cognition. Instead, they suggest that the same network of brain regions is involved in *all* moral cognition. Conversely, although Moll and colleagues can admit that each individ-ual brain region in the identified network is also involved in some nonmoral cognition, it would not be interesting to find a network of brain regions involved in moral cognition if that whole network is also involved in many kinds of *nonmoral* cognition. If the network subserves all judgments—whether moral or not—then it might show something about judgments without showing anything special about morality. Thus, Moll and colleagues seem to suggest that the discovered network of brain regions is distinctively moral.

Similar claims are implied by psychologists who claim to discover "the essence of mo-rality." Recently, Gray, Young, and Waitz wrote, "We investigate whether all moral judg-ments can be explained by appealing to a dyadic template" (2012, 103), and their answer is affirmative. Assuming physicalism, the proposed psychological template must have some neural basis. The psychological template would hardly be a single "essence" if its neural basis were not unified. So these psychologists seem to be committed to the claim that all moral judgments share a distinctive and unified neural basis.

Other moral scientists and philosophers are less explicit but still seem to assume that moral judgments are unified in the brain. For example, Greene and Haidt cite a small sample of moral judgments but draw conclusions about moral judgments in general: "Neuroimaging studies of moral judgment in normal adults, as well as studies of individuals exhibiting aberrant moral behavior, all point to the conclusion, embraced by the social intuitionist model, that emotion is a significant driving force in moral judgment" (2002, 522). Again, notice the lack of qualification, so they seem to be referring to all moral judgments. A generalization from *some* moral judgments to *all* moral judgments can be justified only if moral judgments are unified by some feature that supports those generalizations. Otherwise, how could they rule out the hypothesis that emotion is a significant driving force in some but not all moral judgments? Thus, regardless of whether they are aware of it, scientists who generalize from small samples to universal conclusions must be assuming that moral judgments are unified.

Philosophers notoriously share this assumption. Philosophical moral theories from utilitarianism to Kantianism to virtue theories all claim to apply to morality as such. Even Ross (1930), who postulates seven different prima facie moral duties, assumes that these seven duties share something distinctive that makes them moral duties instead of nonmoral duties. The same assumption is made by metaethical theories of the meanings of moral terms, the epistemic justifiability of moral judgments, and the relation between moral belief and motivation. These philosophical theories almost never admit the possibility that different moral theories might work for different kinds of moral judgments. Thus, although most philosophers do not talk about the brain directly, they seem to assume that moral judgments share some distinctive essence, and again that essence would seem to have some unified neural basis, assuming physicalism.

Admittedly, some philosophers, psychologists, and neuroscientists do not share this assumption. Flanagan (1991, 15–20) and Stich (2006, 181–189) explicitly reject the unity of morality. So do Greene and Haidt in their final conclusion: "There is no specifically moral part of the brain" (2002, 522) and "Morality is probably not a 'natural kind' in the brain" (2002, 523). I agree, and I am indebted to these predecessors.

Unfortunately, however, this lesson is not appreciated widely enough. Many philosophers, psychologists, and neuroscientists still do not agree—or at least they seem not to agree, because they continue to write, theorize, and design experiments as if morality is unified and, more specifically, as if there is some distinctively moral part of the brain. Moreover, even when careful philosophers and scientists add appropriate qualifications, there still remains a significant temptation for nonexpert commentators to overinterpret careful conclusions, such as when the popular media claim that scientists have found "the moral compass in the brain" (Sundby 2010). Claims like these stand in the way of progress.

My goal here is to convince these recalcitrant overgeneralizers to stop. I want to explain why and how morality fails to be unified. Of course, I cannot refute every possible proposal for unifying morality, so I won't try to do that. Instead, I will focus on three main levels at which morality is often taken to be unified. First, I will discuss the content of morality, because variations in content display the challenge for my opponents. Second, I will discuss whether morality is unified at a neural level, because this volume focuses on the brain. Third, I will explore the function of morality, because the most common and popular proposals for unifying morality cite some function. Admittedly, even though these three proposals fail, some other candidate still might succeed in unifying morality.[1] Nonetheless, in the absence of another plausible proposal, I will conclude that nothing unifies morality. But, before I can assess any candidate for unifying morality, I need to clarify the standards that such candidates must meet.

14.1. What Is the Issue?

The question is basically whether morality is like memory. Once upon a time, philosophers and psychologists believed that memory is monolithic. Now memory is understood as a group of distinct phenomena that need to be studied separately (Tulving 2000). Memory includes not only semantic or declarative memory, such as remembering that a bat is a mammal, but also episodic memory, such as remembering seeing a bat yesterday. Memories can also be long-term or short-term (or working) memory, and procedural memory includes remembering how to do things, such as how to ride a bike. Thus, there are many kinds of memory, and they are not unified by any common and distinctive feature. They are not even all about the past, since you can also remember timeless truths, such as that pi is 3.14159 . . ., and you can also remember that you have a meeting tomorrow, even if you do not remember setting up the meeting or even who set it up. These kinds of memory differ not only in their psychological profiles and functions but also in their neural basis, as shown by both fMRI and by patients, such as H. M., whose brain lesions left him with severely impaired episodic memory but largely intact procedural and semantic memory. Such findings led most experts to accept that memory is not unified.

This recognition enabled progress. Neuroscientists could never find a neural basis for memory as such while they lumped together all kinds of memory. Psychologists could never formulate reliable generalizations about memory as long as they failed to distinguish kinds of memories. And philosophers could never settle how memory is justified if they conflated remembering facts and remembering how to ride a bicycle. Although these problems remain hard, progress became easier after recognizing that memory is not a single natural kind.

My thesis is that morality is like memory. Neither of them is unified, and admitting disunity makes progress possible in both areas. Moral neuroscience, psychology, and philosophy will become much more precise and productive if they give up the assumption that moral judgments all share a distinctive essence.

To make this thesis more precise, I first need to specify which class of things my thesis is about—the class that is claimed to be unified or not. The issue here is not about which moral judgments are true or justified or which judgments I (or you) endorse. Instead, the issue is only about which judgments are intended or supposed to be about moral norms as opposed to other kinds of norms, including aesthetic, prudential, economic, legal, conventional, or religious norms. People do distinguish kinds of norms and invoke one kind as opposed to another, but that practice by itself does not show that there are any real differences among those kinds of norms. Just as people might distinguish races even if races are not really distinct biologically, so people might distinguish kinds of norms even if there is no real difference between moral and nonmoral norms. The question here is about real rather than merely apparent differences. Nonetheless, we need to start with the norms that people classify as moral in order to determine whether or not anything really unifies those norms and distinguishes them from so-called nonmoral norms. Hence, I will count a judgment as a *moral* judgment if and only if people who make that judgment do or would think of it as similar enough in important respects to judgments that they take to be exemplars or paradigms of moral judgments. To sidestep controversy, I will focus on judgments that millions of people accept as moral judgments in this way, even if many people reject those moral judgments as false.

Critics might object that I am talking only about the judgments that millions of people (perhaps falsely) count as moral judgments rather than the judgments that really are moral judgments. To see why this objection is misdirected, compare races again. A biologist who wants to determine whether a race is unified biologically needs to start by specifying which people are supposed to be in that race and then asking whether anything that is biologically important is shared by and distinctive of those people. If a critic replies that the biologist who denies the unity of race is looking at people who are not really members of that race, then the critic assumes that there really is a race for people to be a member of. Analogously, critics who respond to my definition by saying that genuinely moral judgments are unified are assuming that there really is a class of genuinely moral norms for judgments to be a member of. That might be right, but we cannot assume it at the start. In order to avoid assuming either that moral judgments are unified or that they are not unified, we need some independent test of which judgments are moral judgments. That is why I appeal to the judgments that millions classify as moral.

Next, I also need to specify what it is for this class to be unified. I will call a group of phenomena *unified* if and only if some single feature that enables useful theoretical generalizations is present in all and only members of that group. Although this requirement is common for definitions, some critics might see it as too stringent: all and only! An alternative account of unity could be statistical, so that a group is unified when its members are more likely to share a trait with other members than with nonmembers. However, this statistical notion is too weak to serve important purposes. If moral judgments are only more likely to have certain features, then the fact that a new judgment has those features cannot show that the new judgment is a moral judgment, and the fact that it lacks that feature cannot show that the new judgment is not a moral judgment. Moreover, if the relation is purely statistical, the feature need not capture what makes a judgment moral. Even if most (or nearly all) cities have a certain sort of public transportation system, and even if most areas with that sort of public transportation system are cities, the public transportation system is still not what makes this area a city. Similarly, a proposed account of what makes moral judgments moral must meet the more stringent test of fitting all and only moral judgments—or at least all and only judgments that millions of people see as moral judgments—in order to provide a test of which judgments are moral and in order to uncover what it is that makes them moral judgments.

My thesis, then, is that judgments that are intended to be about morality rather than some other kind of norm are not unified by any single common and distinctive feature that enables important generalizations about distinctive properties of those judgments. This thesis is compatible with the claim that moral judgments fall within a broader category that is unified. Even if moral judgments are not unified, for example, normative judgments still might be unified, perhaps because they (and only they) have some conceptual relation to reasons or motivation. My thesis is also compatible with unity within some narrower kinds of moral judgments, such as moral judgments about harm or the moral judgments of a certain person, society, or group. My thesis here is only that a particular level of generality—moral judgment—is not unified by any single important feature.

14.2. Is Morality Unified by Its Content?

The most obvious candidate for a unifying feature is content: what moral judgments are about. The idea cannot be simply that moral judgments are about morality, since that would beg the question of whether morality is a unified topic to be about.

Moral judgments are also not unified merely by being about what is right and wrong. DeScioli and Kurzban (2009, 282) say, "This paper examines 'morality,' meaning phenomena surrounding the concepts 'right' and 'wrong.'" Whatever they meant by this, the terms "right" and "wrong" are much too general to give the meaning of morality in particular, because many kinds of rightness and wrongness are independent of morality. There are right and wrong answers on history and math tests as well as right and wrong ways to bake a brioche or build a bridge. Thus, it is wrong (though not immoral) to identify morality with what is right and wrong. Moral judgments are moral because they judge acts to be right or wrong or good or bad in special ways, and those special ways are what need to be defined here.

A more plausible proposal about content claims that all and only moral judgments are about harm to others (Gert 2005; Mill [1859] 2011). In this vein, Grey, Young, and Waitz (2012, 16) write, "On our account, perceived suffering is not a distinct moral domain, but a core feature of all immoral acts." However, some moral judgments are about goods instead of harms. Imagine that a colleague gets tenure; and she will not suffer or be harmed if you fail to give her a celebratory gift, partly because she does not expect any gift, and she is happy already. Nonetheless, many people would still judge that giving her a gift is nice or ideal, and the way in which it is nice is moral as opposed to legal, aesthetic, religious, conventional, or prudential.

Some theorists still might contrast moral ideals like niceness with moral requirements and prohibitions and claim that all moral requirements and prohibitions are about harm to others. Notice that this move already admits that harm to others cannot unify *all* moral judgments, since moral judgments do include judgments about moral ideals. Moreover, harm to others also cannot succeed in unifying even only the moral judgments that are about requirements or prohibitions. This is evident from a quick survey of moral requirements and prohibitions (which expands on Haidt 2011, which builds on Shweder et al. 1997):

Harm:
> *Death*: Do not kill.
> *Disability*: Do not blind, paralyze, or maim.
> *Loss of property*: Do not steal.
> *Physical pain*: Do not torture.
> *Psychological pain*: Do not insult or make people feel bad.

Justice:
> *Retributive*: Do not punish more or less than is deserved.
> *Distributive*: Do not treat people unequally.
> *Procedural*: Give everyone a fair hearing and a fair chance.

Dishonesty:
> Do not lie (or deceive).
> Do not break promises.
> Do not cheat (e.g., in games or in marriage).

Social position:
> *Hierarchy*: Do not disrespect or disobey your parents or elders.
> *Role*: Do your job and duty (e.g., as employee, citizen, or club member).
> *Loyalty* (to an in-group): Be patriotic. Don't rat on friends.

Purity:
> *Sexual*: Do not commit incest or necrophilia.
> *Gustatory*: Do not commit cannibalism.

These categories are vague, incomplete, and overlapping, and these rules need to be qualified. Still, the point here is only to illustrate some of the variety.

The first group of moral prohibitions explicitly concerns harm to others. So does retributive justice, insofar as punishment involves harm. In contrast, harm is not essential to distributive and procedural justice, because unequal tenure gifts as well as procedures for awarding grants or prizes can be unjust apart from harm. Dishonest acts also seem morally forbidden even when they do not cause harms, as in the classic case of deathbed promises (unless we count false beliefs themselves as harms).

The disconnect between harm and moral judgments is even clearer in prohibitions based on social position. Sometimes nobody is harmed when one disobeys one's parents or the law, and yet many common folk and philosophers believe that we always have some (pro tanto) moral obligation to obey our parents and the law. Similarly, burning a flag is often seen as immoral because unpatriotic even when done secretly so that nobody is affected at all. Even when harmless, such acts are still judged as morally wrong by many people who accept such rules of hierarchy, role, and loyalty.

The same point applies to purity. If one eats part of a dead human body in secret when no disease is transferred, no habit begins, and the person died by accident, then cannibalism causes no harm. People might stretch to find some indirect harm, believed harm, or risk of harm, but that tendency does not show that such a tenuous relation to harm is what really makes people judge such acts to be immoral or what makes them classify such judgments as "moral" (cf. Haidt et al. 1993).

Many liberals and libertarians see the moral judgments that are not based on harm as irrelevant to real morality (Haidt and Graham 2007). However, what they mean by this claim seems to be that the people who make those judgments are mistaken. When people say that harmless impurity (allegedly in homosexuality, incest, and cannibalism) and disrespect for authorities (such as parents, the law, or one's country) is immoral, even liberals and libertarians have to admit that those judgments are moral in the sense that they are intended to be about morality. What liberals and libertarians deny is not that these judgments are moral judgments (as opposed to aesthetic, prudential, conventional, legal, or religious judgments). Instead, what they deny is only that these judgments are accurate, acceptable, or true. Otherwise, liberals and libertarians would not really be disagreeing with conservatives but only talking about a different, nonmoral topic.

Moreover, conservatives who claim harmless immorality see these judgments as moral in nature and basically similar to paradigm moral judgments about harm, injustice, and dishonesty. It might not be clear why they see their judgments as moral, but the fact that enough of them do intend their judgments to be about morality and do classify such judgments as moral despite knowing that they are not about harm is enough to show that harm cannot unify all judgments that are moral in the way defined above in section 14.1.

Finally, even if all moral judgments did somehow concern harm, that would not be enough to unify morality unless the notion of harm itself is unified. Harms can be physical (such as death, injury, and disease) or mental (such as loneliness and sadness). Harm is also sometimes defined to include "injustice and violation of [moral?] rights" (Haidt et al. 1993, 613), such as stealing fruit that its owner never notices or needs. Robinson and Kurzban (2007, 1866) add "intangible harms, such as the extent of intrusion of privacy." Gray and Wegner (2011, 258) extend harm so far that "even seemingly non-harm domains are understood in the currency of harm." Gray, Young, and Waitz (2012, 16) even include "spiritual destruction," whatever that is. To cover all kinds of moral judgments, the term "harm" has to be extended so broadly that a happy and healthy secret masturbator is seen as harming himself (at least by those who judge that masturbation is immoral). This stipulation conflicts with common language and causes confusion. It also cannot show that the various harms are unified in any way that could generate any useful generalizations that are distinctive of morality.

That is why moral judgments cannot be unified by harm to others. Of course, moral judgments still might be unified by some other feature of content. However, it is hard to imagine what that other feature of content would be. In the absence of any plausible proposal, I conclude that moral judgments are not unified by their content.

14.3. Is Morality Unified by Its Neural Basis?

What else could unify moral judgments? Since salt comes in various colors but is unified by a shared chemical structure, one might hope to find a physical basis for all and only moral judgments. Such a common physical basis would presumably be located in the brain. Where else? Indeed, some studies of moral judgments might seem to suggest a shared neural basis that is distinctive of moral judgments. Many of Moll's early studies aimed to distinguish the neural basis for moral judgments in contrast with nonmoral judgments (Moll 2005, quoted above). However, recent neuroimaging evidence clearly tips the balance in favor of disunity—that is, in favor of the thesis that no neural system is both distinctive of moral judgments and also shared by all moral judgments. This section surveys a selection of these findings.

14.3.1. IDEALS VERSUS REQUIREMENTS AND PROHIBITIONS

Different brain processes have been discovered for moral judgments about ideals in contrast with requirements and prohibitions. In Moll et al. (2006), subjects were given $128 and knew that they could leave with any of it that they did not give away. These subjects were asked to read about real charitable organizations. Some of these charities dealt with euthanasia, abortion, children's rights, the death penalty, gender equality, war, and nuclear power, so they raised controversial moral issues. Subjects were then given the chance to respond yes" or no to a choice of real payoffs to themselves and to a certain charity. For example,

Pure monetary reward: Yes to +$2 to you and $0 to the charity
Costly donation: Yes to −$2 from you and give +$5 to the charity
Noncostly donation: Yes to $0 to you and +$5 to the charity
Noncostly opposition: No to $0 to you and +$5 to the charity
Costly opposition: No to +$2 to you and +$5 to the charity

One might wonder why people would turn down $2 for themselves in order to prevent $5 going to a charity. The answer is moral judgment. Participants who see abortion as morally prohibited might accept some sacrifice in order to avoid enabling abortion. More generally, subjects who opposed donations to certain charities either at some cost or no gain to themselves presumably based that decision on a moral judgment that those charities violated some moral prohibition; and subjects who gave donations to certain charities at some cost to themselves presumably based that decision on a moral judgment that those charities further some moral ideal.

Moll et al. found that these judgments about moral prohibitions and moral ideals were associated with activation in distinct brain regions. Subjects who donated on the basis of moral ideals showed higher activation in the subgenual region. In contrast, subjects who opposed donations on the basis of moral prohibitions showed higher activation in the lateral orbital frontal cortex. Some regions were activated by both moral ideals and moral prohibitions, including the ventral tegmental area, the striatum, and the anterior prefrontal cortex. However, the ventral tegmental area and the striatum were also activated by pure monetary rewards as well as other kinds of reinforcement expectancy, so they were not activated *only* for moral judgments. The anterior prefrontal cortex was not activated by *all* moral judgments, because it was not activated by noncostly donations or noncostly opposition, so it seems to be related not to moral judgment but to cost to the chooser. Overall, no region of the brain is common and peculiar to both moral ideals and moral prohibitions. Those moral judgments seem to be made by different systems.

Critics might deny either that these donation choices were based on moral judgments or that we should ever have expected moral ideals to have the same neural basis as moral requirements or prohibitions. Even if moral ideals have a distinct neural basis, all moral requirements or prohibitions still might share a common and peculiar neural basis. That would not show that all moral judgments are unified in the brain, but it would still be important.

14.3.2. KINDS OF REQUIREMENTS AND PROHIBITIONS

Another study disconfirms that more limited hypothesis. Schaich Borg, Lieberman, and Kiehl (2008) asked participants in a brain scanner to memorize and recall statements that described neutral controls and target acts that involved three kinds of disgust: pathogen disgust, sexual disgust, and moral disgust. For example,

Control: You have dinner with your sister.
Pathogen disgust: You touch your sister's feces.
Sexual disgust: You give your sister an orgasm.
Moral disgust: You push your sister in front of a bus.

The assumption was that people who memorized these statements and repeated them would be making implicit moral judgments. The behavioral results are crucial here. Subjects rated the acts in sexual and moral disgust statements as equally immoral, but the acts in pathogen disgust statements were rated as much less immoral or not immoral at all. Schaich Borg et al. (2008) also found significant activations in many different brain areas. Pathogen disgust was related to activation in the amygdala, orbital frontal cortex, left inferior frontal gyrus, precuneus, visual cortex, and left fusiform gyrus. Sexual disgust was related to activation in the anterior cingulate, medial prefrontal cortex, insula, posterior cingulate, temporoparietal junction, and middle temporal gyrus. Moral disgust was related to activation in only the inferior parietal lobule. In addition, all disgust stimuli were related to activation in some common areas, including the medial prefrontal cortex, middle temporal gyrus, amygdala, and occipital gyrus.

The crucial point here is that no neural region is common and peculiar to all moral judgments—that is, to judgments regarding moral disgust and sexual disgust but not pathogen disgust. Some brain regions were related to *all* moral judgments in this study, but these areas were related to pathogen disgust where subjects did not make moral judgments. Other brain regions were related to *only* moral judgments—for example, the insula was related to only sexual disgust, about which subjects did make moral judgments—but those areas were not activated by other moral judgments, such as those related to moral disgust. Crucially, no brain regions were common and peculiar to all kinds of moral judgments. In order to show that morality is unified in an interesting way that enables distinctive and significant generalizations, some neural region would have to be both common and peculiar to all moral judgments. Hence, this study supports the disunity thesis.

Unfortunately, the study by Schaich Borg et al. (2008) did not ask subjects to make explicit moral judgments but only to memorize and recall statements that would presumably invoke implicit moral judgments. To see whether this makes a difference, we designed a study (Parkinson et al. 2011) that directly tests the unity hypothesis for explicit moral judgments.

The first step was to construct a set of stimuli that cleanly separates different areas of morality. Over the course of three pilot studies, we developed balanced scenarios that described actions that were (physically) harmful but neither dishonest nor disgusting, separate acts that were dishonest but neither harmful nor disgusting, and a third group of acts that invoked (sexual) disgust but were neither harmful nor dishonest. For example, the second group included undiscovered lies, and the third group included necrophilia without deception. We developed these stimuli so that they would be ambiguous in the specific sense that at least 30 percent of subjects found the act to be morally wrong and at least 30 percent found the act to be not morally wrong. This enabled us to compare brain activations when participants actually judged that an act was morally wrong to the brain activations when they judged that an act was not morally wrong. A final group for comparison included neutral stimuli that were neither harmful nor dishonest nor disgusting and were not judged to be morally wrong.

Our findings confirmed our hypotheses. Harmful acts that were judged morally wrong compared to neutral scenarios were associated with increased activity in the left dorsal lateral prefrontal cortex, anterior cingulate cortex, supplementary motor area, inferior parietal lobe, superior temporal sulcus, and thalamus. In contrast, when participants judged dishonest acts to be morally wrong, there was bilateral activity in the dorsal medial prefrontal cortex (dmPFC), temporal parietal junction extending superiorly into the inferior parietal lobe, and posterior cingulate cortex as well as increased activity in the left dorsal lateral prefrontal cortex. When disgusting acts were judged to be morally wrong, we observed increased activity in the bilateral dorsolateral prefrontal cortex, dmPFC, amygdalae, anterior cingulate cortex, and posterior cingulate cortex, as well as the right temporal pole and left inferior frontal operculum/anterior insula. In summary, none of these areas were common and peculiar to all and only judgments of moral wrongness.

We did, however, find one location of activation that was common to all areas of moral judgment. A conjunction analysis revealed one twenty-eight-voxel cluster in the dmPFC that was independently activated in the comparison of each area of moral wrongdoing compared to neutral scenarios. To investigate whether this region was activated specifically by moral wrongdoing, we applied this cluster as a mask to each individual's data to extract the average response for the not-wrong scenarios in each category type. This secondary analysis revealed that dishonest and harmful scenarios judged to be not-wrong also activated this region more strongly than neutral scenarios. Thus, the activity observed in this region of the dmPFC seems to reflect a process engaged by the moral scenarios that is not peculiar to a moral judgment that the act is wrong. This interpretation is consistent with research showing that activity in this region of the dmPFC is modulated by ambiguity in both social and nonsocial contexts (van Overwalle 2009). By design, our moral scenarios were ambiguous in a way that our neutral scenarios were not, so ambiguity may explain the observed dmPFC activation across areas in the comparison between moral and neutral scenarios. Regardless of the exact mechanisms, the overlapping activation in the dmPFC seems to reflect some process or processes that are not peculiar to moral judgments that something is morally wrong.

Although our study focused on harm, dishonesty, and disgust, other studies have investigated the neural basis of moral judgments about fairness or justice. Robertson et al. (2007) found that areas of the brain reacted differently to sensitivity to harm versus sensitivity to unfairness and dishonesty. Hsu, Anen, and Quartz (2008) found that judgments of equity activated the insula, whereas judgments of efficiency activated more the putamen. These studies and others provide reason to expect that our results (Parkinson et al. 2011), as well as those of Schaich Borg, Lieberman, and Kiehl (2008), would generalize to other areas of morality.

Critics might respond that, even if not all moral judgments are unified by a brain mechanism, there still might be a unified brain mechanism underlying moral judgments of harmful acts in particular. That would not be enough to unify moral judgments in general, but it might satisfy some theorists who reject other kinds of judgments as not really moral judgments. However, Greene et al. (2001, 2004) found different brain activations for moral judgments of harmful acts in personal dilemmas as opposed to impersonal dilemmas. Schaich Borg et al. (2006) also found different brain activations for moral judgments of harmful acts when the harm was intended than when it was foreseen as an unintended side effect. Thus, not all moral judgments activate the same brain regions even when the moral judgments are all specifically about harm. This suggests that a prototypical neural response for a particular judgment, should it exist, will exist at a fine-grained level of analysis many subcategories below "moral judgment" (e.g., a specific kind of harm in a particular context from a distinct perspective). Accordingly, there appears to be slim hope of finding a prototypical neural correlate common and peculiar to all moral judgments.

Critics might reply that I require too much. The circulatory system seems unified, but it is distributed throughout the body instead of being located in only one part of the body. Thus, there can be unity without colocation. Similarly, even if moral judgments are not associated with activity in a single brain area, they still might have a distributed kind of unity. Nonetheless, it is one thing to say that the system might be unified and quite another to say that it actually is unified. If the circulatory system did not include physical connections or similar cell types, then it would not be unified at the physical level. In contrast, there is no evidence that moral judgments are related to anything in the brain that is remotely like the blood, veins, and arteries that make up the circulatory system. Hence, this analogy cannot show that moral judgments are unified at the physical level. Of course, the circulatory system is also unified at the functional level, because its various parts function to spread nutrients and other chemicals through the body. Similarly, even if moral judgments are not unified at the physical or neural level, they still might be unified at the level of function. That is a separate hypothesis that we need to consider next.

14.4. Is Morality Unified by Its Function?

The most popular proposal for unifying moral judgments appeals to function. As we saw above, Greene and Haidt agree with my conclusion in the preceding section when they write, "There is no specifically moral part of the brain" and "Morality is probably not a 'natural kind' in the brain" (2002, 522 and 523). Haidt (2011) also emphasizes that the content of morality covers several distinct "foundations." Nonetheless, Greene and Haidt still both claim that moral judgments share a distinctive function that unifies moral judgments at a different, nonneural level (Haidt 2011; and Greene 2013, 23;

discussed below). Thus, these moral theorists do not agree with my radical thesis that moral judgments are not unified at *any* level.

If moral judgments are unified by some function, then we can cite that function to distinguish moral judgments from nonmoral judgments and also to explain why so many people make moral judgments as well as why they make moral judgments in some cases but not in other cases. However, we still need to determine precisely which function can play these explanatory roles.

In order to specify the function of moral judgments, it seems natural to cite some widespread problem that moral judgments help to solve. Most proposed functional accounts of moral judgments specify the function in this way, but these accounts differ in the particular problem that moral judgments are supposed to solve. The challenge is then to find a single problem that all and only moral judgments solve, are intended to solve, or evolved to solve.

In order to fit the wide variety of moral judgments surveyed above in section 14.2, the relevant function, purpose, or problem must be characterized very broadly. One general problem for all societies is to control conduct by members of the group. This problem can be built into a definition of morality like this: "Morality is considered as the sets of customs and values that are embraced by a cultural group to guide social conduct" (Moll et al. 2005, 799). Although this sort of definition is popular, it cannot be adequate, because it is both too narrow and too broad.

First, it is too narrow, because some moral judgments are not about "social conduct." Many moralists, including Kant (1797, 82–107), condemn masturbation and suicide as immoral even in cases where they know that nobody else is involved or affected. Indeed, these and other moral duties to self have been a major topic in moral theory for centuries. The whole point of this debate is to determine whether acts can be immoral independent of other people. Whichever position you happen to agree with, the judgments on opposing sides are clearly moral (as opposed to aesthetic, economic, legal, etc.). However, the moral judgments that favor duties to self explicitly do not refer to "social conduct." These moral judgments are missed by any definition that limits morality to "social conduct."

Moll's definition is also too broad in other respects. Notice that this definition explicitly includes "customs." However, Turiel (1983) and his followers found that most people distinguish customs or conventions from morality. Many of the conventions or customs that Turiel's subjects distinguished from morality were based on values (even if not moral values) and were "embraced by a cultural group to guide social conduct." After all, "social conduct" includes everything that we do together with other people, and societies often value their own conventions or customs for various reasons.

One simple example is rules of dancing. These rules guide conduct that is social insofar as more than one person is dancing, and different societies value their own forms of dancing. Thus, rules of dancing do seem to be "customs and values that are embraced by a cultural group to guide social conduct," as the above definition says. Nonetheless, idiosyncratic dancing that breaks the social norms is often seen as ugly or weird but not as immoral. Even dancers that hurt their partners by stepping on toes are judged to be uncoordinated but not immoral (unless they do so intentionally or carelessly). Some people might judge sexually explicit dancing to be immoral, but the relevant example here is unconventional dancing that is harmless and nonsexual but still judged to be ugly but not immoral. This example illustrates the general problem that there are many kinds of customs and many kinds of values. Dancing serves a kind of value (aesthetic) that is distinguished from morality. That is why we cannot define moral judgments simply as "the sets of customs and values that are embraced by a cultural group to guide social conduct."

Another instance of the same problem involves the rules of different languages. People who speak the French language might value placing adjectives after nouns, because that order seems more natural to them; and people who speak English might value placing adjectives before nouns, because that order seems more natural to them. These claims might seem silly, but the point here is only that many people value the customs of their own societies, but they still do not think that it is immoral for other societies to have other customs. It is wrong linguistically but not morally to place the adjective after the noun when speaking English.

Next compare laws that govern driving. Some people from Australia and the United Kingdom argue that it is better to drive on the left side of the road, because most people are right handed, so left-side driving allows more drivers to keep their dominant hand on the steering wheel when they shift gears in a manual transmission. Such judgments might seem silly, but that does not matter here. The point here is only that these people value their own customs, but they still do not think that it is immoral to drive on the right in the United States. Of course, it is immoral to intentionally drive on the right in the United Kingdom when this endangers other drivers, but that is a separate matter. People who value driving on the left do not think that it is immoral to drive on the right in countries where right-side driving is safe and legal. Indeed, they usually think that it is immoral to drive on the left in those countries. They see right-side driving as imprudent or inefficient as a custom but not as immoral when it is customary. Thus, this example and the others show that we cannot define moral judgments simply in terms of "the sets of customs and values that are embraced by a cultural group to guide social conduct." That definition includes too much.

In order to avoid these problems, some moral theorists introduce selfishness or self-interest as a target for the function to morality. Here is Greene (2013, 23): "Morality is a set of psychological adaptations that allow otherwise selfish individuals to reap the benefits of cooperation." Compare Haidt (2011, 270): "Moral systems are interlocking sets of values, virtues, norms, practices, identities, institutions, technologies, and evolved psychological mechanisms that work together to suppress or regulate self-interest and make cooperative societies possible." Thus, Greene and Haidt seem to agree that moral judgments evolved to serve a distinctive function of overcoming selfishness in order to enable cooperation.

This story sounds plausible in the abstract until you look more closely. To show why such definitions cannot really unify moral judgments, I will focus on Haidt's more complex version. Notice three features of his definition.

First, Haidt ascribes functions not to moral judgments but rather to "moral systems" as wholes. The problem is that moral systems include many parts, and the relations among those parts are exactly what is at issue here. Haidt might be claiming only that (A) any system of rules that can legitimately be called a moral system must have at least some parts that serve the specified functions. That claim (A) is compatible with recognizing that many other parts of the system do not serve these functions at all. But then it will not be true that (B) any rule that is part of a moral system must serve those functions. Claim (B) could be used to argue that a certain judgment is not a moral judgment, but claim (A) is useless for that purpose. For that reason, I will focus on claim (B) while recognizing that Haidt might have intended only claim (A).

Second, Haidt claims that moral systems "suppress or regulate self-interest and make cooperative societies possible." He does not explicitly say that nothing else serves this function. Hence, his official definition implies that (C) all moral judgments "suppress or regulate self-interest and make cooperative societies possible" but not that (D) *only* moral judgments "suppress or regulate self-interest and make cooperative societies possible." The problem, as before, is that claim (D) could be used to argue that a certain judgment is a moral judgment, but claim (C) is useless for that purpose. For that reason, I will focus on claim (D) while recognizing that Haidt might have intended only claim (C).

Third, Haidt's definition actually ascribes two functions instead of just one. To "suppress or regulate self-interest" is not the same as to "make cooperative societies possible." Which of these is supposed to be the function that unifies morality? This is unclear, so I will discuss them separately.

Consider first Haidt's claim that moral systems "make cooperative societies possible." What exactly does this mean? A minimal interpretation is simply that cooperative society would not be possible without at least some morality. Totally amoral people could not cooperate or live together for long. That seems plausible. Nonetheless, it cannot help us distinguish moral from nonmoral judgments. Even if total amorality would undermine society, there could still be many parts of morality that are not needed to "make cooperative societies possible." If some parts of morality are essential to cooperative society, but other parts are not, then this function is not common and peculiar to all moral judgments.

What would be needed to determine which judgments are moral is the stronger claim that all (and only) moral judgments "make cooperative societies possible." That stronger claim is, however, implausible. The problem can be illustrated by many permissive moral judgments. The judgment that I am morally permitted to spend my money on a yacht is moral in nature even though it is not needed to "make cooperative societies possible." A cooperative society could get along perfectly well, perhaps even better, without this moral judgment, even if it needs some rules in the general area of property.

In addition, many moral prohibitions are not really necessary for society. Just recall the survey of moral judgments in section 14.2, and it will be easy to find many moral judgments that are not necessary for cooperative society. For example, cooperative societies can survive without moral judgments against cannibalism, either because they practice limited cannibalism or because they have an aversion to cannibalism that prevents the practice without leading to a moral judgment.

Another problem is that several kinds of nonmoral rules or judgments are also needed to make cooperative society possible. We saw examples above: language and law. Without any rules of language, we could not communicate in ways that are needed for us to form anything like the societies we have; but it is still not immoral to break those rules of language (even intentionally). Similarly, without any laws, we could not live together in cooperative societies; but we can still judge an act to be illegal without judging it to be immoral. Admittedly, many individual rules of language and law are not necessary to "make cooperative societies possible." It is only language and law as a whole that are needed to "make cooperative societies possible." But that is precisely the situation with morality. Hence, this function cannot be used to show what is distinctive about morality.

The other function that Haidt ascribes to morality is to "suppress or regulate self-interest." (Notice that Greene also alludes to "selfish individuals.") However, some moral judgments seem not to function to "suppress or regulate self-interest"—at least not on an individual level. After all, the judgment that I am morally permitted to spend my money on a yacht is moral in nature even though it does not "suppress or regulate self-interest." Haidt could respond that his definition was meant to apply not to such permissive moral judgments but only to moral judgments about what is forbidden or obligatory. However, this admits that his definition does not work for all moral judgments, since permissive moral judgments constitute a large group of moral judgments.

In addition, many moral judgments about obligations also do not "suppress or regulate self-interest." If I promise my wife to go for a walk with her, then I might judge that my promise creates a moral obligation to go for a walk with her, even while I very much want to do so and it is in my self-interest to do so. On many occasions like this, morality and self-interest coincide. Admittedly, the general rule that we ought to keep our promises does conflict with self-interest in some situations, but such occasional conflicts cannot help us distinguish moral judgments from nonmoral judgments in general.

Finally, it is not *only* moral judgments that "suppress or regulate self-interest." Rules of games also have that function, since it would often be in my self-interest to move my rook on a diagonal when I am playing chess. The same goes for language. I might want to use words contrary to the rules of grammar, but doing so is still ungrammatical, so grammar can also "suppress or regulate self-interest." (Lewis Carroll made this point with Humpty Dumpty.) Indeed, it might be a general feature of all rules (whether moral or not) that they sometimes (though not always) regulate self-interest. Nonetheless, this function of regulating self-interest does not turn rules of chess or grammar into moral rules. We judge chess moves to be illegal and utterances to be ungrammatical without judging them to be immoral. Thus, even when moral judgments do "suppress or regulate self-interest," that function cannot be used to define moral judgments.

It might seem that I cheated by separating the two functions that Haidt mentioned together, so let's consider conjunctions and disjunctions. Can moral judgments be identified as judgments that serve both to regulate self-interest and also to make cooperative society possible? No, because I gave examples of moral judgments that lacked one of these functions, so those judgments also fail the conjunctive requirement. Next, can moral judgments be identified as judgments that serve either to regulate self-interest or to make cooperative society possible? No, because I gave examples of nonmoral judgments that have one of these functions, so those judgments also meet the disjunctive requirement. Thus, moral judgments cannot be unified by taking these two functions together.

To avoid these problems, moral theorists might refer not just to selfishness but also to other kinds of partiality. Warnock (1971), for example, argued that the purpose of morality and of moral judgments is to reduce liability to harm that arises from limited sympathy. The purpose could not be simply to reduce liability to harm in general, since hygienic rules about brushing your teeth reduce liability to harm but are not moral rules. The particular concern of morality, according to Warnock, was that we care about ourselves and our family and friends much more than we care about strangers. This limited sympathy then leads us to do acts that harm others, so we are all in danger when lots of other people have such limits on their sympathy. Morality is supposed to solve this problem by having rules that apply to all people equally. One should not lie, break promises, kill, or rape anyone—even strangers for whom one has no sympathy.

This picture might seem plausible in many cases, but it does not cover all of the judgments that people usually classify as moral. Consider rules about purity. A judgment that it is morally wrong to commit homosexual sodomy will reduce sympathy for homosexuals and the difficulties that they have when prevented from freely expressing their love. Batson and his collaborators (1999) found, for example, that people who judge homosexuality to be immoral do not help out needy homosexuals, even when they just need money to visit their grandparents. Similar points apply to moral judgments about hierarchies and loyalty. When people judge that we must obey our parents and bosses or that we have special duties to our in-group, this judgment will presumably reduce sympathy for people who are not in our in-group or whom our parents or bosses order us to hurt, neglect, or despise. Moral judgments about hierarchies and loyalty function not to reduce limits on sympathy but, instead, to impose limits on sympathy for underclasses and outsiders.

Next consider retributive justice. The rule that punishers must take an eye for an eye and a tooth for a tooth seems to undermine sympathy for people who have committed crimes. On this rule, officials should punish them in proportion to their crime regardless to how much sympathy anyone feels for the criminal. Even those who reject retributivism must recognize such retributivist judgments as moral judgments instead of aesthetic, prudential, legal, or conventional judgments. That shows that not all moral judgments function to expand sympathy. More generally, the problem in morality sometimes is too much sympathy rather than too little. The classic expression that hard cases make bad law does not, as many people assume, mean that difficult cases make bad law. Instead, it refers to cases where you need to be hard on someone. For example, if you need to punish or civilly penalize someone who has done something wrong, but you feel really sorry for her (perhaps because she is sick or had a child die), then you might bend the law so that you will not have to punish her or make her pay damages in a civil case. Here sympathy gets in the way of justice. Since justice is an area of morality, morality does not always serve the function of overcoming limits on sympathy, as Warnock claimed.

Let's consider one more recent attempt to unify morality by its function. Robinson and Kurzban (2007, 1865–1866) claim that "what makes an act immoral is the concurrent belief that those who perform the act should be punished." This proposal is not entirely clear, but it can be interpreted as suggesting that the function of judging an act to be immoral is to distinguish agents who should be punished from those who should not and perhaps also to justify punishing the certain agents. Nonmoral judgments (such as aesthetic, prudential, and conventional judgments) are not supposed to justify punishment in the same way. If so, we can identify moral judgments as those that are intended to tell us who "should be punished."

Unfortunately, this account is again both too broad and too narrow. It is too broad because, for example, there can be fines for illegal parking and penalties for failing to file tax forms on time, even when those acts are not judged to be immoral. In the classic terminology, mala prohibita are punishable, even though they are not mala in se or immoral in themselves. Moreover, even in cases of mala in se, such as murder, there might be strong reasons for criminal laws against some actions, such as active euthanasia, even in circumstances where those acts are not immoral, simply because allowing such acts would lead to too many mistakes. Conversely, Robinson and Kurzban's definition is also too narrow because many acts are seen as immoral even if nobody should punish the agent. Imagine that your neighbor's wife lies to him, and he immediately forgives her. Who should punish her? Him? But he forgave her. You? But it's none of your business. It seems at least possible that, even if her lie was immoral, there is nobody who should punish her, as Robinson and Kurzban's definition requires. (Perhaps she was liable to punishment by her husband before he forgave her, but their definition requires that someone should punish her, and even he should not punish her if he should forgive her as he did.) In addition, recall permissive moral judgments, such as the judgment that it is not immoral to buy a yacht. Permissive judgments do not justify punishment. That is what makes them permissive. Remember also judgments of moral ideals, such as that it is nice to give the tenure gift described above. The judgment that the gift was nice, good, ideal, or supererogatory can be intended as a moral judgment as opposed to a religious, aesthetic, economic, conventional, or legal judgment, even if no punishment would have been justified if the gift had not been given. Thus, neither all nor only moral judgments justify punishment.

Kurzban admits as much in a later development of his views. DeScioli and Kurzban (2009, 282) "argue for two distinct components of moral cognition: One subsystem regulates one's own behavior (conscience) and another mechanism is specialized for judging others (condemnation)." Of course, if different parts of morality have two distinct functions, as they claim, then morality is no more unified than jade is unified when it has two subtypes, jadeite and nephrite. Maybe the claim is instead that each moral judgment has both functions: conscience and condemnation. However, condemnation simply generalizes punishment, so it still cannot account for permissive judgments or ideals, discussed above. Consider also heroism. We can judge someone a moral hero, and that is a moral judgment, even if we do not condemn people who do not live up to such high standards. This case and many others like it show that condemnation plays a role in only some but not all moral judgments. Moreover, we condemn people for nonmoral wrongs, such as ungrammatical sentences, stupidity, invalid arguments, and illegal parking. A special kind of condemnation might seem appropriate for violations of moral prohibitions, but then the problem is to specify that special kind of condemnation (without circularly calling it "moral condemnation"). The general notion of condemnation by itself is not enough to enable us to identify moral judgments, because we condemn lots of things other than immorality. Adding the notion of conscience cannot help here because conscience is defined so broadly as that which "regulates one's own behavior." We can use hygienic rules, such as "Brush your teeth," to regulate our own behavior without judging it immoral to skip brushing our teeth because we are too tired. The same goes for rules of grammar, games, logic, and prudence. In all such cases, we can regulate behavior and condemn rule violations without judging anything immoral. Thus, this new proposal by DeScioli and Kurzban also cannot capture what is distinctive about morality.

Many more possible proposals about the function of morality deserve consideration here. However, instead of extending the list, I want to step back and raise the general question of why functional definitions of morality all fail. Evolutionary psychologists cite evidence that different moral judgments arose from different evolutionary pressures at different times. For example, Lieberman and Hatfield (2006) argue that pathogen disgust (connected to prohibitions on cannibalism) arose from one type of evolutionary pressure; then sexual disgust (connected to prohibitions on incest) arose from a different kind of evolutionary pressure; and then "moral" disgust (such as finding nonsexual sadism disgusting) arose from yet another evolutionary pressure. Moreover, it is hard to see how moral rules against lying or promise breaking could arise before language or why moral rules against harm would not have arisen in some form before language, since our ancestors were subject to harmful aggression long before they could talk. In these cases and others, then, different moral judgments probably arose from different evolutionary pressures in different circumstances. If that is correct, then it should come as no surprise that different kinds of moral judgments serve different evolutionary functions as well as different contemporary functions. This evidence thus provides reason to doubt that any single function could unify all areas of moral judgment. Morality is just too diverse in its history.

Admittedly, there is a large body of fascinating and plausible work about the evolution of morality that I have not discussed. However, most of that literature does not even try to show that all and only moral judgments serve a common and distinctive function. Instead, most studies focus on one or a few particular kinds of moral judgments, as is proper (see section 14.5). Hence, this research cannot undermine my conclusion that different moral judgments have different functions. Indeed, surveying the larger literature would further support the conclusion that morality has no single unifying function, as Machery and Mallon (2010) have argued.

14.5. Does Disunity Matter?

My overall conclusion is that morality is not unified. This conclusion can meet with either of the two prototypical philosophical replies: (1) Oh yeah? (2) So what?

Some critics respond that I have not proven this conclusion. Granted. Since I have not and cannot survey all possible proposals for unifying morality, my conclusion is best characterized as raising a question: If there is something else that unifies all and only moral judgments, what is it? Opponents need to put forward a precise proposal. Only then can we assess it.

Another common response is this: Fine, but who cares? All scientists and philosophers should care. If morality really is like memory, as I suggested, then scientists and philosophers can make more progress if they stop trying to study morality all at once. Here's why.

In many experiments, researchers lump together moral judgments and seek contrasts between moral and nonmoral judgments. These experimenters do not draw distinctions among different kinds of moral judgments or test these kinds separately. Instead, they throw them all into a single bin. I suggest, instead, that scientists should isolate smaller classes of judgments within one region of the map, carefully distinguish from other types of judgments not on the basis as whether they count as moral or not, but rather on the basis of their content and context. Then scenarios should be presented from a single perspective either in the first person, second person, or third person consistently. And then scientists should look for the neural basis or the evolutionary origin or the psychological process behind that smaller class of judgments.

After a series of such smaller-scale experiments, of course, we can ask whether this basis or origin in each area extends to all or only moral judgments. We might eventually find some unifying feature. I doubt it, but I cannot rule out the possibility on the basis of what I have argued here.

This bottom-up method has several advantages. It prevents both false positives and false negatives. First, if researchers lump together different types of moral judgments in empirical studies, they might miss a lot of interesting conclusions. For example, if one class of moral judgments in the mix activates an area of the brain more highly than the baseline, but then other moral judgments activate that same area of the brain less than the baseline, then researchers will miss both of these significant brain activation levels, because they will cancel out each other. Similarly, we might find no significant difference between moral and nonmoral conditions, even though a subset of moral judgments is related to a significant activation increase, simply because the increased activation from a subset of our stimuli is not statistically significant when thrown together with all the other types of moral judgments.

The bottom-up method also helps to avoid false positives. For example, if researchers present ten moral scenarios each from five different areas, and they find an increased activation for that total set of compared to a neutral baseline, then they might conclude that all of the moral judgments tend to activate those areas. However, that entire result might come merely from one or two classes of moral judgments out of the five kinds, even though the other moral judgments do not activate these brain areas at all. If they assume that those other judgments will activate that area, then they will fall into the trap of false positives.

To avoid such mistakes and to make more progress, moral science needs to shift towards taxonomic rigor. The first step is to accept that moral judgment is not unified. I hope that this chapter has convinced readers of that fact. The next step is for researchers to begin to create a working taxonomy that informs future paradigm design and data interpretation. Any such taxonomy should be based on detailed empirical research combined with careful philosophical analysis. By committing to a taxonomic approach, the field can progress toward a deeper understanding of the component processes that define the myriad judgments that we call "moral."

Note

1. Sinnott-Armstrong (2008) and Sinnott-Armstrong and Wheatley (2012, 2014) argue against other ways to unify morality. In this chapter, I draw heavily on that previous work. I am deeply indebted to Thalia Wheatley for our joint research on these issues. I am also grateful to many other friends for comments on this series of articles and to Matthew Liao and Peter DeScioli for comments on an earlier draft of this chapter.

References

Batson, C. D., R. B. Floyd, J. M. Meyer, and A. L. Winner. 1999. "And Who is My Neighbor? Intrinsic Religion as a Source of Universal Compassion." *Journal for the Scientific Study of Religion* 38: 445–457.

DeScioli, P., and R. Kurzban. 2009. "Mysteries of Morality." *Cognition* 112: 281–299.

Flanagan, O. 1991. *Varieties of Moral Personality*. Cambridge, MA: Harvard University Press.

Gert, B. 2005. *Morality: Its Nature and Justification*. New York: Oxford University Press.

Gray, K., and D. M. Wegner. 2011. "Dimensions of Moral Emotions." *Emotion Review* 3: 258–260.

Gray, K., L. Young, and A. Waitz. 2012. "Mind Perception Is the Essence of Morality." *Psychological Inquiry* 23: 101–124.

Greene, J. 2013. *Moral Tribes: Emotion, Reason, and The Gap between Us and Them*. New York: Penguin.

Greene, J., and J. Haidt. 2002. "How (and Where) Does Moral Judgment Work?" *Trends in Cognitive Science* 6: 517–523.

Greene, J. D., L. E. Nystrom, A. D. Engell, J. M. Darley, and J. D. Cohen. 2004. "The Neural Bases of Cognitive Conflict and Control in Moral Judgment." *Neuron* 44: 389–400.

Greene, J. D., R. B. Sommerville, L. E. Nystrom, J. Darley, and J. D. Cohen. 2001. "An fMRI Investigation of Emotional Engagement in Moral Judgment." *Science* 293: 2105–2108.

Haidt, J. 2011. *The Righteous Mind: Why Good People Are Divided by Politics and Religion*. New York: Pantheon.

Haidt, J., and J. Graham. 2007. "When Morality Opposes Justice: Conservatives Have Moral Intuitions That Liberals May Not Recognize." *Social Justice Research* 20: 98–116.

Haidt, J., S. H. Koller, and M. G. Dias. 1993. "Affect, Culture, and Morality, or Is It Wrong to Eat Your Dog?" *Journal of Personality and Social Psychology* 65: 613–628.

Hsu, M., C. Anen, and S. Quartz. 2008. "The Right and the Good: Distributive Justice and Neural Encoding of Equity and Efficiency." *Science* 320: 1092–1095.

Kant, I. [1785] 1959. *Foundations of the Metaphysics of Morals*. Translated by L. W. Beck. Indianapolis: Bobbs-Merrill.

Lieberman, D., and E. Hatfield. 2006. "Lust and Disgust: Cross-Cultural and Evolutionary Perspectives." In *The Psychology of Love*, 2nd ed., edited by R. J. Sternberg and K. Weis, 274–297. New Haven: Yale University Press.

Machery, E., and R. Mallon. 2010. "Evolution of Morality." In *The Oxford Handbook of Moral Psychology*, edited by J. Doris and the Moral Psychology Research Group, 3–46. New York: Oxford University Press.

Mill, J. S. [1859] 2011. *On Liberty*. New York: Simon and Brown.

Moll, J., R. Zahn, R. de Oliveira-Souza, F. Krueger, and J. Grafman. 2005. "The Neural Basis of Human Moral Cognition." *Nature Reviews Neuroscience* 6: 799–809.

Moll, J., F. Krueger, R. Pardini, M. Zahn, R. de Oliveira-Souza, and J. Grafman. 2006. "Human Fronto-Mesolimbic Networks Guide Decisions about Charitable Donation." *Proceedings of the National Academy of Sciences* 103, no. 42: 15623–15628.

Parkinson, C., W. Sinnott-Armstrong, P. Koralus, A. Mendelovici, V. McGeer, and T. Wheatley. 2011. "Is Morality Unified? Evidence That Distinct Neural Systems Underlie Moral Judgments of Harm, Dishonesty, and Disgust." *Journal of Cognitive Neuroscience* 10: 3162–3180.

Robertson, D., J. Snarey, O. Ousley, K. Harenski, F. Bowman, R. Gilkey, and C. Kilts. 2007. "The Neural Processing of Moral Sensitivity to Issues of Justice and Care." *Neuropsychologia* 45: 755–766.

Robinson, P. H., and R. Kurzban. 2007. "Concordance and Conflict in Intuitions of Justice." *Minnesota Law Review* 91: 1829–1907.

Ross, W. D. 1930. *The Right and the Good*. Oxford: Clarendon Press.

Schaich Borg, J., D. Lieberman, and K. A. Kiehl. 2008. "Infection, Incest and Iniquity: Investigating the Neural Correlates of Disgust and Morality." *Journal of Cognitive Neuroscience* 20: 1529–1546.

Shweder, R. A., N. C. Much, M. M. Mahapatra, and L. Park. 1997. "The 'Big Three' of Morality (Autonomy, Community, and Divinity) and the 'Big Three' Explanations of Suffering." In *Morality and Health*, edited by A. M. Brandt and P. Rozin, 119–169. New York: Routledge.

Sinnott-Armstrong, W. 2008. "Is Moral Phenomenology Unified?" *Phenomenology and Cognitive Sciences* 7: 85–97.

Sinnott-Armstrong, W., and T. Wheatley. 2012. "The Disunity of Morality and Why It Matters to Philosophy." *Monist* 95: 355–377.

Sinnott-Armstrong, W., and T. Wheatley. 2014. "Are Moral Judgments Unified?" *Philosophical Psychology* 27: 451–474.

Stich, S. 2006. "Is Morality an Elegant Machine or a Kluge?" *Journal of Cognition and Culture* 6: 181–189.

Sundby, A. 2010. "Study: Magnetic Waves Alter Moral Compass." CBS News, March 30. http://www.cbsnews.com/stories/2010/03/30/tech/main6347079.shtml.

Tulving, E. 2000. "Concepts of Memory." In *The Oxford Handbook of Memory*, edited by E. Tulving and F. I. M. Craik, 33–44. New York: Oxford University Press.

Turiel, E. 1983. *The Development of Social Knowledge: Morality and Convention*. Cambridge: Cambridge University Press.

Van Overwalle, F. 2009. "Social Cognition and the Brain: A Meta-analysis." *Human Brain Mapping* 30: 585–594.

Warnock, G. J. 1971. *The Object of Morality*. London: Methuen.

Index

CPSIA information can be obtained
at www.ICGtesting.com
Printed in the USA
BVHW032242091019
560701BV00002B/43/P